BAM RAILWAY GUIDE

THE SECOND TRANS-SIBERIAN RAILWAY

Author: Athol Yates
Photographs: Tatyana Pozar-Burgar
Editorial Consultant: Rashit Yahin

This first edition published in 1995 by:

Trailblazer Publications

The Old Manse, Tower Road
Hindhead, Surrey GU26 6SU, UK
International fax: +44 01428-607571

Photographs © Tatyana Pozar-Burgar and Athol Yates
Text © Athol Yates, 1995

All rights reserved. Other than brief extracts for purposes of review no part of this publication may be produced in any form without the written consent of the publisher and copyright owner.

Every effort has been made by the author and publisher to ensure that the information contained in this book is accurate and up-to-date. However, the author and publisher are unable to accept responsibility for any inconvenience, loss or injury sustained by anyone as a result of the advice and information given in this guide.

British Cataloguing in Publication Data
A catalogue record for this book is available from the British Library.

ISBN 1-873756-06-2

Printed by Kelso Graphics, The Knowes, Kelso, Roxburghshire TD5 7BH.

Siberian BAM Railway Guidebook

Authors et. al.
Авторы и т. д.

Author

Athol Yates has had a long fascination with Russian politics, history and language. He has travelled extensively throughout Russia as a student, journalist and researcher. He has an Engineering degree and Graduate Diploma in Soviet Studies and studied Russian at Melbourne University, Moscow's Patrice Lumumba University and Hungary's Egar Teachers' Institute.

He is currently writing several books on Russian railways and developing multi-media guides to Russia. He lives in Melbourne, Australia.

Photographs

Tatyana Pozar-Burgar is fascinated with both photography and Russia. Determined to capture the country on film, she recently spent 8 months in Russia taking photos for this book and her exhibitions. She studied Russian at Melbourne and Moscow universities. She works in a Melbourne photographic company and runs a Russian photo library as a hobby.

Editorial Consultant

Rashit Yahin takes enormous pleasure in revealing the natural treasures of the BAM Zone and the North Baikal region to both Russians and Westerners. In many ways, Rashit symbolises the tragedy of the Soviet era and in particular, the delusion under which the BAM builders toiled.

Rashit was born in a prison camp, the son of an imprisoned and exiled Kazakh priest. He was discriminated against as a child of an "enemy of the working class", but against all odds, he obtained an engineering degree and went to work in Moscow at the BAM planning

organisation, BAMproek. Rashit arrived in Severobaikalsk with the first BAM builders in 1974 and worked there until being dismissed for signing a letter of complaint about working conditions sent to the Minister of Railways. He was later re-employed as a tunnel labourer. He is a Master of Chess, a prominent activist in the Eastern Siberian environmental movement, and speaks excellent English. He is currently the Director of the travel company, BAMTour Co, at Severobaikalsk.

Graphic Art
Book design by Athol Yates and cover train graphic by Linda Fu.

Contributors
Editor, Jacinta Nelligan: Without her meticulous editing, moral support and indulgent patience, this book would be just a jumble of words.
Contributor, Richard Todd: Years of study for a Physical Geography Degree and Masters in Environmental Studies shows in the chapter simplifying the complex subject of Siberian geography.
Editorial Consultant, Marina Kuzminovna: Without doubt, Marina is one of the Russian Far East's foremost experts on gulags, Japanese prisoners of war and the history of the BAM. She has written three books on these subjects in Russian. She is currently the Secretary of the Japanese-Russian Friendship Society's Komsomolsk Branch, Chairperson of Memorial which is a group representing those who suffered during the years of Stalinist repression, and is active in local politics. She is also Director of the travel company, Marika.
Russian language editors, Ilya Karachevtsev and Inna Karachevtseva: Thanks for your help.

Special thanks to:
Joseph Lo Bianco, Richard Baldauf, Joseph de Riva O'Phelan and Pauline Bryant, The National Languages and Literacy Institute of Australia.
E. Shagarin, the Russian Federation Embassy in Australia.
Stephen Wheatcroft, Paul Cubberly and Sonya Witheridge, the University of Melbourne.
Brent McCunn, Passport Travel.
Kirill Yakovlevsky, Alex Klementiev, Mikhail Podolon, Natalya Vitalevna Chernetsova, Richard Fleming, John Sload, Angela Brintlinger, Alexei Lebedev and Dave Beachley.

Dear Reader,

The Siberian BAM Railway Guidebook is designed to open up a vast area of Eastern Siberia along the 3,400km Baikal Amur Railway (BAM) famous for its political exiles, pristine environment, indigenous villages, Cold War secrets and communist dreams. Not only is it a guide to the BAM railway but it is also a handbook to the rarely visited region known as the BAM Zone.

This book is unusual in the field of guidebooks as it recognises that it is the culture and daily life of the inhabitants which is most interesting, rather than dry history and monuments. For this reason, the book emphasises human aspects of the BAM Zone, including profiling a wide range of people, discussing the post-Soviet Russian culture and describing the daily life of the inhabitants and the towns.

This book will be of interest to a wide range of people including:
- travellers wanting an understanding of travel options, information on how to organise a trip and practical travel hints,
- railway and fishing enthusiasts,
- business people planning a trip to the region and wanting to know the travel and accommodation options and costs,
- adventure enthusiasts seeking exciting new rafting, climbing, trekking, and motor cycle touring routes,
- students of Russian studies and history wanting a historic and contemporary coverage of a region virtually unknown in the West,
- readers interested in discovering the current situation and challenges faced by real Russians following the collapse of the Soviet Union.

Despite the railway being opened to foreigners in 1991, only about 50 westerners travel the entire length of the BAM each year. However, once people become aware of the Zone's attractions, this number will rise significantly.

I wish all travellers an enjoyable visit to this region and welcome any comments, information and experiences which could be included in the next edition.

Athol Yates, Author,
Trailblazer Publications, The Old Manse, Tower Road
Hindhead, Surrey, GU26 6SU, UK

Table of Contents
Содержание

History of the BAM — 1
  Why the BAM was built — 2
  The BAM's construction history — 9
  Who really built the BAM? — 15
  The engineering challenge — 23
  The Cold War and the BAM — 30

The BAM Zone — 35
  Life in the BAM Zone — 36
  BAM towns — 38
  The mis-understood climate — 48
  The flora — 51
  The fragile environment — 55
  The continual struggle for food — 58
  What do the locals eat? — 61
  Native food — 66
  The fishing wonderland — 67
  Animals of the BAM Zone — 69
  Indigenous people — 69

For the real rail enthusiast — 77
  An empire within an empire — 78
  Rolling stock — 82

Planning a trip — 87
  Getting information on Russia — 88
  Getting information on the BAM Zone — 88
  Travel arrangements — 89
  Getting to the BAM — 95
  General information — 96
  What to Take — 102

En route — 105
  Getting around the BAM Zone — 106
  Trains — 108
  Around a BAM town — 120
  Security and police — 128
  Siberian customs and manners — 133

BAM mainline route description — 135
- Taishet – Bratsk — 136
- Bratsk – Ust-Kut — 140
- Ust-Kut – Severobaikalsk — 147
- Severobaikalsk — 156
- Exploring North Baikal — 164
- Severobaikalsk – Novaya Chara — 175
- Novaya Chara – Tynda — 203
- Tynda — 217
- Tynda – Novy Urgal — 224
- Novy Urgal – Komsomolsk — 244
- Komsomolsk — 259
- Around Komsomolsk — 271
- Komsomolsk – Sovetskaya Gavan — 280

BAM branch lines route descriptions — 297
- Chegdomyn – Novy Urgal – Izvestkovaya — 298
- Komsomolsk – Khabarovsk — 300
- Bamovskaya – Tynda (The Little BAM) — 304
- Khrebtovaya – Ust-Ilimsk — 307
- Tynda – Neryungri – Aldan – Yakutsk (AYAM) — 308

Appendix — A1
- Russian language guide — A2
- Railway dictionary — A4
- Buying a ticket — A6
- Booking accommodation — A10
- Glossary — A11
- Recommended reading — A14
- Timetables — A19

Route maps — M1

Index — I1

History of the BAM

Why the BAM was built	2
The BAM's construction history	9
Who really built the BAM?	15
The engineering challenge	23
The Cold War and the BAM	30

Why the BAM was built
Почемч был построен БАМ

There were two main reasons for building the BAM: military and economic. The military threat posed by Japan and China was the primary justification during the late 1930s, mid 1940s and again in the late 1960s, while the potential economic benefits of the region dominated justifications in the mid 1930s, 1970s and 1980s. There were a number of other reasons for building the railway such as Brezhnev's personal glory, however they were of secondary importance.

The military value of the BAM
Since the Russian conquest of Eastern Siberia and the Russian Far East, the areas have been vulnerable to invasion and there was little Moscow could do about it. The only route to Vladivostok until the late 1800s was the Great Siberian Post Road which was little more than a mud track. In the event of conflict, the road was totally inadequate for quick communications or military support. After decades of procrastination, in 1891 Tsar Alexander III finally ordered the Trans-Siberian Railway to be built. While this single track railway provided a lifeline to the Russian Far East, it was a very fragile one. Many sections of the Trans-Siberian Railway ran virtually alongside the Chinese border which meant that rail traffic could be interrupted with minimal effort.

The vulnerability of the Russian Far East was brought home to Moscow following the area's occupation by American, British and Japanese troops in 1918. It was only in 1922 that the Japanese finally left the Russian mainland.

The Japanese invasion threat resurfaced in 1931 when they occupied Manchuria and set up an independent state of Manchukuo. Inner Mongolia became a Japanese sphere of influence and the same fate appeared inevitable for Outer Mongolia. The Russian Far Eastern territories were outflanked and they could be cut off at a moment's notice by a Japanese military thrust anywhere to the east of Lake Baikal. In addition, in 1935 the Soviet leadership was forced by Japan into a humiliating sale of the valuable East China Railway, which travelled through Manchuria to the sea port of Port Arthur (now called Lushun) in the Yellow Sea. The Japanese bought the railway for just 55 million gold roubles while Russia spent over 500 million on its construction.

The immediate response to the Japanese threat was to improve the Trans-Siberian by laying a second track. As an additional defensive measure, new bridges were built rather than widening existing ones as this doubled the number of targets for enemy bombers.

However, the only real insurance against interdiction was to build a northern rail line outside bombing range. But by the time construction work started on the northern line of the BAM, the Japanese threat had been neutralised with their defeat in the Japanese Mongolian war in 1939. In 1941, all work on the BAM was stopped, with the exception of the Komsomolsk – Sovetskaya Gavin line as all resources were thrown at stopping the Nazi's advance in western Russia. The Komsomolsk – Sovetskaya Gavin line was completed just in time to be the only part of the BAM to play a significant role in the *Great Patriotic War*. In 1945 it was used to ferry troops and equipment to the Pacific coast in preparation for the invasion of the Japanese held end of Sakhalin Island, the Kuril Islands and the northern Japanese island of Hakaido.

The discontinuation of construction work on most of the BAM was unknown to western observers. Perversely, the Soviet media's silence on the BAM was taken as evidence that the project had become a military secret and work on it was accelerating.

By the time Western intelligence services realised that the reason the BAM was not mentioned was because it was not being built, tension had risen between the former communist allies of the Soviet Union and China, and the debate was reopened on the military need for a second Trans-Siberian Railway. Debate within the Soviet Union peaked following the 1969 Sino-Soviet fighting, the rapid construction of underground nuclear shelters in northern China and the proliferation of multi-warheaded nuclear missiles in China. However, a dispassionate analysis would have shown that the increased range of bombers, long lead time for construction of the BAM, and the likelihood of nuclear conflict rather than railway sabotage, had eliminated any significant military advantage likely to be gained by constructing the BAM.

The economic benefit of the BAM

The economic justification for the BAM was best expressed in the Second Soviet 5 Year Plan covering 1933 to 1937. The BAM will "... traverse little investigated regions of Eastern Siberia and bring to life an enormous new territory and its colossal riches - timber, gold, coal - and also make possible the cultivation of great tracts of land suitable for agriculture."

Over the following 60 years, variations on this economic theme were propounded, including that the BAM would implement Lenin's theory of regional development, facilitate development in the Russian Far East, reduce traffic on the congested Trans-Siberian Railway, and create an alternative container traffic route from the Pacific Ocean to Europe,

Siberia had long been seen as a "frozen asset" to be melted for future generations. Extracting this wealth started under the Tsar with furs, gold, diamonds and timber exploitation. However, its enormous mineral wealth was mainly left undisturbed until Stalin's massive industrialisation campaign. Throughout the Soviet Union, large scale industries were built virtually overnight and raw material was needed to feed them. The shortage of hard currency, combined with the Soviet fear of being dependent on imported raw materials, resulted in a nationwide exploration program.

Siberia became a priority area for raw material extraction and processing in Stalin's early five year plans and his coercive apparatus provided the labour and money to achieve it. In the Russian Far East, Komsomolsk at the eastern end of the future BAM was selected to be the centre for heavy industry and in the 1930s rapidly grew into Eastern Siberia's largest shipbuilding and steel production centre.

Following the devastation of the Great Patriotic War, reconstruction of Western Russia took precedence over new industries in Siberia. Siberia lay forgotten until Khrushchov awoke to its economic importance in 1956. As a result, he doubled the capital investment under the sixth 5 Year Plan. In the seventh 5 Year Plan, 10% of the Soviet Union's capital investment was in Siberia with the focus on energy production, raw material extraction and heavy industries.

Over the next 15 years, a quiet debate raged within Russia about the wisdom of investing such large sums in developing Siberia, and in the BAM in particular. The anti-Siberians, as they were maliciously called, believed that investing in European Russia was more productive as it was possible to develop existing mineral reserves at less cost, as the existing infrastructure and labour were already paid for. In addition, wages were less and infrastructure costs lower in the relatively milder climate of European Russia than in Eastern Siberia. The pro-Siberians believed that the economic advantage of European Russia was short-term, as the area was energy-deficient. In addition, as most extraction projects have a very long life, there is a long-term benefit to building processing plants near the source of raw materials and power.

A more subtle argument against the BAM was that its construction would actually be detrimental to the region. The reasoning was that the BAM's massive construction costs would soak up nearly all the investment capital in Siberia and consequently, other projects, particularly those outside the BAM Zone, would not be funded. In addition, there would be enormous pressure to start repaying the investment which would create a mono-culture of cash crops in the region. This imperative would reflect in poor civic services, transient populations and environmental degradation.

One significant factor in convincing Brezhnev to proceed with the BAM was the opportunity it offered for economic blackmail of the west.

The 1973 Arab oil shock combined with the astronomical rise in the price of raw materials in the early 1970s created a world-wide belief that whoever controlled raw material supply could control the industrialised nations. As the Soviet Union contained the world's largest reserves of many raw materials, this belief promised enormous economic and strategic power to the Soviet Union. Two specific events instigated by the Soviet Union proved the correctness of this belief to Brezhnev. Firstly, the Soviets and their agents were engaged in raw material price-rigging schemes in the mid 1970s and some Americans claimed that this was the main cause of the 1974-5 US recession. Secondly, in 1978 and 1979, Soviet and Cuban activities in central and southern Africa contributed to a tenfold increase in the price of cobalt, a doubling of the price of platinum and a similar jump in the price of chromium. In all these cases, the Soviet Union reaped huge profits. Therefore, it was believed that unlocking Siberia's enormous raw material reserves via the BAM would allow the Soviet Union to manipulate the world's markets. Other anticipated benefits of the BAM included opening up a new transport route to carry West Siberian oil and gas to the Pacific Ocean for the lucrative markets of the Japanese and US.

However, the disappointing results of Siberian oil fields and BAM Zone mines, combined with the early 1980s recession which saw the world awash with natural resources, finally destroyed Brezhnev's grand dream of economic power arising from the BAM. Gorbachev was left to pick up the pieces.

The BAM becomes a "white elephant"

Gorbachev inherited a state on the brink of collapse. Years of stagnation, nepotism and gross mismanagement had forced Gorbachev into a corner; either rebuild the Soviet Union or watch it die.

He attempted the former course with his economic policies of *perestroika* (which means restructuring), scrapping of large projects, and financial responsibility. Gorbachev championed a new philosophy called "intensive growth policy" which was similar to the anti-Siberian development position. The new policy involved a more effective use of existing plants and equipment, increased reliance on scientific research and development, modernisation and reduction of waste in industry. The net outcome was a transfer of investment from developing greenfield sites in Eastern Siberian to expanding and modernising existing plants in European Russia.

It was obvious that the BAM could not be justified in terms of opening up Eastern Siberia, so the Ministry of Railways portrayed the line as a cost competitive new transport bridge for container traffic from the Pacific Ocean to Europe, which would also reduce traffic on the congested Trans-Siberian line. However, a close analysis of these claims showed them to be false.

> ### WHY GORBACHEV SHOULD NOT VISIT THE BAM ZONE
>
> Gorbachev's popularity in Russia has always been vastly overrated by western observers. In a 1994 survey, the Russian people were asked which Russian leader lied to them the most. Gorbachev came first, followed by other current leaders with Stalin and Lenin well down the list. In the BAM Zone, Gorbachev is viewed with even greater contempt. His unforgivable errors included calling the BAM "the biggest monument to stagnation", slashing funding to the railway, and, worst of all, destroying the country's economy which accelerated the collapse of the BAM. Rashit Yahin, one of the authors of this book, sums up the mood of the people saying, "We sacrificed our homes, friends and lives to carve a new life out of the wilderness. After working here for 10, 15 and even 20 years, Gorbachev simply said that all this was for nothing and our dreams were all false. Of course we despise him."

Theoretically the BAM route from Sovetskaya Gavin (Pacific Coast) to Taishet (junction of the BAM and the Trans-Siberian) would be attractive for high value container traffic as it is 450km shorter than the Trans-Siberian line from Vladivostok to Taishet. However, four problems prevent the BAM from being a viable alternative. Firstly, the speed of container ships has increased considerably over the last two decades and the time taken for a ship to travel from Japan to Amsterdam is now the same as transport by rail across Russia. Secondly, the route from Hong Kong, through Urumqi (north west China), Kazakhstan and Moscow to Europe is shorter than the BAM. Thirdly, the speed of the BAM is about one third of the average speed of the Trans-Siberian line. Fourthly, theft on Russian railways is a major disincentive, so that all Russian railways, including the BAM, are unattractive.

The claim that the BAM will relieve pressure on the Trans-Siberian is equally false. While the BAM will lead to some relief on the Trans-Siberian section from Vladivostok to Irkutsk, the major congestion is on the section from Novosibirsk to Ekaterinburg, which both lines feed into. In addition, double tracking, electrification and better train control over the last decade on the Vladivostok to Irkutsk section of the Trans-Siberian has resulted in greater traffic flow.

In democratic post-Soviet Russia, the BAM has received even less attention than in Gorbachev's time. This can be attributed partly to the bankruptcy of the Russian government which cannot further fund the railway's development, the general decline in all sectors of the Russian economy and the small number of voters in the BAM Zone. Yeltsin has never visited the region and probably never will.

The uncertain present
The BAM has never lived up to its expectations of becoming a booming industrial and transport zone.

Today, the BAM's single track supports a miniscule 12 freight and passenger trains a day compared to the double tracked Trans-Siberian which carries over 200 a day.

In 1988, the BAM recovered just 25% of its operating costs and even at that rate, it was expected to take until the year 2017 before it would be profitable. Since the collapse of the Russian economy, this date has been pushed back first to 2037 then to 2050. Nowadays, no-one will even hazard a guess.

In the late 1980s, various schemes were proposed to give a boost to the BAM Zone. These included the proposal by the Leningrad Zonal Research Institute of Experimental Planning to develop a recreation and tourism centre around Severobaikalsk at the north of Lake Baikal. This involved boosting the town's population from 35,000 to 140,000. The response from even the government controlled media was, "How would the people be employed?" and "What damage would there be to the fragile lake?" The general response was best summed up by a Severobaikalsk local who said, "How can you believe anything this Institute proposes as they are directly responsible for much of the poor design of our city!". Another poorly considered proposal was to build an enormous agricultural machinery plant at Tydna, employing 8,000 workers. "But why build the factory in permafrost and doom the employees and their families to a life in such harsh conditions?", was the response of one newspaper.

Such dreams have long been abandoned as the government has no money and foreign companies are wary of all investment in Russia.

1993 and 1994 were the worst years for the BAM. During this time, all income was spent on wages and even then, wages were not paid for up to 5 months. Surprisingly, there were no strikes during this time. This time also saw many Russians leave the BAM

> **WHY NO-ONE SPOKE OUT AGAINST THE BAM**
> When Gorbachev came to power, he immediately criticised the BAM and this was quickly echoed throughout the government and media. Reports were quickly produced to demonstrate what a waste of money it was. So if everyone knew it was a white elephant, why didn't anyone protest earlier?
>
> The answer is best illustrated by an anecdote told about an event at Khrushchov's speech denouncing Stalin in 1956. During his criticism of Stalin, there were shouts from the audience demanding to know why he didn't raise his voice against Stalin when he was alive. Khrushchov stopped mid-sentence, glared at the audience and shouted, "Who asked that?". A long silence followed. Quietly he continued, "That's why".

Zone for work elsewhere which drove the local economy further downwards.

The promising future
The worst may be over for the BAM. Passenger numbers are up, freight prices have risen to above cost recovery and some industrial enterprises are making sufficient money to pay their freight bills rather than giving IOUs.

Reducing costs has also been important to minimise losses. Techniques have included reducing the working hours of staff, not replacing departing staff, and bringing back outsourced work into the railway. In addition, non-core railway assets and their liabilities have been transferred to reduce expenditure. For example, large numbers of railway owned flats in Severobaikalsk have been given to the local government and this has reduced railway expenditure in that town by 20%.

Privatising assets has been an important revenue earner and this has included the sale of the Lake Baikal research ships and station cafes.

To ensure that the BAM receives some regular freight income, the Ministry of Railways has ordered the competing Trans-Siberian Railway to send a certain amount of east-west freight along the BAM.

These changes bode well for the BAM, however everything depends on the state of the Russian economy. Only with a growing economy will exploitation of the region's natural resources start, and with this will come greater freight traffic.

WHAT THEY SAID ...

"Let the crumbling green bosom of Siberia be clad in the cement armour of cities, armed with the stone muzzles of factory chimneys, and fettered with the closefitting hoops of railways. Let the *taiga* be burnt and chopped down, let the steppes be trampled underfoot. Let all this be, for it is inevitable. It is only on cement and iron that the fraternal union of all peoples, the iron fraternity of all mankind will be built." V. Zazubrin at the first Siberian Congress of Writers in March 1926, declaring his support for industrialisation and the BAM.

"The BAM will begin operations during the Third Soviet 5 year plan (1938-1942)." Announced in 1938 by the Soviet commissar Vyacheslav M Molotov who later gained infamy for signing the Molotov-Ribbentrop pact, which divided Poland between Nazi Germany and the Soviet Union in 1939.

"We are confident that the short but meaningful word 'BAM' will become a symbol of the enthusiastic work, mass heroism and courage of the youth of the seventies." The first Secretary of the Komsomol Central Committee, Yevgeny Tyazhelnikov announcing that the BAM would become a *Komsomol Shock Project* at the 17th Congress of the Komsomol in April 1974.

The BAM's construction history
История БАМа

From the mid 1800s, building a railway across Siberia was a popular topic among the powerful in St Petersburg, with the two main route options being either north or south of Lake Baikal. After extensive geological and engineering investigation, the northern route was discounted due to the region's geography and limited agricultural potential. So in 1886, work started on the now famous Trans-Siberian Railway and by 1916, the route from Moscow to Vladivostok was complete.

Despite the disappointing assessment of the northern route, Russians and foreigners still believed that such a railway line was viable and even inevitable. One of the most famous development proposals was from a French entrepreneur, Loik de Lobel, acting on behalf of US rail companies in 1904. He proposed a Siberian-Alaskan railway starting near north Baikal, through Yakutsk and then across the Bering Straits to Alaska. The construction would be privately funded on the condition that the bankers had a 90 year lease on all land within 25 km of the railway. Not surprisingly, the Tsar rejected the proposal in 1904.

Following the 1917 revolution, the desire for massive industrial development in Siberia became a mass movement with railways becoming the symbol of progress and the tool for achieving it.

The BAM was an idea whose time had come.

The major dates in the history of the BAM are:
1911   The western segment of the BAM from Taishet to Ust-Kut was planned but the First World War thwarted its construction.
1921   In December, the Congress of Soviets announced the GOELRO plan which proposed a massive program of nationwide electrification including a railway to the north of Lake Baikal. H G Wells summed up the world's opinion of this ambitious plan when he wrote, "Can one image a more courageous project in a vast flat land of forests and illiterate peasants with no technical skill available, and with trade and industry at the last gasp?"
1924   The Planning Commission of the Council of Labour and Defence elaborated a long-term plan for the development of the USSR's railways. The plan included a map on which the BAM appeared. A total of 1,000 km of the projected route was identical to the present day route.
1926   Two engineers, Mazurov and Lvov, surveyed a railway line

route between the Amur River and Sovetskaya Gavin.

1932 On 13 April the Soviet government passed a secret decree to start survey work on the BAM to select the best route. The organisation was based at Svobodny on the Trans-Siberian which was also the headquarters of the Amur railway. Taishet and Sovetskaya Gavin were selected as end points. An extensive survey began of the Taishet – Ust-Kut – Kirensk – Bodaibo – Tynda route under the direction of the engineer M A Petrov on behalf of the People's Commissariat for Railways.

1933 Plans for the BAM were announced in the Second Soviet 5 Year Plan 1933-1937. The BAM "... will traverse little investigated regions of Eastern Siberia and bring to life an enormous new territory and its colossal riches - amber, gold, coal - and also make possible the cultivation of great tracts of land suitable for agriculture. Two-thirds of the BAM will go through the Far Eastern region, the length of which is 1,800km. The line will be completed in the Third Soviet 5 Year Plan".

1933 The first railway builders began laying track from Oldoi (now Bamovskaya) on the Trans-Siberian line towards Tynda.

1937 On 17 August, a new organisation, BAMProek, was created which oversaw all the enterprises and government departments working on different aspects of the BAM. BAMProek reviewed all the route plans and discovered that all the previous surveys were inadequate except for those between Tynda and Urgal. This realisation prompted a massive purge of BAM geologists, administration staff and engineers. One of the victims was the famous explorer Arsenev whose geologist wife was executed. Many of the purge victims ended up in the chain of railway construction gulag camps along the BAM called BAMLag. These camps also had their headquarters at Svobodny.

A single track was completed connecting the Trans-Siberian with Tynda.

1938 Construction of the Taishet – Bratsk – Ust-Kut line began. This line was a state priority as it would link up with the massive Bratsk hydro-electric scheme.

1939 The search for the BAM's optimum route accelerated. Expeditions of surveyors and explorers used 26 aircraft, 133 motor vehicles, 28 tractors and cross-country vehicles, 28 motor boats, 1,500 horses and hundreds of reindeer sleds in their survey work.

1940 The first grand plan of the entire BAM route was completed. It estimated that 284.8 million cubic metres of earth works and 618,000 tonnes of metal bridging would be needed.

Work started on the Komsomolsk – Sovetskaya Gavin section.

The first BAM tunnel at Pivan was completed but then abandoned as a new route was chosen.

1941 Work started on two branch lines, Izvestkovaya – Chegdomyn and Volochayevka 2 – Komsomolsk, connecting the Trans-Siberian with the future BAM.
Work stopped on all of the BAM with the exception of the Komsomolsk – Sovetskaya Gavin line following the Soviet Union's entry into the Second World War.

1942 The railway lines between Bamovskaya and Tynda, Urgal and Dusse-Alinski tunnel, and Komsomolsk and Postyshevo were dismantled and relaid between Satarov and Stalingrad by gulag prisoners during the battle of Stalingrad.

1945 The final route for the BAM was selected and 200 numbered copies of the secret technical details were published.
The Pivan – Sovetskaya Gavin line was opened.

1946 Construction of the western BAM sector resumed.

1947 Track-laying between Taishet and Bratsk (315km) was completed.
Japanese POWs completed relaying a freight line from Komsomolsk to Postyshevo.

1949 The massive Udokan copper deposits were found halfway between Tynda and Severobaikalsk.

1950 Work commenced on a new 500km line from near Komsomolsk to Sakhalin Island. This included a 9km undersea tunnel linking the Russian mainland to the island of Sakhalin.
The Taishet – Ust-Kut section of the line was opened. As the incomplete Bratsk dam wall would eventually be the bridge across the massive Angara River, rails were laid across the ice as a short term measure.

1953 Following Stalin's death, all work on the BAM was discontinued.

1958 The construction of the Bamovskaya – Chulman railway (which would reach the massive Neryungri coal deposit) was proposed at a conference on industrial development of Eastern Siberia, organised by the USSR Academy of Sciences.

1960 Interest in the BAM was rekindled with the USSR Council of Ministers ordering specialists and researchers to draw up technical and economic plans for industrial exploration of the Udokan copper deposits. The reports indicated that the deposit was worth developing.

1961 The Leningrad Institute of Transport supported restarting the construction of the BAM along the 1945 route from Ust-Kut to Tynda through Nizhneangarsk, Taksimo, Chara and Ust-Nyukzha, with a branch line to the Udokan copper deposit. The Institute of Industrial Construction threw its weight behind the proposal with the only change being an alteration to the route on a small section between Vitim and Larba which took into account the district's developing economy and recent surveys.

1967 A new construction plan for the BAM was released by the Moscow Transport Institute which was then responsible for the BAM's overall planning. The guidelines envisaged the building of a single-track railway carrying diesel locomotives with provision for subsequent building of a second track and electrification of the railway.

1970 Plans for the difficult Kunerma – Nizhneangarsk section were completed. This included replacing three short tunnels with a single 6,698m tunnel in the Baikal Mountains.

1972 Re-laying of the Bamovskaya – Tynda route started a few kilometres west of the original 1937 line. The railway bed of the rebuilt line was one metre wider than the old line and the gradient was reduced to 14m per km. The new line was 5 km longer than the pre-war one. To build the 180 km line, 200 bridges had to be constructed, 7 million cubic metres of soil removed and 2,000 hectares of rail cuttings made.

1974 On 4 January, work started on the western end of the BAM. On 9 January, the abandoned village of Polovinka, which was 20km east of Ust-Kut, was selected as the starting point for the winter road to the first BAM town of Zvezdnaya. Rail workers started building the BAM from here even though the line from Ust-Kut had yet to arrive. This started the pattern of leap frog construction that was so important to building the line on schedule.

On 15 March, the General Secretary of the Communist Party, Leonid Brezhnev gave a speech in Alma-Ata stating that the BAM would become a huge *Komsomol* construction project. The BAM's master plan was released calling for its completion in 1982 with high speed services operating in 1983.

In April, the 17th Congress of the Komsomol in Moscow rubber stamped Brezhnev's request and on 2 May, the first detachment of *Komsomol* workers arrived in Ust-Kut, direct from the 17th Congress of the Komsomol to an enormous reception.

On 25 July, the first big shipment of equipment was sent from Ust-Kut to Magistralny by river barge in an effort to build a large bridge there before the railway line arrived from Ust-Kut. The shipment included an 80 ton power station and a large number of prefabricated houses, and it had to navigate 600km of rivers while the distance was only 170km in a straight line.

On 10 September, the first issue of the *Baikal-Amur Railway Construction Worker* newspaper came off the press.

On 6 October at 11:27am local time, the railway crane operator Ivan Zhunin laid the first rail section on the new rail bed at Ust-Kut.

1975 On 18 March, the three newspapers, *Eastern Siberia*, *Trans-Baikal* and *Soviet Far Eastern* all printed a BAM commemorative issue as part of a media strategy to raise interest in the BAM.

On 8 May, the Bamovskaya – Tynda line was completed.

1977 The final design for the BAM was approved. It is interesting to note that construction was already in full swing.

1978 Brezhnev toured Eastern Siberia and the Russian Far East with the BAM being the focus of all his speeches.

The Soviet government now acknowledged that the 1974 construction targets were too optimistic.

1982 The government media organisation, TASS, released figures that showed the BAM was between 70 and 80% completed. However these figures included the Izvestkovaya – Urgal branch line which was finished decades before.

1983 Achievements to date included constructing 126 large bridges across rivers and gorges, 3,335 railway structures, and 200 stations and sidings.

1984 On 29 April, the eastern section of the BAM was joined at the

A track-layer pushing the BAM through the *taiga*. The average speed of track laying was an impressive 1.5km of new track a day on the western end of the BAM.

siding called Miroshnichenko.

On 24 September 1984, the golden spike connecting the eastern and western sections of the BAM was hammered into place at Balbukhta, near Kuanda. No foreign media were invited to attend this historic event as the Soviets did not want questions asked about the line's operational status. In reality, only one third of the BAM's 3,115km of track was fully operational. Of the remaining, some 1,500 km was suitable for partial service and 500km for work trains only. Only one of the BAM's tunnels was fully operational.

1985　The most difficult construction year. Following the completion of the relatively simple track laying, workers were released for tunnelling, bridge laying and construction of railway infrastructure. However, this work required different skills so a mass retraining program took place. Targets would not be met for two years.

1986　Construction targets were still a major problem. Railway troops achieved their goals in the eastern section of the BAM, while members of the *Komsomol* accomplished only half to three quarters of their plans on the western end.

In July, Gorbachev toured the Russian Far East and only mentioned the BAM twice in his Vladivostok speech. This signalled the end of official interest in the BAM.

In August, the director of the BAM, V Gorbunov, complained that money was so tight that only the most important construction projects would proceed. The BAM was only given 150 million roubles ($180 million) for the AYAM when it was estimated that it would need 2 billion roubles ($2.4 billion) to complete it.

1988　In September, Gorbachev gave his famous Siberian Krasnoyarsk speech and didn't mention the BAM at all. The USSR Academy of Sciences' Scientific Council on BAM Problems was disbanded. Both events reflected the official view that the BAM was unimportant to Siberia's future.

Gorbachev described the BAM as the greatest monument to the period of stagnation (период застая) and an example of Brezhnev's personal economic adventurism (авантюризим). Soviet journalists slavishly followed this with many stories about the line's pointlessness.

1989　During the period from November 1989 to March 1990, the BAM became operational along its entire length.

1990　Locals discussed creating a BAM Republic due to Moscow's lack of support for the region. The Ministry of Railway discussed cutting up the BAM and giving it to other regional railways.

However, these railways rejected the offer as they did not want to be lumbered with a loss making operation.
1991 On 18 April during his speech in Japan, Gorbachev highlighted the opportunities for Japanese firms to expand the ports of Vanino at the eastern end of the BAM and to modernise the Russian Far East's roads and railways, including the BAM.
1993 The Berkakit – Aldan section opened for freight traffic.
1994 The construction management of the AYAM was transferred from Moscow to the Republic of Sakha.
The Ministry of Railways announced the need for massive reductions in the number of railway workers.
Several large price rises in freight and passenger tariffs decreased the operating losses on the BAM.
1995 The BAM's future looks more promising with greater revenue.

Who really built the BAM?

Кто действительно построил БАМ?

The Soviet-era propaganda portrays the BAM builders as young communists devoted to building the country and socialism. However, the reality was that communists made up only a small proportion of the builders. The majority were workers attracted by incentives, railway troops, Stalin-era labourers, and German and Japanese prisoners of war.

Young communists flock to the BAM

Following the 17th Congress of the Komsomol in 1974, which rubber stamped Brezhnev's request that the BAM become a *Komsomol Shock Project*, the public face of the BAM became the self-sacrificing young communist. Being called a *Shock Project*, the BAM was elevated to a national priority which meant that it was given precedence over other projects in terms of equipment, materials and staff.

The *Komsomol* was given the responsibility of attracting workers and it did this by a

THE EMBLEM OF THE KOMSOMOL (COMMUNIST YOUTH LEAGUE).

nationwide appeal for volunteers through its tens of thousands of offices, its newspapers and its TV programs. In the early years, they had no trouble attracting workers. For example, the Khabarovsk Region Komsomol was given the responsibility of surveying the Urgal to Komsomolsk route and over 200 surveyors applied for the 50 positions.

Most volunteers probably believed in the ideals of communism and considered it an honour to work on the BAM. A few may have been attracted to working in the 'romantic' great Siberian wilderness, however the vast majority would have been pragmatic enough to view working on the BAM as a wise career move. Rapid promotion was common on *Shock Projects* and it was possible to become a foreman at just 26. This experience gave the workers an enormous head start when they returned to normal life, particularly if they sought a career in the

COMMUNIST PROPAGANDA

Slogans were a popular way of getting a message across and during the Soviet-era they were emblazoned everywhere and universally ignored. A typical slogan is shown to the right which translates to " You are building the BAM and the BAM is building you".

Вы строите БАМ и БАМ создает Вас

DEFACING COMMUNIST PROPAGANDA

It was a serious crime to deface slogans and would result in lengthy prison sentences. However, this did not deter many from pursuing this popular pastime. The most popular defacement was changing the famous words from Karl Marx's *Das Kapital*, "Being determines consciousness" which became "Beating determines consciousness" with changes to only 2 letters.

Communist Party. Examples of this were Victor Lakomov and Tatyana Vasina, both of whom arrived in the first detachment direct from the 17th Congress of the Komsomol in 1974 and later became deputies in the Supreme Soviet of the Russian Federation.

An important *Komsomol* source of labour was the 2 million university students that graduated each year. To be eligible to receive their degree and to repay the State for the cost of education, the students were given a three year work assignment by the *Komsomol*. Many

CAR VOUCHER CRISIS NEARLY HALTS BAM

While the BAM car voucher incentive scheme was successful in attracting workers, it almost led to the first BAM strike and moves to secede from Russia.

In the late 1980's, workers on the BAM and other northern projects were offered a queue jumping scheme in order to buy a new car. To be eligible for the scheme, you had to work in the north or BAM for three years. This enabled you to open a car account and after putting money into it for three more years, you could buy a car voucher. You then took the voucher to a government vehicle supply organisation and swapped it for a car. As well as retaining workers, the scheme built up massive bank reserves and reduced demand for goods already in short supply.

The scheme was a great idea until workers started to redeem their vouchers. The collapse of the Soviet Union's, and then Russia's, economy sharply reduced the supply of cars and increased their price. The government hoped that the price would stabilise and postponed the 1991 distribution of cars for vouchers until 1992. But in January 1992, the price increased again. When the automobile sellers suggested that the holders of vouchers pay the difference between the old and new prices, the northern workers responded with a hunger strike in the city administration building in Yakutsk and a campaign of bombarding government officials at all levels with telephone calls and telegrams. In response President Yeltsin issued a decree "On Additional Measures for Orderly Trade with Special Purpose Vouchers Issued by Sakha Republic (Yakutia) Institutions of the Russian Federation Savings Bank" which allowed the additional cost of cars to be covered by the Yakutia government's selling of diamonds above the 1992 quota. Consequently thousands of voucher holders eagerly rushed to the car manufacturing regions of Samara, Togliatti, Shigulevsk and other places to redeem their vouchers. But the price of cars went up again in April 1992, stopping all redemptions.

This time the government did not do anything and the workers responded with plans for strikes, blocking the BAM and even seceding from the Russian Federation. However, this was at a time when the whole nation was undergoing massive turmoil which was fortunate timing for the government as the protest plans were soon forgotten because everyone had more pressing things to worry about. Today, most of the long-term workers on the BAM still hold the vouchers hoping for redemption even though they know deep down that it will never happen.

served their indenture on the BAM even though the mostly manual work was a waste of their skills.

Free workers attracted by incentives

The majority of workers didn't have the idealism of the *Komsomol* volunteers but were attracted by incentives. When the idea of incentives was proposed in the late 1970s it became a hotly debated subject in ideological circles as it contradicted basic socialist tenets. The crux of the matter was identified in *Soviet Sociology* in Spring, 1983. "Obviously, the primary emphasis on offering people the privilege of receiving scarce goods as a way of attracting a work force to the BAM region cannot be considered an adequate method ... It stimulates consumerist attitudes among young people, paving the way for various kinds of speculation and intrigue, and damage is done to the patriotic spirit which should prevail on an urgent construction project."

THE LOGO OF GlavBAMstroi, THE MAIN CIVILIAN ORGANISATION RESPONSIBLE FOR BUILDING THE BAM

Despite these ideological arguments, pragmatism and the realisation that "no incentives would result in no workers" won out.

One of the first incentives offered was that when workers moved to the BAM, the flats they left behind were not reallocated to someone else. This was comforting to know as being allocated a flat in the first place could take up to 10 years. If the worker did not have a flat to leave behind, by working on the BAM, they would jump the accommodation queue when they returned to normal life.

Jumping the car queue was another major incentive, but problems caused by this scheme nearly resulted in the first BAM strike. See *Car Vouchers Crisis Halts the BAM* insert.

However, the most attractive incentive was the hardship bonuses which boosted wages to over three times the Soviet average. These bonuses, which multiplied the standard Russian wage, included a regional wage allowance of 1.7 for working on the BAM, an additional 1.5 for working in the harsh northern region and another 1.4 to compensate for continual relocation.

BAM workers got the normal 24 working day holidays plus 12 more for working on the BAM, and an additional 12 for working in northern regions. People in hazardous occupations, such as tunnelling and demolitions, received a further 6 extra days. In addition, workers were given free return rail tickets to their choice of destination in the Soviet Union every year and free plane tickets every third year. Furthermore, they were given considerable discounts at holiday resorts for themselves and at *Pioneer* camps for their children.

Railroad troops

The role of the military in building the BAM has been virtually ignored in Soviet history. This is despite the fact that they were responsible for the whole eastern BAM section from Komsomolsk to Tynda where they laid over 1,459km of track and built over 32km of bridges.

The full name of the railway troops is Railway Forces for the Construction and Maintenance of Railways (Железнодорожные войска по строительству и восстановлению).

They wear the standard Russian military uniform with the addition of their own corp badges and are headed by a General Colonel. Until the early 1990s, they were a part of the Ministry of Defence, however nowadays they are under the control of the Ministry of Transport Construction. This Ministry is responsible for the construction of all new railways and roads in Russia.

THE CORP BADGE OF THE RAILWAY TROOPS

In theory their mission is to manage, build and maintain the railway in the event of war. In reality, they are the Ministry of Transport Construction's main contractor, doing 25% of its heavy work such as excavating and ballasting. From the Ministry's viewpoint, railway troops have two attractions. Firstly, being a military unit, they can be ordered to do work anywhere. Secondly, as railway troops' work is considered training, they are paid much less than equivalent civilian workers. In many ways, they have replaced the forced labourers since Stalin's gulags were closed.

Railway troops have a long history in Russia, first being established in 1851 under the Tsar. They played an important part in ensuring troops and supplies reached the war fronts in both the Russian Civil War and the *Great Patriotic War*.

Railway troops are classified as rear echelon forces and have their own academies and training schools. To become an officer, students must complete 4 years at St Petersburg's Higher Command School of Rail Troops and Military Communication. After graduating and serving for 2 years as a Lieutenant, you are promoted to Senior Lieutenant. After 3 more years, you are eligible to become a Captain, then 4 more years to be a Major with another 4 to become a Colonel. After 5 further years of service, you are eligible to study at the Academy of Rear Services and Transport which is essential to climbing the promotional ladder.

As in other corps, soldiers and officers in the railway troops are not allowed to go abroad for 5 years after leaving military service. This is a Cold War security measure which is meaningless considering the work railway troops undertake.

> **THE Word Gulag**
> The word *gulag* (ГУЛаг) derives from the Russian initials of the organisation which ran prison camps, the Main Department of Corrective Labour Camps (Главное Управление Исправительных Лагерей).

The original BAM builders: Gulag prisoners and POWs

During the 1930s and 1940s, the word *BAM* struck fear into the hearts of Russians. Rather than being the great heroic undertaking of Brezhnev's time, working on the BAM in Stalin's-era was synonymous with a Siberian death sentence.

The numerous labour camps along the BAM route were known collectively as BAM Corrective Labour Camps or BAMLag. Despite its inmate population of 400,000 prisoners between 1932 and 1941, BAMLag was just a small cog in Stalin's giant network of labour camps. Until the Russian archives were opened in 1992, it was believed that between 5 and 30 million Soviet citizens were imprisoned in Russian gulags

> **LIFE IN CAMPS**
>
> Regardless of mateship myths about prison life, the truth is that every prisoner stood totally alone. The only important thing was finding food and if this involved betraying fellow prisoners, cheating and lying, so be it. The only solidarity that did occur was along ethnic lines and among professional criminals. The latter group dominated the more docile Russian political prisoners, and to prevent violence the two groups were often separated.
>
> Starving prisoners was never an official policy, but it was the norm due to the Soviet's lack of food in the 1930s and 1940s, and the difficulty of transporting it to remote camps. For prison authorities, keeping prisoners hungry offered several advantages: it created a work incentive, it focused prisoners' attention on getting food rather than escaping, and it ensured continual tension between inmates which deflected anger from prison authorities.
>
> While the camp commanders were usually blamed for the camp's conditions, in reality they had very little control. The camp authorities were pressured from above to increase their output, while they could not control the supply of food, clothing and equipment allocated to their camps. In addition, the military guard was independent of the camp authorities, a situation which frequently caused tension. Finally, political officers oversaw both the camp authorities and the military guard which created even more tension. While this tri-power system prevented power monopolies, it also destroyed cooperation which resulted in reduced camp output.

Camp Food

All prisoners received the same rations, which meant that physically large inmates invariably died first. There were normally five levels of camp rations, called *cauldrons*.

First cauldron: thin soup twice a day and 300g of bread. This was for those who failed to achieve the daily work target and day labourers within the camp.

Second cauldron: thin soup twice a day, 700g of bread and buckwheat in the evening. This was for those who had achieved the daily work target and office workers.

Third cauldron: soup twice a day, 900g of bread, buckwheat and a small piece of meat or fish in the evenings. This was for those achieving 15 to 25% above the norm.

Fourth cauldron: 750g of bread, and a meal twice a day containing some meat or fats. This was for privileged clerical workers.

Fifth cauldron: a meal three times a day which contained fats and 700g of bread. This was for hospitalised inmates.

The daily routine started with the first meal between 4 and 6am and ended with the evening meal between 5 and 7pm. The prisoners' brigade leaders had the prisoners' lives in their hands as they filled in the work certifications which determined the food rations. If the brigade produced above the norm, they were entitled to extra rations. However, the rations were inadequate to compensate for the extra energy expended so the brigade was unlikely to get extra rations for long. Conversely, if the brigade produced less than the norm, their rations were reduced. Falling below 30% of the norm generally resulted in each brigade member being treated as refusing to work which meant *first cauldron* food rations and if the poor performance continued, they went to the isolator (solitary confinement). If a prisoner actually refused to work, he was referred to court and the usual sentence was a firing squad.

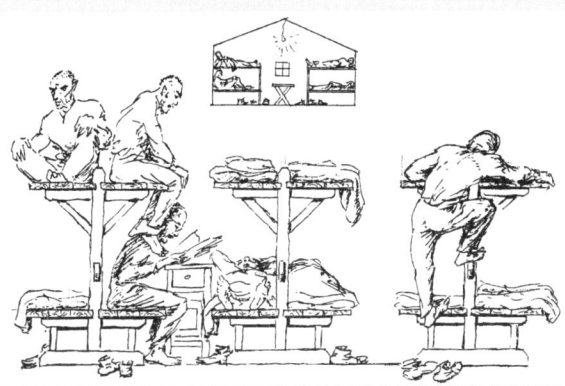

The interior of a prisoners' barracks. Picture reproduced with permission from *The Gulag Handbook* by Jacques Rossi, Overseas Publications Interchange Ltd, London, 1987.

between 1934 and 1953. While the truth is closer to 5 million, this does not diminish the enormous suffering and misery caused by the years of Stalin's brutal repression.

BAMLag was created in 1937 by amalgamating a number of Eastern Siberian gulag complexes with the express aim of guaranteeing a continuous supply of labour for the BAM. Its headquarters was located at Svobodny on the Trans-Siberian line, which was also the head of BAMProek, the BAM project planning enterprise. BAMLag rapidly grew into dozens of camps. It was incorporated into the nationwide Railway Collective Labour Camps Administration or GULZhDS on 4 January 1940 following a purge of the BAMLag management due to perceived poor performance.

Prior to the *Great Patriotic War*, prisoners of the BAMLag built the western end of the BAM from Taishet to Bratsk, the eastern end of the BAM from Komsomolsk to Postyshevo, and the branch lines between Bamovskaya and Tynda and between Izvestkovaya and Urgal. The war stopped further track laying and in 1941/2, most of the rails were torn up and shipped to the Russian-German war front with the prisoners. The only line that was built during the war was the Komsomolsk – Sovetskaya Gavin line which was built by Japanese POWs and Soviet prisoners. After the war, both Russian gulag prisoners and German and Japanese POWs resumed work on several lines and started new ones such as the tunnel under the straits between the mainland and Sakhalin Island. In 1953 when Stalin died, work on the BAM again stopped and the gulags were disbanded with most of the prisoners being released.

The death toll of Japanese and German POWs before they were repatriated in the late 1940s and mid 1950s was enormous. For example, only 10% of the 100,000 German POWs who worked on the western end of the BAM in the OzerLag camp complex, located to the west of Lake Baikal, survived to repatriation. In total, 46,082 Japanese POWs died in the Soviet Union, with most in the Russian Far East and many while working on the BAM.

Today virtually all evidence of the BAMLag camps has disappeared with the notable exception of the chain of tunnel building camps on the shores of the remote Tatar Straits, near Sakhalin Island. However, there are several well preserved non-railway gulag camps within easy reach of the BAM which are certainly worth visiting. The best is the Marble Canyon camp near Chara station which mined uranium ore, and another is Akukan camp near Severobaikalsk which mined mica.

Despite the crucial importance of the gulag prisoners, most of the region's museums unfortunately carry only fragmentary mention of them. This will slowly change as the self-censoring of the past gives way to the truth. If you want an understanding of the reasons for the purges and their history, see the *Recommended reading* section.

Who were the best BAM builders?
Both the railway troops and the civilian constructors regard their work as superior and years after the completion of the BAM, argument still rages about who best completed the work on time, on budget and on specifications. This argument has become more heated in the mid 1990s as both groups compete for a dwindling amount of government construction work.

Ironically, from anecdotal evidence, it appears that the 1930s, 40s and 50s gulag prisoners and POWs built the most durable sections of the railways.

The figures below illustrate the amount of work completed by each of the three main groups of constructors; civilians under GlavBAMstroi which was the main BAM construction agency, railway troops and prisoners. The figures include the BAM proper and related lines including Bratsk – Ust-Kut and Khabarovsk – Komsomolsk but exclude the AYAM. The Little BAM and the line from Komsomolsk to Postyshevo have been included twice as they were rebuilt in the 1970s.

Type of work	GlavBAMstroi	Railway Troops	Prisoners
Line construction (km)	1,641.4	1,459.2	1,458
Embankments (km)	1198.5	1248.4	
Embankments higher than 12m (km)	26	33.9	
Embankments on swamps (km)	212.2	427.5	
Excavations of permafrost (km)	72.1	123.7	
Small bridges (number & km)	410 (8.4km)	434 (9.3km)	
Medium bridges (number & km)	341 (17.3km)	297 (13.9km)	
Big bridges (number & km)	63 (12.0km)	50 (10.7km)	

Source: The GlavBAMstroi and Railway Troops figures are from the Russian railway newspaper, *Gudok*, 13 May 1994.

The engineering challenge
Почему БАМ было трудно построить

Russia's largest ever construction project
Constructing the BAM and the BAM Zone was the largest civil engineering project ever undertaken by the Soviet Union and probably by any country in the world. It devoured the same gigantic amount of resources as were used to conquer space in the 1950s and 1960s.

The Soviet Union is probably the only country in the world that could have undertaken such a massive project as only a single party superpower coupled with a command economy could have marshalled the necessary political will, labour, finances and technical skill.

In the 1970s, probably 20,000 people lived in the BAM Zone with another 300,000 people at the east and west ends around Komsomolsk and Ust-Kut respectively. Today over 1 million live in the area in the Zone's 3 new cities and 100 settlements.

The BAM was a national effort and every republic sent construction units to the BAM. Over 60 of the nation's 100 plus nationalities worked on the line. In addition, 14 of the 15 Republics and 30 *Oblast* governments sponsored individual BAM towns, and built and paid for 500,000 square metres of housing, 18 kindergartens, 12 medical facilities and 4 *banyas* between September 1974 and October 1984.

Numbers Always Win in Soviet Construction

Inadequate planning, massive errors and poor workmanship are all charges levelled at virtually every large Soviet-era construction project,

BAM and BAM Zone Construction Facts*

Length of the BAM	3097.6km
Length of sidings, yards and passing loops	445km
Number of urban settlements built in the BAM Zone	100
Number of cities built in the BAM Zone	3
Number of BAM workers excluding the military in 1981	40,000
Number of BAM workers excluding the military in 1988	60,000
Percentage of workers under 30 in 1984	75%
Embankments	
Total length of embankments	2,446.9km
Embankments higher than 12m	59.9km
Embankments on swamps and marshes	640
Excavations	
Excavations greater than 12m	112.2km
Excavations in permafrost	196km
Excavations at an angle greater than 1:3	122km
Bridges	
Number of small bridges	844
Length of small bridges	17.7km
Number of medium bridges	638
Length of medium bridges	31.3km
Number of large bridges	113
Length of large bridges	22.8km
Tunnels	
Number of tunnels	5
Total length of tunnels	31.7km
Number of railway structures (excluding bridges) built	2,600
Amount of earth moved	570 million m3

These figures only refer to the Russian definition of the BAM and the BAM Zone which runs from Komsomolsk to Ust-Kut.

> ### THE HARSH REALITY OF A FRONTIER WORKER'S LIFE
> Despite the exotic image of working on the Siberian frontier, life in the taiga was basically hell.
>
> One of the hardest jobs was the preliminary survey work carried out by the survey scouts. These true pioneers carried cameras, compasses, tape measures and guns, and scrambled over and through mountains, valleys and swamps mapping the entire BAM Zone. In particular, they explored dangerous mountain ranges looking for evidence of avalanches and rock slides by examining fallen trees, rock fragments and the accumulation of boulders and earth at the bottom of steep inclines. This information was essential as avalanches moving at 50-60m/s travel a long way and the BAM must make a wide detour around these areas.
>
> The only pleasant time of the year for exploration was at the beginning of summer. This short lived bliss would soon be destroyed by swarms of midges and mosquitoes and the only protection was to cover all exposed skin including wearing mosquito nets over your head. As the hungry mosquitoes and deadly tics could bite through one layer of material, it was essential to wear a thick open weave singlet to hold the outer fabric layer 1cm from your skin. As can be imagined, this was uncomfortable when the temperature soared to over 30C.
>
> When the spring weather arrived, the roads quickly turned into quagmires and the river ice broke up, stopping both trucks and river vessels from travelling down them. Helicopters soon became the only means of transport and as the small number of helicopters was needed everywhere to deliver food, fuel and workers, food supplies rapidly dwindled and variety became non-existent. Living on dehydrated potatoes, dried onions and canned food soon took its toll and gums started to swell. The only fresh food surveyors could look forward to was last year's berries found in the thawed June taiga.
>
> Most workers looked forward to the end of the short summer as it brought relief from the insects and tinned food due to the reopening of the roads.

including the BAM. While many of the criticisms were justified, they must be balanced against the fact that invariably, the problems only slowed but never stopped, the ambitious projects.

Unlike the west, it was not money that guaranteed success in the Soviet Union but rather political will. If a problem occurred, then more labour and resources were simply channelled into overcoming it.

The BAM provides an unique insight into the problems of large scale Soviet construction projects as it was being completed just as the Soviet media started to take advantage of Gorbachev's policy of *glasnost* (openness) and to report on the previously 'unreportable'.

Planning problems

Poor planning of the BAM was evident from the start. Following the announcement the BAM would be built, an article in the *Izvestiya* newspaper of May 1974 highlighted that no-one knew what the project would involve, let along how much it would cost. "At this point, it is difficult to say with precision how many stations, settlements and cities will spring up on both sides of the BAM.". It was only in 1977 when construction was in full swing that the plan of the final route, rail infrastructure program and budgets were completed. The BAM planners were aware that problems would inevitably occur and so they set aside 10% of the total budget for unforeseen work and another 15% for rebuilding badly built and temporary structures.

While these amounts may seem high, they are understandable considering the sheer enormity and complexity of the BAM's construction.

The terrain's variety and inaccessibility were 2 of the major impediments facing the planners. As the route passed through 640km of marshes, 120km of landslide-susceptible terrain, and along 1,330km of permafrost and semi-permafrost, re-routeing was a common occurrence. The type of terrain affected the rate of track laying and this was difficult to predict. In 1975 and 1976, tracklaying averaged 1.5km a day in the western end of the BAM but by 1979, it had decreased to between 0.2 and 0.3km a day as the difficulty of the terrain increased and lack of experience showed. As more experience was gained, this increased to 0.4-0.5km a day by the early 1980s.

The quantity and quality of the supplied equipment was also outside the control of the planners. Between 1975 and 1977, 13,000 heavy duty trucks, 1,100 excavators, 2,000 bulldozers, 1,200 mobile cranes were supplied to the BAM. While this may sound an enormous number, most equipment lasted only one season before it became uneconomic to repair. Even the cost of maintaining a vehicle during its one year operation life was enormous. For example, the yearly maintenance cost of a bulldozer was about 12,000 roubles which was almost twice its cost price. The principal reason for the high attrition rate was that the equipment was underpowered. In normal operation, 100hp bulldozers are required for earth moving and 250hp for work in permafrost. However, most of the BAM's bulldozers were converted Kirovets agricultural tractors of 55-75hp.

Similar supply problems occurred for track laying materials. Sleeper supply was a common bottleneck which reached a peak in 1981 when all the sleeper factories supplying the BAM failed to meet their production quotas. Consequently, by the end of the year, the constructors were 130,000 sleepers short. As 2,000 sleepers are needed for each km of track, this meant that an extra 65km of track could have been laid but wasn't.

Another variable outside the planners' control was the weather and its effect on work rates and equipment. When the temperature dropped below -45°C without wind or -35°C with wind, workers legally downed tools. However, bulldozers would seize and axes would shatter before these temperatures were reached, so workers would have to stop earlier than planned.

One problem that can be laid at the feet of the planners was their inability to anticipate the skill shortage following the completion of the relatively simple track laying in 1984. This released large numbers of workers for station and rail facilities construction but they didn't have the skills to do this work. Consequently a massive crash training program was instigated but it took two years before projects were back on target.

Permafrost: The Bane of Constructors

The biggest difficulty faced by the constructors was building on the permanently frozen ground, permafrost. The BAM passes through about 330km of permafrost and about 1,000km of thawed ground dotted with islands of permafrost. The deepest permafrost on the BAM was 600m deep at Udokan near Chara.

The difficulty of constructing on permafrost is that if the insulating surface of moss and grasses is broken or if the ground is compressed, the ice in the soil melts. As frozen water occupies a greater volume than liquid water, the thawed soil subsides. The average depth of subsidence following construction is 90cm but up to 2 metres has been recorded. It normally takes two years for the ground to settle following construction on permafrost. Another option is to not disturb the permafrost by constructing buildings on insolated stilts which leave an airgap between the building and the ground as well as transferring the building's weight to the bedrock rather than the permafrost. This solution is expensive as the cost of constructing permafrost tolerant infrastructure is 2.5 times that of buildings built on solid ground.

Despite knowledge gained from years of experience building the permafrost cities of Norilsk, Yakutsk and Vorkuta in the 1940s, all the construction lessons were forgotten when the BAM was built in the 1970s. In one media report in the early 1980s, it was stated that at 7 major BAM stations, there were over 70 completed structures, such as buildings, sidings and signal systems, which had sagged, collapsed or were otherwise unusable because of design ill-suited to permafrost conditions.

The earliest built towns suffered the most and particularly bad were the towns of Belenkaya, Anosovskaya, Tynda and Khani. However, the worst example of poor permafrost engineering practice was Mogot on the AYAM. It was built in the late 1970s and by spring 1981, the town's heating and water mains had broken, its sewage system had failed and its sidewalks collapsed. Several of the buildings were condemned, including the midwife's station, the administration building and the railway terminal. The basic problem was that most of the buildings' insulated foundation piles were sunk down only 2m rather than until they hit bedrock.

Permafrost slowly swallows the BAM

Laying rail lines on permafrost poses several problems. Firstly, while it takes 2 years for disturbed permafrost to settle, the track layers do not have the luxury of waiting this long. Consequently, it is essential that engineers accurately estimate the subsidence and compensate by building an embankment this much higher. Secondly, as the BAM passes through many geologically different regions of permafrost and semi thawed ground, the most appropriate engineering approach must be used for each. The most common approaches were to either remove the permafrost or build on it. The first method is only suitable in areas of scattered permafrost and involves refilling the excavated hole with rock and ballast. The second, more common method involves building an insulated embankment on the permafrost made of large rocks and boulders at the bottom with ballast at the top.

However, the shortage of building materials and time pressures often resulted in these principles being only partly complied with. The result was that track often had to be relaid after the ground beneath it subsided. Typical of this problem was one report which stated that 10 million roubles a year was being spent in the early 1980s just relaying sagging rail foundations west of Tynda. The best documented track

An ice-wedge thrusts up from the frozen ground to destroy the track. While it is possible to dig it out, a wedge can be hundreds of feet deep so it is easier to re-lay the track around it. Photo courtesy of Tynda's BAM Museum.

problem case was the Little BAM connecting the Trans-Siberian with the BAM, which involved both permafrost and poor quality materials problems. Originally the line was laid with low quality rails on a mixed sand-gravel ballast. This resulted in the 187km trip taking 8 hours, and during four months in 1987, line subsidence and ballast washouts caused three train wrecks. Since 1988, the line has been rebuilt with 1.5 million cubic metres of earthworks and the rails have been replaced with heavy duty rails but still the train crawls along at 46km/h.

Tunnels still block the BAM

Tunnels have been the bane of the BAM and even today, after 20 years of work and billions of roubles spent, not all the tunnels have been completed. It is probable that the last tunnel, the Severomuisk tunnel, will not be finished until the turn of the century.

> **How Much Did The BAM Cost?**
> Officially, the construction cost of the BAM up to 1984 was 9 billion roubles ($10.8 billion) which is suspiciously close to the 1977 Soviet estimates of 8.4 to 9.5 billion roubles. By 1989, the total spent on the BAM and its related lines had officially increased to 10.7 billion roubles. Confusion remains about whether these figures include all of the related lines, the work of the railway troops and the cost of the rail infrastructure. Many western experts believe these figures are understated and should be at least 100% higher.

The cost of the tunnels accounted for an astronomical one third of the BAM's total construction budget. This was because the tunnels go through very complex geological areas, including permafrost, multiple fault lines and underground waterways. A number of new tunnelling techniques had to be developed which further slowed construction.

Work on the tunnels started well before the rail line arrived as it was planned that the tunnels would be completed just as the rails arrived. However, due to faster than expected rail laying, and slower than expected tunnelling, temporary above ground bypasses were built for most tunnels. The only tunnel that was finished before the rails arrived was the Ducce-Alinski Tunnel which was completed in 1954, but did not see its first train until 1982.

In retrospect, several of the tunnels should never have been built as a more cost effective route could have been found had more time been spent on survey work. However, this does not diminish the heroic achievements of the tunnellers. A number of tunnellers died during construction but the Russian authorities have never stated how many. Although some Western experts claim that up to several hundred have died in mishaps, it seems that less than 20 lost their lives in the tunnels west of Tynda. While there are monuments to the tunnellers at each of the tunnels, there is only one memorial to those who died, which is at the Mysoviye tunnels.

There are five tunnels in the BAM, with 4 west and 1 east of Tynda. They are the:
- 15.7km Severomuisk Tunnel which is also known as the North Muya Tunnel (Северомуйский тоннель)
- 5km Mysoviye Tunnel which is made up of 4 tunnels. The tunnel is also known as the Cape Tunnel (Мысовые тоннели)
- 6.7km Baikal Mountain Tunnel (Байкальский тоннель)
- 1.94km Kodar Tunnel (Кодарский тоннель)
- 2km Ducce Alinski Tunnel (Дуссе-Алинский тоннель).

Details of each tunnel are included in the route sections.

The Cold War and the BAM
Холодная Война и БАМ

Western intelligence agencies target the BAM
From the Soviet Union's earliest days, a veil of secrecy cloaked the country. Typical of the silence was the lack of Soviet press coverage of the BAM from the mid 1930s to the early 1970s. During this time, only one announcement was made and that was in 1938 when it was stated that the BAM would be built during the Soviet 1938 to 1942 5 Year Plan.

To justify such a massive undertaking, the west knew that there must be enormous resources in the region and that the BAM was militarily significant. Before the Second World War, both German and Japanese military intelligence sought information on this railway, but its remote location made gathering first hand information very difficult. Getting access to the region was made even harder as it was a closed region due to its gulag camps.

As all information in the Soviet Union was centralised, another intelligence approach was to recruit someone at BAMProek which was the organisation managing the BAM's construction. However, just asking for information on who worked in the organisation, let alone asking these people for facts on the BAM would instantly raise suspicions which in the late 1930's, the war years and the late 1940's would inevitably result in a long jail sentence or execution for the asker.

Western intelligence efforts
Unlike the images portrayed in spy movies and novels, the vast majority of intelligence information is gathered from innocuous sources such as radio, newspapers and general conversations. Often the subject matter is unrelated but by inference, important information can be deduced. For example, in 1941 the Soviet newspaper, *Pravda*, reported that chickens

were airfreighted from Irkutsk to Bodaibo. At the time, the BAM was thought to go through Bodaibo before joining Tynda so this revealed that the line to Bodaibo was a long way from being completed. Another clue was the report in *Pravda* on 2 November 1942, that the people of Yakutsk

---

The New York Times

NEW YORK, FRIDAY, AUGUST 11, 1950

Soviet Completes Far East Rail Link

Road Along Trans-Siberian Route Vital to Army, Says Exiled Scientist

Soviet Russia has completed another strategic railroad to the Soviet Far East, paralleling the route of the double-tracked Trans-Siberian Railroad, Prof. Andre Karpinsky, exiled Russian geologist, reported here yesterday. Professor Karpinsky, who is a nephew of the late Alexander P Karpinsky, noted Soviet geologist and palaeontologist who was president of the Soviet Academy of Sciences from 1917 to 1936, arrived on Wednesday on the United States Army Transport General Langfitt.

He and his wife, Tatiana, were brought to the United States by the international Rescue Commission from a displaced persons camp at Schliesheim near Munich where he had been teaching in a lyceum. They had fallen into the hands of the German Army in the Caucusus in 1943 and were slave labourers in Berlin until the Allied victory.

Professor Karpinsky said the second Soviet Far Eastern Railroad is north of the Trans-Siberian, which skirts the southern border of the Soviet Union, running to Vladivostok. The beginning of construction was reported some years ago, and it was later rumoured that work was progressing, but it had not been known that the road was completed.

Importance of Army Supply

The new railroad, which is important to the supply of the Soviet Far Eastern Armies, runs from Lake Baikal, east of Irkutsk, east to Sovietskaya Gavan, a seaport north of Vladivostok opposite Sakhalin Island. From Sovietskaya Gavan supplies can be taken by ship to new Soviet bases on Sakhalin Island and at other points in the northern Pacific region.

Recent reports have indicated a stepping up of Soviet military activity in the Soviet Far East and the Trans-Siberian has been reported working at capacity moving military supplies.

Professor Karpinsky said that the Baikal-Sovietskaya Gavan Railroad had been completed before he left Russia in 1943 and that students of his had made the geological surveys of the road. He himself had made the geological surveys for the Turkmenistan-Siberian Railroad.

donated presents for the soldiers at the front and these were despatched by train from Irkutsk. This implied that they were flown from Yakutsk to Irkutsk which meant that there was no close railway line otherwise the presents would have rail freighted along the BAM.

A more recent example of using seemingly trivial information involved locating a secret aviation research centre in the city of Komsomolsk at the eastern end of the BAM. Since the late 1930s, Western intelligence services knew of the Komsomolsk Aviation Works, later named the Yuri Gagarin Aviation Works, and its construction of military planes, including the Mig-17 starting in 1967. However, it was only in the early 1970s that the services had a breakthrough and discovered that inside the factory was a secret research and development bureau designing sophisticated military avionics.

> **Mis-information on the BAM Still Abounds**
> Despite the exact route of the BAM being known since the mid 1970s, Western books still contain many errors about the BAM. For example, the back cover of the 1992 edition of one well-known Russian guidebook shows the BAM passing through the Bodaibo area which is 1,000km north of its real route!

This revelation came about by examining a secretly obtained list of Soviet colleges and their courses, and cross tabulating it with other information. Traditionally, the Soviets built advanced technical colleges, VUZs, near related factories and often within these factories were specialised research and development bureaus. To find a particular research and development bureau, you started looking at the courses offered by the VUZ. For example, the VUZ mechanics speciality No 2014 course contains subjects including gyroscopes, flight dynamics and aerodynamics. There were 15 universities and VUZs that offered this course in the Soviet Union and 10 of these were located in cities which had an aerospace industry. Komsomolsk was one of these and further investigation of the courses offered by its VUZ revealed speciality courses for avionics. Further cross tabulating revealed that there was an avionics design bureau run by the aircraft builder Sukhoi.

Soviet counter-intelligence efforts

The secret to destroying the intelligence value of everyday information is to plant mis-information which makes the intelligence assessor unsure of what is correct. The incorrect information on the BAM that prevailed for 40 years can partly be attributed to a clever Soviet mis-information campaign and partly due to Western intelligence services beating up the story to justify a bigger defence budget.

One of the first widely published inaccuracies was aired in the 1943 book by Emil Lengyel, called *Siberia*. "An American traveller in Siberia brought back the story in 1941 of the building of another railway line in the Soviet Far East. He did not see it himself, only heard about it from a young Communist. This line was to have its southern terminus at Komsomolsk and from there run along the Okhotsk Sea, eventually reaching Kamchatka peninsula and the Bering Sea. The building of the railway would be a formidable enterprise on what is probably one of the worst terrains on this globe. It is difficult to see how the Soviets could complete it on short notice, and it is even more difficult to see how they could overcome the obstacles placed in man's way by nature."

Cold War Paranoia Lingers On

Despite the collapse of the repressive Soviet Union and the passing of Russian decrees allowing freedom of movement for foreigners, Cold War paranoia still lingers.

The most obvious form of this paranoia is inaccurate maps which contain imaginary streets, don't show existing towns and move landmarks hundreds of metres.

The logic behind the misleading maps was that in a time of war, captured maps would be of little use to the invading army. However this ignored the fact that space satellites could produce far more accurate maps than the Soviets ever printed. So the only confusion the maps created was for the Russians who used them.

Nowadays the larger cities have accurate maps, but the smaller cities, such as those on the BAM, still have to rely on inaccurate Soviet era maps.

For the traveller, it is important to be aware that any Russian map you buy may be inaccurate.

Another cold war legacy is the reaction of the military to taking photos of railway stations, bridges and tunnels. In the past this was strictly forbidden and even stated on visa applications. Although it has now been deleted on the forms, many officials are not aware that photographing railway infrastructure is no longer stealing a state secret. This problem is more pronounced off the beaten track, such as on the BAM, so the best policy is discretion when taking photos.

In the preparation of this book, the author was interviewed by the former KGB when he was spotted photographing the Vitim River bridge on the BAM, and in another incident, he was detained by an armed guard for taking photos around Khabarovsk's station. If this happens to you, simply explain in a friendly manner and hopefully, everything will be laughed off.

An article in the New York Times, 11 August 1950, is indicative of the mis-information at the time. It is completely wrong in its claim that the line was finished at a time when only about 30% was completed and several sections were abandoned until the project was restarted in the 1970s.

To put this article in perspective, it must be remembered that it was written during the McCarthy-era of communist witch-hunts. On the same page of the paper were two other articles notable for communist paranoia.

One entitled "Reds Say Cake-Bake Song Proves We Are Starving" claims that the American singer, Jack Smith, stated that the communists were using his song lyrics to prove that the masses were starving under capitalism. "Mr Smith said a former Berlin cabaret manager had told him that the words to "If I knew you were coming, I'd have baked a cake" were being used to show that rationing existed in the United States".

The other article concerns the arrest of Rose Lightcap, the wife of a reporter for the *Daily Worker*, a US communist paper. She was charged with being a member of an organisation which "writes, circulates, distributes, prints and publishes and displays written and printed matter advising and teaching the overthrow by force and violence of the government of the United States, to wit, the International Workers Order".

THE BAM ZONE

Life in the BAM Zone	36
BAM towns	38
The mis-understood climate	48
The flora	51
The fragile environment	55
The continual struggle for food	58
What do the locals eat?	61
Native food	66
The fishing wonderland	67
Animals of the BAM Zone	69
Indigenous people	69

Life in the BAM Zone
Жизнь в Зоне БАМа

On the well worn tourist routes of the Trans-Siberian, Moscow and St Petersburg, it is very difficult to experience the real Russia. However in BAM Zone you are guaranteed to see 'pristine' Russia, as very few foreigners have ever travelled to the area. There is no tourist infrastructure in the Zone so you will eat in Russian restaurants, stay in hotels for locals and experience Russian life first hand. In addition, the scarcity of foreigners ensures that you will be greeted with enthusiasm by virtually everyone you meet.

This makes the BAM one of the most interesting routes in Russia and this chapter will provide you with the background necessary to understand how everything works.

BAM Zone dwellers
Despite the BAM being built by over 70 of the Soviet Union's 120 nationalities, the vast majority of BAM Zone dwellers are ethnic Russians. Other nationalities, notably Central Asians, have started settling in the region over the last 5 years after fleeing civil unrest in their countries. Indigenous Siberians make up less than 3% of the population.

Who holds the reins of power?
Technically, the governments of the 5 regions through which the BAM travels govern the BAM Zone. These regions, from west to east, are the Irkutsk *Oblast*, Republic of Buryatiya, Chita *Oblast*, Amur *Oblast* and Khabarovsk *Krai*. Most of the north-south BAM branchline, the AYAM, is governed by the Republic of Sakha (formerly the Republic of Yakutia).

However in practice, the BAM railway controls the lives of locals as it is the major employer, and manages all aspects of town life including apartment buildings, schools and hospitals. While the railway officials are unelected, locals consider that the BAM administration is more concerned with the life in the Zone than the politicians in the capitals of the administrative regions which can be over 1,000km away.

Who pays the wages?
In the past, almost 100 percent of those in the BAM Zone were state employees with the few exceptions being hunters and cooperative workers.

By the mid 1990s, a combination of the economic downturn, the elimination of government subsidies and a scaling down in the number of railway employees, had resulted in many people in the BAM Zone being unemployed or underemployed with just a few hours of work a week. The choice faced by these people was to become either self-sufficient with vegetable gardening and fishing, self-employed which invariably meant purchasing food and clothes elsewhere and selling them locally, or unemployed which entitled you to a paltry state benefit. In early 1995, the official employment rate Russia-wide was 13%, however many believe the figure is closer to 25% and probably slightly less in the BAM Zone.

Although there are already a few medium sized private companies in the BAM Zone, such as gold mining, large scale trading, local food manufacturing and fishing companies, it will be many years before the private sector becomes a significant employer. This can partly be attributed to the lack of experience with self employment but also due to the ambivalent attitude of many Russians to what was until recently "worker exploitation", "speculation" and "economic opportunism".

Entertainment

Without doubt, the greatest source of entertainment in the BAM Zone is television. Most towns have two or more channels including a local and a Moscow-based channel. Part of the interest in TV can be attributed to a faith in the "truthfulness" of pictures compared to years of lies in newspapers, advertisements that show a life only ever dreamed of, and most importantly, a distraction from daily problems.

Books are also an important entertainment with the majority being translated Western detective and romance novels. On the other hand, newspapers readership has plummeted, partly due to their poor quality, conservative editorial position and continual negative focus on politics, economics and other problems.

Cinema going is not that popular as there are only a few towns in the BAM with a cinema and the practice of taking portable cinemas to the other towns has stopped.

The popularity of outdoor and group activities has decreased significantly since the collapse of the Soviet Union. This is because many clubs, such as those involved in climbing, rafting, walking, chess, stamp collecting, flying, parachuting and painting, were sponsored by the trade union movement or the military and these have had their government funding stopped. The demise of the young communist organisations, *Komsomol* and *Pioneers*, has similarly reduced the opportunity for outdoor activities for children. Fortunately, this situation is slowly improving due to activities such as those occurring in Kuanda. See under *Kuanda* in the *BAM mainline route description* chapter for more information. Nowadays the most common forms of outdoor activity are those that produce food, such as fishing, gardening and berry picking.

Travel
Russians are generally not well travelled and the people in the BAM Zone are no exception. This is despite the fact that virtually all inhabitants moved to the Zone from other parts of Russia. The reasons for the lack of travel experience are the Soviet political system which discouraged exploration, the difficulty in obtaining tickets and the lack of tourist facilities. For foreigners, this means that you should always confirm any travel information you are told by a Russian with several other people as the information may be second or third hand.

Future of BAM towns
It is impossible to discuss the future of the BAM towns without considering future trends in the BAM Zone and Russia.

The first trend is that there is a migration from rural regions to the cities. The basic reasons for this are a lack of work, coupled with poor accommodation, a harsh life, poor education prospects and a dwindling rural population. In the worst case, the young of whole villages are leaving with only the old being left behind. This is most vividly illustrated at the village of Bargalino, near Taksimo, where just 12 houses are occupied out of over 100, or in Festivalny near Solnichny.

The second trend is of shrinking government, which is stopping all new state-funded industrial projects for at least a few more years. This means that employment growth is left to the small private sector.

The third trend is that the private sector is creating a type of capital feudalism as in Tokur, near Fevralsk. See under *Tokur* in the *BAM mainline route description* chapter for more information.

Combined, these trends will result in the BAM Zone remaining at its current snail-paced level of development for many years yet. This may be good for travellers, but it is not so good for the BAM Zone inhabitants.

BAM towns
Города БАМа

There are 3 main types of towns in Russia: rural settlements, urban settlements and cities. All have the same elements, which is hardly surprising as every Soviet town was built according to Moscow's universal civic blueprint. This section describes the 3 types of town and the elements common in every town, which will not only help you to orientate yourself in the BAM Zone towns but also in virtually any town in Russia.

Rural settlements (Населенный пункт сельского типа)

Rural settlement is a broad term for any collection of houses whose inhabitants' main occupation is farming, hunting or fishing. The vast majority of the towns in the BAM Zone that existed before the railway are of this type. These settlements are normally made up of single storey wooden houses with no running water. Romantically they could be referred to as 'rustic villages', however this camouflages the tough life of the inhabitants. Rural settlements have a variety of historical names in Russian with most carrying connotations of backwardness. The more common names include *selo* meaning village (село), *derevnya* meaning hamlet (деревня) or *khutor* meaning a few dwellings in a forest (хутор). Examples of these sorts of settlements include Kholodnaya near Severobaikalsk, Ust-Nyukzha near Yuktali and Ust-Muya near Taksimo.

Pre-BAM villages are usually located near river junctions and in valleys protected from the wind. While this was excellent for the villagers, the location of most villages was inconvenient for the railway builders and consequently, the BAM bypassed many of these town. Instead new towns were built on the railway just a few kilometres away from the existing towns. Examples of these pairs of towns include Staraya Chara and Novaya Chara, Urgal 1 and Novy Urgal, and

Baikalskoe on Lake Baikal's northern coast is a typical rural village with most of its inhabitants being fishermen, hunters and farm labourers. The town also contains a sable farm and a seal skin collective factory.

40 The BAM Zone

Fevralskoe and Fevralsk.

Rural settlements are also found around *kolkhoz* or collective farms. These farms were created from collectivising private farms or, more commonly in the BAM Zone, by creating new farm land. They are sometimes fancifully known as agricultural towns (агрогород) and being relatively recent, have more concrete and brick buildings than older villages.

Urban settlements (Посёлок городского типа)

These types of settlements are the most common on the BAM. Technically an urban settlement is defined as a settlement with a minimum population of 3,000 of which over 85% are employed in non-agricultural work. They are really miniature cities and most are designed with plenty of space to expand into full blown cities. The vast majority of urban settlements were built as the BAM was being constructed and they are dominated by 1970s pre-fabricated concrete buildings. Notable exceptions are Nizhneangarsk, Ekimchan and Chegdomyn which still have many wooden buildings.

Kuanda is typical of urban settlements with its low rise apartment blocks, ugly hot water pipes (foreground), and a half-completed look. The apartment blocks are usually built in squares which provide a wind protected centre where children's playgrounds and parks are often located.

Cities (город)
There are only a few cities on the BAM. A city is defined as having a minimum population of 12,000 of which over 85% are employed in non-agricultural work. These include the small cities of Severobaikalsk, Vanino and Tynda, and the big cities of Bratsk and Komsomolsk.

Town planning and layout
As most of the towns in the BAM Zone were built according to Moscow's Russia-wide town planning regulations, they all share a similar city centre layout of a central square bordered by a town administration building, a hotel, and often the railway administration building. If the town is pre-BAM, then the square may have a statue of Lenin on it or if was built with the BAM, then it may have a memorial to those who died in the Second World War. Pre-BAM towns often name their streets after Lenin, peace or the Second World War while new towns named them after communist heroes, BAM builders and the place where the builders came from. The newest towns, such as Verkhnezeisk, are only naming their streets after the BAM builders.

Outside the centre, the towns' layout and development are haphazard. The reason for this is that each settlement was made up of different organisations, such as steel works, forestry mills and construction enterprises, each of which cared firstly for the needs of their organisation and workers. This meant that each organisation built its own premises with their own independent power and water supplies, sideline farms to feed its workers and even worker settlements, again with their own water, electricity and sewage systems.

The worst examples of chaotic planning are Komsomolsk and Amursk. Komsomolsk was founded in 1932 and it was only in 1940 that a city-wide construction plan was developed. However the plan wasn't approved until 1967. Even in the early 1990s, the situation was still disorganised with 13% of housing lacking running water and sewerage, nearly 50 organisations owning and administering different parts of the city's water supply and people living in barracks that were built in the 1930s. Amursk was created in 1955 and in 1965, became the administrative centre of the region. Yet it wasn't until 1973 that a coordinated city plan was developed to try to amalgamate all the interests of the city's industrial enterprises into one.

Most towns have substantial reserved areas for parks, fairgrounds and room to expand. While some towns, such as Severobaikalsk and Sovetskaya Gavin, have developed their areas into parks, most reserved areas are simple cleared areas.

One very noticeable aspect of BAM towns is the depressing lack of colour. In communist days, the only colour was provided by political posters and the summer flower boxes of apartment dwellers. Nowadays the posters have faded and while the flower boxes still brighten the summer somewhat, the only winter colour is small splashes from advertisements for Coca-Cola, Camel cigarettes and Mars Bars.

Town buildings
The following describes the major elements to be found in virtually all towns in the BAM Zone.

Railway station (Железнодорожный вокзал)
This is the central focus and rationale of most BAM towns. There is a marked difference between the stations depending on their year of construction. The 1930s and 1940s stations are either wooden, such as Urgal 1, Vysokogornaya and Ust-Kut, or classic Stalinesque buildings which often have imposing steps and stairways, tall columns, massive lintels and energy inefficient high ceilings, such as the stations in Komsomolsk and Vanino. The 1970s ushered in an era of economical concrete and glass stations typified by the stations at Severobaikalsk, Tynda and Tyngara.

The larger stations are equipped with a waiting room, buffet, a room for mothers and children, ticket windows, baggage rooms, an enquiries office, a bookstall, a first aid point and a railway police office. The

Novy Urgal station reflects the 1970s architectural obsession with plain, easily constructed buildings.

stations sometimes have an overnight transit hotel attached to them providing very basic facilities. The waiting rooms are crowded, stuffy and scented with the odours of pickled cucumber, dried fish, sunflower seeds and water melon.

Most of the stations have railway yards for exchanging locomotives and filling freight wagons, while the larger ones also have several hectares of repair yards. Strangely, some stations use old steam engines to generate hot water and old diesel locomotives to generate electricity for their own use. It is interesting to note that most stations have inefficiently large equipment, such as overhead cranes rather than more useful forklifts, however this probably reflects the Russians' inability to maintain small machines.

Town administration building (Административное управление)
It is easy to locate the town administration building as it is invariably on the main square, flies the Russian flag and stands behind the statue of Lenin. This building runs the town's social and administrative services. If the town is a rural or urban settlement, it is called a *possovet* (посёлковый совет), if it is a city it is called a *gorsovet* (городской совет), or if it is the largest settlement in the region and controls the surrounding area, it is called a *raionsovet* (районный совет). The word *sovet* has the meaning of council rather than of communism.

Railway administration (Железнодорожное управление)
Invariably, this building is larger than the town's administration which reflects its greater power.

Hotel (Гостиница)
The hotel normally faces the city square although at smaller stations it can be at the station. If the accommodation is primarily for railway workers, it may be beside the station, as it is at Verkhnezeisk and Ust-Kut.

Shops (Магазины)
In large towns, shops are dispersed around the town. In small settlements, almost everything is located in one large complex called a TOTs (Торговый Обшественый Центр). TOTs have the big advantage of protecting shoppers from the winter temperatures. In some towns, such as Kunerma, even the cinema and library are located in the TOTs.

Post office (Почта)
Post offices have three sections. One part is for letters and telegrams, another for parcels and the third for telephone calls. While in most towns, all three sections are in the one building, in some towns all three

are frustratingly located in separate buildings, as is the case in Komsomolsk, while in towns like Tynda and Sovetskaya Gavin, just the post and telephone sections are separate.

Bus station (Автовокзал)
In small towns, the bus station is just a shelter at the railway station or on the main square, while in large towns, it is a large building with cafes and shops such as at Aldan and Komsomolsk.

Housing (Жильё)
Most of the BAM towns have the bland Soviet, box-shaped multi-storey flats arranged in pentagons. This layout provides a wind sheltered, snow drift free area for children. Most of the buildings are either 5 storeys which is the maximum height before elevators are required or 10 storeys which is the maximum height that is easily constructed. On the ground floor of the flats are grocery stores.

Russia has the lowest per capita housing allotments in Europe. In 1988 Moscow had an average allocation of 14 square metres of living space per person while in the BAM Zone it was just 6.4 metres. This may have been tolerable for young, single, short-term workers but is a major problem for BAM families.

By the early 1990s, only 310,000 square metres out of planned 1.4 million square metres of permanent housing had been built in the BAM Zone with many of the original inhabitants still living in run down hostels, caravans and ramshackle buildings in temporary settlements.

Worker settlement (Рабочий посёлок)
Worker settlements are self-contained satellite suburbs for employees of particularly large enterprises and consequently, are only found in large towns, such as Komsomolsk, Bratsk and Neryungri. As the enterprise provides most of the civic services and stocks the local stores, the lifestyle of the residents is very dependent on the profitability of the enterprise.

Temporary settlement (Временный посёлок)
Hidden away on the outskirts of most BAM towns are temporary settlements. These settlements were hurriedly thrown together before work started on the town, as they were constructed for the initial builders of the railway and town. The houses are normally single storey wooden hostels, shared houses or transportable buildings.

Theoretically, the residents of the temporary settlements build the permanent town, and then move into the new apartments or depart for the next job. The temporary settlement is then demolished. However due to the shortage of apartments, many people still live in the temporary settlements and consequently, few have been demolished. This situation is best illustrated at Novaya Chara and Verkhnezeisk and described under these towns in the *BAM mainline route description* chapter.

It is interesting to note that a few of the BAM towns were designated as temporary towns and the whole town was actually demolished. These include the tunnel construction towns of Dzelinga and Kodar.

Military settlement (Военный городок)
In the BAM Zone there are only a few towns, such as Sovetskaya Gavin, Vanino and Komsomolsk, which have major military bases. However there are a number of towns where small military garrisons are based to guard important bridges. The garrison compounds are normally at one end of the bridge and can be seen from the train. It is not advisable to photograph them.

Library (Библиотека)
Most towns have a library run by the town administration, however there are a number of towns which have another library run by the railways. The railway library contains technical railway journals and books as well as many of the same books as the local library. Everyone is allowed into both libraries.

Palace of Culture (Дворц Культуры)
Every town's cultural activity is focused around the Palace of Culture. These buildings normally have a large hall for films, theatre, musical performances or school performances. If there is a national holiday, you can be guaranteed that something will be on here. The best and most active Palace of Culture on the BAM is at Severobaikalsk which boasts an excellent indoor garden.

Market (Рынок)
Every town has a free enterprise market where home grown food, car parts, imported clothes and anything else are sold. As well as the market, locals will often sell fresh produce in front of the produce stores.

Central heating plant (Жилищно-эксплуатационное управление)
Hot water and heating for apartments all comes from the town's central heating plant. The water is distributed by above ground pipes which should be covered with insulating material and a galvanised tin protective skin. As most of the pipes are in poor repair with sections of insulation fallen off, plumes of steam rising from the pipes during winter are common sights. The pipes are clearly visible in all towns and are quite an eyesore. The plants do not generate electricity as this is

supplied by high voltage long distance power lines from Bratsk, Zeya or Komsomolsk.

Museum (Музей)
There are two sorts of museums; regional museums and special interest museums. The former normally includes information on the life of past generations, indigenous people, town history and local industry, while the latter includes the BAM, local geology, industry and the military. The best way to see which business, military or government delegations have recently visited any town is to check the museum's visitors book.

Book shop (Дом Книги)
In the past, these shops were an excellent source of books, calendars and maps. Nowadays they principally sell western adventure and crime novels translated into Russian. A few book shops also sell old Russian and Soviet notes, coins, medals and stamps.

Bakery (Булочная)
Bakeries are absolutely essential in every town and a small bakery produces about 300 loaves a day and employs one baker and a number of assistants to lug the ingredients and chop the wood for the ovens.

A typical small market found in any BAM town. Fresh vegetables like these are unfortunately only found in late summer.

How the Towns Differ

The differences between BAM towns depend on when they were built and who built them.

During the 1930s and 1940s most wooden buildings contained classic Russian carved decorations, such as the Urgal-1 station, while large concrete and brick buildings reflected Stalin's love of decorative, classically inspired architecture.

In 1959, Khrushchov declared that Stalinesque architecture was inappropriate with its energy inefficient high ceilings and complex decoration and advocated plainer, more easily constructed buildings. The architects of Amursk applied this decree to the letter and produced a fine example of post-Stalin construction. Consequently Amursk has some of the country's most ugly, concrete box apartment buildings which are totally devoid of decoration.

With the resumption of construction of the BAM in the 1970s, the new towns attempted a middle course of being attractive while functional. The result was square apartment boxes with decorations, and some attempts at originality through incorporating cultural elements of the 70 nationalities that worked on the BAM.

Some of the towns which were sponsored by particular Russian cities or regions and reflect some aspect of the builders' culture are:

BAM Town	Sponsor	Bam Town	Sponsor
Verkhnezeisk	Ufa	Soloni	Tadzhikistan
Suluk	Khabarovsk	Ogoron	Ulenovsk
Tungala	Novosibirsk	Dugda	Moldova
Fevralsk	Moldova	Marevaya	Moscow region
Dipkun	Moscow region	Tumaul	Moscow region
Kichera	Estonia	Postyshevo	Novosibirsk
Severobaikalsk	St Petersburg	Kuanda	Uzbekistan
Tynda	Moscow region	Niya	Georgia
Angoya	Armenia	Taksimo	Beloyrussia, Latvia

In many ways the USSR's national emblem, which contains the phrase *Proletariat of the World Unite* in the official language of the Soviet Union's 14 republics, reflects the multi-republic and ethnic participation in the construction of the BAM.

Bank (Банк)
Every town has the national savings bank, Sberabany Bank (Сбербаный Банк). This bank normally has a large queue as it pays pensions. It will buy and sell foreign currency.

Dacha village (Дачный посёлок)
See the *What do the locals eat?* section in this chapter.

Police (Милиция)
See the *Security and police* section in the *En route* chapter.

Hospital (Больница)
See the *Russian medical facilities* section in the *Planning a trip* chapter.

Banya (Баня)
A *banya* is a Russian wet sauna but the word is also used to mean a Russian bath house which can include a *banya*, Swedish dry sauna, a scrubbing area and a cold pool. The process starts with a number of friends sitting in the sauna and lightly hitting each other with branches of dried birch leaves dipped in water, which leave the skin tingling. After a few minutes you leave and scrub yourself down on a washing table. If you are so inclined you can jump into a cold water pool, before returning to the *banya*. This process is normally repeated 3 times. If there is no pool, people often roll outside in the snow. Avoid getting your hair wet between bouts in the sauna as this can give you a cold. After the *banya* you normally have something to eat, which could be a meal or more likely, just a snack of dried fish and beer. *Banyas* normally have session times so make sure you know when you have to be out before you enter. Birch branches, beer and even fish are on sale at the best of the banyas.

Some Russians like to pour beer, birchwood essence or eucalyptus oil onto the *banya's* hot rocks as this creates delightful aromas. By the end of your *banya* trip, you will feel clean, weary and wonderful. Make sure you are rugged up when you leave as it is really easy to get a chill after the *banya*.

The mis-understood climate
Непонятный климат

Snow and Siberia are often mistakenly thought of as synonymous. Therefore it is surprising for many to learn that Eastern Siberia is one of the driest climates in the world with almost no precipitation in winter and very little during summer. This dryness is mostly due to the fact that Siberia is a long way from the source of most precipitation - the sea. Moist air from the east (Pacific Ocean) and south (North East Asia) is cut off by high mountains, while winds from the west (Atlantic Ocean) lose all their moisture by the time they reach Eastern Siberia after travelling across Europe and most of Russia. To the north (Arctic Ocean), rain bearing winds are never generated.

Another result of being far from the sea is that the air temperature fluctuates wildly due to the absence of the regulatory effect of oceans. In some places, the temperature can vary by 30°C between day and night.

During winter, the rapidly cooling land leads to the formation of a permanent high pressure zone, known as the *Siberian High*. This high pressure zone is stationary over Sakha for the whole winter and results in cloudless skies, no wind and very little precipitation. The effect is further accentuated by the basin shape of the region which traps the cold air near the ground. During summer, the *Siberian High* breaks up and remoteness from the sea becomes the major climatic influence on precipitation. The annual rainfall ranges from 700mm at the coast to just 350mm in Tynda. Along most of the BAM, the snow depth rarely exceeds 30cm but stays on the ground for an average of 190 days a year.

The dryness also means that forest fires are a major problem throughout Eastern Siberia. Due to the short growing season and therefore slow growth rate of vegetation, fire damage is visible for decades. Along the Komsomolsk – Sovetskaya Gavin line, the evidence of the 1976 Khabarovsk Krai forest fire is still very obvious.

Permafrost

Permafrost is ground that is frozen throughout the year. Permafrost has an active layer of about 2m which thaws every spring and freezes each winter. The soil or rock below this active layer never melts, and has a constant temperature of minus 4°C.

The greatest depth of permafrost in Eastern Siberia is 1.5km but the greatest depth in the BAM Zone is 600m at Udokan near Chara. Climatically speaking, the permafrost is a relic of the last ice age, formed between 800,000 and 2.5 million years ago. The modern climate, while extreme, is no longer cold enough to create permafrost. However its aridity is enough to prevent the existing permafrost from melting.

The BAM passes through about 330km of permafrost with scattered thawed islands and about 1,000km of thawed ground dotted with islands of permafrost.

Glaciers

There are 18 places in the former Soviet Union where glaciers are found and 3 of these are in the BAM Zone. It is very surprising that glaciers exist in the Zone, considering its low altitude and that it is over 1,000km south of the next closest glacier.

One glacier site is just south of Severobaikalsk at Mt Cherski. This 1.5 square kilometre glacier is at a height of just 2,588m. Information on how to get to it is under *Severobaikalsk* in the *BAM mainline route description* chapter.

The second glacier site is in the Kodar mountain range. There are 40 known glaciers here, with a total area of 15 square kilometres, and more to be discovered. Each glacier is relatively small, with the longest just under 2km. The Kodar range peaks at 2,999m. The majority of Kodar range glaciers are mountain glaciers which slowly flow down mountain slopes or through valleys in winter and melt slightly in summer. The glaciers are 80m thick on average and move at a maximum speed of several metres a year for smaller ones to several hundred metres a year for large ones. There are also a few valley glaciers which trundle along the valley at 3 to 6 metres a year and some mountain glaciers which don't grow or shrink. Information on how to get to these glaciers is included under *Chara* in the *BAM mainline route description* chapter.

The third glacier site is very small and is near Neryungri.

Earthquakes

Seismic activity is common in the western part of the BAM and up to 802,000 minor tremors a year are felt here. There have been three major earthquakes in the region since recording started.

In 1930-31, the earth's crust subsided at the northern end of Lake

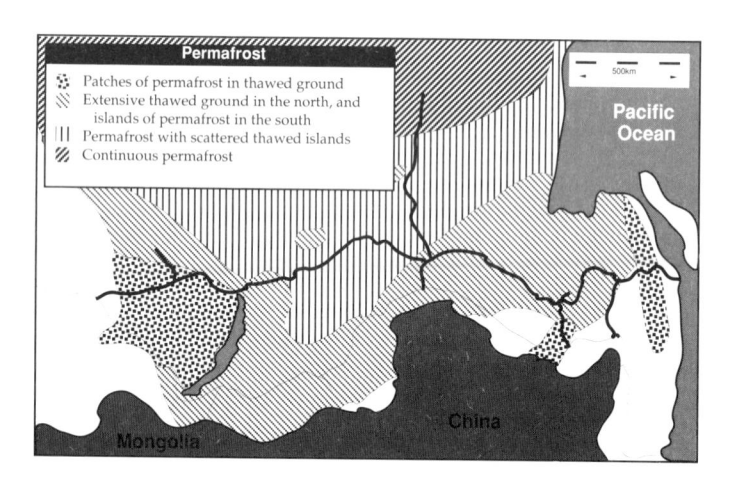

Baikal near the mouth of the Kichera River and the settlement of Nizhneangarsk. The town partly sank into the lake and had to be moved several hundred metres north towards the hills.

The largest earthquake in the BAM region, and the largest in Russian history, was recorded on 27 June 1957. This quake was so big that it is the only Russian one listed in the world's catalogue of earthquake disasters. The epicentre was in the Northern Muya mountains which is now the site of the 15km Severomuinsk BAM tunnel.

A few years after that earthquake, on 29 August 1959, inhabitants in a Lake Baikal town on the shores of the Proval Strait woke to find that some of their houses had rotated 35-40 degrees clockwise due to a massive land slip. Luckily few houses were destroyed due to the extensive use of wood which can easily withstand earthquakes measuring 9 points on the Richter scale. Scientists went to the earthquake's epicentre and found that in places, the lake had sunk by up to 15 metres. These subsidences are part of Lake Baikal's continual growth of 5 to 8km in width every million years.

Over 15 million roubles ($30 million) were allocated to seismic research of the BAM Zone during the early 1970s. One of the interesting discoveries was that permafrost significantly reduced the severity of earthquakes by absorbing their energy through the tens and hundreds of metres of frozen sand, water and rock. Research has found that the removal of the permafrost layer leads to an increase in seismicity by 2-3 points on the Richter scale. For this reason, it was essential that as much of the permafrost ground as possible was not disturbed when the BAM was built.

Rock rivers

Rock avalanches, called rock rivers, are common in some parts of the BAM, particularly in the section from Novaya Chara to Khani. The avalanches are caused by a combination of frost, which shatters rocks, and earth tremors. The avalanches are so common in some sections that vegetation does not have time to take root so hills and even entire mountains are completely bare.

The flora

Флора

The types of vegetation along the BAM Zone vary enormously and include tundra, *taiga*, broad-leaved forests, meadows, swamps and 'drunken' forests.

Tundra

Tundra is a treeless, frozen land where only primitive plants such as lichen and moss can survive. In the Siberian tundra, it rains less than 200mm a year and daylight length varies from 24 hours in summer to complete darkness for a whole month in the middle of winter. Technically, tundra is defined as an area when the mean monthly temperature never exceeds 10°C.

There are two sorts of tundra, arctic tundra and mountain tundra.

Arctic tundra is usually very flat as most of it was levelled by the great glaciers of the Quaternary ice age. These glaciers scraped and crushed rocks on their advance and dropped boulders and stones haphazardly on their retreat. Since the departure of the glaciers, the landscape has changed little as erosion from running water, the major cause of landscaping, has had insufficient time to act. Frost weathering (where water permeates a rock, the frost freezes the water and the rock is shattered as ice takes up more space than the water) is the greatest agent for change and its actions level any remaining features. The net result of frost weathering is that it has produced tonnes of debris which surrounds summits, litters plateaus and clutters up valley floors.

While arctic tundra is now confined to the north of Yakutsk, it once descended into the BAM Zone and its effects can still be seen in the flat land with numerous creeks meandering through it.

Mountain tundra is confined to above 1,700m and has the same barren appearance as arctic tundra. The main sections of mountain tundra the BAM passes through are between Novy Chara and Tynda, and on the AYAM to Aldan.

Taiga

The *taiga* forests of Russia are uncomprehendingly enormous, covering the vast majority of Siberia. *Taiga* is coniferous forest (also known as boreal forest) made up of spruce and larch trees with cones and needle-like leaves. Common *taiga* trees are Dahurian larch, Yeddo spruce, Erman's birch, Khingan fir, Norway spruce, Scots pine, Siberian larch, Siberian fir, Siberian spruce, Ayan spruce and the Siberian Silver Fir.

While both spruce and larch are varieties of conifers, there is a considerable difference between the two which allows them to coexist.

Spruces are evergreen, meaning that their leaves do not fall off during winter. Spruces have leaves which are borne singly on peg-like projections which remain attached to the twig when the leaves fall. The cones develop at the tips of the branches and hang downwards when they are ripe. Spruces have evolved a unique evolutionary mechanism which allows them to retain their foliage all year. In the autumn, the leaves enter a dormant state in which photosynthesis ceases and respiration falls to an extremely low level enabling their leaves to endure the very low winter temperatures, and at the start of spring when the day starts to lengthen, they quickly reactivate. There are about 34 types of spruce.

Spruces can endure shade but require moist, nutrient rich soil. For this reason, the best spruce stands are along river valleys with good drainage. The location of these stands was used by the first settlers to locate good arable land. The spruces are ideally adapted for growing in permanently frozen subsoil as they have a superficial root system which means that they can spread in the thawed top soil.

Larches are a light-loving species and can tolerate various soil types and moisture contents. They can grow in sandy soils, in swamps and on granite ledges. Larches have soft leaves in tufts that fall off in winter. There are about 9 species of larch trees.

The undergrowth of the *taiga* includes heathers such as *Ericaceae vaccinium* and *Ericaceae arctostaphylos*, flowering herbs such as twinflower, wintergreen and creeping orchid. Mosses are usually abundant, but in the driest *taiga*, only lichens grows. During the winter most of the herbs die down to their roots while small shrubs are covered by snow which insulates them from extremes of cold.

Taiga covers the landscape to a height of 1500m on most northern slopes and to 1700m on the southern slopes.

The BAM passing over the Stanovoi Range between Tynda and Novaya Chara reveals the distinct separation between the *taiga* and mountain tundra.

Broad-leaved forests

Despite the predominance of conifers, there are a large variety of other trees along the BAM including the Korean cedar (a light and beautifully hued wood used to produce turpentine oil, rosin, pine oil and plywood), ash (used as a decorative material and in engineering and shipbuilding), aspens (used for match sticks), the Amur cork tree (a good substitute for the classic Algerian cork tree), the Brazilian oak (used as an insulating material in ships, aircraft and refrigerators), Japanese stone pine, rhododendron, and Asiatic white birch.

Other types of terrain

There are three other main types of terrain you will pass through in the BAM Zone; meadows, swamps and drunken forests.

Meadows exist in isolated regions and their small size is one of the major limiting factors for local agriculture. There are two types of meadows: flood plain meadows which are located in river valleys and flood regularly, and dry valley meadows which are located in floodless regions or on hillsides and only exist temporarily following forest fires or logging. As it is very difficult to create flood plain meadows, most new haymaking and pasture meadows are in man-made dry valley meadows.

Natural swamps are not that common in the BAM Zone due to the scant precipitation, dry air, and good drainage of Eastern Siberia. Although there is several hundred kilometres of swamp, most of this is a result of destruction of the natural eco-system during the BAM's construction. Before construction, the forests evaporated the water that lay in the thawed soil above the permafrost. However following the removal of the absorption layer, the water forms a swamp as it cannot penetrate the permafrost, thereby killing the trees. If the area is not further disturbed, the swamp will eventually silt up over hundreds of years, thereby creating a new absorption layer, and the forests will eventually reclaim the area. As further disturbance is inevitable along the BAM, it is inevitable that the amount of swamps will increase.

Drunken forests are a product of the annual freezing and thawing of the soil which causes the earth to swell and shrink, resulting in the soil pushing out stones to the edge of the thaw area. This action often results in regular stone patterns which on flat ground are usually polygons and on sloping ground are lines. The churning of soil tilts over trees and hence their name of 'drunken' forests.

The fragile environment
Хрупкая окружающая среда

The BAM Zone's eco-systems have evolved over tens of thousands of years but can easily be destroyed in months. Due to the long months of icy winter and the short growing season, Siberian eco-systems are biologically very slow. This means that any environmental disturbance will be felt for years, if not decades. For example, following a forest fire, vegetation reaches equilibrium (climax vegetation) within 50 years in the southern republics of the former Soviet Union while it takes 200 years in the BAM Zone.

Siberia's environmental movement started to grow in the 1970s and 1980s with actions to protect Lake Baikal. Great achievements were made, such as stopping logs from being floated down the lake's tributaries because their bark pollutes the lake, reducing industrial pollution into the lake, and eliminating overfishing.

The Soviet government saw the political advantages of supporting environmental protection and even introduced environmental impact statements (EIS) for major new projects in the early 1980s. However there were no specific laws that stated when EISs must be prepared and what types of issues should be addressed. Instead, the Soviet government relied on broad laws which govern the use of water, land, wildlife, air and other natural resources. These laws mandated conservation and the prevention of harmful actions. For example, Article 21 of the 1980 Wildlife Law calls for "the organisation of scientific studies aimed at substantiating measures for the protection of the animal world".

This attitude probably reflects the general Russian view that environmental protection involves saving particular plants and animals rather than eco-systems. While most Russians are willing to sacrifice some factories to protect drinking water or save a particular animal, very few are prepared to make sacrifices for the less tangible benefit of saving an eco-system. The perception of the vastness of Siberia and its apparent ability to absorb human damage reinforces this reluctance.

The BAM and environmental destruction

Despite this attitude, the media did occasionally attack some projects, such as the BAM, for environmental reasons. For example, a 1984 article in Moscow's nationwide *Izvestiya* newspaper criticised the environmental blueprint for the BAM Zone. "We became acquainted with a project ... known as the *Territorial Comprehensive Plan for*

Siberian Cowboys

Since the late 1980s, the newest and possibly greatest environmental threat to the BAM Zone has come from a new breed of post-perestroika Siberian cowboys. These fortune seekers look for any opportunity to make a rouble or dollar and this invariably means illegally exploiting natural resources for short term profit. They believe that 'freedom' means 'freedom to take what they see'. Their most damaging activities involve alluvial gold mining where whole rivers are dredged with no revegetation, clear felling of forests and hunting of endangered animals.

In the past the law enforcement agencies would have stopped this but today, they have no money to even survey the damage. In addition, the profit from illegal activities has enabled huge bribes to be paid, which has resulted in the enforcement agencies becoming party to these crimes.

The two factors currently standing in the way of the cowboys are the indigenous people and the economy.

The indigenous people, who were forced into collective farms in the 1930s and 1940s, are now emerging to reclaim their ancient hunting and fishing lands from logging interests while the downturn of the economy has resulted in less demand for wood in Russia.

Both of these factors will not save the environment in the long term as the only real protection is creating a workable and enforceable legal system, building a cadre of honest Russian and Western business people, and opening the government's allocation of natural resources to public scrutiny. This will take years, maybe decades, to introduce and in the meantime the Eastern Siberian and Russian Far East environment is slowly but steadily being destroyed.

A river destroying gold dredge between Fevralsk and Tokur. Notice the giant picture of Lenin on top of the machine.

Environmental Protection Along the BAM. Its many volumes provide a comprehensive analysis of the territories and resource potential of the BAM Zone and forecast potential pollution and environmental damage. But we failed to find in the plan specific proposals as to how to protect primary topographical features and basic eco-systems ... and what kind of organisational measures are needed to protect the environment. Yet such proposals are essential."

The authors of the article were justified in their concerns about the BAM as it did and still causes considerable environmental damage. The problems can be divided into five categories: the railway line, the daily operation, construction debris, industrial development and population pressures.

- The railway line's very presence has dramatically altered the eco-systems through which it passes. Not only has it affected much of the landscape by diverting rivers, draining swamps and disturbing the permafrost, it has also cut in two the migration path of animals and introduced new species in the permanently cleared reserves alongside the line.
- The daily operation of the railway is a continual cause of large scale environmental pollution. Leaky locomotives drip about 1 litre of oil per 100km onto the rails while raw sewage from the train's toilets falls directly onto the tracks. Both of these pollutants find their way into the waterways. In addition, tens of thousands of tons of diesel soot and unburnt diesel fuel are pumped into the atmosphere each year by the trains.
- Construction debris, such as discarded equipment, rotting camps and left-over construction materials, litters the BAM route and continues to cause pollution as it decays. The biggest construction debris polluters are oil, petrol and chemical drums. As there were no refuelling points along the route when it was being constructed, all vehicles had to carry their own fuel needs. This resulted in a large number of spills and abandoned oil drums along the route.
- Industrial pollution is a major problem due to a combination of poor environmental standards in Russian factories and the climate. Inadequate standards tolerate higher levels of pollution than are internationally accepted and the practice of *storming* (a last minute work frenzy) to meet the monthly target frequently creates a surge of pollution that is high even by lax Russian laws.
- The region's expanding population also causes various forms of pollution such as river silting due to the clearing of forests for pastures, raw sewage overflowing into rivers and mountains of garbage which never seem to decompose.

The continual struggle for food
Непрерывная борьба за пищу

Since the start of the BAM until the mid 1980s and again in the early 1990s, the Zone dwellers have suffered continual food shortages with fresh milk being restricted to children and the sick, choices of vegetables limited to cabbages and potatoes, and meat always scarce.

This is despite a massive self-sufficiency program since the early 1970s that was formalised into Brezhnev's 1978 announcement that, "The newly developed economic regions should be provided with their own agricultural base and should be in a position to supply themselves with their own animal products and vegetables". In the media, the program was justified using a combination of ideology and warped scientific rationalism.

Ideological support came from Lenin himself when he wrote that new enterprises should be built near raw resources rather than carting the resources to be processed hundreds of miles away. In the case of the BAM, this was interpreted to mean that farms should be established near the human resources they needed to feed.

The theories of scientific rationalism, where science could always triumph over nature, also justified the ideas of self-sufficiency in areas not farmed before. Although the last major Soviet attempt to apply science to farming, in Khrushchov's 1950s Virgin Lands campaign, was a massive failure, Soviet technocrats believed that it was simply a matter of fine tuning. The BAM offered a second chance, admittedly a much harder one considering the land's poor potential for agriculture. To ensure that the nation's best minds were working on this project, in 1976 the Research Council on Agricultural Development in the BAM Zone was formed and slightly later the Scientific Council on the Problems of the BAM was created.

However the real reason for the self-sufficiency program was pragmatism. Regardless of the Soviet Union's propaganda of massive technological advances, continual plan overfulfillment and improving living standards, the government realised that virtually all Russian regions barely produced enough to feed themselves, let alone provide a surplus for other areas. In addition, the transport system was so chaotic that surplus food could not be guaranteed to reach its consumer in a fit state. Railway reports of the early 1980s stated that about 35% of rail freighted vegetables were spoiled during shipment over 2,000-3,000km.

To achieve self-sufficiency in the BAM Zone was an ambitious and unrealistic target as in 1978, there were only 27 farms in the entire BAM

The Real *Dacha*

While people living in houses have a garden, most high rise dwellers have a small plot on the outskirts of town to grow vegetables. This land is normally rented from the government for a minimal amount. Over time, the owner often builds a small shed which invariably gets enlarged into a little weekend cottage.

A growing number of people, particularly the unemployed and pensioners, are living permanently in their *dachas* all year round. Their advantages include more space than apartments and a source of food, while their disadvantages include being a long way from shops and no running water or electricity.

Typical of the move from city to *dacha village* are Nikolai and Erena Ushakov of Komsomolsk. Both have retired and they have slowly built their *dacha* over the last 10 years from bought and scavenged material. Despite its lack of electricity and running water, they are immensely proud of their two storey house. The principal source of cooking is natural gas and their tanks are filled every 3 months by a delivery truck.

The garden produces their entire year's supply of potatoes, cucumbers, eggplant, strawberries, sunflower, beans, radish, cabbage, lettuce, corn, onions and tomatoes. A small greenhouse is heated with a wood fire.

The short summer is an exceptionally busy time for Nikolai and Elena with gardening, *kolbasa* making, pickling, jam making, *kvas* and vodka brewing, mushroom collecting and continuing the construction of their *dacha*. In winter, the cold is too much for Elena and she returns to the city to live in their flat which now houses her son's family. Nikolai prefers to live in the *dacha* where he can ice fish and hunt for wild sheep and deer. The long winter evenings are spent making things out of the pelts and eating sunflower seeds by the light of candles.

In many ways, *dacha* life is remarkably similar to Siberian life of 100 years ago.

The extended Uskakov family of Komsomolsk proudly displaying their *dacha*.

Zone which met only 25% of local needs in 5 of the 7 BAM administrative regions and contributed nothing at all in the other two regions.

The magnitude of this problem is illustrated by one directive emanating from the central planning headquarters in Moscow which declared that the BAM Zone should be 65% self sufficient in milk. Using the figures from another government department which stated that each citizen was to receive 185 litres a year of fresh milk, this meant that the 10,600 cows in the region in 1978 had to increase to 144,500 by the late 1980s. Providing fodder for the anticipated number of animals required a massive program of deforestation, reclamation, redirecting water courses and damming. Before the self-sufficiency was stopped, 96,600ha of hay land and 33,000ha of range land were created at the cost of the destruction of numerous river eco-systems.

Increasing vegetable cultivation was just as difficult. There is only an average of 94 frost free days per year which is just sufficient for cold-resistant varieties of cabbage, red beets and carrots. To grow other vegetables requires expensive heated and artificially lit greenhouses. In addition, the new farms would require farmers but few were attracted to work in the BAM Zone with its harsh climate, unworked land and limited potential for farm machinery due to the hilly terrain.

Despite the best efforts of economists, scientists and politicians, the Agricultural Academy of the Siberian Division of the Soviet Academy of Agricultural Sciences finally admitted the defeat of the self-sufficiency policy in 1985 with a statement that the BAM Zone's program was a failure. The Academy reluctantly admitted that while technically all the food could be grown locally, it would be too expensive, and it was recommended that the BAM Zone import 80% of its butter, cheese and grain needs from West Siberia.

Following this announcement, food supply increased until the economic downturn in the early 1990s, when inhabitants of the BAM Zone had to survive on their own resources. The food shortage peaked in 1991 and 1992 but nowadays, food is readily available just as it is anywhere in Russia.

Locally produced food comes from four sources: collective farms, state farms, industrial sideline farms and private garden plots.

Collective farms are farming enterprises supposedly owned by the members, but in reality they are the same as state farms which are simply large commercial farms owned by the government.

Industrial sideline farms are small farms owned by large industrial enterprises which provide food for their workers. These farms are important in attracting and retaining workers in a region where food shortages are common. Examples include the Osetrovo River Port Industrial Farm at Ust-Kut, the Aircraft Plant Farm at Komsomolsk and the Tin Concentrator Farm at Solnechny. Sideline farms create a number of problems. Firstly, the operation of a sideline farm distracts the management of the industrial enterprise from its principal task. Secondly, the more self-sufficient an enterprise becomes, the more insular it becomes. Thirdly, as the free market forces started to take effect in the late 1980s and early 1990s, some enterprises realised that they could make more money with their sideline farms than their principal business. This resulted in resources being directed to the farms with a corresponding fall in industrial output.

Private garden plots were and are essential in supplementing the limited quantities and varieties of food available in state stores. Most people keep a small garden around their houses while flat dwellers were entitled in the 1980s to a 600 square metre plot of land on the outskirts of the town. In the late 1980s, about 40% of all of Moscow's food was produced in small garden plots and in the BAM region, there can be no doubt that it would have been even higher. To extend the short growing season, most gardens have a greenhouse maintained at an optimal 28°C. These extend the growing season to mid September and if it is heated by a slow burning stove or by a hot water pipe, to mid October. Although in the past, some enterprise-owned glasshouses were heated and lit all year round, the price of electricity and hot water has risen astronomically in the last few years and this is no longer practical. Seeds can occasionally be bought in the local shops, but many people make a yearly pilgrimage to Moscow where there are seed shops which stock unusual varieties such as Khol-Rabi.

What do the locals eat?

Чем питаются местные жители?

The meals eaten by locals in the BAM Zone are classically Russian. This means that they are of limited variety, mostly fried and noted for their absence of spices. In the summer months, there is an abundance of home grown vegetables but in winter, the choice is reduced to a few staples such as potatoes, cabbages and onions.

Despite the fact that the residents of the BAM came from all over the former Soviet Union, the food is fairly uniform, particularly the commercially available bread and cakes. This is an interesting comment on the food imperialism of Russia.

The basis of all Russian meals is bread and tea. There are only two types of bread: black and white. The black is a heavy rye bread which lasts for over a week without going stale. The white is delicious when

62 The BAM Zone

Native Food

1. Amur barberry
2. blueberry
3. woodbine
4. wild strawberry
5. cowberry
6. raspberry
7. sea buckthorn
8. blackcurrant
9. small cranberry
10. redcurrant
11. Mongolian dandelion
12. wild onion
13. Siberian cedar
14. bracken fern
15. hazelnut
16. rowantree, mountain ash
17. wildrose, dogrose
18. hawthorn

Native Food

Name	Picking time	Preparation	Notes
Siberian cedar (кедр сибирский)	September to October	The needles are boiled to make a stomach soothing tea and vitamin C drink. Pine nuts are found in the cones. They are eaten raw or crushed for oil.	This tree lies down in winter parallel with the ground and springs upright when it thaws. Found in the *taiga*. The tree produces cones once every 5 or 6 years.
Amur barberry (барбарис амурский)	September to the fall of snow	Used in jam or as meat seasoning.	Found in broad-leaved forests along the upper Amur River.
bird cherry tree (черёмуха)	mid July to August	Eaten raw and the seeds ground for cooking spice or coffee. The grounds are also used for a stomach soothing drink.	Found in light *taiga* and along rivers. The beautiful trees have white flowers and black berries.
blackcurrant (смородина чёрная)	mid June to mid July	Eaten raw or used in jam.	Found in light *taiga* and along rivers.
blueberry (голубника)	mid July to August	Eaten raw or used in jam.	Found near waterways.
bracken fern (папоротник)	May to mid June	Boil the shoots and fry with garlic and egg.	Found in light *taiga* and around swamps. Beware of the rhizome (roots) which are poisonous and will give you stomach, liver and bowel problems.
cowberry, red whortleberry, red bilberry, mountain cranberry (брусника)	September to snow fall	Eaten raw or used in jam or in *kompot* fruit drink.	Found in *taiga*. The red berry survives all winter under the snow and last year's crop can be eaten just after the thaw. It is very popular with the Chinese and Japanese.
hawthorn (боярышник)	September to October	Eaten raw or used in jam.	A red fruit with pink or white blossoms.
hazelnut (лесной орех)	September	Roasted.	Found in broad-leaved forest.
Mongolian dandelion (одуванчик монгольский)	from late May	The leaves are eaten raw in salads.	Found in meadows. A variety of dandelion with a yellow flower.
raspberry (малина)	early August	Eaten raw or used in jam or in tea.	Found in meadows, light *taiga* and along rivers.
redcurrant (смородина красная)	mid July to August	Eaten raw or used in jam.	Found in meadows, light *taiga* and along rivers.

Native Food cont.

Name	Picking time	Preparation	Notes
rowan tree, mountain ash (рябина)	September to October	Eaten raw or used in jam.	Found in broad-leaved forests.
sea buckthorn (облепиха)	June	Used to make *kompot* fruit drink.	
small cranberry (клюква болотная)	August	Eaten raw or used in jam or *kompot* fruit drink.	Found near waterways. The red berry survives all winter under snow and last year's crop can be eaten just after the thaw.
wild onion (черемша)	Mid June to mid July	Eaten raw or pickled. Tastes like spring onions.	Found in light *taiga*. Sold as bunches of leaves.
wild rose, dog rose (шиповник)	August to September	Eaten raw or used to make rose tea and rose flavoured liqueur.	Found in light *taiga*, meadows and along rivers.
wild strawberry (земляника)	end June to July	Eaten raw.	Found in light *taiga*, meadows and along rivers. Not as nice or large as normal strawberries but quite edible.
woodbine (жимолость)	late June to August	Eaten raw or used in jam.	

fresh but goes bland and stale within a few hours. Tea is made by pouring hot water onto leaves in a small container. This concentrated tea is kept for the day and when needed, small amounts of it are poured into a cup and boiling water is added. The tea is different from the common Indian or Ceylonese varieties as it does not go bitter when stewed. At most meals there will be sweets which can be a substitute for sugar in tea.

A typical worker's lunch will be a slab of bread, an onion, tea and *salo* or *kolbasa*. *Salo* is salt or smoke cured pig fat. *Kolbasa* is either a conventional western salami or a sausage-salami which has a texture of sausage but is smoked and can be eaten without cooking.

Typical snack food is beer, dried fish and sunflower seeds. The dried fish consists of a whole fish and to eat it you rip off the skin and tear off the chewy dried fish flesh. Sunflower seeds are bought by the cupful at the market or still attached to the giant flower head which is more fun eating.

A typical dinner includes shallow fried potato chips and a slab of meat. Common variations include fried macaroni with meat, boiled fish and fried slices of *kolbasa*. During winter most vegetables are pickled, while in summer the vegetables will be fresh.

As well as tea, coffee and boiled water, a popular drink is *kompot* which is made from stewed fruit. Vodka is the most common alcoholic drink, as beer is frowned upon as a workers' drink. However this attitude is changing with the increasing popularity of imported beer. Milk is hardly ever drunk by healthy adults.

Preserving food

Once food is grown, it has to be preserved so that there is something to eat over the long winter.

Vegetables are normally pickled in a mixture of vinegar, sugar, black currant leaves and dill.

Fish is salted which simply involves gutting the fish and tossing lots of salt on it. The salt sucks the fluid out of the fish and the salt slurry is regularly drained off and replaced by fresh salt. After 24 hours, the fish can be hung out in the open and after two weeks, the breeze and sun produces long-life dried, salted fish. Another option is to leave the fish in salt for a few days and then eat it raw like salty sushi. A third option is to fillet the fish, cover it with salt and keep replacing the salt until no more moisture comes out. The fish is then packed with salt and sealed in a barrel. Fish can also be smoked but this will not keep for as long. Smoking is done by filling the bottom of a metal container with green

A typical afternoon tea of apples, jam, tea and bread for the adults and dinner of meat and potatoes for children.

leaves, and above this, lying the fish on a metal grill. A lid is then placed on the container and a fire lit underneath it. It takes about 1 hour to smoke a fish.

Red meat can be either frozen or smoked. In houses that do not have refrigerators or electricity, the meat is kept in an underground coolstore. This coolstore is kept cold all summer long by blocks of ice cut from frozen lakes and rivers in winter. Smoking is normally reserved for salami-like *kolbasa* and as most people prefer to buy it rather than make it, *kolbasa* smoking is a dying art.

Kolbasa is invariably made from pork and is made as the weather cools in late autumn. The process starts with slitting the throat of the pig and catching the drained blood. The skin on the pig is then singed with a blow torch which removes the hair. The animal is then gutted and the intestines are cleaned out to be used as the *kolbasa* skins. Meanwhile the flesh of the pig is minced and stuffed into the remaining intestines. Salt, pepper and paprika are added to give flavour and help preservation. The *kolbasa* are then hung up in a smoking shed with the *salo* and after 24 to 48 hours are ready to be eaten. *Kolbasa* can be stored for over a year without going off. Some people use the remaining organs and the blood by boiling them, mincing them up, mixing them with rice and finally stuffing them into the intestines to make a rice-based black pudding. *Kolbasa* is not made from reindeer or rabbit as their meat has too little fat and their intestines are too large.

Native food
Местная пища

Collecting native food is a major social event as well as providing an important dietary supplement. Going to the forests or fields collecting berries, mushrooms, nuts and roots is not just limited to rural folk but is also an activity city dwellers love.

A number of native foods in Eastern Siberia are not found in European Russia and for the initial explorers, many had an unpleasant taste. An example of this is *cheremsha*, a leafy vegetable that tastes like spring onion. Back in 1850, the Eastern Siberian Governor General N Muravev-Amurski, on one of his explorations of the Amur, noted that "I bravely ate *cheremsha* to prevent scurvy" as an example for his men. At that time, spring onions was unheard of in Russia. Nowadays, most Russians in the BAM Zone eat *cheremsha* and Westerners will enjoy it.

The *native food table* lists the native foods along the BAM Zone. The picking time is for the western section of the BAM between

Severobaikalsk and Novy Urgal. At the eastern end of the BAM, the picking time may be a month earlier. Participating in a picking expedition with Russians is a highly recommended, enjoyable and educational experience.

Mushrooms (грибы)
Collecting mushrooms is probably Russia's most popular outdoor activity. There are 3,000 varieties of mushrooms in the former Soviet Union, however there are only a few hundred which are edible with the most common being the white mushroom (белый), rough stemmed boletus (подберёзовик) and orange caped boletus (подосиновик). Mushrooms can be eaten raw, salted, pickled or fried. Mushrooms pop up from June to September depending on the rain. As with other native food, if you don't know if it is edible, don't eat it.

The fishing wonderland
Рыбалка

The BAM Zone contains some of the best fishing places in Russia and in most places, the fish stocks are increasing. This is partly due to the decrease in fishing following the collapse of government subsidised fishing enterprises and partly because of the increase in breeding following a reduction in pollution as industrial enterprises shut down.

Virtually everyone in the BAM Zone fishes as it provides both a recreation and an important source of food. However there are only a small number who are truly fanatical fishermen and have an excellent knowledge of all the fish in their region. These people are introducing foreigners to the delights of Russian fishing and in return, foreigners have spread the concept of throwing back rare fish

---

CAVIAR (Икра)

There are 3 sorts of caviar, or fish eggs; black sturgeon caviar (kaluga sturgeon, Siberian sturgeon, beluga sturgeon), soft red salmon caviar (dog-salmon, taimen, red sockeye salmon, humpback salmon), and other fish caviar (black carp, black Amur bream, whitefish, Amur pike, grayling, silver carp, sea urchin, Amur pike).

The first two types of caviar are commercially produced by pasteurising, pressing and salting eggs taken from live fish. Many fishermen make their own caviar by scooping out the fish eggs from the fish into a container. A stick with a nail through it is then rotated like a beater in the container to break up the membrane between the eggs. After a few minutes, salt is added and the caviar is ready to eat. However it is best to leave it for a few days as it improves with age.

In August and September, fish are spawning and locals sell fresh caviar for $3 a glass jar at the BAM stations. The sight of hundreds of dead fish following the spawning is disconcerting for some.

so they can continue to breed. During summer, locals use a combination of bait, lures and fly fishing to catch fish. In winter, there is only one method which is to cut a hole in the ice and dangle a line. The fanatical fishermen have several prepared camps along rivers which they use depending on the weather and season. During winter, they often build a shelter over their hole cut in the ice so they can stay there for several days at a time. For additional information on fishing in the region, see the *BAM Zone Fishing Guide* in the *Recommended reading* section.

Places to fish

The best places to fish on the BAM are around Kuanda, Verkhnezeisk, Postyshevo and Komsomolsk. A brief summary of the fish in these areas follows with detailed information on how to organise a fishing trip listed under the respective towns in the *BAM mainline route description* chapter. The laws governing fishing vary from region to region, and fishing is prohibited at some places at certain times of year. However generally a licence is not needed unless you catch over 50kg of fish or use a net.

Kuanda is surrounded by over 30 lakes, and numerous rivers which flow into the long Vitim River. It is one of the few places left in Russia where you can find the mighty taimen, however even there you will have to travel several hundred kilometres up the Vitim to be guaranteed

Fishing in the *taiga* can be dangerous, particularly after the bears arise from hibernation. Fishing tackle is often carried in a briefcase.

a catch. In the surrounding lakes and rivers are grayling, Amur pike, whitefish, Soldatov's catfish and the endemic targun.

Verkhnezeisk is on the Zeya Reservoir which is becoming a rich fishing area. Fish include Amur pike, Soldatov's catfish, taimen, Amur id, grayling and *Brachymstax* salmon.

Postyshevo is a 10 minute walk from the Amgun River which is famous as one of the best fishing rivers in Eastern Siberia. In late summer and autumn, you can flyfish for dog salmon and hunchback salmon, while in winter you can icefish for *Brachymstax* salmon, taimen and grayling.

Komsomolsk is on the Amur River which is fed by 120,000 big and little rivers. The Amur is stocked with 99 different species of fish, which is the greatest variety in any Russian river. The main fish caught are the dog salmon and humpback salmon. Other fish caught include silver carp, kaluga, skygazer, *Erythroculter Mongolicus* and Siberian sturgeon. While the fish stocks in the river are dwindling due to overfishing and pollution, there are still a great deal of fish in its tributaries.

Animals of the BAM Zone
Животные в Зоне БАМа

There is a large variety of animals in the BAM Zone, as it encompasses the vastly different habitats of *taiga*, broad-leaved forests, meadows, swamps and mountain tundra.

The *taiga* is a harsh environment for animals with an abundance of food in summer and very little in winter. Consequently, the animal density is quite small. For example, in the Bodaibo Zakaznik there are only 10 sables and 50 squirrels for every 10,000 square km. Animal variety is greatest in the *taiga* of the east and decreases as you move westward. Broad-leaved forests contain the greatest variety of native animals of all habitats while meadows are inhabited by many introduced species from European Russia. Mountain tundra supports only a small number of species due to the vegetation's lack of protection and food.

Indigenous people
Местные Жители

The indigenous peoples of Eastern Siberia and the Russian Far East, like many indigenous peoples all over the world, are facing cultural

Some BAM Animals

Siberian Chipmunk and Squirrels (бурундук, белка): The chipmunk, squirrel and flying squirrel are ideally suited to the vast *taiga* as they can eat the conifers' bark and cones. The best squirrel pelts in Russia come from the Barguzin area where local pride in the animal is shown by the heraldic symbol of a squirrel sitting on a silver ground.

Bears (медведь): Every year bears kill one or two people in the BAM Zone and the Russian Far East. Attacks invariably happen at the end of winter when the bears awake from their hibernation and are very hungry. Most deaths occur in areas far from human settlement so you are perfectly safe in a town. If you do go trekking in remote areas, a guide with a rifle is normally only essential when the bears are hungry. But remember, it's better to be safe than sorry.

Sables (соболь): While sables are still hunted in Siberia, over 75% of them come from farms. Despite years of scientific breeding, raising sables in captivity is still very difficult due to rapid transfers of disease. In the BAM Zone there are about 10 sable farms, and these are worth a visit. The most precious sable is the Vitim or Barguzin black sable. This animal only lives in Russia and was saved from extinction when hunting was prohibited in 1912 for 3 years and again from 1935 to 41. These animals cannot be raised in captivity and are extremely rare outside of the Barguzin *Zapovednik* on the Lake Baikal eastern shore, and small areas of the Urals where they have been introduced.

Musk-rat (ондатра): Also known as musquash, these animals have been used for centuries to make the popular Russian musk-rat fur cap. Due to over hunting, these hats haven't been available for several years in Russian shops. In addition, musk-rats are used by fishermen to make lures for the taimen fish.

Animals of the BAM Zone 71

Legend

1. hare (заяц)
2. marmot, Mongolian bobak (сурок, тарбаган)
3. musk deer (кабарга)
4. wolf (волк)
5. reindeer (олень)
6. roe deer (косуля
7. pine marten
8. Ussuri wild boar (Уссурийский кабан)

Amur Tiger

The Amur tiger is the second rarest of the five species of tigers worldwide, and like other tigers around the world, it is facing extinction. There are about 20 Amur tigers left in north east China, a few in North Korea and the majority in two reserves in the Russian Far East. The largest reserve is the Lazovsky *Zapovednik* near Vladivostok with a tiger population of about 300 while about 100 tigers live in the Sikhote-Alin *Zapovednik* north east of Khabarovsk.

At one time the tiger roamed the whole of the Russian Far East but by the 1930s, it had been exterminated everywhere except in a few pockets. In the mid 1930s a determined effort to preserve the tiger resulted in the creation of the Sikhote-Alin *Zapovednik* in 1935, a five-year ban (1936 - 1940) on hunting the red deer which is the tiger's main prey, a massive restriction in the number of hunting licences issued after 1941 and a ban on the capture of tiger cubs.

The tiger population slowly rose until the mid 1980s. Since then the numbers have dwindled, principally because of logging of the tigers' habitat and expanding agricultural land which has brought tigers closer to humans, with the animals invariably coming off the worse. There have been a number of incidents of tigers taking domestic animals, including dogs, and in March 1986, a sighting of a tiger in a main city street in Vladivostok. In the latter case, the cat was pursued 200km before it was shot.

Officially, only 35 tigers have been legally or illegally shot each year from 1985 to 1990. However the actual number of killings far exceeded this because of a combination of the collapse of the Soviet Union, the destruction of the scientific and law enforcement agencies, and the opening of the border with China which resulted in a surge of poaching. Tiger bone is particularly valuable in the folk medicine of China, Taiwan, North and South Korea and other Asian countries.

A more accurate hunting toll is about 70 tigers a year and another 10 die each year from natural causes. This far exceeds the annual birthrate.

Other factors in the reduction of the tiger population include the ease of purchasing rifles, poor regulation of hunting, continual destruction of habitat and the absence of a clear legal base for the use of natural resources.

annihilation or even extinction. Centuries of Chinese, Russian and Soviet assimilation policies, alcohol, disease and unemployment have all taken their toll. Today, several indigenous groups have been reduced to just a few hundred members.

There are only 800,000 indigenous people in the whole of Siberia, making up just 3% of the region's total population. About 15,000 of these lead a nomadic lifestyle with the rest living in collective farms and fisheries, or working in Russian cities and villages.

Siberian indigenous people can be divided into three main groups.

The largest is the Buryat who were part of Genghis Khan's great empire. They were a people of grass lands who led a nomadic life based on horse and cattle breeding, but following Russian colonisation have

AMUR TIGER ACTION PLAN

To combat the dwindling numbers of tigers, the *Amur Tiger Action Plan* was launched in 1993 in Khabarovsk and coordinated by the Wildlife Foundation. The Foundation is a non-government environmental group, made up of 6 Far Eastern nature reserves, 3 scientific institutes, a number of indigenous people's associations and several foreign environmental non-government organisations.

The main objective of the Foundation is to preserve the Russian Far East's unique biodiversity. This involves the protection of rare and endangered species such as the Amur tiger, the red wolf and the Japanese and hooded cranes. The Foundation is working towards the development of a network of protected territories to combat habitat loss.

The *Amur Tiger Action Plan* demands the creation of a new protected territory for the conservation of tiger habitat in Khabarovsk Krai. The plan calls for coordinated development of conservation measures and viable economic alternatives for local people. The Foundation has also assisted in the development of an anti-poaching campaign for Primorye and Khabarovsk Krais, initiated by the Tiger Trust, the World Wildlife Fund and the Russian Ministry of Ecology.

The Foundation invites all interested individuals or institutions to become members. Membership is free. The Foundation is interested in attracting collaborative grants, foreign scientists, ecologists, botanists and education groups.

To raise desperately needed research money, the Wildlife Foundation organises photo tourism of the tiger and other animals.

The Wildlife Foundation,
680049, Russia,
Khabarovsk-49, Lev
Tolstoy Street 15-A.
Tel: (4212) 21 12 98
Fax: (4212) 22 04 10
Email:
wildlife@wf.khabarovsk.su

been integrated into mainstream Russian society.

The second largest group are the Tunguso-Manchurian tribes which can be further divided into two groups: the Tungusic (northern peoples: Evenki, Even and Negidais) and Manchurian (or southern: Nanais, Ulchas, Oroks Oroch and Udehes). The Tungus people arose from a mixing of aboriginal tribes from Northern Siberia with tribes from Southern Siberia and Manchuria. The first Tungus people appeared in the Lake Baikal area and migrated north and east sometime after 1,000AD.

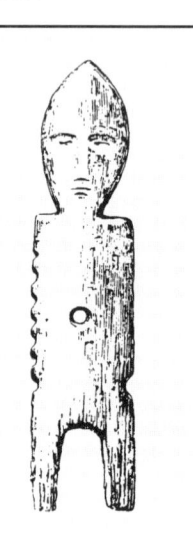

The third and smallest group is the Nivkhi. This race has a separate language and culture, and the Nivkhi people are believed to be the original inhabitants of the area. They are a maritime people living mainly on fishing and seal hunting. Another distinctive characteristic is that they cremated their dead unlike their neighbours who usually used air burials which involved putting corpses in trees. The Nivkhi share many characteristics with the North American Inuit people.

Shamanism

While both Lamaism (Tibetan style Buddhism) and Christianity are widespread in Eastern Siberia, Shamanism is the religion most widely associated with the region. Shamanism takes many forms with each tribe and clan having different traditions and practices. However all forms are based on the belief in a universe consisting of three worlds linked by a river. The upper world is inhabited by gods, the middle by people and the lower by the spirits of the dead. In the human world, nature is dominated by occult forces from the other two worlds.

A shaman is not a priest and does not officiate at ceremonies but is a person who has been blessed with the sacred power of spirit contact. The shaman's work is mostly to do with healing, divination, clairvoyance, magical bodyguard creation and guiding the dead into the underworld.

A *massi* idol which sits in the corner of a house protecting the occupants. The shaman invests the massi with a guardian spirit from the lower world and by feeding the spirit through the hole in the idol's stomach or mouth, the occupants believe that it will keep the spirit's strength up while purifying the food. *Massis* are produced by an idol maker to the shaman's orders and are not considered art but practical items.

Shamanism is an aggressive discipline involving constant combat with occult forces, demons and evil spirits. The contact and battles are achieved during an ecstatic state induced by dancing, drum beating and occasionally by eating hallucinogenic Fly Algaric mushrooms.

The Future of the Indigenous People

Since the fall of the communist government, little has changed for the indigenous people of Siberia. Although officially indigenous people are no longer labelled culturally deficient or forced to work on collectives, racism and stereotyping often prevent indigenous people from achieving their full potential.

Most indigenous peoples live on the verge of poverty and have a shortening life expectancy. Unemployment is widespread, alcoholism is rampant, traditional occupations looked down upon, and children of indigenous people are still being educated in Russian in boarding schools. In addition, the accelerating destruction of the environment, combined with unfettered immigration, is putting further pressure on indigenous cultures.

One of the few positive aspects of the collapse of communism for the indigenous people has been the ability to protest. Recent protests have stopped environmental logging and dredging practices, stopped logging of certain habitats that disrupt the food chain and won back sovereignty over traditional hunting and fishing grounds. With the decentralisation

Indigenous Peoples in the BAM Zone

Ethnicity	Population and location
Evenki (Tungus)	40,000 in total (including populations in Mongolia and China), 28.000* in the former Soviet Union. Their lands are bounded by the Ensei River to the west, the tundra between the Ensei and Lena Rivers to the north, the Sea of Okhotsk to the east and the Amur River to the south.
Even (Lamut)	12,800*. They are found east of the Lena River.
Negidais	400 - 500* people. They live along the Amgun and Amur Rivers between Komsomolsk and Nikolaevsk.
Nanais (Goldy)	13,100. They are found along the lower reaches of the Amur River and right tributaries of the Ussuri River.
Ulchas (Manguny)	923`. They are found on the lower reaches of the Amur River.
Oroki	190`. They live on the Easten side of the Sakhalin Island.
Oroch	1,200*. They live in just 2 areas near Sovetskaya Gavan and Komsomolsk.
Udehes	1,902. They live along the Kungari and Aniui Rivers.
Buryat	353,000. They are found in the Buryatiya Republic
Nivkhi (Gilyaks)	4,400. They live on the lower Amur River and Sakhalin Island

1979 Census   `1989 Census

of power from Moscow to the provinces, now is the best and possibly last chance many indigenous communities will have to make changes that for once will benefit them rather than the state or private industry.

Contacts
Oroki: Nadezhda Aleksandrovna Laigun, Native Affairs Officer, 39 Kommunisticheskii Prospekt, Yuzhno-Sakhalinsk, 693011 (Надежда Александровна Лаигун, 693011, Южно-Сахалинск Про. Коммуницический 39).
Oroki: Tatyana Roon, Sakhalin Regional Museum, 29 Kommunisticheskii Prospekt, Yuzhno-Sakhalinsk, 693011 (татяна Роон, 693011, Южно-Сахалинск, Музей, Про. Коммуницический 29).
Nanai: Valeri Makhailovich Belgy, Chairman, The Nanai People's Association, Khabarovsk Krai, Nanaiski Raion, Troitskoe, ul Pazo, d8, kv 2 (Бельгы Балерий Махайлович, Хабаровск край, Нанайский район, посолок Троицкое, ул Пазо, д 8, кв 2).
Nanai and Orochi: Zoya Stepanovna Lapshana, Regional Museum, pr Mira 8, Komsomolsk-na-Amur tel: 422-60 (Зоя Степановна Лапшана; Комсомольск-на-Амуре; Музей краеведческий; пр Мира 8).
Nivki and Ulchi: Vyacheslav Orlov, Head of Collection, Nikolaevsk Museum, Ul Gogol, Nikolaevsk-na-Amure, 682430, tel: 2-23-47, fax: 2-22-66 (att. museum) (Вячеслав Валерьевич Орлов, главчий хранетель, 682430 г. Николаевск-ча-Амуре; ул Гоголя).

Russia is experiencing a rebirth of interest in shamanism by both indigenous people and Russians. Shaman spiritual services are now big business.

For the Real Rail Enthusiast

An empire within an empire   78

Rolling stock   82

From a railway enthusiast's point of view, the BAM is one of Russia's most interesting railways. Unlike the rest of the Russian railways, the BAM's facilities, locomotives and wagons are new which has meant that the BAM incorporates the latest advances in management and equipment. In addition, no other railway in the world runs through such a harsh environment as the BAM Zone and observing the solutions to operating in this climate is fascinating.

The following sections explain some of the mysteries of all Russian railways and should help you understand your journey better.

An empire within an empire
Империя в империи

The Russian Ministry of Railways is an enormous organisation by any measure and prior to the collapse of the Soviet Union, it ran the world's largest railway. It managed over 3 million employees and organised the transport of 4,000 billion tonne-km of freight and 411 billion passenger-km. To put this in perspective, this is about 2.5 times the total freight on all North American railways and 2 times the passenger-km of the UK, France, Germany and Italy combined.

Today the railways of the Russian Federation consist of 19 railway administrations, of which the BAM is one.

Like all Soviet enterprises, the Ministry of Railways learned that unless it controlled all inputs to its organisation, there was no guarantee that it would receive what it ordered. This meant that the Ministry grew into an empire with over two third of its workers employed in non-core activities such as hospitals, schools, vacation assistance, housing administration, water supply and farms. This is particularly apparent on the BAM where nearly every town is owned and run by various departments of the BAM railway.

The best illustration of this empire is the railway telephone system. The Russian Ministry of Railways operates one of the world's largest private telephone networks with over a million telephone lines. Of these, 60% are located at railway stations and offices, 30% in the homes of railway employees and 10% at commercial establishments. In larger towns, there is a combination of railway and civil phones, but in many BAM towns there are only railway phones. Although there are connections between the civil and railway phone systems, this is extremely difficult to organise and it is often necessary to call the main railway telephone switchboard in Tynda or Moscow to get such a connection. The phone lines are also sometimes used as dedicated computer lines, however, these are rare. There are no railway fibre optic cables along the BAM nor are any planned.

Why trains don't crash

Despite the fact that the BAM is a single track with trains going in both directions, there have been no recorded head on collisions. This excellent track record is due to many complementary safety systems, with the most important being signals.

The BAM uses a 2-block, 3 aspect colour light autoblocking signal system which basically means that the railway is divided up into sections of not less than 2.5km and controlled by a three colour signal. If the light is green then it means that the next two blocks are empty of trains, if it is yellow then only one block is empty and if it is red then there is a train in the next block and it is impossible to enter. Stations are located about 40km apart on the BAM and only once all of the blocks between the stations are green, are trains going the other direction allowed to enter. When this happens, the signals facing the new train are switched on and those facing the other direction are turned off.

Under the rails next to the signal post is a electromagnetic pickup

Pereval station is typical of the little stations dotted along the BAM every 35-40km. Life at these small stations is lonely as often the closest humans are at the next station. In the photo, the station master is holding a white disc as the train speeds by to confirm that it is safe for the train to proceed.

which identifies when a train passes over it. If you look out the window as the train passes a signal, you will see it change from green to red as soon as the locomotive reaches it. A 25volt cable running along the entire length of the BAM carries this information to the closest stations. An automatic system in the locomotives ensures that unless the train is brought to a halt by the driver within 12 seconds of passing into a 'red' block, the brakes will automatically be applied. This 'deadman's handle' ensures that if the driver dies, the train stops automatically. There is an override but this only works if the train is going less than 20km/h and if both the driver and his assistance push an override button every 8 seconds.

Inside the cab, there is a display of 3 coloured lamps which mirror the outside signals. In addition, there is a white lamp which lights if the outside signals are not working. A report in the railway newspaper, *Gudok*, stated that onboard signalling systems have a failure rate of only 2.2%.

While not a safety measure, the 'black box' recorder in the locomotive cab is used to continually improve the safety of the line by finding the cause of any problems such as derailments or crashes. The black box on the train records on paper the speed, signals passed and distance travelled and stands in the right hand corner of the cab.

So how do trains going in the opposite direction pass? Basically, a train pulls into a siding off the main line called a 'passing loop' and when all the lights are green in the blocks through which it has just passed, the train coming from the opposite direction passes the stopped train. If the loop is long and the trains arrive at the same time, they can pass each other while moving and this is called a 'flying pass'. The vast majority of the passing loops on the BAM are 1,050m long sidings so the trains have to stop to let others pass. However, there are a few sections where flying passes occur and these include the section between Chara and Khani.

How trains communicate

As well as signals, train movement is controlled by radios between the closest stations and the locomotive cab. Dotted along the BAM every 35-40km is a station which houses among other things, a signal controller and 150MHz radio transmitter. There are 14,000 of these radio transmitters along Russian railways, making the railways one of the world's largest radio systems for private communications.

In the locomotive is a radio which has a range of up to 80km, enabling the driver to talk to 2 stations in each direction, and via the station's relay, to the central train controller. To ensure that there is never a minute without the train being in touch with a station, a wire runs along the length of tunnels to carry the signal outside.

The cabs are also fitted with another radio which allows the driver to communicate with the head conductor on the train. A third radio frequency is used around the station to control local shunting, maintenance and rail movements. The station controller uses a loud speaker broadcasting to the entire station while the workers reply using a 2kg walkie-talkie which has a range of about 1km.

Drivers: the railway elite

In Tsarist times, train drivers were considered the bourgeoisie of railway workers and the job was often passed down from father to son. Despite the early years of communism, when they were persecuted for their lack of support during the October revolution, drivers today are still considered the railway elite.

Locomotives have a crew of two: driver and assistant driver. Despite about 50% of rail employees being women, there are no female drivers on the BAM. There are two ways of becoming a driver. Firstly, attend a two year course at a railway institute, passing both theory and practical exams. Secondly, start out as a locomotive fitter, then cover 30,000 miles as an assistant driver before taking the final drivers' examination.

Locomotive crews are the best paid on the railway, earning 30% more than the average for all railway staff. (Track maintenance staff receive 6% less, signals and telecommunications staff 8% less, and station staff receive 24% less.) While each different type of traffic, such as passenger, freight and shunting, attracts a different wage, the difference is quite small compared to the loadings for work hours and

---

THE ELEMENTS OF A MONTHLY PAY PACKET FOR A GRADE 1 LOCOMOTIVE DRIVER

Basic pay

Loadings

Night work 2200-0600	40% loading
Lodging away from home	30% loading
Overtime	50% loading for the first 2 hours per week
	100% loading for remaining hours per week

Additional payments
- Qualification Pay: A 15-25% loading based on skill, experience, freedom from accidents, quality of work, reliability, time-keeping, and successful passing of tests and courses.
- Bonus - up to a 70% loading can be earned from various bonuses for meeting production targets.
- Annual increments starting at 5%, and increasing by 1.5% for every year of service after one year.

From *Railway Sector Survey of Russia, Belarus, Ukraine and Kazakhstan*, 1993, by the European Bank for Reconstruction and Development.

work location. These loadings can boost the drivers' pay to that of the basic pay of the Director of the BAM.

There are also a number of hardship pay loadings for BAM railway workers, similar to those for BAM construction workers, which can boost their wage to nearly double that of their European Russian counterparts (See *The engineering challenge* section in the *History of the BAM* chapter).

Conditions for drivers are similar to those for other rail employees, such as a retirement age of 55 after a minimum of 25 years of service, annual leave of up to 56 days per year, free medical care and sick pay based on the average earnings for the previous two months.

Ivan Nivolaevich Kostylev, a TEM2 shunter driver based at Novy Urgal.

Like the rest of Russia's railways there are numerous bylaws which attract financial and service penalties. The 45 Ministry of Railway, BAM railway and local railway department bylaws include going faster than permitted, being consistently late and ignoring a red signal. A common punishment is being transferred to a non-driving job for 6 months with a subsequent cut in pay. Drivers often complain about the number and triviality of many of the regulations, and also about the large number of clerical staff whose sole job is to pore over the driver's black box records and their time sheets searching for violations.

Rolling stock

Подвижной состав

The BAM's work horses

If you are a steam buff, the locomotives on the BAM will be a disappointment. However, if you are interested in electrics and diesels, then the engines on the BAM will be of considerable interest. The BAM runs only a few types of Russia's most powerful and newest locomotives, and the drivers are invariably only too pleased to show you around their machines.

The most common electric locomotives are the VL80 and VL85. The designation VL comes from the initials of Vladimir Ilich Lenin. The 8 axle VL80 is normally used to pull 900 ton passenger trains, while the heavy duty VL85 is used in a two or three unit configuration to pull freight trains of up to 10,000 tons. While the VL85 has the power, it is not a total success as its heavy weight rapidly wears the rails. As the BAM is only electrified from Taishet to Taksimo, the electric locomotives are based at this section's regional administration in Severobaikalsk.

Diesel locomotives run on the rest of the BAM and these are normally 3 and 4 unit 3TE10M, 4TE10S and 4TE130S locomotives.

For shunting, the most common locomotives are the TEM2 and the TEM. In the past, the Czech built ChME3 shunter was popular but a lack of parts has disabled virtually all these engines. The ChME3 were part of a barter agreement between the Soviet Union and the Eastern Bloc countries with the Czechs receiving main line locomotives in return.

The harsh conditions of the BAM Zone take their toll on the locomotives and they are unavailable due to technical faults about 10% of the time, which is double the rate of European Russia.

Passenger wagons

Despite Russia's massive passenger carriage fleet of 62,840 cars, which include dining, suburban and long distance sleeping carriages, there is still a shortage of passenger rolling stock. This is because East Germany made the vast majority of these cars and since the collapse of the Soviet Union, the Russians do not have the hard currency to buy carriages to replace damaged ones.

BAM long distance passenger trains are normally about 15 to 20 carriages long with a baggage and postal van attached. Their gross weight is about 900 tonnes. For information on the sleeping and

BAM LOCOMOTIVES

Type	Diesel/Electric	Rated Power	Max speed km/h	Weight tonnes	Year
TE-3	Diesel	4,000 hp	100	2 x 126	1953
2TE-10M	Diesel	2 x 3,000 hp	100	2 X 129	1981
2TE-121	Diesel	2 x 4,000 hp	100	2 X 150	1980
4TE-130S	Diesel	4 x 3,000 hp	100-120	4 x 138	1982
2TE-136	Diesel	2 x 6,000 hp	100-120	2 x 200	1984
TEM-2V	Diesel	1,200 hp	100	123.6	1960
TEM-7	Diesel	2,000 hp	100	180	1981
TEM-12	Diesel	1,200 hp	40-80	100	1978
VL60K	Electric	4,590kW/h	100	138	1962
VL80R	Electric	6,520kW/h	110	192	1980
VL85	Electric	10,000kW/h	120	288	1983
VL86F	Electric	10,800kW/h	120	288	1985

restaurant cars refer to the *Getting around the BAM Zone* section in the *En route* chapter.

Specialist trains

As the railway is Russia's principal means of transport, it is not surprising that there are a large number of speciality trains. These include repair, fire, prisoner, armoured and postal trains. On the BAM, the most common ones you will see are the repair trains, fire trains and snow ploughs.

Repair trains (Восстановление поездов)
Repair trains are self contained trains on 24 hour a day standby ready to repair track that has collapsed or to right derailed trains. A repair train normally consists of a locomotive with up to 12 carriages which include sleeping quarters for 30 men, a canteen, a crane, a bulldozer, an all terrain tracked vehicle and a generator. The train also normally has 5 wagons carrying pre-assembled 25m segments of track. As the priority is to get the line back in operation, the most common repair work is to bulldoze the damage track off the line and lay the pre-assembled segments in its place.

A diesel TEM3 shunter in Tynda goods yards. Russian locomotives are invariably painted either green, blue or maroon and the difference is due to the paint availability at the time.

Rolling stock 85

A 2TE136 twin unit diesel locomotive ready to haul a long-distance 900 tonne passenger train from Novy Urgal.

The repair trains technically report to the BAM HQ at Tynda, but in reality are controlled by the BAM's regional headquarters of Severobaikalsk, Tynda and Novy Urgal. As the majority of the repair workers' time is spent waiting for work, their compounds normally have excellent facilities, such as the sauna and swimming pool in the compound at Severobaikalsk.

Repair trains are spaced strategically along the line, normally about 400km apart. However in areas of high need, they are located as close as 150km.

Some of the repair equipment looks like it was converted from military vehicles which is not surprising as this was a common practice. For example, the Railway's Transport Machinery Research Institute and the Kiev Technical Design Centre modified the T-55 battle tank to produce a kind of bulldozer. This vehicle is ideal for clearing away piles of smashed freight cars that block tracks after derailments. In addition, the all terrain tracked vehicle is similar to an armoured personnel carrier but carries 10 workers in its belly rather than soldiers.

Fire trains (Пожарный поезд)
Fire trains are essential to putting out the frequent fires along the BAM which are caused by the locomotives, passengers or lightning strikes.

The fire trains, which consist of a combined engine and accommodation, water tanks and a generator to power the hoses, are not designed to put out large fires, but simply protect the railway line and railway structures.

Snow ploughs (Снегоуборочная машина)
In winter, one of the joys of the BAM is watching the snow ploughs at work. There are three types of ploughs.

The first and most common type is the basic snow plough (струг) which is simply a blade fitted onto a diesel shunting engine. This plough can speed along, clearing the line at 35kmph, and can ram through 2m high snow drifts.

The second type is the rotary snow plough (Роторный снегоочиститель) which scoops up the snow and ejects it out the side in a continuous stream of snow.

The third type, known as the snow collectors train (СМ), consists of three wagons. The first scoops up the snow and transfers it by conveyor belt to the second and third wagons which store the snow. Once the wagons get filled up, they are taken elsewhere and the snow is dumped. This type of snow collector is used in areas where snow can't be ejected out the side, such as in narrow valleys, rail yards or towns.

PLANNING A TRIP

Getting information on Russia	88
Getting information on the BAM Zone	88
Travel arrangements	89
Getting to the BAM	95
General information	96
What to take	102

One of the secrets to satisfying travelling is preparation. Don't leave background reading, travel arrangements and packing to the last minute as you will invariably forget something. Reading this chapter and making a list of what you need to do before departure is highly recommended.

Getting information on Russia
Как получить информацию о России

The maxim "You get out what you put in" is just as true for travelling as it is for anything else. For this reason, it is advisable to read as widely as possible about Russia before travelling. The list of recommended reading at the back of this book provides a good start.

As the Russian political and economic situation is changing rapidly, the best source of up to date information is the media and information superhighway. When watching the media remember that only bad news sells and that most of the media's coverage of Russia is negative. Typical of this tendency to over exaggerate was the so-called "Food Crisis" in 1991 and the 1994/5 "Crime Wave". Electronic bulletin boards and listservers are excellent sources of information as you can ask questions and get answers from recently returned travellers without delay. See the *Recommended reading* section for more information on these two information sources.

Another source of information is guidebooks on Russia but unfortunately, most are out of date within two years of being printed. All guidebooks have something to offer, but don't take their word as gospel, particularly on prices. Fortunately the BAM Zone, like other remote areas of Russia, is mostly immune to the changes sweeping the major Russia cities, so the information in this book will be accurate for far longer.

Getting information on the BAM Zone
Как получить информацию о БАМе

Getting useful information on the BAM Zone is extremely difficult because besides this guide, the only other books on the Zone focus on the region's economic, military and industrial aspects. These books were mostly written during the Reagan-era Arms Race period when the BAM was viewed with concern in the West.

The only detailed information for travellers on the BAM are the *BAM Zone Fishing Guide* and the *Siberian Lena and Amur Rivers Guide*, both listed in the *Recommended reading* section.

A few guidebooks on Russia include information on the BAM, such as *Russia by Rail* by Athol Yates, the *Trans-Siberian Handbook* by Bryn Thomas, the *Trans-Siberian Guide* by Robert Strauss and *Lonely Planet's Siberian Guide*. Understandably, these books devote just a few pages to the BAM as it is just one of many railways in Russia.

Even in Russian, there is very little information about the BAM. There have been a number of glossy photo albums, communist propaganda hero-constructor novels and technical books but these contain little practical information for the traveller. While it won't help you when preparing for a trip, once you are over there it's worthwhile going with your guide to the libraries in the BAM Zone and asking if they have any maps or other information on your particular areas of interest. Sometimes, tucked away on the shelves, are maps of trekking routes in the mountains, fishing guides or other rare finds.

Another source of information once you are over there are local Russian papers which provide information on upcoming public celebrations, museum displays, or interesting things to see and do. There are newspapers in the following towns: Severobaikalsk [Severny Baikal (Северный Байкал)], Taksimo, Chara [Charaskaya Pravda (Чарская Правда)], Tynda [Avangard (Авангард)], Novy Urgal, Komsomolsk [Dalnevostochny Komsomolsk (Дальневосточный Комсомольск)], Sovetskaya Gavin and Nikolaevsk. Don't forget to get the Tynda-based BAM railway newspaper (БАМ) which covers the whole line. Papers are normally sold at railway station kiosks or from the newspaper offices.

Travel arrangements
Подготовка к путешествию

As the BAM Zone is rarely visited by foreigners, there are few English or German speakers there and even fewer tourist facilities. While the lack of tourists ensures that you get to experience the real Siberia, it is also harder to travel in the area. This makes some Russian language essential but a short Russian language course plus this book should make it possible to travel the BAM Zone without help. If you have no Russian language knowledge, it is recommended that you join an organised tour.

Finding a travel agent

As the BAM is virtually unknown in the West, it is hardly unexpected that very few travel companies have even heard of it, let alone offer trips to the region. However as more travellers discover this region, it is expected that other companies will start to offer BAM tours. The author would be grateful if you could send this information to us so that we can include it in the next edition of this book.

International companies

Red Bear Tours, Australia. This company organises a fully inclusive 10 day tour of the BAM Zone as well as specialist itineraries. They can even organise just the visas and you do the rest yourself, or the entire travel arrangements for a complete tour of Russia. Red Bear Tours' research manager, Athol Yates, is the principal author of this book. STA Travel in the United Kingdom, and Monkey Business in Hong Kong and Beijing market Red Bear Tours trips.

Red Bear Tours, 320 Glenferrie Rd, Malvern, Melbourne, Victoria, 3144 Australia, ☎ (613) 824 7183, fax (613) 822 3956, email bmccunn@werple03.mira.net.au

Monkey Business, Block E, 4th Floor, Flat 6, Chungking Mansions, Kowloon, Hong Kong, ☎ (852) 723 1376, fax (852) 723 6653.

BAMTour Europe, C/o Julian Pignat, 2 Ch. Mouille-Galland, 1214 Vernier, Switzerland, ☎ /fax (4122) 340 1530.

BAMTour USA, 119 12th St NY, Washington DC 20005, USA, ☎ (202) 544 6999, fax (202) 544 6944.

There are a number of Russian companies in the BAM Zone that can organise part or all of your tour. The main ones are listed below with additional information about each listed under the respective town in the *BAM route description* chapters. Choosing between companies can be difficult but the following guidelines may help.

- Ask for their government issued, international tourist operations licence number.
- While they may be experts and can organise everything in their own town, how will they, and with whom will they organise activities in other towns?
- Can they issue visa invitations?
- Can you pay only a deposit and the rest once you arrive?
- Do they have a hard currency bank account so you can electronically transfer money?
- Most important of all, be very explicit about the services you want, and suggest a price. See under *Costs* later in this section.

From experience, it is best to write a letter to the company as most companies seem to change their fax numbers frequently.

BAM wide companies

BAMTour, Severobaikalsk. This company is run by Rashit Yakhin, one of the authors of this book. BAMTour is the best known company organising tours on the BAM and in the north Lake Baikal region, including seal watching. Rashit is one of the most knowledgeable residents in the region, having worked on the BAM in the early 1970s. BAMTour Co, 671717, Severobaikalsk, ul Oktyabrya 16-2, ☎ & fax (30139) 21-560, telex 154215 DWC SU (attention: BAMTour).

Marika, Komsomolsk. The company is headed by Marina Aleksandrovna Kuzminovna who is one of the Russian Far East's experts on gulags, Japanese prisoners of war and the history of the BAM. She has written three books on these subjects. Marika, ul Shikhanova 10, ☎ (42172) 347-63, fax (42172) 402-69.

Exotour, Komsomolsk. Adventure travel in the eastern end of the BAM is best organised through Exotour. This company's main activity is running outdoor programs for Russian and foreign youth and sportsmen. It is also the central point of contact for Russian and foreign special interest groups and runs a network of about 60 specialists who organise archaeological, ornithological, caving, rafting, skiing and ethnological trips. The company is run by the helpful Alexander F Shelopugin. Exotour Tourist Centre, pr Mira 43, ☎ & fax (42172) 47-632.

Largi, Komsomolsk. This company's main activity is running outdoor programs. The company is run by Aleksandr Melnichenko. Largi, pr Mira 52, office 26, ☎ (42172) 43-435, fax (42172) 402-69.

GeyaBAM, Tynda. This company is run by Vladimir Kraenoperd and has only organised a few foreign groups in the past. GeyaBAM, Amurskaya Oblast, Tynda, 676080, ul Profsyuznaya 4-42, ☎ (41656) 27-683, fax (41656) 32-335, telex 154128 KREDI SU. They also have a Moscow affiliate which is easier to fax and they will pass the fax on. The Moscow company's fax is (095) 230-2919.

BAMtourist, Tynda: This company is run by Natalya Anatolevna Philonenko. BAMtourist, ☎ (41656) 220-27, fax (41656) 209-47, Amurskaya Oblast, Tynda, 676080, ul Krasnaya Presnya 35, kv 3.

BAM Railway Company, Tourism Department, Tynda. This organisation, run by Lyudmila Yurevna Feninets, is part of the BAM Railway and can organise complete carriages without trouble. Tourism Department, BAM, Amurskaya Oblast, Tynda, 676080, ul Krasnaya Presnya 47, ☎ (41656) 2-17-16, fax (41656) 23-329, telex 154215 DWC SU.

Amur turist, Blagoveshchensk: This company organises river boat cruises on the Amur River from China to the Pacific Ocean. It is run by president, Gennady Nikolaevich Trusnin. Amurturist, ul

Kuznechnaya 1, Amurskaya Oblast, Blagoveshchensk, ☎ (41622) 277 98, 903-77 or 231-22, fax (41622) 277-98, 231-22, telex 154113 TURNE SU.

Eurasia Trans Inc, Khabarovsk: This company can book any tickets in the BAM Zone which you have to pick up in their office in Khabarovsk. To book tickets, contact Valentina G Neretina, Head of Service Department or Victor I Kozub, Director General, Eurasia Trans Inc, Khabarovsk 680000, ul Turgeneva 64, ☎ (4212) 22-60-67, 38-42-61, fax (4212) 33-27-26 telex 141174 Rotor SU.

Local companies

The following companies specialise in programs mainly in their town or local region.

Intourist, Bratsk, organises general travel in the region.
Tourist Club Kedr, Zheleznogorsk Ilimsk, is one of Eastern Siberia's most active adventure clubs.
Sputnik, Neryungri, organises general travel programs in the region.
BAM Tourist Centre for Children, Kuanda, organises adventure programs for children and also for adult mountain climbers and adventurers. Highly recommended.
Sputnik, Komsomolsk, mainly organises tours for Russians wanting to travel abroad.
Bureau of Travel and Excursions, Aldan, organises general travel programs in the region.

In addition to the above, there are several individuals and organisations that may provide special interest advice and programs. Experts on indigenous peoples can be found at Komsomolsk museum. Experts on fishing can be found at Kuanda and Postyshevo. Experts on animal and bird watching can be found at Exotour in Komsomolsk (see above) and the Wildlife Foundation of Khabarovsk. The Wildlife Foundation, 680049, Russia, Khabarovsk-49, Lev Tolstoi Street 15-A, ☎ (4212) 21 12 98, fax (4212) 22 04 10, email wildlife@wf.khabarovsk.su.

Costs

There is very little price stability in Russia and giving prices is extremely difficult. Therefore the following should be considered as guidelines only.

Basically, the BAM Zone is cheaper for travellers than the big cities in European Russia as there is no tourist culture. This means that most services do not distinguish between locals and Russians. The notable exceptions are hotels which normally charge foreigners three times the local's price. However these hotels are still cheaper than elsewhere in the country, and in some places, such as Severobaikalsk and Tynda, it is possible to stay in hotels, which do not have inflated foreigner prices. This means that accommodation can be organised for as little as $5 a night at railway hostels to $30 a night, being the cheapest accommodation in Komsomolsk.

In addition, BAM stations, with the exception of Bratsk, don't charge a price surcharge on rail tickets for foreigners. This may eventually change but probably not until there is an influx of foreigners, which will be many years yet. Overnight rail tickets in a four berth cabin are normally about $20.

Budget about $10 a meal in restaurants with no alcohol and $4 in a canteen.

If you organise local services, which is the cheapest but most unreliable way to get assistance, typical costs are $30 a day for an interpreter, $30-50 a day for a guide, $2 a litre for petrol, $10 a day for catamaran or kayak hire, $30 a day for motor boat hire and driver excluding petrol, $50 a day for car hire and driver excluding petrol, and $10 a day for homestay excluding meals.

If you get a local company to organise a special program, budget $100 a day. Remember the communication costs which quickly add up when faxing Russia.

A typical all inclusive 10 day package tour of the BAM Zone from Khabarovsk to Irkutsk sold by Red Bear Tours is $1300, while they organise special itineraries for about $140 a day.

Visas

A Russian visa is essential for visitors to Russia. In the Soviet days, the state travel monopoly, Intourist, would only provide a visa for as many days as accommodation was booked. However those days are gone and now companies will provide visas for as many days as requested. To get a visa, you must have a visa invitation which should be organised by your travel agent or the company that you are dealing with in Russia. You attach this visa invitation to your Russian visa application form and send it to your local Russian consulate. It is advisable to get one visa invitation that covers your whole time in Russia rather than one for the BAM Zone and another one for elsewhere. As Russian visa rules and regulations change all the time, you should contact your local travel agent for the latest information.

When to go

The decision about when to go depends on a number of factors, notably the weather and your interests.

The temperature table gives you some ideas of the temperatures of towns in the BAM Zone and compares them with Moscow and St Petersburg. For general sightseeing, the best time to visit is from June to August.

Average temperature °C

	Jan	Feb	Mar	Apr	May	June	July	Aug	Sep	Oct	Nov	Dec
Moscow	-9	-6	0	10	19	21	23	22	16	9	2	-5
St Petersburg	-5	-1	1	7	14	19	22	19	14	7	1	-3
Irkutsk	-18	-14	-6	2	11	19	21	19	11	3	-16	-16
Khabarovsk	-23	-17	-9	3	10	17	20	20	13	4	8	-19
Komsomolsk	-26	-9	-3	5	12	21	23	10	18	0	-9	-18
Nikolaevsk	-27	-20	-12	-3	7	11	17	17	11	2	-10	-20
Kirensk	-27	-22	-11	-2	7	15	19	15	7	-2	-15	-25
Aldan	-27	-24	-16	-6	3	13	17	13	6	-6	-20	-27
Bomnak	-32	-24	-14	-1	8	15	18	15	7	-3	-20	-30

For special interest activities, refer to the following:
- Trekking: It is best to go after June when the deadly bush tic has gone (see under *Health requirements* later in this chapter).
- Fishing: For the best times to fish and when to see the fish spawning, see the *Fishing wonderland* section in the *BAM Zone* chapter.
- Bird watching: Refer to the book, *A Field Guide to Birds of the USSR*, listed in the *Recommended reading* section.
- Seal watching: It is best to go in May (see under *Severobaikalsk* in the *BAM mainline route description* chapter).
- Rafting: See under *Kuanda* in the *BAM mainline route description* chapter.

Another factor to consider is the availability of fresh food. This is particularly important if you are a vegetarian. Although food is available all year round, the end of summer is the only time when there are plenty of fresh vegetables. Collecting indigenous berries, nuts and mushrooms is an enjoyable experience and a table in the *Native food* section in the *BAM Zone* chapter lists when these ripen.

Parades, festivals and special events occur throughout the year and they are worth seeing.

Large towns are the best place to see big events such as Army and Navy Day, and Russian Orthodox Christmas, while small towns are often the best to see small celebrations such as International Women's Day and International Children's Day. Indoor events, such as school performances or photo exhibitions, are normally held in each town's Palace of Culture, while outdoor events, such as parades or concerts, are held along the main street or in the main square. Some events are only celebrated in one or two towns, such as Geologists' Day at the mineral town of Solnichny, while others are celebrated everywhere, such Rail Workers' Day. Try to coordinate your program with a celebration as they provide glimpses of a side of Russia rarely seen by outsiders. For the egotistical, visit your sister city on World Sister Cities' Day and you will be guaranteed attention.

Holidays

1-2 January	New Year
7 January	Russian Orthodox Christmas
23 February	Army and Navy Day
8 March	International Women's Day
7 April	World Health Day
First Sunday in April	Geologists' Day
22 April	Lenin Memorial Day (unofficial)
Last Sunday in April	World Sister Cities' Day
1-2 May	May Day
9 May	Great Patriotic War Victory Day
Late May	School year ends (school concerts are common)
1 June	International Children's Day
12 June	Russian Independence Day (post-communist)
Last Sunday in June	Russian Youth Day
20 July	International Chess Day
Second Sunday in July	Fishermen's Day
First Sunday in August	Rail Workers' Day
Second Sunday in August	Builders' Day
22 August	Holiday in honour of the defeat of the 1993 coup
Third Sunday in September	Forestry Workers Day
7 November	Anniversary of the October Revolution (unofficial)
10 November	World Youth Day
17 November	International Students' Day
Last Sunday in August	Miners' Day
19 November	Rocket and Artillery Forces' Day

Getting to the BAM

Как доехать до БАМа

It is not possible to reach the BAM directly by either international train or plane. However it can be reached by direct train or plane from most large Russian cities such as Moscow, Irkutsk, Khabarovsk and Vladivostok.

The most popular way to get to the BAM is to travel along the Trans-Siberian until Taishet in the west or Khabarovsk in the east and then join the BAM. The BAM runs between these two stations and this route is parallel to the eastern end of the Trans-Siberian.

A public festival in Komsomolsk celebrating the end of the school year. Get your guide to find out if anything special is happening in town or read the local newspapers so you don't miss a fascinating insight into the life of Russians.

General information
Основная информация

Selected itineraries

The two most comprehensive BAM Zone itineraries are either an east-west or west-east 14 day trip from Khabarovsk to Irkutsk, or a 9 day loop trip starting and finishing in Khabarovsk. It is also possible to do a trip straight through from Khabarovsk to Moscow via the BAM with only one change of trains at Tynda. Below are several itineraries and a number of options which could be added to the main trip.

Most tours of the BAM start or end at either Khabarovsk or Irkutsk, and there are direct Trans-Siberian trains from these cities to Moscow in the west and Vladivostok in the east.

14 day east-west or west-east tour starting in Khabarovsk and ending in Irkutsk

Day 1: Depart Khabarovsk by evening train for Komsomolsk.
Day 2: Morning arrival in Komsomolsk. Tour the town.
Day 3: Day tour to Amursk. Evening train departure for Novy Urgal.
Day 4: Tour Novy Urgal and Chegdomyn. Evening train departure for Tynda.
Day 5: Tour Tynda and a local indigenous village.
Day 6: Morning train departure for Chara.
Day 7-10: Walk to the best preserved gulag camp in Siberia at Marble Canyon.
Day 10: Evening train departure to Severobaikalsk.
Day 11-13: Explore the town and visit gulag camp, indigenous village and glaciers, watch seals, or simply wander around.
Day 14: Morning departure by hydrofoil down Lake Baikal to Irkutsk (hydrofoil operates from 15 June to 15 September) or take the train to Irkutsk or Moscow.

9 day far eastern loop starting and ending in Khabarovsk

Day 1: Depart Khabarovsk by evening train for Komsomolsk.
Day 2: Morning arrival in Komsomolsk. Tour the town.
Day 3: Day tour to Amursk. Evening train departure for Novy Urgal.
Day 4: Tour Novy Urgal and Chegdomyn. Evening train departure for Tynda.
Day 5: Tour Tynda and a local indigenous village.
Day 6: Morning train departure for Bamovskaya which is the junction of the BAM and Trans-Siberian. Continue onwards to Blagoveshchensk and arrive in the evening.
Day 7: Tour Blagoveshchensk and evening train departure for Birobidzhan.
Day 8: Tour the town.
Day 9: Morning train departure and mid-morning arrival in Khabarovsk.

3 day Sovetskaya Gavin option starting in Khabarovsk and ending in Komsomolsk

Day 1: Depart Khabarovsk by plane to Sovetskaya Gavin. Tour the town and the 1930s anti-Japanese fortifications.
Day 2: Tour Vanino, see spawning fish (August and September) and depart on evening train for Komsomolsk. Another option is to catch the ferry to Sakhalin Island.

Day 3: Arrive in Komsomolsk and join the 14 day east-west tour, 9 day far east loop or return to Khabarovsk.

4 day Aldan option starting in Tynda and ending in Tynda
Day 1: Depart Tynda by evening train to Neryungri. Visit the giant coal mine and tour the town.
Day 2: Travel by train or bus to Aldan.
Day 3: Tour Aldan gold factories and visit mine.
Day 4: Return by train, bus or plane to Tynda. Another option would be to continue on by bus to Yakutsk and then take a scheduled Russian ship down the Lena to Ust-Kut on the BAM. The downstream trip from Ust-Kut to Yakutsk takes 5 days while the upstream trip from Yakutsk to Ust-Kut takes 7 days.

Russian medical facilities

The standard Russian hospital is considerably less well equipped and supplied than those in the West. However most doctors are just as competent, so if you land in a hospital for stitches or need an x-ray, don't be too concerned. Because of the shortage of medical equipment, hospitals are forced to reuse syringes so it is best to take a few for yourself. Russian hospitals will expect you to pay for your treatment.

In Moscow and St Petersburg there are a number of western medical services and your embassy can give you a list of them. However this is of little help in the BAM Zone so if you need an operation, contact your embassy and arrange for evacuation to a Western country. It is for this reason that the highest level of medical insurance is absolutely essential in Russia.

Health requirements

There are no mandatory vaccinations for travelling in the BAM Zone or anywhere else in Russia. It is recommended that you have tetanus and hepatitis innoculations, and take precautions against typhoid and diphtheria. You should check with your local doctor or travellers medical centre for the latest requirements.

The most common problem is stomach trouble and the best prevention is to boil all the water that you drink.

If you are going to be in Russia for more than a few weeks, it is advisable to take vitamin tablets as it is difficult to get a balanced meal most of the year.

At the beginning of spring, some people will suffer blood noses and headaches caused by the forest blooming. After a day or so, the problem disappears.

The only serious problem is caused by the Ixodes tics. These aggressive creatures appear from the start of spring to late June and cause fever, excruciating headache, vomiting and central nervous disorders. Victims either die or remain crippled for life with their neck, arm and leg muscles paralysed. The condition was called Kozhevnikov epilepsy until the 1930s when it was found to be inflicted by a bite of the Ixodes tic carrying the encephalitis virus which is in the blood of wild animals. The disease is called Russian Spring Fever.

While it is possible to get innoculations against the tic, it is much better to do as locals do and simply avoid going into *taiga* before June. The tic is not present in the BAM Zone towns at this time.

There are several varieties of tic including grey ones, black ones and black ones with a red stripe around their belly. The tics prefer valleys in *taiga*, broad-leaved forest and cleared tracts of forest.

The tics position themselves in bushes, waiting for warm blooded creatures to walk by and then drop onto them. They then crawl imperceptibly under the skin, leaving only the tail end of their abdomens sticking out, giving them the appearance of a black cucumber seed on your skin. To pull one out without breaking off its head is impossible. The only reliable way of getting rid of them is to pour paraffin or salt onto the skin and they will crawl out.

If you do have to go in the *taiga* in the dangerous months, you should wear protective clothing and consider a course of innoculations. The Russian protective clothing consists of a woven singlet of thick weave that ensures that your outer protective garment stays about 1cm from your skin. The outer garment is a polo neck jumper with a hood and long sleeves made of light-weight material impervious to insects. You should always wear long pants and tuck them into your socks or put a rubber band around your trouser legs to prevent tics from crawling up your legs. As an added precaution, you should spray your clothing with insect repellent. It is essential that after returning from the *taiga* that you check every inch of your body for tics, particularly warm skin creases, and get someone to check your hair, back and other parts you can't see.

Innoculations are inconvenient as the serum is difficult to obtain outside Europe. There is also a Russian serum but it is difficult to find. The immune globulin serum is made by a Viennese company, Immuno, and one dose will provide protection for up to 4 weeks while 2 shots, 2 weeks apart will provide protection for a longer time. The Russian vaccine involves three injections with a gap of a few days between each and another shot after 6 months, with an annual booster for year round protection.

If you do get bitten, it is essential that you get medical help immediately as treatment can save your life.

This encephalitis tic should not to be confused with either the tic-

100   Planning a trip

> **PAINFUL INJECTIONS ARE BETTER THAN THE DISEASE**
>
> This jab hurts," warned the nurse.
>
> The girl holding the syringe was very young but her expression was so serious and concentrated that I involuntarily grinned. I was already 24 that spring in Chita and seemed to myself next to this green graduate from medical college to be an old *taiga* hand with a lot of sights behind him, having worked in the upper reaches of the Zeya river.
>
> *Various types of Ixodes tics*
>
> Tics never really gave me the creeps until one day I saw a woman who had encephalitis. Her face would jerk from time to time in a ghastly smile. It was said she suffered from splitting headaches and this had been going on for several years already. Even when the attack had passed, her eyes expressed lassitude and an expectation of pain. I looked at her and vowed to myself that just in case I would stop drinking unboiled reindeer milk and that I would give myself a careful examination after every walk in the *taiga*. That was all very well if one was coming back to a warm and spacious cabin but what if one was returning from an expedition to a cramped and tiny tent?
>
> The syringe was a pretty large one, the kind they call a vet's. About 16-gauge at a rough estimate. The nurse, however had an astonishingly light hand.
>
> "Is that all?" I asked, feeling a cold wet dab beneath my shoulder blade. I tucked my shirt into my trousers, buckled my belt and said good-bye. I had more than enough to do that day. "Be careful! Be careful! ..." protested the nurse, worried.
>
> I paid no attention as I was already making for the door. I was just about to grab the handle when I suddenly felt my spine judder as if I had been given a heavy blow with a log. A cramp instantly paralysed my back, chest, neck and whole body. I couldn't move an inch. I felt like I was drowning under an ice floe.
>
> Dumbfounded, gasping for air and eyes bulging, I slowly turned towards the nurse. "What did I tell you! ..." she shouted angrily, though I could see she felt sorry for me.
>
> From the short story, Touchdown at Leprindo by Sergei Bogatko, in *The Great Baikal-Amur Railway*, 1977, Moscow.

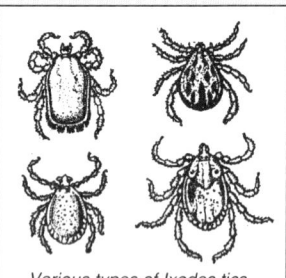

borne Siberian typhus or Japanese encephalitis, both of which do not occur in the BAM Zone but nearby in the lower areas of the Russian Far East and Amur regions. Siberian (or North Asian) typhus is a disease similar to Rocky Mountain Spotted Fever. It is caused by a bacteria (*rickettsia sibirica*) and can be treated with the doxycycline or ciprofloxacin antibiotics. The mosquito-borne Japanese encephalitis is common in rice-growing areas and vaccinations are available in the West.

Physical fitness
A moderate degree of physical fitness is needed in Russia. As there has been no consideration for the disabled in Russia, mobility challenged people should consider carefully before travelling in this country.

Insurance
You should take out medical and travel insurance. A high level of insurance (similar to Western Europe) is advisable to allow you to recover the cost of Western medical services in Russia, and international evacuation.

Language
Russian is a Slavic language and uses the Cyrillic script. At first the alphabet appears complicated but it can be quickly mastered. If you take the time to do this, you will find navigating around much easier and more enjoyable. While some guidebooks recommend taking a basic Russian language textbook and reading it on the train, very few people seem to find the time to read it then. A much better idea is to learn some Russian before you leave home or do a short course in Moscow.

Electricity
The electricity supply in Russia is 220 volt AC, 50Hz and a standard European two pronged plug is used. Adaptors should be purchased before you leave home as they cannot be easily bought in Russia.

Money, travellers cheques and credit cards
Russia's currency is the rouble, which used to consist of 100 kopeks. However since the massive inflation of the early 1990s, kopeks have been withdrawn and the smallest denominations are now 1, 5, 10, 20, 50 and 100 rouble coins. Notes include 100, 200, 500, 1000, 5000, 10,000, 50,000 and 100,000 roubles. Notes with Lenin's head or the old Soviet Union national symbols on them have been superseded and are not legal tender.

The exchange rate is a moving target due to inflation. In every town there is at least one currency exchange point, which in small towns is the bank. As the rouble is a free floating currency, there is no blackmarket rate any more.

US cash is the best method of carrying hard currency in Russia. Travellers cheques are difficult to cash except in Moscow and St Petersburg, nor are credit cards widely accepted. It is virtually impossible to get cash advances from your credit card in the BAM Zone and even if you can, you will be charged a hefty commission. For a one month stay on an organised tour, it is worth bringing at least US$200-500 in cash, with smaller notes ($1, 5 and 10) being particularly useful.

Keep your money in a money belt or similar on your body at all times. You should also carry a wallet with a small amount of Russian and hard currency in it which is your normal source of money. As well as enabling you to get to your money quickly, the wallet can be lost and you won't lose too much.

It is best to carry and accept only new, crisp and unmarked US dollar notes. This is because there are always rumours in Russia about forged US notes and many banks will turn down notes that are not in excellent condition. Strangely, some banks will refuse to accept US notes that are more than a few years old. This is because if there has been a change in note design, such as the US$100 note in 1989, many Russians mistakenly believe that the old notes are not legal tender any more. Their belief comes from the Russian government's practice of replacing old currency with new notes and then outlawing the old currency within a few months.

What to take
Что брать?

Prepare for your trip well in advance and avoid last minute packing. This will ensure that you enjoy your trip without worrying about buying things you forgot to bring. The following ideas may help in your selection of what to take.

As the supply of personal items is extremely unpredictable, it is recommended that you take everything you need.

A backpack or soft suitcase is preferable to a hard suitcase as the former are easier to carry on and off trains and buses. If you do take a case, carry two small ones rather than one big one, and bring a two wheeled trolley to move them around. Wheels built into suitcases are of limited use as the stations and pavements in Russia are very rough. Carry a small day pack for day trips. Do not carry excess luggage as there are no porters and excess luggage on flights is expensive.

On the train you will find it comfortable to take slip-on scuffs.

A heavy duty water bottle which will withstand boiling water from the train's *samovar* is vital. When cooled, this water becomes your drinking water for the next day.

A spare set of passport photos should always be carried in case you need another visa. Also take a photocopy of your visa and the first three pages of your passport and keep them separate from your passport.

Bring all the clothes you need and do not rely on buying clothes when you arrive.

What to Take Checklist

- ❏ 2 pin electricity adaptor
- ❏ 2.5m length of rope as a clothes line
- ❏ alarm clock
- ❏ anti-tinea cream
- ❏ baby powder
- ❏ books & magazines
- ❏ business cards
- ❏ camera batteries
- ❏ camera film
- ❏ can & bottle opener
- ❏ contact lens solution
- ❏ contraceptives
- ❏ curry & other spices
- ❏ diary
- ❏ electric immersion coil
- ❏ guidebooks & maps
- ❏ hat, gloves & scarf
- ❏ heavy duty water bottle
- ❏ knife, fork & spoon
- ❏ laundry detergent
- ❏ lip chaff stick
- ❏ medical kit & medications
- ❏ money belt
- ❏ mosquito repellent
- ❏ nail clippers
- ❏ paper, envelopes & pens
- ❏ passport
- ❏ photocopies of visa & passport
- ❏ plastic bags
- ❏ pocket dictionary
- ❏ pocket knife
- ❏ pocket mirror
- ❏ resealable containers
- ❏ sanitary items
- ❏ sewing kit
- ❏ shaver
- ❏ slip-on scuffs
- ❏ soap, shampoo & comb
- ❏ souvenirs
- ❏ spare set of passport photos
- ❏ strong plastic cup
- ❏ suitcase trolley
- ❏ sun glasses
- ❏ sunscreen
- ❏ tea, coffee, sugar & milk
- ❏ tissues
- ❏ toilet paper
- ❏ toothpaste
- ❏ universal sink/bath plug
- ❏ vitamin tablets
- ❏ wallet
- ❏ watch

The best sort of gifts to take are souvenirs from your country such as US flags or kangaroo stick pins, baseball caps, T-shirts, glossy picture books, maps, or travel videos. Pens, calculators and digital watches with your company's logo emblazoned on them are essential if you are travelling on business. The days are gone when Russians wanted jeans or runners as nowadays, these can be bought in Russia.

You should always carry around a pack of good quality unopened biscuits or chocolates, which you can buy in Russia, as your contribution if you are invited to share a meal.

You should carry plastic bags as they are not handed out in shops or markets.

A pen and paper are always useful and a good way of carrying them is to buy a pocket sized notebook and staple or glue to its cover a plastic sheath which can hold a pen.

A small medical kit should be carried. It should include several syringes, band-aids, antiseptic, head-ache tablets, antiseptic gauze, personal medication and insect repellent.

If you play a musical instrument that is portable, take it along as playing is a good way of making friends.

What to leave at home

Always photocopy your valuable documents, such as passport, credit cards and travellers cheques, before you leave home and give the photocopies to someone whom you can notify if you lose them.

What to buy and not to buy

It is prohibited to take antiques, old artworks and medals out of Russia. If you are buying new paintings, make sure you get an official receipt stating that the goods can be exported and the year of their production. This also applies to *samovars*.

While many things are cheap in Russia, such as excellent enamel pots, remember that you have to carry purchases out, as mailing goods is very difficult and unreliable.

Clothing

Casual clothes are the norm in Russia even when attending high-art events. The BAM Zone's summer weather is very pleasant, so light clothing is normally adequate. During May and September sharp changes in temperature occur and warmer clothing is needed. A rain coat, umbrella and overcoat are essential for these months. During winter, extra warm clothing is essential as temperatures go as low as minus 40°C. It is recommended that you take lined boots, padded full length skiing jacket, thermal underwear, a woollen hat, woollen pants (jeans are not warm enough) and thick gloves.

EN ROUTE

Getting around the BAM Zone	106
Trains	108
Around a BAM town	120
Security and police	128
Siberian customs and manners	133

Getting around the BAM Zone
Путешествие по Зоне БАМа

There are 4 main ways of travelling in the BAM Zone: cars, planes, river vessels and trains.

Cars (машины)
While there are roads connecting towns, most are little more than dirt tracks which become impassible bogs in spring and autumn. In winter, excellent roads appear in the guise of frozen rivers. The notable exceptions are the paved roads connecting Bratsk to Irkutsk, the Trans-Siberian railway to Yakutsk (Amur-Yakutsk Highway) and Komsomolsk to Khabarovsk. There are no car rental companies in the BAM Zone.

Aircraft (самолёт)
Internal plane travel in Russia is not recommended both for safety and reliability reasons. The break-up of Russia's national air company, Aeroflot, into many small regional companies which had neither sufficient training, employees nor spare parts, resulted in a number of crashes. However, the biggest problem was that most planes never took off due to a lack of fuel and aircraft. The mid 1990s rationalisation of air companies and the tightening of safety standards has resulted in the number of scheduled flights being reduced but these are now much more likely to depart. While fuel supplies are still a problem, the greater impediment to flying is the weather. Fogs, wind, snow storms and howling rains can delay planes for several days or more. Another problem with local internal flights, eg Bodaibo to Chara, rather than long distance flights, eg Moscow to Komsomolsk, is that they are virtually impossible to book outside Russia.

For these reasons it is better to travel by train, for while it is slower, at least you are guaranteed to get there.

In the past, hiring a helicopter has been reasonably cheap but nowadays, the going rate is about $500-800 an hour. The standard helicopter for rental is the MI-8 and these are owned by the military, Aeroflot and specialist organisations. Generally, the military pilots are less experienced at mountain flying than civilian crews and the most experienced crews work for the rescue organisations KSS or KSO (КСС - Контрольно-спасательная служба, КСО - Контрольно-спасательный отряд) or forestry protection rangers (Лес охрана). Remember there are various grades of pilots, with the highest grade being permitted to land on unprepared sites. So before you hire, check their credentials.

River vessels

Excluding small motor boats, there are two sorts of passenger vessels which ply Russia's rivers and lakes; hydrofoils and river cruisers. While hydrofoils travel about three times faster than river cruisers, cruisers are a more elegant way of travelling and an excellent way to meet Russians.

Hydrofoils (подводная лодка)
Hydrofoils, commonly known as *raketa* (ракета), *kometa* (комета) and *meteor* (метеор), look quite futuristic with sleek lines and bubble windows. Hydrofoils travel only during daylight due to the danger of hitting an unseen object.

The most common hydrofoil is the *meteor* which seats the passengers in three sections: the front, middle and rear. There are large expanses of perspex in each section which provide good viewing from all window seats. The front section is popular as it allows you to see the entire river ahead, as the perspex wraps right around. The bridge is reached from this area. During the cooler months, the front section becomes very cold and is often closed. The middle section contains the majority of seats and a small kiosk. It provides hot water and in the past hot meals but more than likely today, it will just sell confectionary and beer. Between the middle and rear section is an open air walkway. While the fresh air

The space age looking *Meteor* hydrofoil.

is pleasant, the noise from the engines underneath the walkway makes conversation difficult. As you descend the walkway to the rear section you pass two toilets on the right and the crew's room on the left. The rear section is the warmest as it is closest to the engines but also the noisiest. While they are pleasant to travel on, hydrofoils have the feel of long-distance buses. Within the BAM Zone, hydrofoils travel along the Amur River from Komsomolsk to Khabarovsk, the Lena River from Ust-Kut both upstream and downstream, and Lake Baikal from Severobaikalsk to Irkutsk.

River cruisers (Теплоход)
This is by far the more elegant way of travelling. These three deck ships can carry several hundred passengers and are like small ocean liners. The ones configured to be tourist vessels have single, double and triple person rooms, restaurant, banya, cinema, souvenir kiosk and bar. However the working ships are more simple and have a restaurant, a small number of 1 and 2 person rooms, and many 4 and 8 person rooms. Cruisers stop every few hours at larger towns for up to 30 minutes which gives you time to stretch your legs on land. Tips for travelling on these vessels are the same as for those on trains; take your own food, bring a long book and meet the locals. Within the BAM Zone, cruisers only travel along the Lena between the BAM station of Ust-Kut and Yakutsk.

Trains
Поезд

Types of trains
The major classes of trains are the fast, passenger and suburban trains.

Fast trains (скорый поезд) are long-distance express trains stopping only at the largest stations. These trains are typically up to 24 carriages long. In the BAM Zone, the trains don't deserve this title. For example, the average speed of the Tynda to Severobaikalsk 'fast' train is just 47km/h.

Passenger trains (пасса)ирский поезд) are also intercity trains but they normally only go a few hundred kilometres, stopping regularly for locals to get on and off. The average speed of the passenger train on the Tydna to Severobaikalsk section is 41km/h.

Suburban trains (пригородный поезд) are normally electric suburban trains like those in the west. However, in the BAM Zone they refer to trains that travel up to 300km or 4 hours, connecting a big town

Looking out the corridor window as the train passes over the Muya Mountain Range. Notice that the snow has yet to melt even though it was already May.

with the surrounding villages. Suburban trains normally consist of a diesel locomotive and one or two *obshchi* carriages.

A recent development are *firmenny* trains (Фирменный поезд) which are fast trains leased to private companies. This allows the railways to charge a higher ticket charge than the government permits. The condition of the train is normally better than on a government fast train but this does not justify the 50% additional cost. Tickets are bought at the station just like any other rail ticket. On some routes, such as train №15 from Irkutsk to Bratsk, *firmenny* trains are the only option.

Types of berths

There are four types of berths; *obshchi*, *platskartny*, *coupe* and *SV*.

Obshchi (общий) is the lowest class of carriage and it is an old *platskartny* wagon with no bedding. Up to 87 people can be crammed into a carriage and there is no seat numbering. They are normally dirty, stuffy and hell if you have to sleep on them overnight. They are okay to travel on for a few hours but, without any padding, they get uncomfortable quickly. These carriages are normally only attached to passenger trains and used by workmen or fishermen.

Platskartny (платцкартный) are the most common type of carriage in Russia but not the most pleasant to travel in. They are a sleeping wagon which has 2 tiers of berths in open compartments on one side of the corridor with a row of berths arranged lengthwise down the other side.

These cars accommodate 58 passengers. Mattresses and pillows are supplied. By an ingenious mechanism, the aisle berths can be lifted up and down to make aisle seats and tables. These carriages are noisy, stuffy and lack security. Avoid getting the berth next to the toilet otherwise you get the banging door next to your head which vibrates your bunk as well. It is not recommended to travel in *platskartny* unless you sleep well and have nothing valuable on you.

Coupe (купейный) carriages are the most enjoyable way to travel as they offer privacy, security and comfort. A *coupe* wagon consists of eight or nine 4 bunk enclosed cabins and as you will be sharing the cabin with Russians, there is plenty of opportunity to practice your hand signals or test a phrase book. There are two types of *coupe*, an older type which has 36 berths and normally has white laminex and the new one which has 32 berths, brown laminex and more padding. *Coupe* compartments are described in detail below.

SV (СВ - спальный вагон) are sometimes called *myaky* (мягкий) carriages. These cars have 9 two berth compartments, each containing 1 two-tier set of berths or 2 berths on the same level. These carriages are not common on the BAM.

Coupe compartment

The four berth *coupe* compartments are separated from the corridor by a sliding door which can be locked from the inside. The conductor has a key which can open this lock from the outside. As an additional safety device, there is a flick down lock high up on the inside of the door which cannot be opened from the outside. Some people go to the trouble of jamming a cork in this lock which ensures that no-one can open it by devious means from the outside.

The two top bunks can be put up during the day to give you more head room. Under the bottom two bunks are luggage spaces which are very secure as they can't be reached unless you get off the bunk. The corridor has a false ceiling which makes space for a luggage shelf accessible from your compartment. At the end of each bed is a reading lamp and the 2 or 3 way switch near the door controls the main cabin lights. The loudspeaker volume knob is usually above the window. There is a bottle opener under the table. If the table is in the way, you can fold it up.

Although the bunks are well padded, a mattress and pillow are supplied. You will need to hire a linen set which includes two sheets, a pillow case and small towel. Don't lose any of these as you will have to pay for them. The hire charge is about $1.

In winter, blankets are supplied but during summer, you have to ask for them. As the conductor has only a few which are normally reserved for children, you may have to beg to get one. In winter the windows are locked and the heater is turned way up which ironically means that you swelter under just sheets. To make matters worse, the windows can only be opened with a special key. The only ventilation is a roof vent which can be turned on and off.

There are advantages and disadvantages to sleeping in the upper bunk. While this berth allows you to go to bed when you want and gives you more privacy, it is hotter, difficult to climb up to and much brighter being closer to the main cabin light which is a pain if you want to sleep.

The worst compartment is the last one, with berth numbers 33-36. This one is closest to the smelly toilet, over the wheels which gives you a rough ride and is closest to the banging corridor door. The compartment with berth numbers 13 to 16 gives the best ride.

You cannot reserve a particular berth unless you tell a very good story to the booking staff.

Life in a *coupe* carriage

Life in the carriage is dominated by the conductor called the *provodnik* (проводник). There are normally two *provodniks* on fast and passenger trains. They share a cabin at the end of the carriage. Their job is to ensure that the carriage is clean, everyone has tickets and no problems

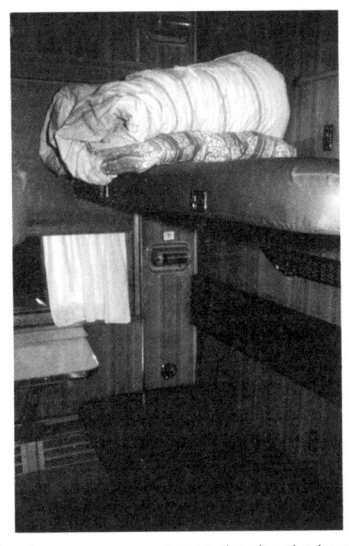

The right hand side of a *coupe* compartment showing the lower and upper berth. Mattresses are rolled up when not needed.

112 En route

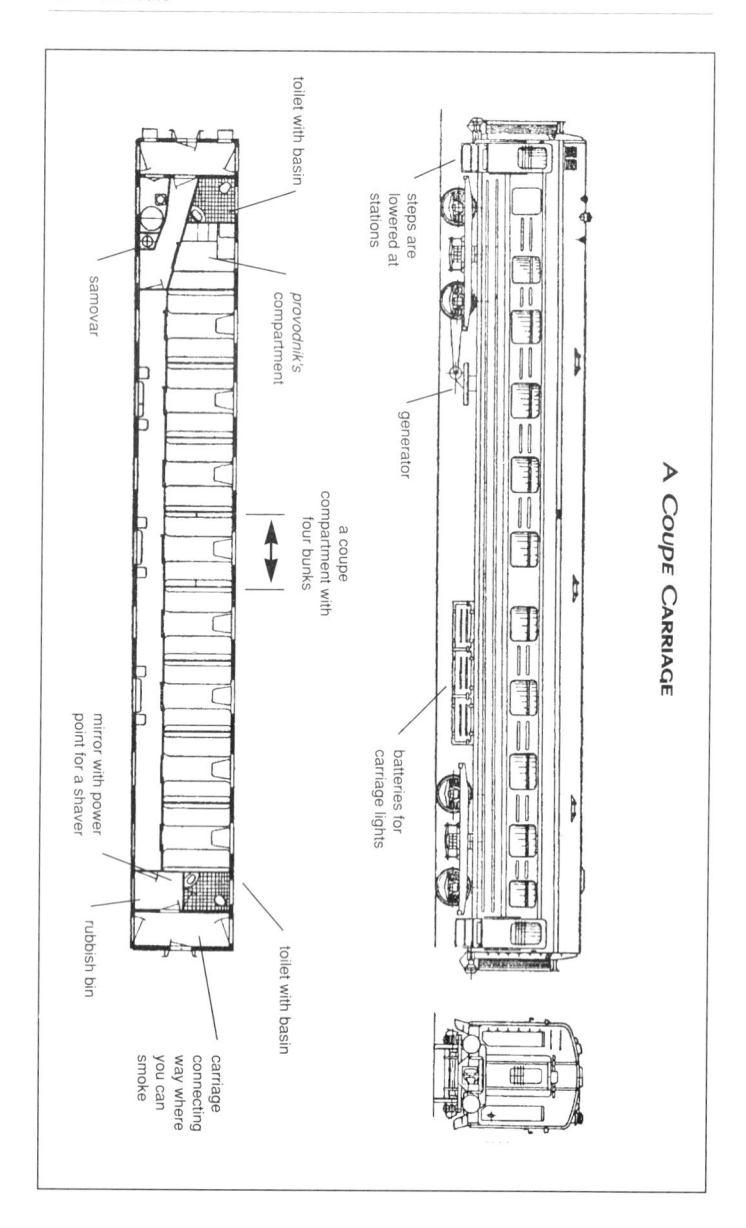

A Coupe Carriage

occur. The most zealous *provodniks* will put down a mat in the wagon's entrance so that no-one tramps dirt or snow through their carriage. During summer holidays, the professional *provodniks* are replaced by students who often just wear a track suit with the railways winged emblem pinned on it. At least once a day, all the cabins will be swept and the corridor mopped.

If you have any problems, such as wanting to move to another berth, go to the *provodnik* and if the matter is not resolved to your satisfaction, go to the chief conductor who is normally located in the centre of the train.

There is a rubbish bin at the end of the corridor infront of the toilet. Unfortunately environmental awareness has yet to reach most of the *provodniks* as they normally empty the bin by throwing the rubbish out of the train as it is moving.

At the end of the corridor near the *provodnik's* compartment is a hot water urn or *samovar* (самовар). You can use this water for tea, coffee, soup and dehydrated Chinese noodles. Some *samovars* have a flat top which means that you can cook a meal on them. Most *samovars* are electric, however there are a few coal ones left. A temperature gauge on the side of the *samovar* indicates the temperature and only use the water when it is in the red band. Although there is a drinking water tap near

Three *provodniks* or conductors in front of a standard 36 berth *coupe* carriage.

the *samavour*, a better source of drinking water is to pour the *samovar* water into a heavy duty canteen at night and in the morning it will be cool enough to drink. If the water is not hot in your *samovar*, try the next carriage and if all else fails, go to the restaurant car and ask them.

There are no showers on the train so you have to use the basin in the toilet to wash in. The water is turned on by pushing up the lever just behind the spout. Bring your own soap. There is an electric power point near the toilet which is designed for shavers but this often does not work.

The worst aspect of the carriage is the toilet. This is normally unpleasant and most people use it by squatting on its rim rather than sitting on it. Bring your own toilet paper and a reserve roll just in case.

Smoking is forbidden in the carriages with the exception of the connecting ways at the end of each carriage.

In the corridor, there are seats which you can flip down. Often, the corridor windows are the only ones that can be opened and sitting here in the fresh breeze is extremely enjoyable.

Wear comfortable clothes on the train; a tracksuit and slip on scuffs are ideal.

Getting off in the middle of nowhere

Officially trains only stop at scheduled stops. However in the BAM Zone where there are only a few trains a day, trains will stop for people

---

WHAT HAPPENS IF YOU CAN'T GET A TICKET

There are 3 main reasons why you can't get a ticket. Firstly, you don't have time as the ticket office normally stops selling tickets 5 minutes before train departure, secondly, because there are no berths, and thirdly, because tickets are only sold a few hours before the train arrives. The third reason applies only to trains which do not originate in your departure place. This is because until the train is approaching your station and the chief conductor has counted up the number of vacant berths and radioed this ahead, no tickets can be sold. This results in a mad scramble to get tickets in the one or two hours before the train arrives.

If you try to jump on a train without a ticket, you will first have to ask the chief conductor if there are any places and if you can buy a ticket on board. If you are allowed on, you will have to pay a fine of $3 to $10.

If you have tried to get a ticket but are told there are no places at the station, you can wait for the train and ask the chief conductor and any of the carriage conductors if there are spare berths. Sometimes due to a communication problem there may be a berth but more likely, they will obtain you one by subterfuge. In the latter case, you will normally pay the conductors the cost of a ticket plus a hefty 'assistance' charge. Travelling in this fashion is illegal and the ticket inspectors can have you thrown off the train or arrested.

You could always try to travel free, known as travelling like a rabbit (как кролик) but the ticket inspectors, conductors and railway police are bound to catch you.

to get on and off at unscheduled stops. You will see this particularly in summer as hiking groups get off in the middle of nowhere. To get off somewhere special, your best bet is to talk directly with the driver, although the chief conductor or your carriage conductor might organise it on your behalf. If you are lucky, the driver will invite you into the cab so that you can get off quickly.

Dining cars

Most trains have a restaurant car which normally has just one entree and one main course. They will often sell alcohol which is strange as it is illegal to drink on a train. If you do drink, keep it discreet as this saves any hassles. Two thirds of the dining car contains seats while the remainder is occupied by a kitchen, pantry, scullery and refrigerators. There are 12 four seat tables together with a table for the supervisor who is also the cashier.

On the BAM, there are also some brand new wagons which consist of a buffet selling processed food and 4 *coupe* compartments.

Travel Tips and Facts

- The kilometre markings beside the railway line are of little use to the traveller. They simply mark the distance from the boundary of an administrative region of the railway. The BAM's mainline spans 3 major and 2 minor regions. Some of the stations are known by a number of kilometres such Raz. 555 which is 555km from the start of the Severobaikalsk administrative region. Confusingly sometimes the number and distance do not coincide due to relaying of the track. For example, Raz. 885 is actually 850km from Severobaikalsk.
- There is an unwritten rule that at bed time, all males leave the compartment so the females can change.
- As travelling can be hot, the Russians often wear tracksuit trousers and no top. Shorts are another option but are not popular in Russia except with the fashionable hip and sportsmen.
- Trains going in opposite directions don't stop for the same length of time at the same station. In addition, if the train is late, it will depart earlier than its scheduled stopping time. So when you get off, always ask the conductor how long you will wait here.
- Locomotives are changed at the end of administrative regions and this normally takes 40 minutes.
- Carry a cloth to clean the windows of your carriage.
- If you are a woman always say you're married, travel with a male companion or wear a wedding ring.
- Get up first and go to the toilet before breakfast and well before the end of the trip to beat the rush. Remember the toilet is locked just before the train arrives at a station and will be opened until you are moving again.
- If the toilet door is locked you can still wash your utensils at the water tap near the *samovar*.

Buying A Ticket

Once upon a time, you could book tickets over the phone and they would be delivered to you. Nowadays, only the private companies offer such a service and not yet in any of the towns in the BAM Zone. So the only real choice is to go to the station and buy the ticket yourself.

Step 1: Which train?

The first step is to find out which train you want to go on. Check the timetable which will be displayed in the booking hall. It will state the train's number, the time of departure and on which days of the week it travels.

Things to remember:

- The train number indicates which way it is heading. If the number is even it means that it is going to the east and if odd, the train is heading westward towards Moscow.
- The time quoted on timetables is invariably Moscow time. In a country covering 8 time zones, this is the only way the system would work. The BAM spans 3 time zones with the time zone borders at the borders of administrative areas. From the eastern end to the border of the Republic of Buryatiya and Amur Oblast (stations of Raz. Shivery and Kora) the time difference with Moscow is 5 hours, from here to the borders of the Amur Oblast and Khabarovsk Krai (stations of Ulma and Etyrken) the time difference is 6 hours. Within the Khabarovsk Krai, the difference is 7 hours. In rare cases, where timetables are written in local time it will state this at the top of the timetable. The clock in the booking hall is normally set to Moscow time.
- Most trains depart every day, however some run on odd number days (1st, 3rd, 5th etc) and some on even days (2nd, 4th, 6th etc). In addition, a few trains only run in summer or winter.

Write down the train number, date of departure, the class of cabin, and your destination. If you don't speak Russian, write this information on the booking card blank in the appendix. Have your passport and visa ready in the rare case that the ticket seller asks for it.

Step 2: Which window?

There are several sorts of ticket windows, known as *kassa,* in the booking hall and it is important to queue at the correct one as you can waste hours by queuing at the wrong one. The best practice is to go to the information window and ask if there are any tickets for the train you want to go on, and if there are, which ticket window are they sold from. In addition, ask the price of the ticket. Although there are windows which say for pensioners, military and railway personnel, these are normally irrelevant except in the largest of cities. Before queuing, check the opening hours of the window as each *kassa* has a different closing time. It may be better to queue up at a closed *kassa* which will open in an hour than to wait in a long line where the *kassa* might close before you get to the head of the queue.

A good practice is to leave your bags with your partner so that you can push your way through the queue without worrying about your belongings. If there are 3 of you, 2 should queue with one shielding the other from the Russians trying to push in ahead of you. The person guarding the luggage should stack it in a corner near the information window which is the safest place in the hall.

> **Step 3: Buying the ticket**
> When you get to the window, tell the cashier the train number, date of departure, class of cabin, and your destination. If you don't speak Russian, given them the filled in booking card in the appendix. Good luck!

Rail tickets

Booking rail tickets in Russia is probably considerably easier today than at any time in the past. The basic reason for this is that supply is now greater than demand due to the increase in the cost of tickets. Despite the price rise, overnight rail tickets are still considerably cheaper than in the West, Russian plane tickets, and even hotels rooms in Russia.

To help you buy your own tickets, a Russian-English dictionary of words and phases used in booking is contained in the appendix as well as a booking card blank which can be filled in and handed to the ticket seller to eliminate the need to speak Russian.

In reading this section, please remember that Russian rail travel is continually changing and costs, procedures and regulations may have changed.

Ticket prices

Ticket prices are made up of three components: a booking fee, the class of ticket and the distance to be travelled. The booking fee is about $2. The cheapest class of ticket is *obshchi*, followed by *platskartny*, *coupe* and *SV* with each class being about 1.5 to 2 times the cost of the previous class. The cost per kilometre reduces with distance.

Ticket prices depend on the direction. This odd situation arises when you cross an administrative railway boundary between Russia's 19 railways as each railway has its own tariff charges. The BAM spans 3 of these 19 railways.

Tickets on trains that are leased to a private company (*firmenny* trains) cost about twice that of government trains.

Theoretically ticket prices for foreigners can be up to 3 times that of locals, however in the BAM Zone this is rarely enforced. Foreigner tickets are normally sold at stations which have an Intourist ticket window and Bratsk is the only such station in the BAM Zone.

Eventually the BAM will be brought into line with the rest of Russia and different tariffs for foreigners and local's tickets will be enforced. When this happens and you travel using a local's ticket, your conductor will report you to the head conductor and they will demand that you make up the difference in ticket prices. You will get an official receipt which you must keep in case a ticket inspector gets on your train. While you may be able to only get local's tickets from small stations, if you have obtained the local's ticket dishonestly from a station that sells

> ## What do the tickets look like?
> There are several types of tickets with the most common for foreigners outside the BAM Zone being the Intourist ticket which is a folded card with a red stripe across it and a ticket stapled into it.
>
> The most common in the BAM Zone is the local's ticket which is a long paper ticket with all the classes of berths printed on it. The seller cuts off the options you have not paid for, writes in the destination, your train, compartment and berth numbers, and then dates it with a hole punch.
>
> If you are travelling between large stations, then you may be issued a thick cardboard ticket which has the train number and destination station printed on it. The seller then just has to write the carriage and berth number on it and date stamp it. These tickets are normally issued for *platskartny* berths but occasionally for *coupes* as well. Strangely, some stations issue a combination of the two with a cardboard ticket plus a long paper ticket stating the premium for a *platskartny* to *coupe* upgrade. This process negates all the time savings of the cardboard tickets.
>
> There are a number of other tickets for use by railway personnel, the military and government officials and these are normally square paper tickets with blue ink. If these are offered to you, refuse them as it will be illegal for you to travel on them.

foreigner tickets, you may have to pay a fine as well as making up the difference. You can try to bribe the conductor and may get away with paying less, but then again, you may pay more than the upgrade price.

At the beginning of 1995, the cost of an overnight *coupe* for locals was about $20.

Visas and tickets
Technically, you can only buy tickets to those destinations listed on your visa. However, only at a very few stations on the BAM, notably Tynda, will you be asked to produce your visa. In addition, you will only get a ticket to the Republic of Sakha, if a Sakhian town is listed on your visa.

Booking tickets in advance
In the BAM Zone, you can buy a ticket for most trains up to 15 days in advance from all stations and up to 31 days from major stations. Only Moscow can issue tickets 45 days in advance. It is possible to get tickets further in advance but this requires connections.

Names on tickets
Nowadays, tickets do not normally carry the name of the purchaser on them. This was introduced at a time when ticket prices were low and speculators were buying the tickets and reselling them for a profit. This stopped in 1993 when the price of tickets went up substantially and the ticket supply outstripped demand. The only tickets which now carry names are those used on international trains.

Trains 119

Long Paper Ticket (usually for *coupes* berths)

Hole punch. Gives the date of departure.

Place of departure

Destination

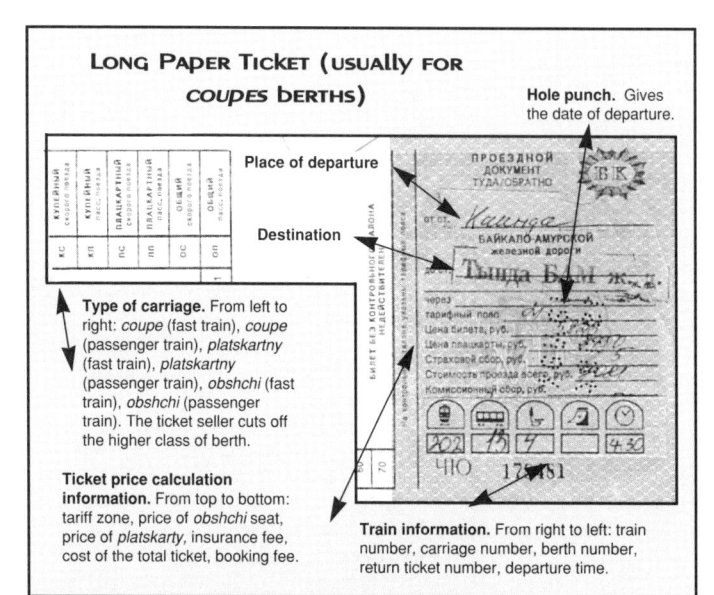

Type of carriage. From left to right: *coupe* (fast train), *coupe* (passenger train), *platskartny* (fast train), *platskartny* (passenger train), *obshchi* (fast train), *obshchi* (passenger train). The ticket seller cuts off the higher class of berth.

Ticket price calculation information. From top to bottom: tariff zone, price of *obshchi* seat, price of *platskarty*, insurance fee, cost of the total ticket, booking fee.

Train information. From right to left: train number, carriage number, berth number, return ticket number, departure time.

Small Cardboard Ticket (usually for *platskartny* berths)

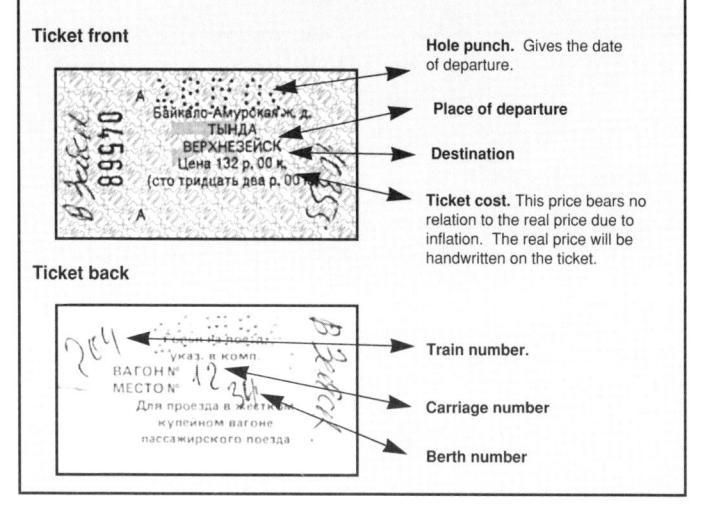

Ticket front

Hole punch. Gives the date of departure.

Place of departure

Destination

Ticket cost. This price bears no relation to the real price due to inflation. The real price will be handwritten on the ticket.

Ticket back

Train number.

Carriage number

Berth number

If you are buying a ticket from another person, check that no-one's name is written on it, on the off chance that the rule has been reintroduced. The only way for a ticket to be legally renamed is for the ticket selling staff to overstamp the original name with an official stamp and write your name on it.

Return tickets
It is possible to buy return tickets but only from some stations, and only 5 days or more before commencing the outgoing journey. There is no price discount for return tickets.

Changing your ticket
It is possible to change your ticket at the *kassa* where you bought the ticket from but it is best to get it right the first time and avoid the hassles. If you want to depart on an earlier train, the ticket is simply redated and you pay the booking fee of a few dollars. If you want to depart on a later train, a new ticket is issued and you pay the booking fee. If you don't want to travel and return your ticket 24 hours ahead of departure, you get a full refund minus the booking fee. It you return it between 6 and 24 hours from departure, you lose 50% of the ticket price if it was a *platskartny* berth or 18% if it was a *coupe*. If you are late and miss your train by less than 3 hours, you lose everything if you had a *platskartny* ticket or about 50% if it was a *coupe* ticket. If you arrive at the station more than 3 hours after the train has left, you will have to fill in some forms which are sent off to the central booking office for a decision.

Around a BAM town
Путешествие по городу

Orienting yourself
The maps in this book plus the description in the *BAM Town* section in *The BAM Zone* chapter are your best guide to finding your way around any BAM town. If you still have trouble finding something, you can always go to the police station where they invariably have a large map of the town and surrounding region on the wall.

If you want to visit a particular place, don't give up after being told by several people that they have never heard of it. Often locals have only been in the area for a few years and many have a poor regional knowledge. And even if someone tells you exactly how to get somewhere, keep asking until you get independent confirmation of it.

Finding toilets is always hard in Russia. In big towns there is the occasional public toilet but your best bet is any large public building such as cinemas, museums and restaurants. You will normally have to pay a few roubles to enter a public toilet, or pay the museum entry fee. In small towns, there is normally a toilet near the station and that's about all. So the best advice is to go just before you get off the train, and always use a toilet when you find one.

Getting around town

Trolley cars and buses offer a cheap way of getting around as well as giving you a tour of the town. If you get on the wrong bus, don't worry as it will eventually return to where you got on. To travel on trolley cars and buses, you need to buy a ticket which you self-validate. Tickets are normally bought in strips of 10 at roadside kiosks or on the vehicle. Generally buses with numbers below 100 travel within the city and above 100 travel to nearby towns.

Taxis are another option but are quite expensive. Remember three rules when dealing with taxis. Firstly, do not get a taxi near a hotel because if the driver thinks that you are a foreigner, he will insist on an outrageous sum. Secondly, never get into a taxi before you have negotiated a price. Thirdly, never get into a taxi if there is someone else in it, for obvious safety reasons. There are two sorts of taxis; official taxis which are yellow with a taxi sign on them, and unofficial taxis which are private cars that stop when people put out their hands. While official taxis have distance meters in them, no-one ever uses them as inflation has made them impractical.

Where to stay

There is a hotel in virtually all but the smallest towns in the BAM Zone.

The best hotels are equivalent to basic tourist level hotels found in Moscow. They have private facilities and services such as hairdressers and restaurants, and are only found in Komsomolsk, Tynda and Bratsk. In these hotels, there will invariably be a forbidding *dezhurnaya* (дежурная) or floor attendant who will supply you with flasks of hot water and tea, and is the guardian of room keys. On the ground floor, there is normally a luggage storage room where you pay per item per day.

More common in the BAM Zone is the local Russian hotel which has about 20 rooms. A few have twin bed rooms with private facilities while most have 2, 3 or 4 beds per room and share communal facilities. The best hotel rooms are called *lyuks* (люкс) and most hotels have at least one such room. *Lyuks* is a relative term and it just means that it is the best of all the rooms in that one hotel. The vast majority of the local hotels are owned by the BAM railway but anyone can stay in them. If they are used by locomotive crews who have finished their shift and are staying overnight before returning home the next day, they will have a canteen attached which is often open 24 hours a day. These Locomotive Brigade Hostels (дом отдыха Локомотивой Бригады) are spaced every 4 hour rail journey apart on the BAM.

Other options include holiday homes (дом отдыха) such as those at Severobaikalsk and Cape Kotelnikovski hot springs, and sanatoriums (саниторий) such as those at Kuldur and Aninski. These are like small hotels well away from the town with a number of single, double and triple rooms with communal facilities. They will normally have a canteen, sauna and pool.

Unfortunately there is only one place on the BAM where there are cottages (коттедж), which is at Severobaikalsk. Here there are 4 cottages which are self contained houses with their own kitchen, lounge room and three bedrooms.

The roughest kind of accommodation is in small towns and villages which have no hotel. Here you can stay in the municipal building, *possovet*, which will contain a room with a bed but often no running water.

A good way to experience Russian life is to stay with a family in *homestay*. This is still rare in the BAM Zone but can be organised if you ask the company you are dealing with. To minimise the clash of cultures, you should remember the following when living with a Russian family.
- You should organise a time each day for your meals.
- Be prepared to pay your family for additional services such as organising theatre tickets, sightseeing and taxis. Ask beforehand how much it will cost before agreeing to it and set an upper limit on how much you want to pay.
- Be prepared to supplement the household's food shopping when you visit the markets. Buy fruit or goods that they normally do not have.

Booking accommodation
It is best to book accommodation in advance. While this does not guarantee you a bed as hotels rarely reply to confirm or decline your request, it will increase your chances. The best way to book is simply to send a telegram to the hotel. Hotels are listed under the respective towns in the *BAM route description* chapters with a telegram booking request blank in the *Appendix*.

Washing
There are no coin operated laundrettes in Russia, however there are organisations where you can take your laundry. Unfortunately these are only located in large cities and they take several days to wash and dry

Around a BAM town   123

clothes. Your best bets are the hotels and if they don't have such a service, ask the *derzhurnaya* or the receptionist if they know someone who could do it for you. Rather than going to this trouble, most travellers prefer to do washing themselves.

Where to eat
There are three main places to eat in Russia; canteens, cafes/bars, and restaurants. The variety, presentation and quality of food are invariably worse than in the west and it is for this reason that Russians prefer to eat at home than out.

Canteens (столовая): These are basic eating places for workers and virtually all stations and towns have them. They normally serve three meals a day but close quite early. If the town is small, this may be the only place where you can buy hot food. The food is normally of average quality, but is cheap and quick.

Cafes (кафе) and **bars** (бар): These places are normally private establishments and have better surroundings but a worse selection than the canteens. Some only have one meal, such as Komsomolsk's Pilmeni Cafe (a pilmeni is a meat dumpling), while a few will have several courses, such as the Odin Cafe in Vanino. Alcohol is sometimes available.

A typical local Russian hotel room. Double beds are rare, the fridges and televisions rarely work, and the phone seems to only ring in the middle of the night.

Restaurants (ресторан): These establishments seem to serve the same bland dishes throughout the country. People don't come here for the food but the alcohol and the band.

The best Russian food is home cooked, particularly by someone who knows the older recipes which incorporate native food. Unfortunately, this knowledge has mostly been replaced by Soviet style stodge recipes. Hopefully with the increasing availability of herbs and spices, there will be a greater interest in different cuisines in the future.

What to eat

Nowadays, almost all western foods, from herbal tea to Mars Bars, are available in the large BAM towns. While this provides a good security net, Russian food will be cheaper and shopping for it is an educational experience. The food in the BAM Zone is about twice the cost of that in Moscow and about 1.5 that of Irkutsk and Khabarovsk. The reason for this is that BAM Zone wages are higher than the rest of the country due to the hardship allowances, and because food has to be freighted in.

Russian food that is commonly available all year round in state food shops includes *kolbasa*, cheese, bread, pickled vegetables, preserved fruit, tins of jam, jars of cooked *kasha*, macaroni, rice, milk, butter, cream, dehydrated Chinese noodles, frozen fish, slabs of meat, *salo*, eggs, tinned meat, biscuits and dried fruit.

Wilted vegetables can be obtained for most of the year, supplemented by locally grown fresh vegetables in late summer.

Vegetarians

Being a vegetarian in Russia is not easy. Meat is served with every meal and many Russians believe that vegetarian simply means that you will not eat solid lumps of red meat. If you are a vegetarian, or have another dietary requirement, you should inform your Russian host when the invitation to their home is made. Be warned, vegetarians find it difficult to eat a balanced diet in Russian where not eating meat is considered eccentric. So bring some supplies and vitamin tablets. The one advantage of being vegetarian is that you will be safe from meat food

A great vegetarian food is sea cabbage or morskaya kapusta (морская капуста). This is seaweed cut into thin strips in a little oil. It can be eaten straight out of the tin or as a salad. It is common in shops as the Russians don't particularly like it.

poisoning, however this is very rare in the rural areas of Russia, particularly in winter.

Telephones, telegrams, mail, faxes and email

Telephones, telegrams and mail are normally available at the post office. Post offices are divided into two main sections, occasionally located in separate buildings. The first is the postal office, where you send postal items and telegrams, and the second is the intercity and international telephone exchange. Both sections are difficult to work with.

The postal section of the post office has three main counters: normal for letters and postcards, *banderoli* (бандероли) for books and documents, and *posylki* (посылки) for other items. The normal section also serves as the poste restante (востребование). Unfortunately, the three sections are also occasionally in different buildings, such as at Komsomolsk. Be aware that the postal service is very unreliable and often items that are valuable never leave the country. To increase the chance of your mail making it, send everything by registered post (заказной). While it is technically possible to mail books and other things, it is recommended that you don't do this. It is both very time consuming and frustrating. To export a book, you need to pay a tax based on the book's cost. Remember when you send parcels, don't seal them before going to the Post Office as they need to be examined.

Food Tips

- Preserved jars of fruit are a great travelling food as you can not only eat the fruit but drink the juice. For wine lovers, you can get preserved grapes in wine.
- A good summer breakfast is a mixture of crushed biscuits, fresh berries and sour cream.
- To stop butter going rancid for up to 5 days on long train trips, put it in salt water.
- Don't eat dried fruit before washing it at least once. Some Russians soak it overnight before eating it.
- Chinese noodles are great on trains, particularly those that come with a disposable polystyrene container. The *samovar* at the end of the carriage provides the hot water.
- Take some small resealable plastic containers to prevent butter, eggs, tea, coffee etc from being crushed.
- Take a tube of milk if you like it in your tea or coffee.
- Pack all your food in a large carry bag on the train as this is more convenient than continually opening your backpack.
- While most of the meat products in Russia are safe to eat, it is best not to buy meat products off railway platforms.
- When buying bottles of beers, make sure they are freshly bottled as Russian beer only lasts about 7 days before it starts to lose its fizz. The word for fresh beer is *svezhnoe pivo* (свежое пиво).

Airmail letters normally take 3 weeks to travel from Moscow to anywhere in the West but from the BAM Zone, add an extra month. If you send material by land and sea mail, allow 3 to 6 months for the item to arrive.

The telephone section of the post office is called *Peregovorny Punt* (Переговорный Пункт). Even if you don't want to make a call, you should visit one of these chaotic places to hear tens of Russians in individual phone booths yelling to overcome the poor line quality and each other's shouting.

To make a call, you need to fill in a form stating the town, phone number, name of the receiving party, and the length of time you want to talk for. You then pay for the call and wait until your name and telephone booth number is called over the loudspeaker. As soon as you pick up the phone in the booth, your time starts. The operator will tell you over the phone when there is 30 seconds left. If your call can't get through, you get a refund. A typical wait is from 15 minutes to 1 hour but if you want it to be put through quicker, you can pay a premium for a quick *srochny* (срочный) call. Frequently in the BAM Zone it will be impossible to get an international line and so you may have to make several trips to the *Peregovorny Punt*. In some places, there are intercity direct dial pay phones (междугородний автомат) which can instantly connect you with other cities in Russia. These take tokens which you buy from the cashier. Due to a strange twist of logic, these automatic phones are about twice as expensive as booking a call with the cashier. In Komsomolsk and Bratsk, there are credit card international phones in the biggest hotels which provide instant but incredibly expensive communication. For example a call from Komsomolsk to New York will cost $15 a minute.

SHOPPING THE RUSSIAN WAY

Don't expect Western-style service in shops, as it is unknown to the majority of Russians. The staff in stores may seem indifferent or even rude but there is no point getting annoyed or upset. At least it makes for great holiday stories when you get home. When you enter a store, watch what the other shoppers are doing and copy them. The procedure can differ a bit, but generally there are 4 steps to buying goods in a Russian store.
1   Decide exactly what you want to buy.
2   Find out the total price for all the things you want. Get an assistant to write it down for you.
3   Pay the total cost to the cashier and get your receipt. There is often only one cashier and you might have to queue. If the queue is long, then have a friend stand in it while you check out the things you want to buy.
4   Take your receipt back to the counter, show it to the assistant and pick up your goods, which will often have been wrapped while you were paying.

It is also possible to make an intercity and international call from most Russian houses by booking a call with the operator.

Direct dialling into the BAM Zone from abroad is usually not a problem providing you are calling a normal phone number. If

> **EMERGENCIES**
> To get assistance by phone, dial the following numbers. If you don't speak Russian, get help from a Russian.
> 01 Fire
> 02 Police
> 03 Ambulance
> 07 Long distance telephone connections
> 09 Directory assistance

you are trying to call a railway number (ie a phone number on the Russia-wide railway phone system), then it is virtually impossible as you have to use a normal phone number to call the railway operator, who will then redirect your call to the railway phone network.

If you are making an international call, remember that the BAM Zone is between 5 and 7 hours infront of Moscow which is 3 hours ahead of London in winter and 2 hours ahead in summer, and 7 hours behind Sydney in winter and 8 hours in summer.

Telegrams are the easiest way to communicate internationally as any post office will send them. They are also relatively cheap. Unlike telexes, which only a few post offices can send, telegrams are sent to the address of the recipients via their country's national post office. They normally are delivered a day or two after they are sent. Telegrams are commonly used within Russia to book accommodation and meetings.

Most large post offices have a public fax machine.

While email is common in European Russia, there are very few email providers in the BAM Zone. Komsomolsk and Bratsk have networks and it is expected that Tynda and Neryungri will get networks within a few years.

Tips and bribes

Tipping is not normally done as a reward for good service, but is more of an ostentatious display of wealth or as a bribe. If you want to show your gratitude, give a small gift such as a stick pin, baseball cap, pen or cheap digital watch.

Bribes, known as *vzyatka* (взятка), are common in Russia but unless you are well versed in Russian and the Russian ways, don't ever attempt this. If you are travelling with a Russian let them do it. A better approach for foreigners is to be patient and go through the official channels and if a bribe is expected, let the Russian initiate it. In the BAM Zone where foreigners are rare, being asked for a bribe is incredibly rare. However, an appropriate response to someone's 'assistance' in getting a railway ticket, a tour of a closed museum or a reserved room in a hotel, is a small gift.

Entertainment

While there is always a large range of entertainment in Moscow, such as the circus, ballet, opera, classical music, football matches and pop concerts, there is very little in the BAM Zone. In Bratsk or Komsomolsk there are the occasional performances, but elsewhere the only regular evening activities are films and television. As there will invariably be a concert, parade or performance on one of the official holidays, consult the calendar in the *Planning a trip* chapter, so you don't miss it.

Locals entertain themselves by going to the *banya* or *dacha* on the weekends, and outdoor activities such as fishing, picnics or berry and mushroom picking. If you get asked, go along with the Russians on these outings as it's always interesting.

Queuing

Queuing is a fact of life in Russia, and because of this, the Russians are resigned to it. Getting frustrated or impatient will do no good. The Russians have developed a few strategies for coping with long queues, and you can use them too. The first is to get someone else to stand in the queue for you - a child or friend, perhaps - so don't be surprised if the person in front of you suddenly swaps places with another person. The second thing is to ask the person in front or behind you to mind your place in the queue. This is very common, and it can be both good and bad. It can mean that when you are 2 people from the cashier, after waiting for 15 minutes in a store, 2 or 3 more people will materialise and take their rightful places ahead of you. This is annoying, but they were there first! On the positive side, you can do the same thing; if you are dying of thirst in a slow moving queue, then you can ask the person in front or behind you to mind your place - just the word *pozhalusta* (please) with a gesture to the door and your watch should be enough to get the idea across, and Russians are quite happy to mind your place.

Security and police
Безопасность и милиция

Being a Westerner you instantly attract attention and envy in Russia. For a very small group of Russians, this can mean an opportunity for their quick gain and your quick loss. Fortunately the BAM Zone is considerably safer than Moscow and probably safer than most Western cities. Common sense is the best safeguard and here are a few rules.
- Minimise the things you carry around.
- Dress down and blend in with Russians.

- Carry money and documents next to your body in a money belt, never in a bag.
- Carry a wallet with enough money in it for the day and nothing else so if you lose this 'sacrificial' wallet, it does not matter.
- Be discrete and don't draw attention to yourself by talking loudly in English or carrying a camera around your neck.

Types of police

Regardless of horror stories of corrupt police, they are your best bet for getting reliable information. The vast majority of police are honest and trustworthy with foreigners. As all police officers have to do military service before they enter the force, the youngest officers are 21 and have proved themselves to be reliable and trustworthy.

There are very few female police officers. The police identity card is the standard red vinyl flip-open card carried by all Russians so unless you read Russian, flashing an identity card means nothing. Police come in many guises, including civilian police, railway police, traffic police and railway property guards, and it is useful to know their areas of responsibility as they are very reluctant, if not prohibited, to work outside them.

Police identification

It is often hard to distinguish between the types of police as they mostly wear either a military uniform or the civilian police blue uniform, a blue peaked cap with a red band, black baton, short range radio and pistol.

Civilian police (Милиция): These are your average police officers who are responsible for common crime. Most street police teams consist of one plain clothes officer and one in uniform.

Railway police (Железнодорожная милиция): These police, also known as transport police (Транспортная милиция), wear the normal police uniform but are employed by the Ministry of Railways. There is a railway police officer at every railway station, and they will sometimes travel on trains. If a problem does occur on a train, the chief conductor can radio the next station and the railway police will be ready to storm aboard.

A typical small BAM town, such as Verkhnezeisk, has a complement of 13 civilian police and 8 railway police.

GAI police (ГАИ-Государственная Автомобильная Инспекция): These police man traffic intersections along major roads. Drivers show them enormous respect as they can levy hefty fines or confiscate your car. When they point their black and white striped baton at your car, you must pull over. The officer will eventually stroll over and demand your driver's licence and passport. They are experts at finding something wrong with your documents or car, but a bribe can get you on your way with the minimum of inconvenience. During the day, they will normally wear a pistol and baton but at night, particularly at the more remote GAI posts, they will carry automatic pistols.

Railway property guards (Военнизированная охрана): These paramilitary officers guard freight yards and other railway property. They normally wear army uniforms, carry machine pistols and occasionally, patrol with German shepherds. Most are ex-soldiers, many of whom have fought in Afghanistan or returned from Germany. There are very few guards that travel on freight trains with the exception of high value refrigerated wagons. These three carriage sets are looked after by one person in specially built quarters in one of the carriages. Occasionally civilians will travel in freight wagons with their cargoes but these people have no police power.

Railway troops (Железнодорожная войска по строительству и

GAI policemen flagging down cars to check drivers' licences and car registration documents.

восстановлению): While the vast majority of troops within the Railway Forces for the Construction and Maintenance of Railways are involved in building railways, a small percentage guard the ends of bridges and tunnels. This means that they are often based in the middle of nowhere and have a profoundly boring job. Despite the fact that they are not part of the Ministry of Defence, their uniform is identical to that of normal soldiers except they have their own railway insignia. The current government policy is to replace the bridge guarding soldiers with civilian guards.

Military police (Патруль): These soldiers wander the streets and stations looking for military personnel on unauthorised leave. There is always one officer and at least one enlisted man. They wear a large badge or red arm band emblazoned with the word Патруль (Patrol), and carry a pistol, baton and radio. Most of these police are normal soldiers rostered to this duty but full-time military police are identified by an arm patch with a "K" meaning Commandant Corp on it.

FSK police (ФСК): These police are part of the old KGB which has been renamed FSK (Federal Counter-Intelligence Service (Федеральная Слу)ба Контрразведки)). The FSK investigates crimes against the state and across administrative borders. These police are most often encountered if you are caught photographing something that they consider inappropriate such as a railway bridge.

Border guards (Пограничник): While these guards wear the Russian military uniform, they are actually part of the Ministry of Internal Affairs. Probably the only time you will meet them will be as you enter and leave the country. They have their own navy, airforce and ground troops, and wear a green band around their peaked caps.

Cossacks (Казакы): These self appointed, volunteer, paramilitary soldiers should be avoided. The Cossacks first explored Siberia and their descendants feel that by wearing the old Cossack uniform, consisting of a Russian military uniform with a yellow stripe down the trousers and a yellow hat band around a peaked cap, they are recapturing their true heritage, which entitles them to respect. As most of the Cossacks are louts, the average Russian eyes them warily. An uneasy truce exists between the regular police and the Cossacks. They are not allowed to carry guns but carry truncheons and long whips.

Cossacks believe in the three principles of common ownership, military service in support of the state and regional autonomy. These principles made them ideal tools for the Tsar in conquering new land and guarding boarders but have little relevance today. Thankfully there are only a few Cossacks in the BAM Zone as their power base is in the Don region in southern European Russia.

Crime on the railways

There are many stories of crimes on railways. The majority are exaggerations, distortions or complete fabrications. The most outrageous story in recent years has been the so-called Sleeping Gas Incident on the Moscow-St Petersburg train. This story involved an entire carriage being put to sleep by sleeping gas and everyone being robbed. After a week of international media coverage, the Russian journalist who wrote the story admitted that it was fictitious but she still maintained that she did lose her purse when she was asleep.

Having said this, crime does exist on railways and a few simple precautions will substantially reduce your chances of being a victim. These include locking the cabin from the inside when you are asleep by the normal lock and the flick down lock, putting valuables under the sleeping bench which means that they can't be reached without lifting your bed, dressing down on trains, not displaying cameras, talking softly and always carrying valuables on your body.

Some people feel the need to chain and padlock their bags but this is excessive. It is a good idea to always leave someone in the cabin to look after the luggage. If everyone has to leave, ask the conductor to lock your cabin.

Although valuables can be left in a small safe that is located in the chief conductor's cabin, this is not recommended.

If there is a problem, first go to your train conductor who will call the head conductor, who in turn will notify the police if it is warranted.

Siberian customs and manners
Традиции Сибири

Russia and its people are radically different in attitude and customs to Westerners. Being receptive and noticing their behaviour can save you a great deal of misunderstanding and offence. It is often said that the Russians are rude and abrupt. This may be true in business spheres but in personal matters they are probably more open and willing to please than Westerners.

Simple courtesy will often go a long way, and if you are not sure of the appropriateness of your actions, ask.

A common problem is what to take as a present for the host when visiting a Russian house. Flowers are ideal to be given to a female host as is a bottle of alcoholic drink for a male host. What kind of drink to take? Usually, something stronger than 30% proof.

Alcoholic beverages are usually drunk neat and in the "bottoms up" style. If you mix your vodka with juice or water, Russians may find it very strange, and call it "a spoilt drink". Moreover, if you are a man it will be appreciated if you drink it straight and straight down. A strong opinion some Russians have is that if you make a toast but do not drink it all in one gulp, then you are not sincere. So, if you propose in your toast something like, "for the well-being of the host" or "to Russia", make sure that you drink it to the end.

To minimise vodka damage, eat butter or fat before you drink as this will line your stomach with a protective layer which will slow the rate of alcohol absorption. Always follow vodka with a water or fruit juice chaser, and something to eat. It is not advisable to sip vodka but gulp it down quickly without leaving it in your mouth. In addition, don't mix alcoholic drinks.

Women attending Neryungri's new Russian Orthodox church. Devout female believers will wear a scarf to church from pubety. When visiting churches, make sure that you are dressed appropriately. Men should not wear shorts and women should not wear trousers when visiting a church. In some churches, you may be allowed to take pictures of the interior. However church officials will disapprove of you taking pictures of yourself in front of a background of icons. Smoking is not allowed within church property.

The legal drinking age in Russia is 18 years old.

It is customary in Russia to show respect for older people and this means that when travelling on public transport, it is the accepted norm to give your seats up to elderly people, women and small children. People may make disapproving remarks if you do not. In addition, it is polite to use a person's first and patronymic name if they are older than you. The patronymic name is the modified version of the person's father's name. For example, if your name is Brent and your father's name is Alexander, your full formal name with the patronymic would be Brent Alexandrovich. The additional suffix to make the first name into a patronymic for men is "-ovich", and for women is "-ovna".

Another difference between Westerners and Russians is that Russians usually don't greet strangers by saying the Russian equivalent of "How are you?" which is *Kak delo*?. A Russian when asked such a question may think that you are genuinely interested in how they are, and they may start to tell you about their fortunes and misfortunes! In Russia the most common way of greeting people is by saying *Zdrastvuite* which means "be healthy". Men usually greet each other by a handshake.

Another custom in Russia is to take off your hat and shoes when entering a house. It is believed that the custom originates from the traditions of old Russia, when it was necessary for a warrior to take his helmet and armour off in order to show the host of the house that he trusted him and did not consider him an enemy.

Another worthwhile thing to remember is that the Russian society is very heterogeneous. Westerners often call everyone who lives in the territory of the former Soviet Union a Russian. However, there are about 120 nations and nationalities inhabiting Russia and an equal number of languages are spoken. Some nationalities may take offence if you call them Russian while others may feel honoured.

For Australians, probably the most worthwhile advice is that the Australian way of expressing affection, by making fun of the person you are speaking with, is totally inappropriate in Russia unless you know the person very well. Russians usually mean what they say, and therefore, understand other people accordingly.

BAM Mainline Route Description

Taishet – Bratsk	136
Bratsk – Ust-Kut	140
Ust-Kut – Severobaikalsk	147
Severobaikalsk	156
Exploring North Baikal	164
Severobaikalsk – Novaya Chara	175
Novaya Chara – Tynda	203
Tynda	217
Tynda – Novy Urgal	224
Novy Urgal – Komsomolsk	244
Komsomolsk	259
Around Komsomolsk	271
Komsomolsk – Sovetskaya Gavan	280

Route Description Legend

✗ station only

🏠 village

▦ town

Taishet – Bratsk
Тайшет - Братск

Taishet (Тайшет)   0km
☎ area code: 395-63, ✉ Irkutsk Oblast, Taishet
Иркутская Область, г. Тайшет

This town with its population of 70,000 straddles the junction of the BAM and the Trans-Siberian railways. Being a small town, you can explore it in few hours.

Taishet is famous in gulag literature as it was a transit camp for Stalin-era prisoners heading east and west. In addition, Taishet was a major camp of Ozerlag, the gulag complex which built the Taishet-Bratsk section of the BAM. The building of this section started in earnest following the end of WWII and at the height of construction, there were over 300 camps dotted along the 350km stretch from Taishet to Bratsk with a total population of 100,000 prisoners. In *The Gulag Archipelago*, Solzhenitsyn wrote, "And Taishet, where its factory for creosoting railroad ties (where, they say, creosote penetrates the skin and bones and its vapours fill the lungs - and that is death)." The factory which makes the ties, or railway sleepers, still operates.

Getting there and away
Trains on both the Trans-Siberian and BAM railways stop here. From the north on the Trans-Siberian, trains arrive from Moscow (72:15 hours), Ekaterinburg (43:15 hours), Novosibirsk (22:00 hours) and Krasnoyarsk (7:45 hours). To the south, they arrive from Irkutsk (11:35 hours), Chita (30:45 hours), Khabarovsk (74:00 hours) and Vladivostok (87:30 hours). From the east on the BAM, trains arrive from Bratsk (6:30 hours), Ust-Kut (16:15 hours), Severobaikalsk (22:00 hours) and Tynda (44:00 hours). On a minor branchline from the south west trains arrive from Sayanskaya (саянская, 6:10 hours).
Taishet is located on the M53 Moscow-Irkutsk highway.
Planes arrive at Taishet from Bratsk, Irkutsk and Krasnoyarsk.

Where to stay
The best accommodation in town is the Hotel Birusa, opposite the railway station. It is a 4 storey building with 60 rooms. Prices are $8 for deluxe, $5 for twin share, $6 for single rooms. All have toilets and showers. Hotel Birusa, ul Transportnaya, ☎ 303-18 (Гостиница Бируса, ул. Транспортная). Another option is the hostel at the station. They

have 1 room with 13 beds for men and several rooms for women. Cost is $2 a bed, ☎ 524-23. The 3 storey Locomotive Brigade Hostel for locomotive drivers is another option. It has twin and triple rooms from $1.50 per person, ul Suvorova, ☎ 526-76 (Дом Отдыха Локомотивой Бригады, ул. Суворова). To get permission to stay there, you need to ask the chief of the locomotive repair shop, ☎ 437-77 or his deputy, ☎ 538-01.

Where to eat
The Birusa restaurant in the Hotel Birusa is okay. On the opposite side of the street and 100m down from Hotel Birusa is a canteen in a 2 storey building. Open weekdays 7:00-19:00 and weekends 10:00-23:00. A 24 hour canteen operates in the Locomotive Brigade Hostel.

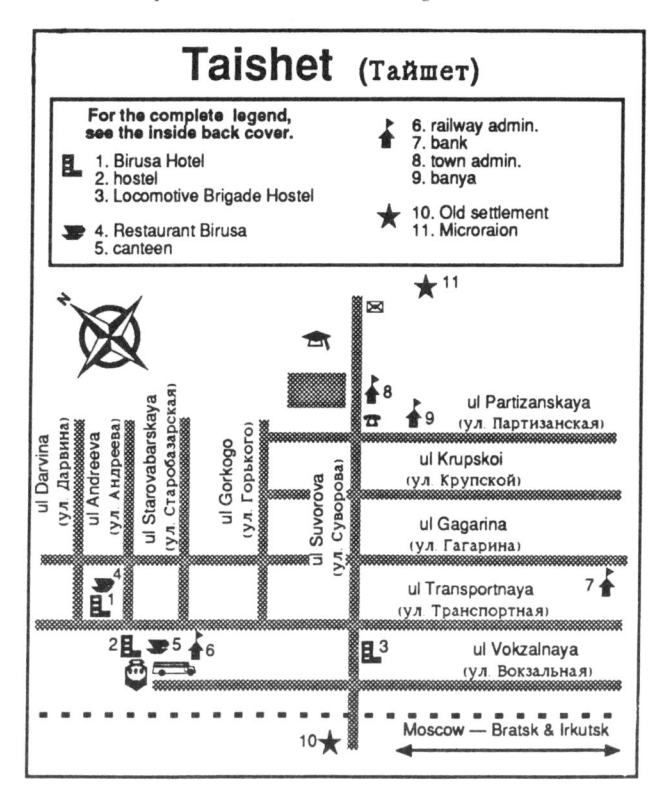

Taishet (Тайшет)

For the complete legend, see the inside back cover.
1. Birusa Hotel
2. hostel
3. Locomotive Brigade Hostel
4. Restaurant Birusa
5. canteen
6. railway admin.
7. bank
8. town admin.
9. banya
10. Old settlement
11. Microraion

Getting around
The town is divided into a new settlement which is where the station, apartment blocks and administrative centre are located and the old part which is on the other side of the railway line. The bus station is located in front of the station. Buses №1 and №3 go past the market which is located in the old settlement while Bus №4 goes to the new district (микрорайон) out of town a little way.

If you have several hours to spend, you can take a pleasant 25-30 minute car trip to the Birusa River where *dachas* are located.

Sosnovye Rodniki (Сосновые Родники) 129km
The station's name, which translates as pinewood springs, is different from the town which is called Oktyabrski (Октябрьский). The town is located on the right bank of the Chuna River and its main industry is lumber. Timber is floated down the 1,203km Chuna River, which is called the Uda River in its uppercourse, and loaded into railway wagons at Sosnovye Rodniki. The river freezes in late October or early November and is ice free in late April or early May.

Chuna (Чуна) 142km
Chuna was another major gulag camp centre and its camps included №19 Wood Processing Plant, №04 Deportation Camp and brick making works.

Vikhorevka (Вихоревка) 269km
Vikhorevka is 35km southwest of Bratsk. It has a population of 35,000 and was officially founded in 1957, despite gulag camps operating there since the mid 1940s.

Vikhorevka was the site of the prison hospital for the camps located along the entire length of the Taishet – Bratsk railroad. The town is now the headquarters of the Taishet – Lena administration of the East Siberian Railway.

Morgudon (Моргудон) 283km
Morgudon is the junction of the BAM and a spur line to the centre of Bratsk. Only suburban trains stop here so you have to get off at Anzebi to change for the suburban train. The 20km spur line was completed in 1971. The stations on the line are: Morgudon, Barulnaya (Багульная) 7km, Bratsk Porozhski (Братск Поро)ский) 17km, and Port Novobratsk (Порт Новобратск) 20km.

Anzebi (Анзеби) 292km
This is the best BAM station to change trains for the suburban train that goes to the centre of Bratsk. The adjacent settlement on the

Vikhorevka River is called Chekanovsi (Чекановский) after A L Chekanovsi, a famous explorer of central Siberia (1833-1876). Chekanovsi was born in the Ukraine, but was a Pole by nationality. He took part in the Polish Uprising of 1863-65 and for his troubles was exiled to Siberia. However the Russian Geographic Society appreciated his geographical training and commissioned him to conduct geographic surveys of the Irkutsk region in 1869-71. He later explored the upper Lena and Olensk Rivers and a number of towns in the region have statues and memorial plaques to him. See under *Bratsk* for more information.

Galachinski (Галачинский)   303km
Only suburban trains stop at this small station. See under *Bratsk* for more information.

Bratskoe More (Братское Море)   314km
Only suburban trains stop at this small station. See under *Bratsk* for more information.

Gulag Camp No 410, Vikhorevka:
A Prisoner's Account

"It was daytime when we arrived in Vikhorevka, a small settlement not far from the Bratsk Hydro-electric power plant. When I saw the prison building from the outside, I was surprised to see how gloomy a place could be made to be. This squat, grey, one storey concrete building, located on the perimeter of the settlement, was surrounded by an old, grey wooden fence and an off-limits zone with watchtowers. The walls, floors and the ceilings of the prison were cast with cement and iron bars into a cold block. This indestructible reinforced-concrete vault was built in the wintertime. Thus, in order to make the concrete harden as quickly as possible, salt had been added to it. The result, however, was that the floors, walls and ceiling were constantly wet. With a creak of the door and a squeak of the hinges, I was locked into my cell of 15 square metres. I was at home. Directly opposite the door was a window under which stood a large plank bed for eight persons. It was made of thick wooden blocks held together by iron clamps that were spaced some 30 to 40 cm apart from one another. Ice glimmered in the indentations in the floor. The window was also covered with a thick layer of ice. Drops of water clung to the ceiling; water trickled down the wall.

A single oven, positioned between two cells, was used for heating. Yet, because it was placed behind iron bars, we could not even warm ourselves up on it. We received two billets of firewood a day, about a quarter of a log, for use in the oven. The oven was only moderately warm and naturally could not, as a result, heat the cells. Our bodies were the only source of heat in these reinforced concrete cubicles. Light could hardly penetrate the ice layering on the iron barred windows. Over the door, there was a light bulb of not more than 25 watts. The yellow gleam could hardly illuminate the cell".

From *A World Apart* by Gustav Herling.

Padunskie Porogi (Падунские Пороги)   325km

This station services the suburbs of Padun (Падун) and Energetik (Энергетик) on the west bank of the Bratsk dam. See under *Bratsk* for more information.

Gidrostroitel (Гидростройтель)   339km

This station services the residential area of Gidrostroitel which is also known as Osinovka (Осиновка) on the east bank of the Bratsk dam. See under *Bratsk* for more information.

Bratsk – Ust-Kut
·Братск - Усть-Кут

Bratsk (Братск)
☎ area code: 39531 Bratsk
✉ Irkutsk Oblast, Bratsk, postal codes: Bratsk More 665707, Padun 665701, Energetik 665709, Иркутская Область, г Братск

Bratsk is fascinating, principally as an example of what not to do when you are creating a gigantic industrial complex in the middle of the *taiga*. Despite being in the top ten most polluted cities in Russia, Bratsk is still awe inspiring considering the massive achievement of constructing a modern city of 280,000, a giant dam and massive industrial complexes in just 2 decades. Two days is the maximum you will need to see all of Bratsk, however looking out the window of an express train may be enough for most travellers.

Orientation
Bratsk is not one town but a ring of connected settlements around the man-made Bratsk Sea (Братское море) which is a large reservoir created by the Bratsk dam.

The administrative centre of Bratsk is at Centralny, as are the Taiga and Bratsk hotels, but unfortunately there is no BAM station here. However Bratsk Centralny can be reached by an electric train from the BAM station of Anzebi which is 12km away.

The station of Padunskie Porogi services the suburbs of Padun and Energetik. The station's name derives from the Padun rapids which existed before the dam was built. This station is the closest to Hotel Turist. Padun contains the most attractive part of Bratsk as it has a pleasant promenade, with an old log watchtower and the city's only working church. Bratsk airport is to the north of Padunskie Porogi and can be reached by a 40 minute bus trip which starts from in front of the station. GSK-Bratsk Hydro-electric Construction Conglomerate (Братск ГСК-Гидроэлектрический строительний Комплекс), which is the biggest construction enterprise in the whole of Siberia, is located in Padun. In addition, the town also has several health sanatoriums for armed forces personnel but why they would be located in such a polluted place is still a military secret.

History
The Bratsk area with its rich agricultural lands was an important staging area for exploring and colonising Eastern Siberia and the Russian Far East. The word *bratsk* comes from the Russian words Bratskie Lyudi (Братские люди) which was given to the local indigenous people, the

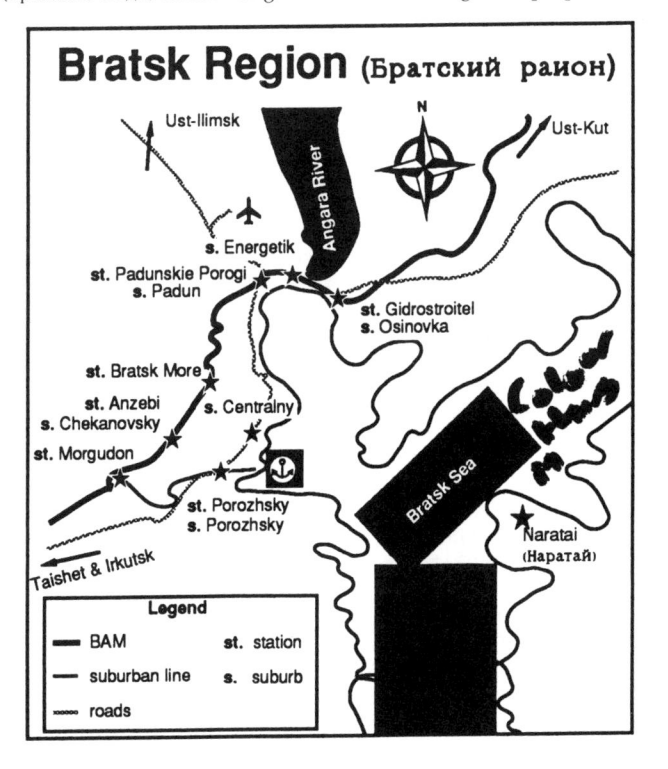

Buryats. Bratskie Lyudi means *fraternal people*. Old Bratsk was founded as a fort in 1631 but has long since disappeared under the giant Bratsk Sea.

As well as being an excellent farming region, the region provided much of the industrial base for development in the late 1890s. In 1895, the Nikolaevsk pig iron works began operation on the Dolonovka River, not far from Bratsk. The works built steamers which sailed on the Angara, produced equipment for the gold fields on the Lena, and forged rails for the Trans-Siberian railway. They were closed in 1899 when Irkutsk was connected to Moscow by the Trans-Siberian and cheaper steel could be shipped in.

In 1954, the decision was taken to build the Bratsk hydro-electric station and it rapidly became a gem in the nation's industrialisation crown. The reservoir is one of the largest in the world, being 169.3 cubic kilometres in volume with a surface area of 5,470 square kilometres. Within 7 years of the start of the dam's construction, electricity was being generated and in conjunction with the nearby Ust-Ilimsk hydro-electric station, the region now generates a mammoth 4.5% of the nation's electricity. To utilise this enormous amount of power, large industrial complexes were simultaneously built. These include the LPK Bratsk Timber Complex (ЛПК-Лесопромышленный комплекс) (1965) and BRAZ Bratsk Aluminium Complex (БРАЗ-Братский Алюминийзавод) (1966).

The planning and construction of Bratsk has been a series of errors but considering that the city arose out of virgin *taiga*, it is hardly surprising.

One of the first major mistakes was the underestimation of the speed that the reservoir would fill. In all, 249 settlements had to be moved and most villagers had to shift to their new towns before they were completed. In addition, the rising water quickly submerged the forests in the Bratsk-Ilimsk basin before they could be harvested which was a massive waste. Incidentally, the flooding resulted in a major downturn in agricultural production as the best farming land was in the submerged valleys. The novel, *Farewell to Matyora* by Valentin Rasputin, tells of the flooding of the Bratsk region and the resulting social problems of the resettled villagers.

Another major planning error was the vast under-utilisation of the dam's energy. Although on the drawing board the planned industrial complexes would consume all the electricity, in reality the plants were simply too big to operate at full capacity and therefore couldn't reach their theoretical energy consumption. For example, the paper and pulp mill has enormous problems obtaining the 7 million cubic metres of raw materials it needs annually. Even the Soviet media acknowledged the complex's problems and in 1971, the industrial journal *Sotsialisticheskaya*

Industriya stated that "there had been serious negligence in the building of the complex".

However the greatest problem is air pollution. The belching of the industrial smokestacks regularly blackens the skies over Bratsk and poisons the water. When the wind blows across town, the smell from the paper and pulp plant is dreadful. The biggest threat to life comes from the fertiliser factory. Every year there are accidental releases of nitrogen gas and the clouds float over the city. The city administration's solution was to install loud speakers on poles which advise you to stay indoors when an accident has occurred. This problem is compounded by the fact that despite the city plan showing industrial and residential zones, there is virtually no green belt between them. As might be expected, Bratsk has an active environmental movement.

Getting there and away
Bratsk can be reached by Trans-Siberian trains which join the BAM at Taishet (6:30 hours) from cities including Moscow (78:15 hours), Ekaterinburg (49:45 hours), Novosibirsk (28:30 hours) and Krasnoyarsk (14:15 hours). There is also a train from Bratsk to Irkutsk (18:00 hours). To the east there are trains from Ust-Ilimsk (8:30 hours), Ust-Kut (16:00 hours), Severobaikalsk (16:00 hours) and Tynda (38:00 hours).

There are daily buses to Ust-Ilimsk in the north east. To reach Bratsk by car from the west, you must first go to the town of Tulun (Тулун) which is 180km south of Bratsk on the M53 Moscow-Irkutsk highway.

There are daily flights from Krasnoyarsk, Irkutsk (one hour and $80 one way), Moscow, Novosibirsk, Omsk and Vladivostok. Other destinations include Ekaterinburg (6 times a week), Khabarovsk (3 times a week), Magadan (twice a week) and Yakutsk (once a week). The Aeroflot office at ul Deputatskaya 17 is open 8:00 to 19:00.

There used to be a 13 hour hydrofoil up the Angara River to Irkutsk but this was discontinued in 1994 due to a lack of passengers. It may be revived in the future so it is worth asking about when you get there.

Getting around
Both the Taiga and Bratsk hotels, and the central bus station on ul Yuzhnaya, are located in Centralny. Bus №110 travels from the bus station every hour, past the Hotel Taiga to the airport and takes 50 minutes. Bus №7A travels between the bus station and the closest BAM station of Anzebi. Opposite the Hotel Taiga and down the street at ul Mira 27 is the post office with a bookshop opposite. Next door to the post office is a large food shop with imported food. Hotel Turist is located near Padunskie Porogi station and can be reached by a 10 minute trip on Bus №103.

Where to stay
Hotel Taiga is a medium quality Intourist hotel, with a restaurant on the first floor and cafe on the ground floor. It is expensive at $40 single and $50 double rooms with private facilities. Hotel Taiga, ul Mira 35, ☎ 443-979 (Гостиница Тайга, ул. Мира 35). Hotel Turist is the best in town but is as expensive as Hotel Taiga. Hotel Turist, Energetik, ul Naymushina 28, ☎ 370-995 (Гостиница Турист, Энергетик, ул. Наумышина 28). Hotel Bratsk is very basic, has a restaurant and costs $24-46 for a single room. Hotel Bratsk, ul Deputatskaya 32, ☎ 446-44 (Гостиница Братск, ул. Депутатская 32). There is also a hotel at the airport.

What to see
Bratsk Intourist offers 2 hour tours of Bratsk for $20.

Any visit to Bratsk would not be complete without seeing the 50th Anniversary of Great October Bratsk Hydro-electric Station, BGES (БГЭС-Братская Гидроэлектрическая Станция). This dam consists of a 506m concrete wall with 3.5km of earth walls on its left and right. The BAM line runs along the top of the dam and gives an excellent view of the Bratsk reservoir on one side and the Angara River on the other. You enter the powerhouse by walking down the steps from the top of the dam. It goes without saying that there is no mention in the powerhouse's displays of the tens of thousands of Gulag prisoners who laboured and died building the dam and the region's industrial complexes. There are plenty of buses that go along the top of the dam where you can get off. These include №4,102, 103, 104 and 107. It is a 40 minute walk from the Padunskie Porogi station. It is well worth a visit and Intourist Bratsk provides a 2 hour tour for $45.

On the outskirts of Bratsk at Angara Village is an open-air ethnographic museum containing an Evenki camp, a watchtower and a fort from Bratsk's early years, and several houses of past generations. It is open in summer from 10:00 to 17:00 except Mondays. Intourist Bratsk provides tours to the museum for $40, however you can organise a visit yourself by hiring a taxi for the day.

Although the hydrofoil to Irkutsk no longer runs, there are still local ferries which travel to *dacha villages* and nearby settlements. Visiting one of these places makes a pleasant day outing. Boats leave from the piers at Gidrostroitel and Port Novobratsk from late May to the end of September.

Getting assistance
Bratsk Intourist is located on second floor of the Hotel Taiga, ☎ 443 95, fax 446-522.

Vidim (Видим) 463km
Vidim is located on the Vidim River, which is one of the many rivers that flow into Bratsk Sea. Its population of 6,600 is mainly involved in the timber industry. A good road connects Vidim with Zayarsk on the Bratsk reservoir and Zheleznogorsk-Ilimski.

Zhelezny (Железный) 546km
This small station should not to be confused with the nearby town Zheleznogorsk-Ilimski which is 8km away.

Korshunikha-Angarskaya
(Коршуниха-Ангарская) 554km
☎ area code: 39566 ✉ 665680, Irkutsk Oblast, Nizhneilimski Raion, Zheleznogorsk-Ilimski 665680, Иркутская Область, Нижнеилимский Район, г. Железногорск-Илимский

Although the railway station is called Korshunikha-Angarskaya, the surrounding town is known as Zheleznogorsk-Ilimski (Железногорск-Илимский). The station gets its name from the abandoned village of Korshunovski which is about 30km away.

Despite being a mining town, Zheleznogorsk-Ilimski is one of the cleanest towns on the BAM and has a lot to offer travellers. The settlement was founded in 1948 when iron ore deposits were discovered, it became a city in 1963 and is now the administrative centre of Nizhneilimsky *Raion* with a population of 33,000. It is located 16km from the Ilim River. A good road connects Zheleznogorsk-Ilimsky with Vidim and Ust-Kut.

Where to stay
Hotel Magnetit is an excellent hotel and many rooms have both toilet and shower. Costs are $9 double and $6 single rooms. The hotel is a 5 minute walk from the station. Hotel Magnetit, ☎ 214-60 director, ☎ 217-58 reception, fax 226-05 (att: Hotel Magnetit) (Гостиница Магнетит).

Where to eat
There is a restaurant in Hotel Magnetit, and a canteen on the opposite side of the street which is open 8:00-18:00 daily.

What to see
A 15 minute walk up the main street will bring you to Yangel Square (Площадь Янгела) where you will find the post office, Mayor's office, three museums, and a monument to aircraft and spacecraft designer Mikhail Yangel. The museums consist of a local regional museum, a

museum to Mikhail Yangel's life and work and a museum of Japan-Friendship. For the past 15 years, Zheleznogorsk-Ilimski has had a sister city relationship with the Japanese city of Sakata and both cities have hosted many sister-city cultural and sporting groups. The museums are open Tuesday to Sunday, 9:00-17:00, closed 13:00-14:00. The Director of all museums is Nadezhda Novikova (Надежда Новикова) ☎ 20-792.

Getting assistance
Zheleznogorsk-Ilimsky is home to one of Eastern Siberia's most active adventure clubs, the Tourist Club Kedr (Туристический клуб «Кедр»). The club is well known throughout the region, particularly in the Lake Baikal area. Members hold many climbing records and have discovered a number of glaciers and climbing routes to peaks. Their members are willing guides for rafting, biking, mountaineering and trekking trips in summer, and skiing in winter. It is possible to explore caves all year

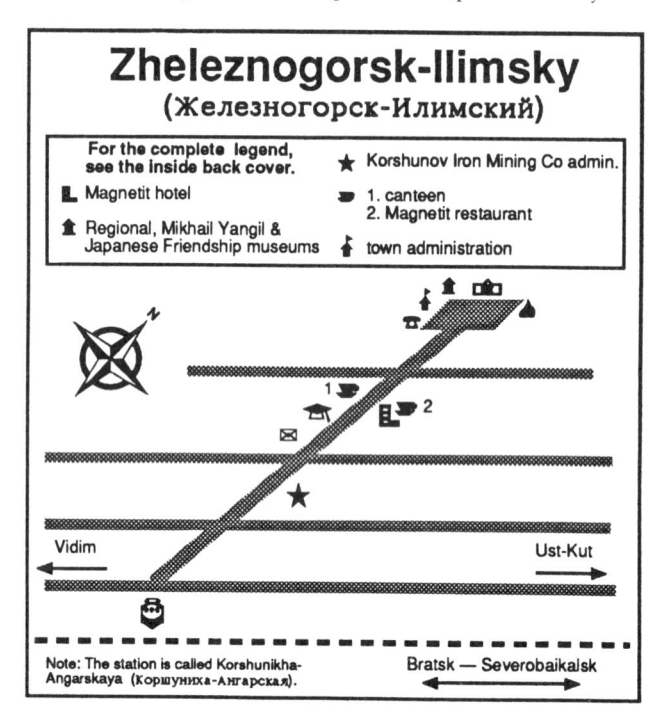

Zheleznogorsk-Ilimsky
(Железногорск-Илимский)

For the complete legend, see the inside back cover.
- **L** Magnetit hotel
- **血** Regional, Mikhail Yangil & Japanese Friendship museums
- ★ Korshunov Iron Mining Co admin.
- 1. canteen
- 2. Magnetit restaurant
- town administration

← Vidim   Ust-Kut →

Note: The station is called Korshunikha-Angarskaya (Коршуниха-Ангарская).

Bratsk — Severobaikalsk

> ### From Peasant to Rocket Scientist
> Mikhail Yangel (1911-1971) is a Soviet success story; the child of peasants who became one of Russia's greatest rocket scientists. During his life and immediately after his death, his achievements were unknown as they were a state secret and it has been only in the last 15 years that their release has made him into a local celebrity.
>
> He was born in the village of Zyryanovo (Зыряново) and in 1926 he went to Moscow. In 1931 Yangel entered the Moscow Institute of Aviation, he worked developing aircraft and space craft until he died in 1971. His work was instrumental in putting the world's first astronaut, Yuri Gagarin, into space in 1961. There is a museum to his life in Zheleznogorsk-Ilimsk and another in his family home in Zyryanovo. This house-museum contains much of his family's original furniture and many of his personal belongings are on display, including the suitcases taken on his trip to the USA in 1935. You can reach Zyryanovo village by a 90 minute bus trip from Zheleznogorsk-Ilimsky.

round but it is best to visit them in winter when the cave temperature is warmer than outside. Guides charge $10-40 a day. The club also manufactures rucksacks and inflatable rafts, using imported fabric, which are excellent and reasonably priced. Most equipment can also be hired for $5 a day. The club can also organise homestay for $10 a day. Contact Anatoly Semilet, 8th Kvartal, 4th hostel, kv 430, ☎ 284-73 home, ☎ 228-28 work, fax 226-05 (Анатолы Семилет, квартал 8, Обще)итие 4, кв 430) or Mrs Raisa Fisher, ☎ 285-29 home, ☎ 2943-70 work.

Khrebtovaya (Хребтовая)   575km
Khrebtovaya is the junction of the BAM and the branch line to Ust-Ilimsk. The town is located on the Bratsk-Ust-Kut highway, 220km northeast of Bratsk. For information on the Ust-Ilimsk branch line, see the *Khrebtovaya – Ust-Ilmisk* section on the *Northern Branch Line Route Description* chapter.

Ust-Kut – Severobaikalsk
Усть-Кут - Северовайкальск

Ust-Kut (Усть-Кут) 715km
☎ area code: 395-65
✉ area code: 665780, Irkutskaya Oblast, Ust-Kut
665780, Иркутская Область, г. Усть-Кут

Ust-Kut is one of the most vibrant towns on the BAM, as it is a major rail and river terminal for the Lena River and the Republic of Sakha (formerly Yakutia).

Ust-Kut is 40km long and lies at the junction of the mighty 4,400km Lena River and the 408km Kut River. The town sits astride the BAM which runs parallel with the Lena River. Present day Ust-Kut was created in 1954 by amalgamating several settlements. From west to east they are Kirzavod (Кирзавод), Ust-Kut, Lena (Лена), Rechniki (Речники), Rechniki-2 (Речники-2), Geologists (Геологики), Neftebaza(Нефтебаза) and Yakurim (Якурим).

This amalgamation causes confusion with travellers as the main passenger station in not Ust-Kut but Lena. A short walk from Lena station will bring you to the Lena River Passenger Station, known as Osterovo.

The freight port is located near Ust-Kut station. In the late 1980s, this port shipped 80% of all cargo for the Yakutia region.

History
Ust-Kut was founded by the famous explorer Yerofei Khabarov in 1631 and it rapidly became an important trading port as it supplied most of Eastern Siberia with food and equipment until the 20th Century. Rich deposits of salt were discovered nearby which were exploited until the beginning of the revolution. Rail traffic first reached Lena in 1958 when a temporary railway was laid across the Bratsk reservoir. The town now has a population of 70,000 and has one of the nation's few river transport institutes.

What to see
The most interesting sight is the freight port. Bus № 1 goes to the freight port and onwards to Lena station.

Another option is to visit the balneological-pelotherapeutic mud spa which is renowned throughout Russia but unknown abroad. The spa uses diluted sodium chloride brine containing bromine and silt mud from Lake Ust-Kutskoe. The baths are used to treat muscular, gynaecological and peripheral nervous system disorders. The spa is 3km from Ust-Kut and the easiest way to get there is to take a taxi.

Lena (Лена) 722km
This is the main passenger station rather than Ust-Kut as travellers for the river vessels that travel to the Republic of Sakha depart from nearby Osterovo River Passenger Station.

Getting there and away
Trains reach Ust-Kut from Moscow (88:30 hours), Irkutsk (27:50 hours), Taishet (16:15 hours), Bratsk (7:00 hours), Severobaikalsk (8:15 hours), and Tynda (36:40 hours).

The town has air links with Irkutsk, Bodaibo, Yakutsk, Chita,

Kirensk, Lensk, Mirny, Olekminsk, Kirenga, Mama and many other smaller settlements.

From late May to September, it is possible to go by regular passenger boat down the Lena to Yakutsk (3 days, 13 hours), and up the

> ## The Celebrated Killer
>
> While Yerofei Khabarov may have been one of Siberia's greatest explorers and was even honoured with the city of Khabarovsk being named after him, he was also one of Russia's most brutal conquerors. Khabarov arrived in Ust-Kut in 1631 from European Russia with a small fortune from his early trading ventures. He initially started farming, then founded a salt works, before branching out into corn wholesaling. However due to his hot-temper, heavy handedness and brutal treatment of peasants, in 1641 all his enterprises were appropriated by the State.
>
> He moved down the Lena River to Kirensk and started farming again. A group of peasants were sent from Yakutsk to settle in this region a few years later which Khabarov tried to discourage with violence. Frustrated by the peasants' encroachment, Khabarov sailed to Yakutsk, collected 150 mercenaries and unexpectedly appeared before the governor to ask for permission to sail to the Amur River. Confronted with so many soldiers, the Governor was only too pleased to get rid of the trouble maker, and Khabarov's force sailed further down the Lena River in March 1649 to the Olekma River then onwards to the Amur River. He returned to Yakutsk in May 1650 with few spoils but news that there was grain in the Amur valley and it could be transported to Yakutsk in just two weeks at a significantly cheaper cost than grain from European Russia.
>
> Later that year he returned to the Amur River with a larger group of mercenaries, cannons and provisions, and decimated many indigenous Daurian villages. Even among the callous Russian explorers, Khabarov's deeds were considered barbaric. Khabarov took thousands of prisoners yet few lived, and he administered punishment as a weapon of fear not justice. His treatment of women was particularly offensive. He built up harems at each stop but when he and his Cossacks moved on, they simply abandoned or executed the women as more were to be found in the next settlement.
>
> The taking of tribute, women and provisions from the Amur region infuriated the Chinese rulers and when Khabarov was camping on the site of present day Khabarovsk, a Chinese army attacked. The Chinese lost and, ironically, the captured provisions allowed Khabarov and his men to winter in comfort.
>
> As soon as word of Khabarov's conquest of the Amur valley reached Yakutsk and the rest of Russia, hundreds of volunteers flocked to him. As these men were attracted by spoils and owed no allegiance to Khabarov, they resented his harsh and arbitrary treatment. Within a short time, his force rebelled and imprisoned him. He was eventually transported to Moscow not as a hero conqueror but as a despot.
>
> In Moscow, the Tsar confiscated his property and sentenced him to death. However, Khabarov was able to convince the Tsar that his conquests were in the best interests of the state and that they had opened up the unknown riches of the Amur. Pragmatism won the Tsar over and he restored Khabarov's property and made him a nobleman or 'boyar' with control over several villages in the Ilimsk region which is 220km north east of Ust-Kut. He retired to this area which is now under the Ust-Ilimsk reservoir.

Lena to Zhigalvo (11 hours). A good road connects Ust-Kut with Novaya Igirma and Khrebtovaya.

What to see
The city museum contains information on the BAM and the region, and is located near the Osterovo River Passenger Station.

It is also possible to tour the river fleet shipyard known as REB which was founded in the 17th Century. To get there take Bus № 6 to the other side of the river.

For steam rail enthusiasts, 500m from the east end of Lena station are three rusting steam engines, including one built by the American Locomotive Company in February 1945. Its number is 72649.

Getting around
The main bus station is in front of Lena station. Bus № 1 goes to Ust-Kut, № 2 to Kirpichny Zavod *Microraion*, № 3 to Nephtevaza *Microraion*, № 4 to the hospital complex near *Microraion* Rechniki, № 6 to the other side of the Lena River close to REB, № 101 to the airport, and № 102 to Yakurim *Microraion*.

Where to stay
The best and most expensive hotel in town is the new, 9 storey 220 bed Lena Hotel. It is opposite the railway station and the price for a two room suite is $53, twin share $33, and single bed $27. All rooms have full facilities. The hotel also houses the Irkutsktourist Travel Company. Lena Hotel, ul Kirova 88, ☎ 21-507, fax 20-729 or 21-500 (att: Lena Hotel) (Гостиница Лена, ул. Кирова 88)

Osterovo River Passenger Station also has a few rooms including five 4-person bed rooms at $5 a person, and three twin bed rooms at $7.50 a person, ☎ 214-80.

The best railway accommodation is the Moststroi 9 Hotel. It has single and double rooms with all facilities and is a 10 minute walk from Lena station. ☎ 2-25-22. The hotel is next to the Locomotive Brigade Hostel which also has a 24 hour canteen.

Information: Irkutsktourist Travel Company, located in the Lena Hotel, can book rail and boat tickets, and arrange excursions. Its main business is organising travel for Russians and it has been operating for 9 years. The Director is Elvira Musatova, ☎ 21-880, fax 20-729 or 21-500 (att: Irkutsktourist) (Иркутсктурист, ул. Кирова 88).

Lena-Vostochnaya (Лена-Восточная) 736km
On the west bank of the Lena is the station Lena-Vostochnaya which is the official start of the BAM railway.

After leaving Lena-Vostochnaya, the train passes over the first bridge built after Brezhnev announced that the BAM was to be built. The 418m bridge was completed in 1975.

The area between the Lena River and the Baikal Range is famous for its scenic beauty, and is one of the most pleasant stretches on the BAM.

Zvezdnaya (Звездная) 786km

In February 1974, construction work started on Zvezdny settlement. The town became famous throughout the USSR as the first of

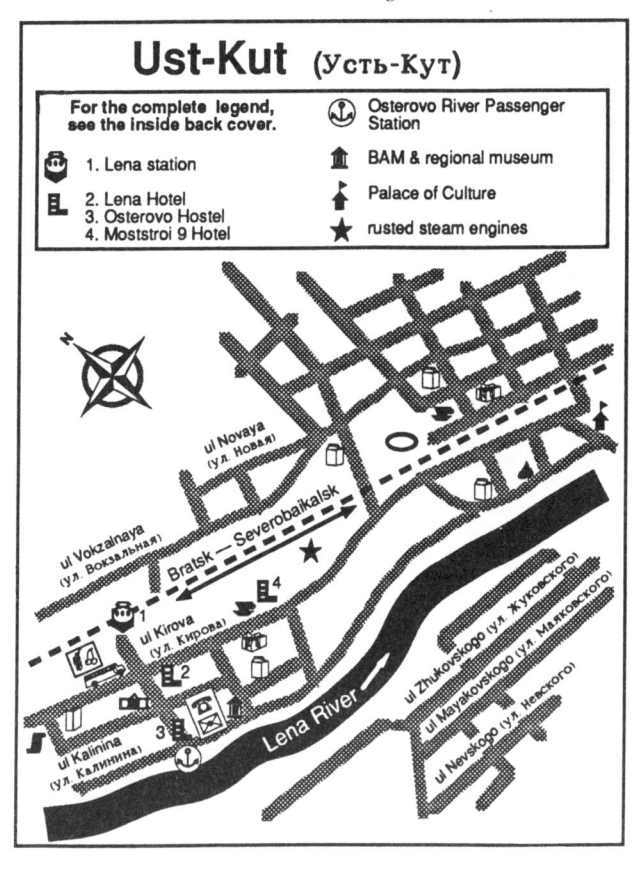

THE MIGHTY LENA RIVER (Рика Лена)

The mighty Lena River is the second biggest river in water volume in Russia (after the Yenisi), yet it is virtually unknown outside of Russia. The 4,400km river starts in the mountains to the west of Lake Baikal and snakes through north eastern Siberia until it floods into the Laptevikh Sea in the Arctic Ocean. Since the mid 1600s, the river has been the lifeline to the capital of north eastern Siberia, Yakutsk, supplying it with grain, salt, guns and adventurers. It was from here that the exploration, conquest and eventual colonisation of eastern Siberia and the Russian Far East were launched.

Like the vast majority of Russian rivers, the Lena flows north. This makes sailing downstream from the major southern river port at Ust-Kut to Yakutsk three days shorter than going in the reverse direction.

The river is navigable from about 150km from its source to the Arctic sea, however regular services only ply the river from Ust-Kut north to Yakutsk and from Ust-Kut south to Zhigalovo. It is usually ice free from May to September and its frozen surface is so solid that it can be safely driven on in February. Its June temperature ranges from 14°C to 19°C.

What is particularly surprising about the Lena is the amount of river passenger traffic it carries when all around central Siberia everything is dead. Even Irkutsk can only support one hydrofoil route every second day to the north of Lake Baikal.

The Lena is a godsend for travellers as it is one of the most interesting ways of exploring hidden corners of Russia. As few foreigners have ever travelled these routes, you are guaranteed an extraordinary insight into the lives of river villages, both Russian and indigenous. In addition, the complete lack of Intourist's presence, except in Yakutsk, means that the price of tickets and accommodation is very reasonable.

Travelling on the Lena River
Both regular hydrofoils and river cruisers ply the Lena River. From Ust-Kut, regular hydrofoils travel upstream to Zhigalovo and downstream to Peledui (Пеледый) which is about 40% of the way to Yakutsk. River cruisers also sail downstream from Ust-Kut to Yakutsk and occasionally as far as Khandyga.

Booking
Tickets are bought at the river stations (Речной Вокзал) or if the town is small, on the vessel. You can either do this by requesting a local travel company to buy it in advance (however they will be reluctant to just sell you a ticket as there is little profit in it for them) or to buy yourself once you arrive directly at the river station. The ticket offices normally open half an hour before departure of the hydrofoils while tickets for river cruisers can be bought during normal business hours. As the price of tickets is expensive for locals, there are invariably spare berths. Remember to keep hold of your ticket as you may be asked to show it during the trip and when you get off the boat. The major river stations are at Ust-Kut and Yakutsk. Ust-Kut's Osetrovo River Port, ul Kalinina 8, ☎ 26-397 dispatcher, ☎ 26-506 chief, fax 20-728 and 21-500 (att: Osetrovo River Port) ☎ 23-253 general (Осетровный Речной Порт, ул. Калинина 8).

For more information on travelling on the Lena River, including places of interest, route description and suggested itineraries see *The Lena and Amur Rivers Guidebook* in the *Recommended reading* section.

Hydrofoil Timetable from Ust-Kut to Zhigalovo (South of Ust-Kut)

Place	Time of Arrival	Km from Ust-Kut	Cost $
Ust-Kut (Усть-Кут)	8:00 depart	0	
Turuka (Турука)	8:45	22	2.40
Omolo (Омолой)	10:20	75	7
Boyarsk (Бояск)	11:10	100	9
Koknina (Кокнина)	11:50	121	11
Dyadina (Дядина)	14:25	202	14
Surovso (Сурово)	14:55	217	17
Golovskoe (Головское)	15:30	234	18
Konoshanovo (Коношаново)	16:05	252	19
Gruznovka (Грузновка)	17:10	288	21
Molodezhny (Молодежный)	17:40	303	22
Ust-Ilga (Усть-Илга)	18:05	315	22
Zhigalovo (Жигалово)	19:00	342	24

River Cruiser Timetable from Ust-Kut to Yakutsk (North of Ust-Kut)

Place	Time of Arrival	Km from Ust-Kut	Cost $
Ust-Kut Усть-Кут	9:00 depart	0	
Kirensk Киренск	5:00	301	33
Vizirny Визирный	21:30	622	51
Vitim Витим	3:30	743	56
Peledui Пеледуй	5:00	767	59
Lensk Ленск	14:10	910	69
Saldykel Салдыкель	16:45	1,008	122
Nuya Нюя	18:20	1,037	122
Tinnaya Тиннаыа	2040	1,083	76
Chapaevo Чапаево	22:10	1,111	76
Macha Мача	24:00	1,151	76
Delge Дельгей	3:35	1,232	76
Olekminsk Олекминск	10:30	1,301	134
Khorintsy Хоринцы	15:10	1,426	138
Uritskoe Урицкое	18:00	1,485	142
Sanyyakhtakh Саныяхтах	22:20	1,581	142
Malykan Малыкан	0:35	1,622	145
Isitskaya Иситская	2:40	1,661	145
Pokrovsk Покровск	12:40	1,893	103
Yakutsk Якутск	18:00	1,988	106
Khandyga Хандыга		2,637	132

Hydrofoil Timetable from Ust-Kut to Peledui (North of Ust-Kut)

Place	Time of Arrival	Km from Ust-Kut	Cost $
Ust-Kut Усть-Кут	7:00 depart	0	
Markovo Марково	9:15	138	13
Kirensk Киренск	13:15	301	2
Korshunovo Коршуново	16:30	513	35
Vizirny Визирный	18:40	622	41
Vitim Витим	20:35	743	46
Peledui Пеледуй	21:00	767	50

several hundred new towns to spring up in the path of the BAM. It was named after the cosmonaut settlement of Zvezdny near Moscow but commemorates terrestrial rather than cosmic pioneers. There is a memorial board in the town listing the 14 male and 2 female Komsomol youths who were the 'first' pioneers to arrive at the future town site located on the banks of the Tayura River. In reality, Zvezdny was built on the site of an old village called Tayura.

Zvezdny today is a combination of rustic wooden cottages, new concrete buildings and an impressive station. The town has shrunk considerably since the 1970s as the promised new industry which justified its construction never materialised.

Kirenga (Киренга) 890km

Kirenga is a very small railway settlement with the nearest town being Magistralny (Магистральный) which is 12km to the east. There are regular buses between the two places. Magistralny is a sizeable town of 10,000 on the Kirenga River and its main industry is timber. The river port is called Klyuchi (Ключи) but since the construction of the BAM, few craft ply the river. A one hour drive to the north will bring you to the small town of Kazachinskoe (Казачинское), the capital of the *Raion*. This isolated town was founded in 1776 and its inhabitants' main occupations are farming, hunting and fishing. Until the arrival of the BAM with its large influx of workers, expeditions used to visit Kazachinskoe to study ancient Russian dialects which had been preserved by descendants of early settlers.

There is a Locomotive Brigade Hostel with a canteen in Kirenga.

Ulkan (Улькан) 931km

This town of 10,000 is located on the Ulkan River and confusingly, has the same name as another town at the confluence of the Ulkan and Lena Rivers about 150km to the north west. The BAM town of Ulkan was constructed by the Crimean Regional Komsomol Party which is reflected in road names such as Crimea Street. About 1km from Ulkan is the ancient village of Yukhta (Юхта) which is surrounded by two smaller villages called Tarasova (Тарасова) and Munok (Мунок). A total of 51 men, virtually the entire able bodied male population of the 3 villages, departed to fight in the Great Patriotic War. Sadly not one returned and consequently, the villages have become virtual ghost towns. The war memorial in Yukhta lists the names of those who died.

Between Ulkan and Kunerma are several hot water springs which are regarded as having great healing power. There are no tourist facilities at these springs.

Kunerma (Кунерма) 983km

Kunerma is a nice place to visit on a day trip from Severobaikalsk, as to get here you pass through scenic mountains. The town is also attractive as it consists of a number of wooden two storey apartment blocks, a recently refurbished station and a single shopping complex. Only 700 people live here and it provides an interesting insight into small town life. It is also a very popular fishing destination as there is a well stocked lake nearby.

As well as the daily trains from Tynda to Moscow, suburban trains terminate here from Severobaikalsk. There are three suburban services to Severobaikalsk daily. There is no accommodation in the town.

After leaving Kunerma, the train loops around the Goudzhekit River valley towards the 2,000m above sea level Baikal Mountains and through the 6.7km Baikal Mountain Tunnel (Байкальский тоннель). This tunnel was the easiest of all the BAM tunnels to build and took only 3.8 years to complete. It was opened on 1 October 1984, however from 1979 to 1984 trains ran over the mountains on a dangerous 15km bypass from the towns of Delbichinda (Дельбичинда) and Daban on either side of the mountains. The remains of this bypass can be seen about 5km from the western entrance of the tunnel on the right side. About 500m to the right of the Baikal Mountain Tunnel entrance is another rail line going into a tunnel. This was an exploration tunnel and extends for less than 100m. To visit the exploration tunnel and the bypass, you need to get off at Delbichinda and walk about 10km.

Daban (Дабан) 1,015km

As soon as you emerge from the eastern tunnel entrance, you come to the station of Daban. The stop, at 1,500m above sea level, is a popular starting point for hikers and cross-country skiers. The only building at this stop is the station and there is no accommodation here.

As you descend from the mountain, you will see the Goudzhekit River on your left and after a few kilometres, a solitary red brick chimney in a large field. This is all that remains of the town which was constructed for the 3,000 tunnellers who built the tunnel. Eliminating all traces of construction and returning the area to its natural condition was an important element in the BAM's environmental policy. A further 3km from the tunnel's exit on the left side is the military camp which supplies guards for the tunnel entrances.

Between Daban and Goudzhekit, you cross the signless border separating the Irkutsk Region and the Buryatia Republic.

Goudzhekit (Гоуд)екит) 1,029km

This town was once a holiday resort and although its trade has died with the economy, it still has its attractions, including hot springs, a swimming pool and a small, basic hotel.

Tyya (Тыя) 1,043km

On most rail maps this stop is called a rail siding or is simply not mentioned. However, near the station is the medium sized town of Solnechny (Солнечный). Near the town is a 340m down hill ski run with a tow and ski rental. Three suburban trains a day stop at Tyya.

Just outside Tyya on the left is a disused shooting range beside a small house on a lake. In the Soviet-era, these ranges were financed by the Ministry of Defence as a way of maintaining military skills among citizens.

Severobaikalsk
Северобайкальск

Severobaikalsk (Северобайкальск) 1,064km
☎ area code: 301-39
✉ 671717 Republic of Buryatiya, Severobaikalsk
671717 Республика Бурятия, г. Северобайкальск

Severobaikalsk is the capital of the western end of the BAM and probably the most popular destination on the line. The town provides excellent access to the North Baikal attractions, which include trekking and mountaineering in the Baikal Mountains, indigenous villages, a Stalin-era gulag, downhill skiing, sailing around the north end of the lake and seal watching.

In terms of tourist infrastructure, the city is also blessed with a range of accommodation, several reasonable restaurants and good transport links with Irkutsk (hydrofoil and plane) and Moscow (train).

The town is stark but following the 1994 program of street scaping and tree planting, it should be attractive in a few years. (Why it has taken 15 years for the City Council to plant trees is a mystery.)

The history of Severobaikalsk provides a fascinating insight into the way BAM towns have changed with the railway's fortune and post-Soviet economic collapse.

Severobaikalsk has a population of 35,000 and grew out of the virgin *taiga* with the arrival of the BAM constructors. The city was planned by the Leningrad Zonal Research Institute of Experimental Planning which is blamed by most inhabitants for the town's badly designed apartment blocks and lack of suitable housing. At first glance the apartment blocks look like standard Russian ones, however a closer look reveals that they don't have balconies. For Russians, balconies are invaluable as they are a storage area and giant refrigerator in the winter. The reason for this massive oversight was that the buildings were designed for the hot climates of Central Asia by the Leningrad Institute and simply

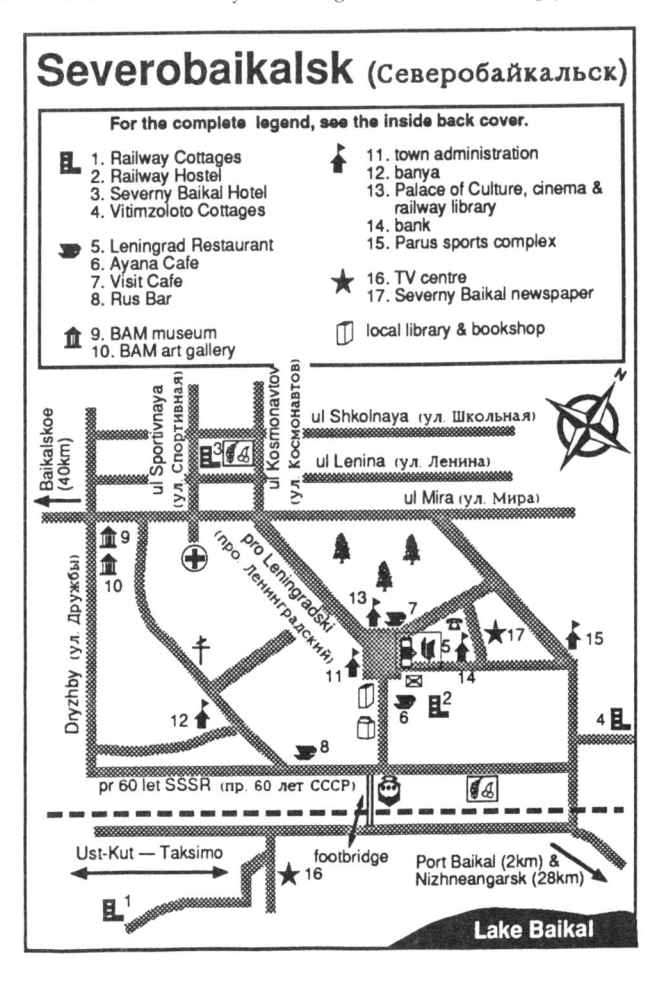

Severobaikalsk (Северобайкальск)

For the complete legend, see the inside back cover.

1. Railway Cottages
2. Railway Hostel
3. Severny Baikal Hotel
4. Vitimzoloto Cottages

5. Leningrad Restaurant
6. Ayana Cafe
7. Visit Cafe
8. Rus Bar

9. BAM museum
10. BAM art gallery

11. town administration
12. banya
13. Palace of Culture, cinema & railway library
14. bank
15. Parus sports complex

16. TV centre
17. Severny Baikal newspaper

local library & bookshop

- Baikalskoe (40km)
- ul Sportivnaya (ул. Спортивная)
- ul Kosmonavtov (ул. Космонавтов)
- ul Shkolnaya (ул. Школьная)
- ul Lenina (ул. Ленина)
- ul Mira (ул. Мира)
- pro Leningradski (про. Ленинградский)
- Dryzhby (ул. Дружбы)
- pr 60 let SSSR (пр. 60 лет СССР)
- Ust-Kut — Taksimo
- footbridge
- Port Baikal (2km) & Nizhneangarsk (28km)
- Lake Baikal

transplanted to Severobaikalsk. While northern Russian building designs could have been used, only the Central Asian ones were earthquake resistant which was essential for the seismically unstable north Baikal area.

Another problem was, and still is, an oversupply of some types of accommodation and undersupply of other types. In the early 1970s the Institute predicted that 80% of the settlers would be bachelors and ordered the construction of mostly single room flats and hostels. In reality it turned out that 80% of the long-term inhabitants were married couples with young families.

Another interesting fact is that the best years of the town were in the late 1970s and early 1980s when the town was being sponsored by Leningrad's *Komsomol*. In these years, the town had access to many restricted goods, but when the BAM arrived, most of the workers with their privileges moved on. Leningrad's sponsorship finally ended in 1984 and today the only remnant of the original constructors is a detachment of the *LenBAMstroi* (Leningrad BAM Construction) organisation. Since the slowdown of construction work on the BAM in the early 1990s, *LenBAMstroi* 's 600 workers have had very little to do and are on unpaid leave for months at a time.

While most organisations like *LenBAMstroi* and the Severobaikalsk

Siberians produce much of their own food and many keep animals. This local is grazing her household goat on the outskirts of Severobaikalsk.

City Council wait for non-eventuating money and work from Moscow, a few locals have tried to develop new industries and inspire optimism. Unfortunately residual Soviet-era centralised control and secrecy have limited the success of such projects.

One such attempt was the international 1990 Expertise Conference, held in Severobaikalsk. Participants included the Californian Earth Institute, UNESCO, Moscow-based Russian government and scientific officials, and a handful of local representatives. The conference's aim was to develop an economic and environmental strategic plan for the Lake Baikal region. Despite recommendations being made, the conference report was never released in Russia. However, the report was freely available in the US and Rashit Yakhin, head of BAMTour and local environmental activist, obtained a copy. He translated it back into Russian and organised its publication in Severobaikalsk, creating a political storm. The reason the report was never released in Russia was because its main recommendation to list Lake Baikal on the World Heritage Register was totally unacceptable to local authorities. This would entail establishing a ring of national parks around the lake which would restrict industry, tourism and town development.

Another project is the City of Sun which is described later in this section.

Getting assistance

Severobaikalsk is home to the best known company organising tours on the BAM and in the north Lake Baikal region. Rashit Yakhin heads the company, BAMTour, and he is one of the oldest residents in Severobaikalsk, having worked on the railway in the early 1970s. BAMTour Co, 671717, Severobaikalsk, ul Oktyabrskaya 16-2 ☎ and fax 21-560, telex 154215 DWC SU (attention: BAMTour) (БАМТур Со, 671717, Северобайкальск, ул. Октябрьская 16-2, Директор Рашит Яхин).

Getting there and away

There are daily trains arriving from the west including Ust-Kut (9 hours), Taishet (21:20 hours), Moscow (94 hours) and from the east Nizhneangarsk (40 minutes), Taksimo (9:20 hours), Novi Chara (14:45 hours), Tynda (29 hours) and Neryungri (34 hours). There is no airport at Severobaikalsk but the one at Nizhneangarsk (50 minutes by bus) has flights to Taksimo, Ulan Ude and sporadically, Irkutsk. From early February to 10 April, it is safe to drive down the frozen Lake Baikal to Irkutsk. There are no commercial services on the ice road. The hydrofoil runs between Severobaikalsk and Irkutsk (8:40 hours) from 15 June to 15 September.

Hydrofoils

The *Kometa* hydrofoil which plies between Irkutsk and Severobaikalsk is an interesting ride, for although it has only one official stop on the lake, the hydrofoil will stop anywhere enroute for any local or traveller who prearranges it. For this reason when you are travelling on the hydrofoil, you will observe motor boats meeting your vessel and transferring mail, food or passengers. For many isolated communities and individual hunters, the hydrofoil is their only link with the rest of the world. The one official stop on the trip is halfway down the lake at Bukhta Bazarnaya (Бухта Базарная) which is on the mainland near Olkhon Island (Остров Ольхон). There are basic cabins for rent, a camping site and a canteen at this stop.

Tickets for the hydrofoil cannot be booked in advance and have to be bought on board. So it is a good idea to get to the pier early and stand in the queue. There is only one hydrofoil and as it takes the whole day to travel the length of the lake, departures from Severobaikalsk are every second day.

At the southern end of Lake Baikal, the hydrofoil docks at Port Baikal which is located at the mouth of the Angara River on Lake Baikal. Passengers then transfer to a river ferry to travel down the Angara for 50 minutes until they reach Irkutsk. As the ferry takes only about two thirds of the passengers that the hydrofoil carries, unless you are first onto the ferry, you have a two hour wait until it returns. There is no accommodation at Port Baikal but if you can travel across the river to Listvyanka, or get off the hydrofoil when, and if, it docks there, you can stay at Intourist's Hotel Baikal there. Port Baikal is a very attractive town and is the start of a small coastal railway which was part of the Trans-Siberian before a detour was built at the turn of the century.

Although the trip down the lake is long, be grateful that there is a hydrofoil for before its introduction in 1986, the boat trip between Irkutsk and Severobaikalsk took 5 days.

Getting around

Everything in Severobaikalsk is within walking distance, with the exception of the port from which the hydrofoil departs, and the port's

Hydrofoil Timetable Between Port Baikal and Nizhneangarsk

From Port Baikal		Place	From Nizhneangarsk		Dist.
Arrive	Depart		Depart	Arrive	(km)
-	9:20	Port Baikal (Порт Байкал)	-	17:30	628
9:30	9:40	Listvyanka (Листвянка)	17:20	17:10	621
13:30	13:40	Buxta Bazarnaya (Бухта Базарная)	13:20	13:10	403
19:50	20:00	Severobaikalsk (Северобайкальск)	7:00	6:40	18
20:20	-	Nizhneangarsk (Нижниенгаранск)	6:20	-	0

Nord Hotel. To get to the port, take Bus № 1 from the central bus station in front of the railway station. Bus № 3 goes past the BAM museum and near the Sever Hotel.

What to see

BAM Museum and Gallery: The museum has a display on the first BAM explorers to this region and a railway model showing the stretch with the 4 Mysoviye tunnels between Severobaikalsk and Nizhneangarsk. It also has information on the Decembrists exiled to this area in the 1820s, but lacks any reference to the region's Stalin-era gulags. It also has a small exhibition of Buryat traditional costumes and jewellery, and celebrations of the 250th anniversary of Buddhism in the Buryat republic in 1991. BAM Museum, ul Mira 2 (ул. Мира 2). Open 10-18 but not Mondays. Around the corner from the museum is an art gallery which contains a good range of local artists. BAM Art Gallery, ul Druzhba (ул. Дружба).

Art and Culture: Without doubt, Severobaikalsk is the most active cultural centre on the BAM and most activity is focused around the excellent Palace of Culture. This delightful building has a small indoor

Severobaikalsk's newly constructed Russian Orthodox Church heralds the post-Soviet revitalisation of religion.

garden and a large hall, and is always putting on theatrical and musical performances. If it is a national holiday, you can be guaranteed that something worth seeing will be on there.

The town also boasts 6 well-known painters and poets, and 1 composer. For aspiring artists, there is also an art school. The school and the Palace of Culture staff are only too pleased to show anyone around their facilities.

Art School: Special arts schools are an important element in the curriculum of Russian education and graduating from one is a prerequisite for entry into an art institute or university. Entry to the school is open to students aged between 7 and 16 and classes normally run for 2 hours a day after normal school hours. Fees were just $0.25 a month in 1994 but this is expected to rise as market forces spread their insidious influence through the Russian education sector.

Currently the school is located in the City Council building but will move to the soon to be completed Art School complex near the post office. School Iskusstv, ul 60 let SSSR, dom 30, kv 6, Director Lyudmila Stepanovna Davydova, ☎ 222-68 home, 215-43 work (ул. 60 лет СССР, д 30, кв 6, Школа искусств, Директор Давыдова Людмила Степановна).

Severobaikalsk Yacht Club: The club possesses 30 boats including five 6 person yachts. Sailing is an excellent way of travelling around the north end of Lake Baikal, enabling you to stop in at villages and hot springs. The Severobaikalsk regatta occurs at the end of July and several children's sailing camps are run during the sailing season from June to October. Most of the fleet was bought in 1988, and in the early 1990s an attempt was made to buy excellent aluminium yachts from the Yuri Gagarin Aircraft Factory in Komsomolsk-na-Amure (which also makes advanced Su-27 fighter aircraft). However, just before the boats were delivered, a Japanese company signed a contract with the factory to purchase all future boats for sale in

The Severobaikalsk regatta occurs at the end of July and several children's sailing camps are run during the sailing season from June to October.

Japan and the deal fell through. Georgi Ekimok, ul 60 let CCCP, dom 14, kv 125, ☎ 2-45-56 (Георгий Екимок, ул. 60 лет СССР, д 14, кв 125).

Where to stay
There is a wide range of accommodation in Severobaikalsk with the best being 4 guest cottages owned by the railways. Each has two bathrooms, toilet, sitting room, kitchen and three bedrooms. It is possible to rent them per room or the entire house. They can be reached by a 10 minute walk from the station, and they have an excellent view of the coast. The complex has a separate sauna with a small indoor pool, and will soon include a small restaurant. Another of the cottages' advantages is that they have their own hot water systems which means that you aren't inconvenienced by the summer maintenance shut down of the town's hot water system. The railway cottages are located near ul Sibirskaya (ул. Сибирская). Booking is done via BAMTour and costs $15 a night per person.

The Vitim Zoloto gold company guest cottages are also good, however they are further out of town. This complex consists of 3 cottages, one each for 2, 3 and 4 people, a sauna, pool and canteen. To book, contact Viktor & Evreniya Kuznitsov, Guest Cottages, Vitim Zoloto (Дом Отдыха, Витим Золото, Виктор и Евгения Кузнецовы). Accommodation is $15 a night per person.

The only reasonable hotel in town is Hotel Nord (Гостиница Норд, Порт Северобайкальск) at the port where the hydrofoil arrives. The hotel is expensive and is 2km from the centre of Severobaikalsk. Bus № 1 and the bus to Nizhneangarsk stop near the hotel.

Another option is to stay at the Railway Hostel in the centre of town. Its location is shown on the map but is difficult to find. It can't be reached from ul Leningradski as its only entrance is from the courtyard on the other side of the building.

The worst accommodation is the Sever Hotel which can be reached on Bus № 3 departing from the station. The bus trip takes 20 minutes. The hotel has no hot water or showers, and only squat toilets. $15 per night per person. ☎ 77-12 (Гостиница Северный Баийкал).

Where to eat
Severobaikalsk has a surprising number of good restaurants and cafes including the Leningrad restaurant which prides itself on once serving a US ambassador. Other good places to eat include the Ayana and Visit cafes. Above the Visit cafe is a small bar/restaurant which deserves a special tourist award as the rest rooms are the best in the whole of the BAM. The Rus bar brews its own beer on the premises. There is also a restaurant/casino at Hotel Nord. There are two canteens inside the station which offer the cheapest meals in town.

Exploring North Baikal
Северный Байкал окрестности

There are a large number of interesting travel options around Severobaikalsk which will appeal to those interested in history, adventure, nature and culture. The following are some suggestions and the destinations are explained in detail in the rest of this section.
- Day bike ride to Nizhneangarsk, Duskhachan and Kholodnoe, and return by train or bus.
- Day hike to Akikan Gulag camp and the nearby indigenous village of Kholodnoe.
- Day bike or bus trip to Baikalskoe village.
- Day train trip to Solnechny settlement (hot springs and skiing) or Kunerma (fishing and Baikal mountain railway tunnel exploration). For information on these two destinations, turn to the respective town's description in the route section.
- Ice fishing on the frozen Lake Baikal between March and April.
- Rafting down the Tyya or Verkhyanaya Angara Rivers to Lake Baikal.
- Take a boat to the east coast of Lake Baikal then hike to Lake Frolikha.
- Cross-country skiing across the frozen Lake Baikal.
- Trekking along the shore of Lake Baikal.
- Mountain and glacier climbing in the Baikal Mountain Range.
- Nature tours and hunting tours based at the Ayaya lodge.
- Seal watching.

Between Severobaikalsk and Nizhneangarsk

The trip between Severobaikalsk and Nizhneangarsk is very scenic as both the road and railway run along the northern shores of Lake Baikal. When the BAM was being built, a temporary railway line ran right beside the road on Lake Baikal's shore linking both towns but due to the problems of landslides, snow avalanches and pollution, the line was relocated several hundred metres inland. This decision required the digging of 4 tunnels collectively known as the 5km Mysoviye Tunnels and the building of several rock shields on this 28km stretch. The original railway line is still operational and while there has been discussion about converting it into a summer scenic railway, nothing definite has eventuated.

Along the road route is what must be Russia's most artistic bus shelters. Built by volunteers of the BAM Tunnel Construction

Company's Tunnel Detachment № 16, each shelter is decorated using mosaic tiles and has a specific theme. From east to west the themes are: *Glory to the tunnel builders*, *Lake Baikal is the most precious asset in Siberia*, *Take care of nature*, and *Let the sun always shine*.

At the second bus shelter from Severobaikalsk is an underground mining vehicle mounted on a plinth. The monument has the inscription: *MoAZ No143, 25 ton underground tractor used on the construction of the Cape tunnels from 1975-1982. The No 2 Tunnel was opened on 16 October 1982 in honour of 20 years of defence of the USSR. Tunnel detachment No 16 of BAM Tunnel Construction Enterprise.*

If you go 300m down the dirt road to the left of the plinth, you come across what looks like the front of a giant aircraft hanger set into the mountain. This is actually a concrete plant. Further on is a bridge in front of the № 2 tunnel. Don't approach too closely as the guard has a giant dog.

Between the last bus shelter and Nizhneangarsk is the only monument on the BAM dedicated to the small number of tunnellers who died building the railway.

5km Mysoviye Tunnels
(Мысовые тоннели)
The Mysoviye Tunnels, which translated means Cape Tunnels, consist of four tunnels with lengths from east to west of 1.5km, 2km, 0.5km and 2km. They were built by Tunnel Detachment No 16 which today is still located in Nizhneangarsk. Work started in 1978 and finished in 1989.

Northern coast of Lake Baikal
The major attractions to the north of Lake Baikal are the Akikan gulag camp, the indigenous village of Kholodnoe, the railway town of Kichera and adventure routes.

The best way to get to the area is on the local suburban train that runs twice daily from Severobaikalsk to Kichera. The

The Severobaikalsk tunnel is the only one on the BAM that was built wide enough to take a second track. While the need for a second track will not eventuate for a decade at least, it makes good economic sense to prepare for this eventuality. This is because widening an existing tunnel requires the removal of the tunnel's concrete casing which is dangerous and as expensive as digging a new tunnel.

route the train takes is Nizhneangarsk 1 (15 min), Nizhneangarsk 2 (30 min), Dushkachan 1 (41 min), Dushkachan 2 (49 min), Dushkachan 3 (56 min), Kholodnoe (62 min) and Kichera (82 min). You should tell the conductor you want to get off at a particular stop before you depart from Severobaikalsk as several stops are by request only.

Kholodnoe (Холодное)

Kholodnoe is a village of the indigenous Evenk people from the Baikal area. The village is trying to keep its traditional way of life alive with *tchums* (similar to Mongolian yurts), hunting, reindeer herd raising, fishing and animal husbandry. The village also runs a polar fox farm. A small museum in the school displays traditional Evenk utensils and religious items. To get to Kholodnoe, get off at the rail stop called Kholodnoe, which does not even have a platform, and then walk down the tarred road at right angles to the railway for 20 minutes. A bus also runs several times a day between Severobaikalsk and Kholodnoe village.

Akikan Gulag (Акикана ГУЛаг)
The highlight of a visit to North Baikal is the Akikan Gulag. The camp operated in the late 1930s, mining mica which was used as electrical insulation. It was closed just prior to the Great Patriotic War when a man-made substitute for mica was found. The camp is located in the Akikan valley alongside the Akikan Stream. Today, the remnants of those terrible years are plainly visible and consist of several collapsed wooden and stone buildings, towers and barbed wire fences. 400m further up the valley on the left are three mine shafts where mica veins can still be seen. The shafts are buttressed with wooden logs but are unsafe to enter. Winches and overhead ore buckets litter the area.

The hike to the camp and back takes about 4 hours from Kholodnoe village or railway station.

One of the many Kholodnoe residents without a job following the collapse of the Soviet Union. Previously he was the gardener of the hothouse of the local school which has now closed due to lack of funds.

From the railway station, you walk along a tarred road for about 1 hour towards Kichera. This route takes you over the Kholodnoe River, up a long hill until you reach the 42km marker on the hill's summit. A further 200m past a long stretch of white highway protection barriers is an overgrown dirt logging track off to the left. After about 1 hour of walking along this track you pass under power lines and after another hour the track changes into a walking path that winds up the Akikan valley. The path beside the Akikan stream is easy to follow and there are logs and planks washed down from the camp laid over the stream and muddy parts of the path to aid you. The path leads directly to the camp.

Discarded gulag mining equipment litters the Akikan valley. This ore bucket transported the mica by an overhead cableway from the mines dug into the side of the hill to the processing area in the camp.

The walk up the valley is fairly strenuous and so you should plan to have your lunch at the camp before returning. The best time to visit the camp is in July and August after the Ixodes tic has disappeared. The tic is common only from May to late June. Only very fit cross-country skiers should attempt this route in winter.

Kichera (Кичера)
For information on this town, see *Kichera* station later in this section.

Verkhyanaya Zaimka (Верхняя Заимка)

This old Russian village is a good place to launch rafts for a trip down the Class 3 Verkhyanaya Zaimka River to Lake Baikal. This easy trip lets you pass by the 25km long and 500m wide Yarki Island (Остров Ярки) which was once a settlement of the Evenk but has been partially submerged with the rising of Lake Baikal following the damming of the lake's only outlet, the Angara River, near Irkutsk. To get to Verkhyanaya Zaimka village, you can go by train to Kichera and then walk the 10km or take a once a day bus from Severobaikalsk. There is no accommodation in the village.

Gulag Camp Buildings

Camps prior to the Second World War were very rudimentary, with the typical camp consisting of the prisoner zone surrounded by a fence of wooden planks and wire, and perimeter guard towers. Guard barracks and offices were made of timber but prisoners often slept in freezing tents unless there was plenty of nearby wood.

No bedding was provided so prisoners slept in their own clothes, fearing to take anything off in case it was stolen. Wooden prisoner barracks had a metal stove but when it worked, it would only radiate heat for 5 to 6 metres. Often there was no fuel for the stoves despite the abundance of wood in Siberia. This was because the prisoners had to meet their work quotas before wood could be collected. In addition, the collection of wood depended on the whim of the guards who often were too lazy to accompany the prisoners.

Following the end of the Second World War, barbed-wire fences around the camp zones were strengthened and enlarged, iron bars were put into the windows of the barracks, visits to neighbouring barracks were forbidden, the prisoners' rights to correspond with their families were restricted, the number of guards increased, and inmates were ordered always to have their numbers attached to their garments. These changes were caused by the influx of POWs and anti-Soviet partisans who could not be intimidated as easily as the pre-war peasant inmates. Their hatred of the Soviet power united them against the camp authorities. The non-Russians took their anti-Soviet hatred out on the ethnic Russian prisoners which eventually led to these two groups being segregated. The post-war prisoners organised numerous protests and strikes, and there were several mass breakouts. Although hundreds were shot during these actions, the actions did result in a general improvement in food and conditions throughout Soviet camps.

Picture reproduced with permission from *The Gulag Handbook* by Jacques Rossi, Overseas Publications Interchange Ltd, London, 1987.

Exploring North Baikal 169

North eastern coast of Lake Baikal

The major attraction in this area is an easy 3-4 day hike to Lake Frolikha (Озеро Фролиха). On the lake, which is 7km inland from Ayaya Bay (Губа Аяя) on Lake Baikal's coast, are hot springs and beautiful views. Most travellers camp overnight on the lake. There is a well marked trail from Ayaya Bay to the lake. Rather than returning from Lake Frolikha to Ayaya Bay, a better choice is a 15km hike to Khakusy Bay (Губа Хакусы) where there is a holiday camp consisting of cottages, canteen and hot springs. To get to Ayaya Bay from Severobaikalsk, you need to hire a boat to travel the 40km. As the area is part of a *zakaznik* nature sanctuary, you will need to get a permit from Gorispolkom, ☎ 66-19 in Severobaikalsk. You may also be able to get the permit from the rangers at Lake Frolikha.

During winter you can cross-country ski the 50km across the frozen Lake Baikal to Khakusy Bay. You will need to sleep on the lake one night before getting to the holiday camp.

North western coast of Lake Baikal

The northwest of Lake Baikal is a popular wilderness recreation area as it contains the beautiful Baikal Mountain range, crystal clear lakes and pristine wilderness. You can start from the old Russian fishing village of Baikalskoe, the Cape Kotelnikovski hot springs resort or the well appointed Ayaya lodge.

The highest peak in the range is Mount Chersky (Гора Черского) at 2,588m. The lands surrounding the mountain are among the most beautiful around the lake. Here one can enjoy the emerald Gitara Lake, waterfall cascades, glaciers and snow-covered peaks. Mount Chersky is the most difficult mountain in the region and there are glaciers at its foot. The best time to climb is from mid July to August and no attempt has been made to climb it in winter. It takes 4 days to cover the 80km to Mount

Vanya, an Evenki fisherman and hunter, lives on the shores of Lake Baikal and is self-sufficient with the exception of bread and salt. In the past he was a drunkard which led to his wife and children leaving him, and the amputation of his fingers after he fell asleep in the snow following a drinking spree. Nowadays, he never drinks and prefers his solitary life to that of stagnating village life.

Chersky, starting and returning to Cape Kotelnikovski. Extra days and special equipment are needed to scale the peak.

There are a number of clubs that can provide adventure guides including the Severobaikalsk Adventure Club (contact through BAMTour) and Kedr Adventure Club based at Zheleznogorsk-Ilimsky.

The best hiking and adventure map for this region area is the English language *Across the North West Baikal Area* map produced by BAMTour. It has topographical details of the area including suggested routes and a list of the passes and their difficulties. Copies can be obtained from Red Bear Tours, 320B Glenferrie Rd, Malvern, Melbourne, Victoria, 3144 Australia for $15.00.

Baikalskoe (Байкальское)

This village is connected to Severobaikalsk by an excellent 40km highway which is also good for bike riding. About 15km from Severobaikalsk you will get an excellent view of the large Onakarshanskaya Bay (Онакорчанская бухта). This place is sacred for the indigenous Buryats and was consecrated by a Lama from a monastery near Ulan Ude in 1992. At the top of the hill is a viewing area with a tree to which strips of clothing are tied and under which gifts are

The inside and outside of Bolshoi Cheremshanyi Lodge's traditional Russian underground ice cellar which uses blocks of ice cut in winter to refrigerate the cellar all year round. Seal blubber is contained in the milk cans, seal oil in the fuel cans, salted fish in the wooden barrels. Animal skins draped over the top protects the fish from insects and contamination, while letting it 'breathe'.

laid. The gifts, which include anything valuable such as cigarettes, vodka, bullets and money, symbolise gratitude for the beautiful places on earth such as this bay. It is in this bay that Sun City (described below) will be built.

From this place, you also see the fourth largest of the 24 islands in Lake Baikal, Bigachan Island (Острова Бигачан). This remote island had one notable visitor in the early 1980s when Brezhnev had a secret picnic there. So as to ensure that the General Secretary of the Communist Party had a completely relaxing time undisturbed by noise, his overzealous staff ordered the closure of Severobaikalsk and Nizhneangarsk ports, as well as a ban on all motor boats!

A further 10km towards Baikalskoe, you pass the Slyudyanski Lake (Слюдянский) on the left where a children's summer ecology camp is located.

Baikalskoe is an ancient Russian village previously called Kharemika (Харемика) and contains the only seal hunting and seal pelt collective in north Baikal. This collective buys seal meat and skins from mainly indigenous hunters and makes seal skin hats and boots. You can visit the collective's seal clothing workshop which is near the pier.

Before the arrival of Russians in the 1600s, the cliff near the town was used for sacrifices by the Evenk people. Archaeologists have found numerous pots and other artefacts here which can now be seen in the Irkutsk ethnographical museum. A polar fox farm is located about 1km further on from the town. In the near future, the company Ayaya (mentioned below) will be opening a small guest house for transit visitors to their lodge down south on the lake.

A bus runs three times a day between Severobaikalsk and Baikalskoe. Very old maps show an airport in Baikalskoe but the airstrip has long since been turned into a potato field.

Cape Kotelnikovski Hot Spring Resort (Мыс Котельниковский)
This tourist base is one of the best kept secrets in north Baikal. It was built by BAM tunnel workers as a holiday resort. It consists of excellent accommodation for 16 people (2 single, 1 double and 4 triple rooms), a canteen, sauna and outdoor and indoor pools heated by 86°C hot spring water. It is used by hikers, tourists sailing the lakes, or people wanting a day away from Severobaikalsk. To stay here costs $5 per person per night, or to just swim in the pools cost $0.50. If you intend to stay and require food, it is worth booking by telephone radio through BAMTour. In summer, the springs can be reached by motor boat from Baikalskoe ($50 return boat hire) and in winter, by car over the frozen lake.

Bolshoi Cheremshanyi Lodge (Большой Черемшаный лодј)
130km south of Severobaikalsk is a remote, well appointed lodge which

can be a base for seal watching or trekking in the Baikal Mountain Range. Situated on 65,000 hectares with a 50km shoreline, the lodge consists of two buildings with a kitchen, a recreation room and five bedrooms with beds for 10 people. The lodge is maintained by two hunters/fishermen and observing their lifestyle is one of the most interesting aspects of staying at the lodge.

The lodge is one of the very few privately owned resorts on north Lake Baikal and the pride of the Ayaya company. The company's main occupation is building and trading but has constructed this base and is building an office and guest cottage in Baikalskoe village in anticipation of the region's tourism boom. Its construction without government funds and shady dealings is testament to the determination of Mikhail Maligin, Ayaya's director. The buildings and fittings were either made by the company and Mikhail's father, or scrounged, such as the ex-military electric generators.

As the mainly meat-based meals prepared by the hunters may not be to everyone's liking, Mikhail is only too pleased to make special arrangements if told in advance.

The easiest way to get to the lodge is to take the hydrofoil from either Irkutsk or Severobaikalsk and arrange for one of the hunters to

---

SEAL WATCHING

The Baikal seal or *nerpa* (Байкальская нерпа) is an endangered species, and is already virtually extinct in the southern part of Lake Baikal. The main killers are not hunters but pollution and starvation from diminishing fishing stocks. The population of nerpas in northern Baikal is stable despite 3,000 being hunted each year.

Although there are no regular trips offering *nerpa* seal watching, it is possible to organise it from Severobaikalsk. The best time to see seals is towards late May and early June when the ice has virtually all gone and the seals bask on the ice that remains in protected bays. During summer they live mostly near Bolshoi Ushkani Island (Остров Большой Ушканий), about 250km from Severobaikalsk. As you may need several days to travel to this isolated area and view the seals, a recommended program is to travel on the hydrofoil to the Ayaya Lodge (which is only 15km from the island) and stay there.

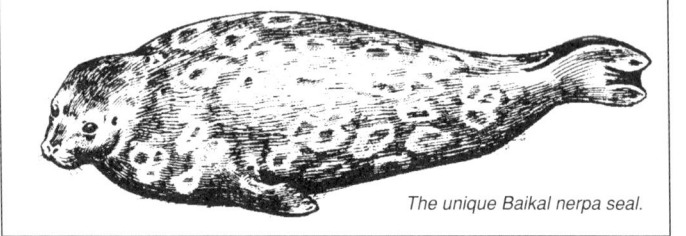

The unique Baikal nerpa seal.

Seal Hunting

Permission for hunting in northern Baikal is granted to only 30 to 40 hunters each year, the majority of whom are indigenous people with a 65 seal quota. For many, seals are an important source of food and money as the meat is salted for winter, and seal blubber and pelts sold to the state. The only buyer of seal products is the seal collective in Baikalskoe village and due to low prices and a small market, there does not appear to be a black market for the animals. The state pays only $0.60/kg for seal blubber and meat and $15 for pelts which means an average seal is worth only $30. Many of the hunters are also fishery inspectors which ensures that unknown vessels are quickly spotted and unlicensed hunters arrested.

Nerpa hunting requires considerable patience and one seal a day is considered a successful day. Hunting is only permitted after seal breeding from 20 April until the disappearance of the ice in June. Seals bask in the sun while sleeping on the ice and as the ice melts they become restricted to protected bays. Hunters cruise the open lake looking for bays with ice and to enable them to get as close as possible without disturbing the mammals, the hunters wear white coats and hats, and put a white sheet over the front of the motor boat. Hunters use only 22 calibre rifles which means that they must approach within 40m of the seals. Boats are normally brought to within 200m of the seals before the motor is turned off and then paddled the last 160m. Once the seals are within range, the hunter whistles which makes the seals raise their head, thereby offering a clean target. Unless a seal is shot in the head and killed outright, the wounded seal will slip into the water and disappear.

Unfortunately, it appears that about 50% of the seals shot are wounded and most injured *nerpas* probably die from their head wounds.

Hunters in white smocks scanning for seals.

Cosmic Energy To Save Russia?

Societies in turmoil often pin their hopes on radical solutions. Since the collapse of communism, Russians have flocked to promises of salvation from groups as diverse as the Russian Orthodox Church, evangelical American religions, Czarist monarchists, white magicians and even mass hypnotists.

Severobaikalsk has its own version of 'The Way' out of Russia's moral, economic and political morass. The solution is a new settlement on the banks of Lake Baikal called the City of Sun (Город солнца). The first stage of the town will consist of 45 cottages, a tourist complex and a cultural consciousness centre, while the second stage involves constructing an academic centre focusing on ecological problems.

What makes the City of Sun different from other new townships is its design philosophy. All the buildings and even the town's layout are designed in accordance with the principles of Elena Ivanovna Reorich (Елена Ивановна Реорич) and her theories of cosmic energies. Elena developed a teaching called Agni Yoga or Living Ethics (Живая этика) while living in India with her husband, the famous Russian artist Nicholas Roerich. Her belief is that everything is in a state of energy flux and this energy inhabits everything. Some call the force 'cosmic energy', while others call it 'thought' or 'psychic energy'. The application of her theories to architecture is called Sacred Geometry which studies the way structures obstruct or enhance the energy and the context in which people inhabit the structure. The energy is particularly concentrated in the corners of buildings and in the most simplistic example, sleeping in the corners will enable you to capture significant amounts of it. For those interested in her teaching, contact the Nicholas Roerich Museum, 319 West 107th Street, New York, NY 10025-2799, ☎ (212) 864 7752, fax (212) 864 7704.

The City of Sun project is the brainchild of Vladimir Mikhailovich Yankovski, president of a local timber industrial complex and former member of the regional parliament. "The City's harmony will generate amazing results and scientists working here will in just two months achieve what will normally take 2 years", he boasts. "The aim of this project is to demonstrate the enormous benefits of cosmic energy city design and it will become the model for all Russian towns."

The City of the Sun will be 8km from Severobaikalsk on the shores of Lake Baikal's Onakarshanskaya Bay (Онакорчанская бухта). This pristine bay is a sacred site of the indigenous Buryat people and has been consecrated by the Lama from the region's religious centre.

As part of the town's objective to achieve harmony with nature, it will be powered by solar energy and each building will have its own dry toilet, which will prevent any waste from flowing into the lake.

According to Vladimir, the City of Sun project has financial support from the Richard Nixon Foundation and the grandson of Alfred Noble, inventor of dynamite and creator of the Noble Peace Prize trust, who incidentally was also educated in St Petersburg. In September 1994, the township design was finalised and the final governmental approvals were being sought. I expect that the town's first stage will be finished by 1996 and with international assistance to spread its success across our country, we can build a new Russia."

Vladimir Mikhailovich Yankovski, President Baikalski Dom, pr. Leningradskoe 5, kv 94, ☎ 52-402, 36-25 (rail) (Владимир Михайлович Янковский, Президент Лесопромышленная компания АО «Байкальский дом»).

meet the hydrofoil at sea. Another way is to take a boat from Severobaikalsk (6 hours) or from the other side of the lake at Ust-Barguzin (Усть-Баргузин) (5 hours) which can be reached from Ulan Ude.

Bookings can be made with Mikhail Maligin, Director, Firm Ayaya, c/o BAMTour, or Firm Ayaya, pr Leningradskoe 6, kv 91 (пр. ленинградское дом 6, кв 91).

Severobaikalsk – Novaya Chara
Северобайкальск - Новая Чара

Severobaikalsk (Северобайкальск) 1,064km
For information on Severobaikalsk, see the *Severobaikalsk* section earlier in this chapter.

Nizhneangarsk 1 & 2 (Нижнеангарск 1 -2) 1,104 km
Republic of Buryatiya, Nizhneangarsk
Республика Бурятия, г. Нижнеангарск

Nizhneangarsk is the Russian equivalent of a low density, sprawling suburb. It is wedged on a 20km strip between Lake Baikal and steep mountains, with each end bounded by the Nizhneangarsk railway station. The Nizhneangarsk station is not actually 20km long but consists of two stations Nizhneangarsk 1 (closest to Severobaikalsk) and Nizhneangarsk 2. Nizhneangarsk's large man made harbour and the town's centre are at Nizhneangarsk 1 station while the airport is located at Nizhneangarsk 2. Strangely the largest station is remote Nizhneangarsk 2 and it is the only stop in Nizhneangarsk for the Tynda-Moscow express.

Prior to the BAM, the 2,000 residents of Nizhneangarsk were mostly fishermen. Following the start of the BAM, the town rapidly expanded and now boasts 10,000 citizens, the headquarters of the BAM Tunnel Construction organisation (БАМТоннелСтрой) and the seat of the regional government. Despite being the regional power, Nizhneangarsk is smaller than neighbouring Severobaikalsk.

The modern history of the town provides an interesting insight into the enormous planning problems of such a gigantic project as the BAM. In the early 1970s, Nizhneangarsk was selected as the centre of the western end of the BAM and it was anticipated that about 75,000 people would live there. At that time, Severobaikalsk was regarded as the site

Nizhneangarsk
(Нижнеангарск)

Beware! The map is deceptive as the distance between the two stations is 5km.

For the complete legend, see the inside back cover.

1. Nizhneangarsk 2 (main)
2. Nizhneangarsk 1
3. BAM Tunnel Construction guest cottages
4. BAM Tunnel Construction Hostel
5. canteen
6. canteen
7. town admin.
8. BAM Tunnel Construction admin.
9. Palace of Culture
10. bank
11. water rescue station
12. banya
13. fish factory
14. abandoned hospital

★ hydrofoil docking point

of just a small workers' town. However, after the construction of a few large buildings, it became apparent that the marshy ground was not at all suitable. This problem is illustrated by the town's hospital which now lies abandoned as it sinks slowly into the ground. The hospital was built in 1976 and closed in 1993 when further repairs became impossible. The hospital is now housed in what was the town's hotel, next to the City Council building. The marshy ground has meant that no buildings more than 2 storey high can be built and that all buildings are restricted to the narrow strip of suitable land along the railway wedged between the marsh and the mountains. As a result of this experience, the site of the headquarters of the western end of the BAM was transferred to Severobaikalsk. However, this was after the building of the Nizhneangarsk airport which also now serves as Severobaikalsk's airport.

Another inadequately researched planning decision was the construction of the large Nizhneangarsk port and pier complex. This vastly under-utilised facility was designed to receive BAM building materials in the mid 1970s so that the work could commence on the section east of Nizhneangarsk before the BAM reached Nizhneangarsk from the west. However, the work on the western section of the BAM progressed much faster than anticipated and the rails arrived at the same time as the port was completed. The railway connected to the Trans-Siberian offered a 365 day a year and much cheaper service for shipping material compared to the Irkutsk-Nizhneangarsk ferry. Consequently, the port was never used for what it was intended for and today, it just serves a small fishing fleet and the hydrofoil that plies the Nizhneangarsk-Irkutsk route.

Getting there and away
Two daily fast trains stop at Nizhneangarsk from Tynda (28:30 hours) and Severobaikalsk (30 min), and two daily suburban trains stop at Nizhneangarsk on their run between Severobaikalsk and Kichera / Novi Uoyan (40 min / 2:40 hours) in the east. There is a regular bus running between Nizhneangarsk and Severobaikalsk which takes 40 minutes for the 28km trip.

Planes fly from Taksimo, Ulan Ude, and Irkutsk. AN-2 seaplanes and MI-8 helicopters are based at the airport and can be hired for trips. Nizhneangarsk is the final stop for the Irkutsk hydrofoil (9 hours) although the main passenger pickup point is Severobaikalsk. Details on the hydrofoil are included in the section on Severobaikalsk.

Getting around
It takes a couple of hours to walk from one end of the town to the other so a better way is to catch the local bus as it runs from Severobaikalsk,

through Nizhneangarsk 1 to the airport. About 10 minutes by foot further eastward is the Nizhneangarsk 2 station.

Accommodation
Since the town's hotel has been taken over by the hospital, there is limited accommodation in the town. The only options are the BAM Tunnel Construction guest cottages for visiting dignitaries and the very basic BAM Tunnel Construction Organisation hotel for visiting workers. However, the best option is to stay in Severobaikalsk where there is a much bigger variety of accommodation.

What to see
The town is pleasant to stroll around with its mainly wooden buildings. Despite most of the town being built since the mid 1970s, Nizhneangarsk is one of the very few BAM towns which is not dominated by five storey concrete flats and prefabricated buildings. Even the two storey City Council building is wooden. An architectural oddity is the wooden boat rental and water rescue station on the lake's edge.

The fish processing factory is worth a visit as it is an eye opener to Russian methods and working conditions. The plant makes delicious smoked or salted Omul.

Where to eat
The town does not have a restaurant but has two canteens which are shown on the map.

Kholodnaya (Холодная)   1,120km
For information on Kholodnaya, see the *Exploring North Baikal* section earlier in this chapter.

Kichera (Кичера)   1,141km
Kichera is a BAM railway town with a population of 3,000. The town was built by the Estonian Young Communist Party and its architecture is notably Baltic influenced. Kichera has one of the region's best and most innovative schools with its teaching methods influenced by Elena Ivanovna Reorich and her theories of *Living Ethics*. These are described in *Cosmic Energy To Save Russia?* in the *Severobaikalsk* section earlier in this chapter. The Kichera River runs through the town and along the railway.

Dzelinga (Дзелинга)   1,171km

Although there is not even a platform at this stop, in the future Dzelinga will boast a small station and a sanatorium based around the Dzelinga hot water springs. Construction has already started on the railway owned sanatorium and it will include accommodation for 50, a cafeteria, a 25m pool and a sauna. Particular attention has been given to maintaining a healthy, pristine environment and consequently an electric boiler will supply hot water rather than a standard coal powered boiler which produces clouds of dust and smoke. The complex will be open to both Russians and foreigners probably by the end of 1995.

Anamakit (Анамакит)   1,242km

Between Anamakit and Novi Uoyan, the BAM crosses over the Verkhnaya Angara River (р. Верхная Ангара) which is the largest river that flows into the northern end of Lake Baikal. This 438km river is navigable in motor launches 270km from its mouth, which is about 100km away. The river is frozen from the end of October to early May.

Novy Uoyan (Новый Уоян)   1,257km

Novy Uoyan was founded in 1976 as a support base for railway and tunnel construction. Goods were hauled up the Verkhnaya Angara river during summer and autumn or driven up it in winter. Construction teams worked in primitive conditions, driving their railway in both directions to join up with the railway coming from the east and west.

The town is 7km from the old village of Uoyan (Уоян) which is one of the largest landings on the Verkhnaya Angara River. There are no regular services on the river to Lake Baikal.

The Latvians built the town which is reflected in its architecture.

Only about 6,000 people now live in Novy Uoyan compared to 10,000 in its heyday.

Children playing on the shores of Lake Baikal. In the background are traditional wooden fishing boats.

Kyukhelbekerskaya (Кюхельбекерская) 1,330km

The railway station is named after the Decembrist Kyukhelberker, while the nearby town is called Yanchukan (Янчукан). Wilhelm Kyukhelberker (1797-1856) was a kind and hopeless idealist, a somewhat eccentric poet and critic, and a friend of Pushkin from their school days. Kyukhelberker received a severe prison sentence due to his participation in the Decembrist uprising and was sent to Siberia. The last time Pushkin saw him was on 15 October 1827 when Pushkin happened to see a group of *troikas* full of prisoners stopping at a way station. When he went to have a closer look he recognised Kyukhelberker among the prisoners. They embraced, but were quickly dragged apart by the police, and Kyukhelberker was taken to his exile and eventual death in Siberia.

After leaving Kyukhelberkerskaya, you travel through a series of steep valleys as you gain height to cross over the mountains. You will notice the vegetation change from larch forest to scraggy dwarf stone pine forest and mountain tundra as you climb to above 1,200m.

Raz. 635km (Раз. 635км) 1,385km

The stop is known as Raz. 635km or Okusikan (Окусикан), and is the western escarpment base for the tunnellers who are building the 15.7km Severomuisk Tunnel (Северомуйский тоннель). The nearby small workers' settlement is called Tonnelni (Тоннельный) and is destined for demolition once the tunnel is finished. When this occurs, the existing 54km North Muya Bypass with its three stops of Raz. 651km, Raz. 673km and Raz. 686km will also be closed.

The trip over the bypass is very exciting and it is unfortunate that most trains do it during the night. The train travels at about 30km/h and offers excellent views as you snake up the mountains. The peak is invariably snow capped even in summer. As you travel down the eastern escarpment towards Severomuisk you can see the partly completed Severomuisk tunnel portal. Between the tunnel portal and the town, you pass through three small tunnels.

North Muya Bypass

When it became obvious that the Severomuisk tunnel would not be finished on time, a temporary above ground bypass was built across the mountains. This 28km bypass was completed in 1987 and designed to last only until 1992 when the tunnel was expected to have been completed. The gradient was extremely steep, being a 40m change in altitude for every km. It was so dangerous that rolling stock was restricted to 15 km/h and only freight traffic was allowed. A 1987 report in *Sotsialisticheskaya Industriya* described the bypass's condition. "Two or three electric locomotives pull the cars. The grades and the drops are so steep that, when the cars are heading down hill, the engineers literally ride on the locomotives' running boards so they'll be able to jump off in time if there's an accident."

Once it became apparent that the 1992 completion date would not be met, a second bypass was built. This 54km bypass contains two short tunnels and was completed in 1989. This is the current bypass and although it's safe for light weight passenger trains, there are regular derailments of the heavily laden goods trains.

Severomuisk (Северомуйск)

This has to be one of the most depressing towns in the BAM Zone. It is a sad collection of ramshackle buildings, non-existent roads and despair. It was founded in April 1977 as a temporary settlement for the miners of the Severomuisk Tunnel. It was expected that by 1984, the original completion date for the tunnel, the town would be demolished and the area restored to its original condition. The only people expected to remain in the area are a small number of maintenance workers and the tunnel's military guard.

Although the tunnel is a long way from being completed, most of the miners have left, leaving behind only those who can't leave because they have no place to go.

While the final straw for many tunnellers was the lack of any pay for 4 months in late 1994 from the tunnel building company, BAM Tunnel Construction Agency (BAMTonnelstroi (БАМТоннелСтрой)), the site had been losing workers since the peak of construction in the late 1980s when there were 9,000 workers on site. The first exodus was caused by the collapse of the Soviet economy in the late 1980s and with it, the biggest incentive of working on the BAM which was access to a new car. Next came the disintegration of the Soviet Union which resulted in Ukrainians, Balts and other non-Russians being classified as foreign workers who attracted hefty government taxes. The final exodus was caused by the BAM's refusal in the early 1990s to improve the rudimentary city facilities despite the fact that people had lived there for 15 years and would have to live there for probably another 10.

The tunnel's entrance is 10km from Severomuisk station and while it is possible to walk up to the entrance, it is impossible to enter unless you are on an organised visit. Severomuisk has an airport with irregular flights to Tynda and Ulan Ude, a cafe and a hostel run by the BAMTonnelstroi.

In anticipation of the completion of the tunnel and the razing of Severomuisk, most Russian maps do not show the location of the town.

15.7km Severomuisk Tunnel (Северомуйский тоннель)

The Severomuisk Tunnel, which translated means North Muya Tunnel, is the only BAM tunnel yet to be completed. Eventually, it will be 15.7km long, making it the fourth longest railway tunnel in the world.

When work started on the tunnel in 1978, it was estimated that it would be finished by 1984. However by beginning of 1995, 950m still remained to be dug and all work had stopped due to lack of funds.

Even if work resumed tomorrow, it is virtually impossible for the tunnel to be finished by the turn of the century. World experience has shown that a zone of unstable rock half a kilometre thick can delay tunnel construction for five years.

Although the BAM can't afford to continue building the tunnel, it also can't afford to just board it up and return when money comes available. If it does the latter, it will only be a few months before cumulative damage from water seepage makes the tunnel so unsafe that it would be virtually impossible for work to resume. While it would be possible to permanently mothball the tunnel, the cost of doing so is estimated to be three times the cost of completing it. Consequently all the money allocated to the tunnel is being spent on simply maintaining the existing works.

The slower than expected rate of the tunnel's construction is due to the horrendous geological structure of the Muya Mountain Range. These mountains contain four major fault lines and are located in a highly seismic area which experiences 400 earth tremors a year on average. However the biggest dangers faced by the tunnellers are the range's numerous underground lakes and rivers. After just a few metres of drilling, the tunnellers encountered streams of water and the epic of water drainage began. The further the tunnel went, the more water entered it. The subterranean water is at pressures up to 35 atmospheres which means that water is always breaking through the tunnel walls. The huge granite fault lines offer a conduit for underground rivers, and they must be approached very carefully.

The decision to build the North Muya tunnel was fundamentally wrong, according to Vladimir Ignatovich, chief geologist for the Buryat Geological Production Association (Buryatgeologia) which surveyed the original BAM line. "Back when the route was being surveyed, we warned the designers at Novosibirsk's Siberian State Transport Design Institute and the Leningrad State Subway Design Institute about the highly complex conditions in the BAM's Buryatiya sector ... We felt it would be better to bypass it from the south with minimal excavation work. However the shortest path was chosen, a 15km tunnel."

The tunnel is actually two tunnels; a small service tunnel and the main tunnel. The service tunnel is drilled parallel and ahead of the main tunnel which provides a warning of impending difficulties for the main

Severomuisk Tunnel Disaster

"It happened towards morning. Kozhemyakin's brigade of tunnellers was preparing to turn over the work face to the next shift. They had done more than their norm. The next day was to have been their day off, so everybody was in excellent spirits. And then disaster struck. The granite wall in front of the face, which had seemed stronger than anything on earth, suddenly shuddered. An alarming rumble came from deep within the mountain and then everything began to thunder. The forbidding wall of rock toppled and with enormous force, a torrent of water carrying sand and rocks poured into the face. The drilling unit, which weighed many tons, was instantly hurled back dozens of metres as if it were a piece of fluff. The lights went out. Only the lamps on the tunnellers' hard hats glimmered faintly through the spray of water and the thick fog rising from the thermal springs. The hot roaring mass rushed swiftly through the tunnel, sweeping up everything in its path", Vladimir Aslanbekovich Vessolov. *Pravda*, 28 February 1983, reporting on an event in September 1979.

What had happened on that morning in September 1979 was that the drilling team had hit an unexpected fault line containing a 140m deep underground lake. The reservoir contained a massive 12,000 cubic metres of water, sand and rocks. The water surged into the gallery in just a matter of seconds, drowning several miners. Had most of the miners not escaped to the service tunnel, then the death toll would have been significantly higher.

The disaster highlighted the inadequate geological work to date and so extensive surveys were carried out. To drain the underground lake, another tunnel was dug under the existing tunnel and the water was pumped out.

18 months after the disaster, on 10 October 1981, work recommenced on the tunnel which now was narrower as the need for a second track was dropped.

The typical Soviet and now post-communist Russian obsession with secrecy has meant that the death toll from this disaster has never been published. While some Western commentators claim that several hundred workers died, probably only between 4 and 10 tunnellers died. There are no memorials to those who died in Severomuisk.

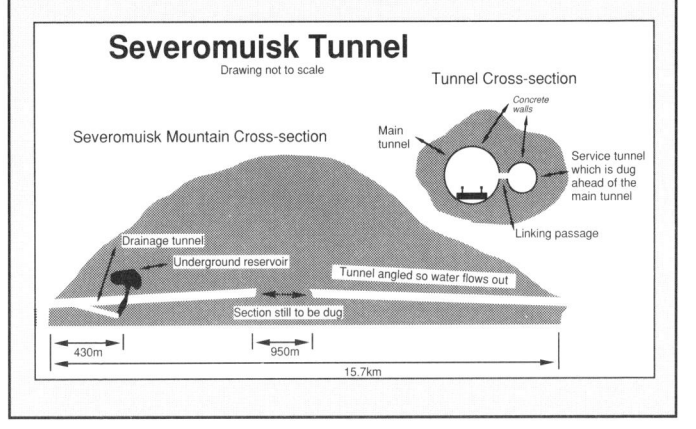

drilling crews as well as a safety passage if one of the tunnels floods or collapses. By early 1995, the service tunnel was 416m ahead of the main tunnel and had only 534m of digging remaining.

When the sheer difficulty of constructing the tunnel was recognised, international tunnel experts were invited from Germany, France, Japan, USA and Finland. Unfortunately the unique situation of the Severomuisk Tunnel meant that western experience was of limited value. Consequently, the Soviet builders were forced to develop new technology including a method of pumping liquid nitrogen into the rocks which freezes the water and temporarily stops water seepage. The tunnel would then be coated with concrete which would permanently seal out the water. Along both sides of the tunnel are drainage channels which, when the tunnel is completed, will drain all the water by gravitation, eliminating the need for costly pumping.

Ulgi (Ульги)

The stop is named after *ulgi* which is a general term for Buryatian indigenous epic folk songs and folktales. The folk songs, known as *baatryn ulgers* or *baatarlag tuul*, tell the adventures of valiant heroes who battle with the forces of evil and the songs range from several hundred to several thousand lines long. The folktales, known as *iavgan ulgers* or *urtu*, are usually short heroic tales. Epic folksongs are sung by performers known as *ulgerch* to the accompaniment of the *khur*, a bowed stringed instrument and of the *tovshuur*, a plucked stringed instrument. Nowadays, *ulgis* are also recited without musical instruments.

Muyakan (Муякан)   1,400km

The station derives it name from both the Muyakan River and also the nearby 120km Muyakan Mountain Range. From Muyakan to Taksimo the route is very scenic as you travel along the valleys of the Muyakan and then the Muya Rivers with the Verkhneangarski Mountain Range (Верхнеангарский Хребет) on the left and the Yuzhno-amurski Mountain Range (Южно-амурский Хребет) on the right. Unfortunately, evening fogs are common in the valleys so the best time to travel through it is in the morning. The Muya River is rich in fish including taimen, grayling, tugun and whitefish.

Taksimo (Таксимо)   1,484km
☭ Republic of Buryatiya, Muiski Raion, Taksimo
Республика Бурятия, Муйский район, п. Таксимо

Taksimo's history dates back to the late Tsarist's times when its isolation made it a safe base camp for bandits. After the 1917 socialist revolution, this same isolation attracted White Army soldiers, priests and others who fled the persecution of the communists.

Modern Taksimo was built by the Belarussians and Latvians although it is very difficult to see their influences. The town has a population of about 14,000 and is the capital of the 28,000 strong Muiski *Raion*.

Taksimo is the end of the electrified section of the BAM and electric locomotives are changed here for diesel ones.

The major industries of the region are railways, gold mining and forestry. Sand is also exported and this is very noticeable beside the railway just east of the town. The soil is very poor for agriculture so most household vegetable plots have a thick layer of rich swamp moss, which is an ideal growing medium, laid over the sandy soil.

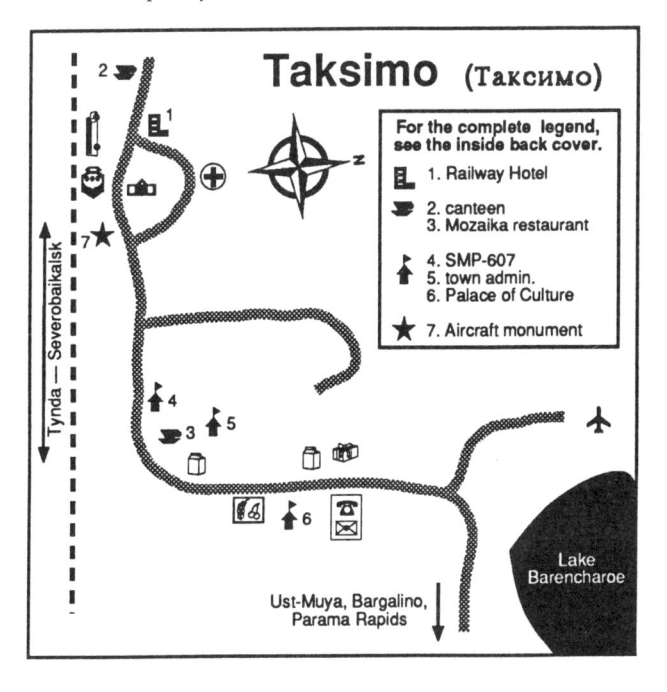

South of Taksimo is a huge asbestos reserve known as the Molodezhnaya deposit. Access to this resource was one of the many justifications for building the BAM in the early 1970s, however the market for asbestos rapidly contracted as the health effects became known. Consequently the 41km branch line to the deposit has yet to be started and probably never will be. Despite this, a team of 8 were still working on the plans for the future mine as late as 1994. Incidentally the proposed mining town is to be called Korchagin after the main communist hero in Nikolai Ostrovsky's socialist realist novel, *How the Steel Was Tempered*.

In the past, a small number of foreign businessmen have come to Taksimo and despite everyone's great expectations little has eventuated. A tragic story told by a Taksimo policeman illustrates what can go wrong. In 1990, the forestry commission signed a contract to organise a bear hunting trip for a group of Germans. Two workers were sent to clear a helicopter landing pad in a remote area where bears were known to live. However as they were travelling down the Vitim River, an ice sheet fell on their boat and both drowned. Consequently the landing pad was not cleared and when the helicopter arrived, it found nowhere to land and was forced to return to base. The arguments over who should pay for the fuel and the wasted time resulted in the contract being cancelled. Nowadays, the businessmen in Taksimo are more wary of proposals and demand money up front.

In front of the station is a 1930s Tupalov ANT-4 on a plinth. This was one of the original planes that conducted the aerial surveys for the BAM in the 1930s. The plane crashed nearby into Lake Barencharoe (Баренчарое Озеро) and in the 1970s its wreckage was discovered and restored voluntarily by the railway builders.

Getting there and away
There are daily trains arriving from the west including Severobaikalsk (9:20 hours), Ust-Kut (18:20 hours), Taishet (31 hours) and Moscow (103 hours), and from the east Novaya Chara (5:50 hours), Tynda (22 hours) and Neryungri (27 hours). Planes arrive from Ulan Ude, Bratsk, Nizhneangarsk, Yakutsk and Bagdarin which is halfway to Ulan Ude.

Technically it is possible during summer to go by boat down the Vitim River to Bodaibo and then to the Lena River. However fluctuating water levels and two difficult rapids prevent regular services, and nowadays only rafters travel this route.

It is possible to drive to Bodaibo in the north but you will have to catch a lift or hire a car as there are no regular bus services from Taksimo. Despite what some Russian books say, the 125km road to Bodaibo is just a dirt track. The best place to find a lift is at the railway station as Bodaibo gold mining company buses often meet trains and take the workers to the gold fields.

Getting around
Like most BAM towns, Taksimo has two parts. The older temporary settlement away from the railway station and the permanent modern settlement around the station. A bus travels between the two settlements on the way to the airport which is 1.5km from the station.

Where to stay
The only hotel in town is the ATCh Railway Hotel, ul Sovetskaya 11 (Гостиница АТЧ, ул. Советская 11) ☎ 56-81.

Where to eat
The only restaurant is the expensive Mozaika (Мозаика ресторан) which is in the *TOTs* shopping complex. There is also a canteen which is being renovated near the hotel.

Around Taksimo
If you are interested in gold mining, there are a number of operations you could visit. The town is the headquarters of Vitim Zoloto which is one of the region's biggest gold producers. All of the operations involve surface mining, mostly using the simple technique of bulldozing the top 10 metres of soil into giant washing trays, using a hose to wash away the dirt and rock and extracting the gold once it settles on the tray's bottom. Environmentally disastrous mercury leaching was discontinued about 10 years ago according to company officials. The miners work 15 days at the camp site and then have 15 days off. Some workers like to spend their holidays at the company owned Vitim Zoloto cottages in Severobaikalsk. (Foreigners can also stay at these cottages and they are

described under *Severobaikalsk*). The best places to see gold mining are at Irakinda (Иракинда) 60km south by a poor road, or at Kalakan (Калакан) which is 120km south up the Vitim River to its junction with the Kalakan river. There is no road to Kalakan but you can drive there down the Vitim River when it is frozen. To organise a visit to one of these sites, contact Vitim Zoloto on ☎ 54-249, or ☎ 826 (rail).

One of the most interesting places around Taksimo is the Parama Rapids on the Vitim River and its nearby towns of Ust-Muya, Muya, Bargalino and Nelyaty. These can be reached from Taksimo or Kuanda.

Parama Rapids and the surrounding towns

Parama Rapids

The Parama Rapids on the Vitim River are among Russia's best rafting rapids. They are only suitable for very experienced rafters and before the collapse of the Soviet Union, about 8 groups a year would raft down them. Nowadays the lack of government sports assistance makes the trip to the rapids prohibitively expensive for ordinary Russians and consequently no one has travelled down it since the late 1980s, according to the region's only ranger.

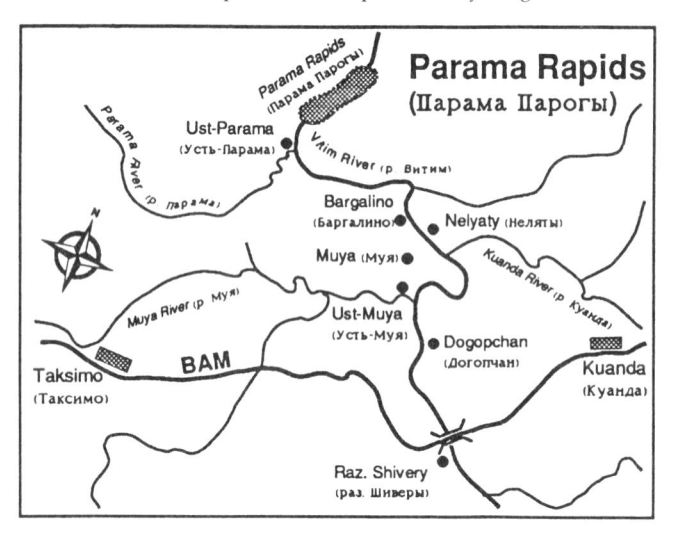

The rapids are formed when the Vitim River narrows from 1km in flood to just 150m. It takes about 10 minutes to descend the rapids and about 2 hours to walk up them. The rapids are very dangerous and it is only safe to travel down them when the water is at a certain level. Even the indigenous people are wary of the river, calling it Ugryum Reka which means *grim river*.

Until recently, barges and log rafts floated down the rapids and while most traversed it safely, a disaster occurred in 1989 when a captain ignored the advice of the pilot that the water level was too high. The tug lost its two 150 ton barges which blocked the rapids for other vessels for the rest of the season. The obstacles were eventually removed by waiting until the winter freezing of the rapids, drilling holes through the ice and packing explosives around the barge. The exploded remains were small enough to be washed downstream in the thaw.

The rapids are shaped like an elongated S and halfway down them is a large flat topped rock. According to local legends, this was where two escaped prisoners from Chara's Marble Canyon gulag camp were finally caught by the guards in 1946. They had travelled 240km without food and were found exhausted asleep on the rock. Rather than taking them back to camp for execution, they were shot in their sleep and their corpses left as a warning. One local claims that his mother remembers seeing the skeletons in the early 1950s.

To inspect the rapids, you need to beach your craft at an obvious place on the right about 500m from the start of the rapids. From here, there is a walking track that cuts off a bend in the river which means that after about 25 minutes walking, you arrive at the centre of the rapids.

In the centre of the river near where you beach is a large rock which is the old measuring stick used to indicate when it was safe to travel the rapids. If the rock is exposed, log rafts can safely traverse the rapids without breaking up. If the water level is above the rock but less than 2.5m above it, then it is safe for motor launches and rafts. Above this, it is highly dangerous for any crossing.

The current measuring stick is now located at the ranger's house at Ust-Parama. It measures the total depth of the river. A 14m level equates to water just submerging the rock which means that a 16.5m water level is safe for rafters. The best time of the year to find the rapids at below 16.5m is in the second half of July. In August the water level will usually fall below 16.5m about twice but it could be anytime in the month. You are guaranteed a safe water level from mid September but the water is then too cold for rafting.

It you want to travel the rapids in style, the only sort of motorised boats that can safely traverse them are the T-63 boats which are 18x3.5m with a 0.8m draft and can carry 4 people, and the KC-100 which can carry 10 people. Despite what boastful locals may say, normal dinghys with outboard motors cannot safely cross the rapids.

THE RANGER

Siberia has been a destination of forced exile for centuries and it is rare to find someone who is happy to live in exile. However the Parama park ranger and his wife, Petr Ivanovich Saukov and Roza Alexandrovna, are happy on their own. Petr, born in 1924, worked for decades in Moscow as a nuclear physicist and once he retired, sought a place of quiet reflection. He chose the area at the junction of the Parama and Vitim Rivers which was the site of Ust-Paramsk village (Усть-Парамск). Today nothing remains of the town except the Saukovs' house.

The local logging collective, Muyaski Leskhoz (Муяский лесхоз), pays him a small wage, which supplements his pension, to observe what and who travels past the junction. He reports any suspicious activity via radio to Ust-Muya and Taksimo.

Meeting Petr and Roza is invaluable, not only for their local knowledge but also to gain an insight into the life of isolated Russians. They are proud to show off their self built house with its enormous larder full of preserved fruits and vegetables, underground cellar kept cool in the summer months by ice cut from the Vitim River in winter, and their garden with the traditional vegetables plus the more exotic vegetables such as khol-rabi, swedes and capsicums. If you are lucky enough to be invited to lunch, you will eat in the outdoor kitchen which is the traditional eating place for rural Russians. Few locals now maintain this tradition but the experience of eating freshly caught fish, pickled vegetables and baked bread in the wooden floored open kitchen while overlooking the river is truly memorable. They also have a small detached cottage of 4 beds and you may stay here if your trip is organised in advance.

Petr Ivanovich and Roza Alexandrovna in their outdoor kitchen.

Surrounding towns

To get to the Parama Rapids you need to go through the nearby towns of Ust-Muya, Muya, Bargalino and Nelyaty. There is a reasonable dirt road between Ust-Muya and Muya (6km) and onwards to Bargalino (6km)

Ust-Muya (Усть-Муя) is the newest of the three villages as it was founded in 1947 to supply logs to the gold mines in Bodaibo. Large log rafts took 4 days to float the 500km down river to Bodaibo. Many exiled nationalities, notably the Volga Germans, resettled here after horrendous voyages which took them through the prison towns of Norilsk and Bodaibo far in the north. The town underwent a boom during the years of BAM construction as again, wood was in great demand. In those days, the town even boasted a runway where IL-14 planes would occasionally land. In the early 1980s, 400 timber workers laboured in the town. Today only 60 timber jobs remain. Of today's remaining workforce of 300, 200 of these work in Taksimo. As daily commuting is impractical due to the distance and poor road condition, the workers live in Taksimo hostels for 15 or 20 days before returning to Ust-Muya for a similar number of days off. A ferry connects the southern bank Taksimo road to Ust-Muya and it is large enough to take 2 big trucks or 4 cars.

Muya (Муя) was founded in Tsarist times and is 3km from the junction of the Vitim and Muya Rivers. Last century it was a major staging post for the barges which were floated down the Vitim River from Romanovka near the Trans-Siberian to Bodaibo. Today there are about 100 houses in the town with the main occupations being hunting and fishing.

Bargalino is worth seeing as it is a living ghost town. The town was founded in the 1800s and once boasted a 1km long street of wooden Siberian houses. However the disappearance of rural jobs has created a mass exodus to the cities. Today there remain just 12 occupied houses in Bargalino.

Despite their isolation, there are a surprising number of phones in the towns. There are 100 lines in Ust Muya, 2 in Bargalino and 20 in Muya.

Nelyaty (Неляты) is on the eastern bank of the Vitim. There is a bad dirt road which connects the town to Kuanda. Nelyaty does not have telephones but the town can be contacted via a radio telephone from Taksimo at 15:00 daily. Like the inhabitants of Muya, the main occupation in Nelyaty is hunting, notably for squirrels, sables, hares, foxes, otters and occasionally for moose, bison, goats and bears.

Getting there and away

You can get to the Parama Rapids from both Taksimo or Kuanda. The trip from Taksimo involves driving on a reasonable dirt road to the Muya River (1:40 hours), and taking a motor boat down the Muya River, to the Vitim River, past Bargalino and Ust-Parama, to the rapids (2 hours). The trip from Kuanda involves going 8km north by road to the river and taking a motor boat down the 90km Kuanda River to the Vitim River (3 hours). This junction is just upstream of Nelyaty and opposite Bargalino. Remember that coming back against the current takes twice as long.

Organising a trip
A trip to this region requires local knowledge and coordination and the best person to do this is the pleasant Chief of the Regional Administration, Victor Serkin, or his assistant, Yury Dmitriya. Victor is responsible for the Muyskaya *Raion* which comprises Ust-Muya, Muya and Bargalino. Victor Serkin, Chief of Muyskaya Administration, 671414, Muyaski *Raion*, Selo Ust-Muya, Glavadministrator, Victor Serkin, ☎ 1-80 (work), 1-41 (home) (671414 Муяский район, село Усть-Муя, Главадмистратор, Виктор Серкин).

Victor Stepanovich Ryzhni, who runs the BAM Turist Adventure Centre for Children can also assist in organising the trip from Kuanda. For more information on the Centre, see under *Kuanda*.

One of the best rafting routes in Eastern Siberia
The Parama Rapids is one of three rapids in the region which make up one of the most challenging rafting routes in Eastern Siberia. The 840km route starts near the little village of Uakit (Уакит). The easiest way to get to Uakit is to fly from Ulan Ude to Bagdarin (Багдарин), then onwards to Uakit (Уакит) in a light plane. From Uakit, you take a motor boat 100km down the Uakit River until it joins the Tsipa River (р. Ципа). Assemble your rafts here. The first set of rapids are 50km away. After another 170km, you reach the Vitim River. After a further 160km you arrive at the Parama Rapids and a further 120km downstream are the Uronski Rapids (Уронский). These are even larger than the Parama Rapids. After another 240km you finally reach Bodaibo.

Shivery (Шиверы) 1,548km
Between Taksimo and Shivery you pass over the 560m long Vitim River bridge. This is a popular fishing spot and there is a small village on the western bank. The actual stop of Shivery is about 1km from the bridge. Beside the new bridge is an older one which was built quickly in order to meet the official opening date of the BAM in 1984. The river is the border between the Republic of Buryatiya and the Amur *Oblast*. The border also designates a time zone change. In Buryatiya, the time difference is 5 hours from Moscow while in Amur *Oblast*, it is 6 hours.

✕ Gorbachevskaya (Горбачевская) 1,576km

This stop is not named after Mikhail Gorbachev, but after the Decembrist, Ivan Ivanovich Gorbachevski (1800-1869). The revolutionary Gorbachevski came from the Ukrainian nobility and inherited a small estate upon the death of his mother. However he refused it and gave it to the peasants for their use, completely and without compensation. At the end of 1823 he was accepted into the Society of United Slavs. He soon became one of its most active figures and carried on revolutionary propaganda among soldiers and officers. An advocate of executing the royal family, Gorbachevski counted himself among those who would make an attempt on the life of Alexander I. During the uprising of the Chernigov Regiment in 1825, he tried to rouse the neighbouring military units and was arrested. In 1826 he was sentenced to life at hard labour, which he served in the Siberian cities of Chita and Petrovski Zabaikalski which is where he died. He wrote a book, *Memoirs*, which is a valuable source for studying the history of the Decembrists.

🏠 Kuanda (Куанда) 1,577km

Kuanda is famous in Soviet propaganda as it was here in September 1984 that the celebration of the BAM's completion was held. The actual golden spike joining the east and west sections of the BAM was hammered in about 15km to the east at Balbukhta (Балбухта) but as there were no facilities there, the celebration was moved to Kuanda.

In anticipation of the completion ceremony, Kuanda was built as a model town. Interestingly, Western media was not invited to the opening which, in retrospect, was a error of judgement on the Russians' behalf. For although the BAM was not as completed as claimed, the exclusion meant that the project is not well known in the West despite its being one of this century's greatest engineering achievements.

Walking down the main street of Kuanda provides a fascinating insight into the minds of the Soviet elite and how they wished their towns to look. The main street consists of attractive two storey wooden houses with each pair of houses having a shared wall. This style of house is called a maisonette in English. Around each house is a medium sized garden and a picket fence facing the tarred street. Most unusually, there are a number of benches along the side of the road where locals sit and talk. There are even raised roadside garbage collection platforms which is a godsend. In most towns which still have garbage services (many Russian towns have cut this service to save money), the garbage truck honks its horn when it stops to accept rubbish. Locals are expected to bring out their garbage and throw it into the back of the truck. As most Russian garbage trucks are tip trucks, throwing rubbish high enough is difficult for many people. Occasionally the truck driver and his assistant will help but most of the time they just sit in their cabs. The raised platforms in Kuanda allow people to stand at a level from which it is easy to tip rubbish in.

However as soon as you walk off the main street, you see the reality of a Russian town. In this sense Kuanda is the same as the other BAM towns with its potholed roads, rotting rubbish piles, concrete apartment blocks, perpetually half built buildings and a general perception of a community lacking pride. As in other towns, strolling a little further away will bring you to the temporary settlement built for the builders of Kuanda.

The Uzbek Young Communist Party sponsored Kuanda and you can see Uzbek influence in some of the town's houses, the railway station and in the excellent internal courtyard of the hotel. However it is not the buildings that will attract travellers but region's excellent outdoor activities including mountaineering, trekking, fishing, and animal and bird watching.

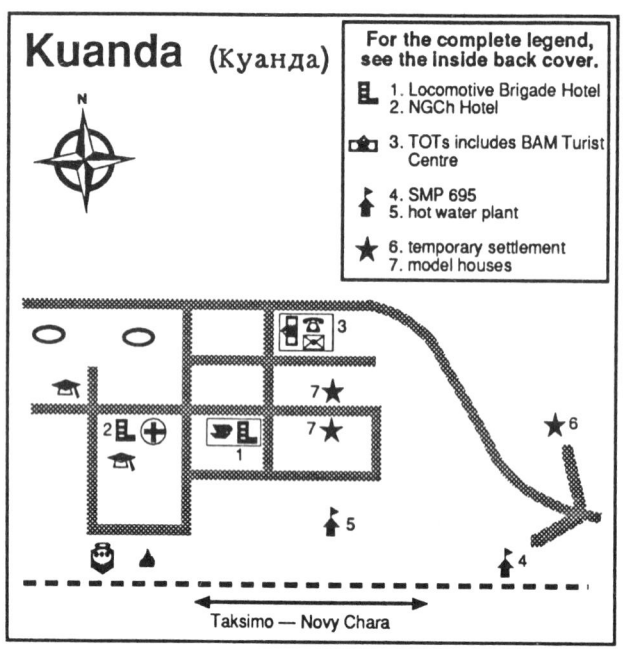

Kuanda (Куанда)

For the complete legend, see the inside back cover.

1. Locomotive Brigade Hotel
2. NGCh Hotel
3. TOTs includes BAM Turist Centre
4. SMP 695
5. hot water plant
6. temporary settlement
7. model houses

Taksimo — Novy Chara

Getting there and away
There are daily trains arriving from the west including Taksimo (2:10 hours), Severobaikalsk (11:30 hours), Taishet (33 hours) and Moscow (106 hours), and from the east Novaya Chara (3:30 hours), Tynda (17 hours) and Neryungri (22 hours). The closest airport is at Novaya Chara.

What to see
About the only noteworthy thing to see in town is the sculpture on the station's platform. It symbolises the joining of the BAM and consists of two giant pillars with one connecting rail on which *Kuanda* is etched. From the outer sides of each pillar protrude dozens of rails with names of other BAM stations etched on them.

Where to stay
There are two hotels in town. The Locomotive Brigade Hotel ☎ 2-51 (Дом Отдыха Локомотивой Бригады) which has 40 basic rooms and charges about $2 per person per night. You will be impressed with the internal courtyard with its fountains but unfortunately, the rooms are not up to the same standard.

The second hotel is virtually next door to the Locomotive Brigade

Kuanda's model houses which everybody would like but few will ever obtain.

Hotel and consists of a floor of a multi-storey building. NGCh Hotel, ☎ 241 (Гостиница НГЧ-3). Its price is the same as the other hotel for Russians but foreigners have to pay 3 times the price.

Where to eat
The only canteen in town is in the Locomotive Brigade Hotel. It is managed by Alexandrovna Lubov who will proudly show you her cookbook of foreign recipes. If you can give her advance warning of your visit she will try to cook your national dish according to this book which will be a challenge considering the lack of ingredients. She is also very pleased to learn new recipes so if you are vegetarian you can work together on preparing a feast.

Trips around the region
Suggestions for trips around the region include:
- Fishing. Described below.
- Rafting the Parama Rapids and downstream to Bodaibo. Described under *Taksimo*.
- Walking to the Marble Canyon Gulag Camps. Described under *Novaya Chara*.
- Mountain and glacier climbing in the Kodar ranges. Described below.
- Exploring the Kodar volcanoes. There are a number of dead volcanoes about 70km south of Lake Leprindo. The only way to get there is by helicopter or a minimum of 3 days of boating and walking to get to the closest volcano and 8 days to the largest one. The area is stunning with water courses flowing down lava tubes and the craters are very distinct due to the lack of erosion. Aku volcano is the largest with a 800m diameter crater, while Chepe, which means gap in Yakutian, is 750m high and has a 150m deep crater. Other volcanoes include the Syni and Gora-Zarod.
- Day trip motor boating or driving up the Kuanda River to its source which is a small hot water spring. In winter, it is very beautiful with clouds of steam rising above the snow but in summer it is dull.

The fishing capital of the BAM Zone
Kuanda is often referred to as the fishing capital of the BAM Zone. The town is surrounded by over 30 large lakes including the beautiful Lake Leprindo. These contain several unique fish as well as rare ones such as the carnivorous taimen. Since the collapse of the Russian economy and the exodus of many people from the country to the city, fish stocks have actually increased in Siberian waterways. Several years ago, the vast majority of fish were sold to Kuanda's Cooperative PEPO for sale in the rest of Russia. However PEPO has since collapsed and today, very little

fish is exported outside the region. In addition, the scaling down of industrial enterprises has resulted in less environmentally damaging pollution.

Types of fish
Locally available fish include: the large predatory *taimen, karas, shchuka, som, omul, elits, nolim* and *soroga*. In addition there is the unique targun (таргун) which is more tasty than the omul. These fish normally grow up to 20cm long and from about the 20 July to 10 September they start to move down the Kuanda River to the Vitim. Special nets are used to catch the fish called targunovi breden (таргуновий бреден). You do not cook this fish but simply sprinkle salt on them and in about 30 minutes they are ready to eat.

Permission is not needed to catch any of the local fish providing you do not catch over 50kg of fish with a net. However there are particular seasons for each fish.

Detailed information on the region's fishing can be founded in the booklet, *The BAM Zone Fishing Guide*, listed in the *Recommended reading* section.

A SIBERIAN FISHING TALE

Fishermen around the world like to tell stories of the giant fish that got away but in this tale it didn't. "Back in 1985, I was fishing on the Chara River, about 30km from Old Chara. I pulled out my net one morning to discover a hole torn in it. Knowing that this was done by a big taimen, I returned that evening with a stronger net. Again in the morning, the net had a hole in it so again I had to go back home and get my largest net. The next morning it also had a rip in it! So I went back to the village and asked my neighbour for his strongest net. That evening I waited in my boat beside the net and when I saw that something was tangled in the net, I picked up my axe and tried to bash it. Unfortunately the thrashing of the taimen nearly overturned my boat and while I was preventing myself from being thrown out, I lost my axe. However I was able to drag the entangled taimen into my boat after an hour and rode it like a bucking horse, stabbing it with a knife as it thrashed around the half submerged boat. It weighed 90kg and was 2.2m long! From just its head, I made two pails of fish soup!" Mikhail Stepanovich, father of the Fisherman's Union member, Ivan Innokentevich Byankin. A more popular way of subduing a taimen is to shoot it when it gets tangled in the net.

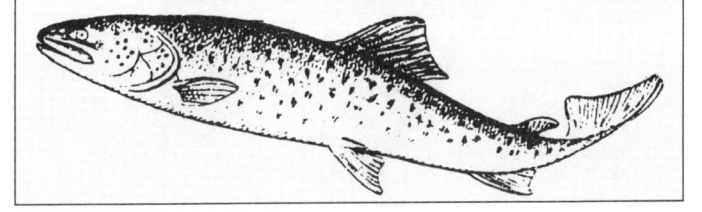

Fishing trips

Day fishing trip options include taking the train to Shivery and fishing on the banks of the Vitim River, or going by car to the Kuanda River. For the serious fishermen, it is recommended to go upstream of the Vitim River bridge by motor boat or motor boat along the Kuanda River.

For those who want to be guaranteed to catch a taimen, which grow up to 2m and weigh 80kg, you need to travel 160km up the Vitim to the Tsipa River, then travel another 160km to just below the first set of rapids. The actual travelling will take 3 days upstream and 2 days downstream.

Even if you are not interested in fishing, the trip up the Vitim and Tsipa is still worthwhile as you will inevitably see many animals including bears, wild goats and deer.

Camping Out When It Is -50°C

For Russian fishing enthusiasts, the season is not important. Winter fishing involves drilling a hole in the ice and building a tent over it. Sleeping bags are obviously very important. Above -15°C, bird feather bags known as *pokhovy spalni meshok* (поховый спалний мешок) are okay, however below -5°C, the 15kg camel skin bags known as *verblyuzhi spalni meshok* (верблюжий спалний мешок) are essential. When sleeping out in the middle of winter, most fishermen use the fire and tent arrangement illustrated. The fire in this configuration will last all night and the open tent prevents condensation while providing reflected heat. This sort of heat is much better than direct heat as a larger expanse is heated, allowing several people to benefit from the one fire.

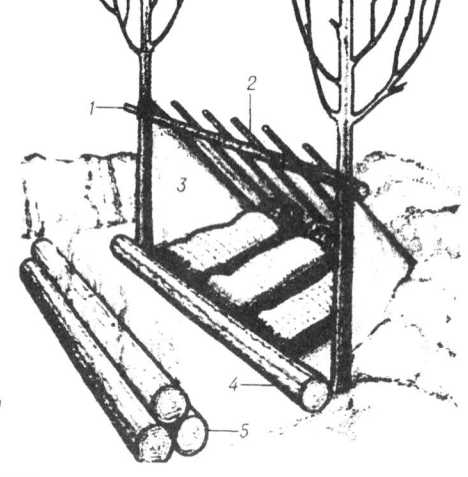

Legend
1: Roof support
2: Reflecting sheet
3: Side sheets to stop wind
4: Log to protect your feet from direct heat
4: 3 log fire which will burn all night

Finding a good fishing guide

Despite the fact that most Siberians fish, it is difficult to find a truly knowledgable fisherman who can take you to proven fishing spots for a range of fish. The best guides are members of the Fishermens' Union which is a group of professional and fanatical fishermen. The Union is very small with just 3 members in Kuanda, 4 in Nelyaty and 5 in Chara. Most have several prepared camps which maximises your fishing time. Contact Ivan Innokentevich Byankin who will put you in touch with other members of the union. His address is 674161 Kuanda, ul Druzhba Narodov 8, ☎ 4-45 (Rail) (Иван Иннокентьевич Бянкин, 74161 Каларский район, ст. Куанда, ул. Дружба Народов 8).

To give fishermen some idea of the cost, Ivan Innokentevich priced a three day fishing trip at $170 which includes $30 a day for a fisherman guide, $20 for renting the boat and motor and $20 a day for fuel.

BAM Turist Centre for Children

Within the BAM Zone, Kuanda has earned a reputation as a children's centre for outdoor education due to the creation of the BAM Turist Centre for Children.

In the years of the Soviet Union, outdoor activities for children were run by the communist youth organisations, the *Komsomol*, *Pioneer* or *Oktyabr*. They usually organised holiday camps where activities included pre-army indoctrination, civic improvement projects and occasionally, comprehensive outdoor education.

However since the collapse of communism most of these thousands of camps have disappeared. The Russian government is slowly creating new holiday camps but in 1993, just 11 new ones were formed in the whole of Russia. One of these was the BAM Turist Centre.

The main function of the Centre is to provide outdoor activities such as camping, skiing, rafting and mountaineering trips, survival classes and physical fitness camps during school holidays. The Centre has

Young children are common in the BAM towns but teenagers are rare as most board at schools in larger towns or have left home to seek work elsewhere.

established a permanent campsite near the Kodar volcanoes where groups stay for up to 18 days with as many as 30 in a group. The leader of the group is a qualified instructor and selected teachers are invited to accompany the group. A volunteer doctor also accompanies the group. During the school year, the Centre coordinates a range of classes along the BAM such as navigation and photography.

The BAM Turist Centre was an initiative of the current manager, Victor Stepanovich Ryzhi, and the principal of the local school, Victor Nikolaevich Gurulev. Victor Stepanovich is well qualified to run the Centre as he is a Russian Candidate Master of Sport and has won many national awards.

Foreign school and sports groups are welcome to use the facilities of the Centre, according to Victor Stepanovich. "The local school has French and German teachers who can work as interpreters as well as a swimming pool, sauna and canteen, and our Centre has most of the necessary camping gear. Most importantly, the surrounding region is very beautiful and offers challenges for even the most experienced sports people. In addition, the quality of staff at our Tourist Centre and others around Russia is excellent. This is because in the communist days the state run trade unions subsidised sports clubs. Nowadays there is no money for clubs so there is a lot of competition among professional sportsmen to work in organisations like ours."

Victor Stepanovich Ryzhi, BAM Turist Centre for Children, 675161 Kalarski *Raion*, Station Kuanda, ul Marta 8, kv 1-4, ☎ 4-41 (Виктор Степанович Рыжий, Дорожная станция юник туристов БАМ, 674161 Каларский район, ст. Куанда, ул. Марта 8, 1-4).

Victor Nikolaevich Gurulev, Srednaya School, 675161 Kalarski Raion, Station Kuanda, ☎ 3-66 (h), 2-40 (w) (Виктор Николаевич Гурулев, Средная Школа, 674161 Каларский район, ст. Куанда)

Mountain and glacier climbing in the Kodar Mountain Ranges
The 200km long Kodar Mountain Range is one of the natural and historical highlights of the BAM Zone. For those interested in the dark side of Soviet history, one of the country's best preserved gulag camps, called Marble Canyon, is in this range. For the adventurer, the range also contains some of the most difficult to climb mountains and glaciers in Russia. The Marble Canyon camp is described under *Novaya Chara*.

The highest peak in the range is Mount BAM at 3,072m with the nearby town of Novaya Chara just 700m above sea level. Up to 1,500m on the northern slopes and 1,700m on the southern ones are deciduous forest and stunted birch trees. This gradually gives way to thickets of Japanese stone pines and scraggy birches as you approach the treeline. Above this are barren alpine summits and mountain tundra. To the south of the Kodar mountains is the Chara Valley which is the coldest in the region. Its January temperatures can go as low as minus 49°C. A temperature inversion ensures that the air remains cold despite the cloudless sky and lack of wind. This results in a strange atmospheric condition in which the higher you go, the warmer it gets. For example when you set off for a mountaineering trip it may be minus 40°C in Novaya Chara but only minus 25°C at the top of Mount BAM.

The main climbing mountains are around Chara. Some are exceptionally hard to climb, reflected in their names such as Fang and Tower, and their difficulty attracted the 1989, 1990 and 1991 USSR Mountaineering Championships. Foreign groups have also climbed them in the past. As well as being very difficult, their attraction for alpinists is that they are easy to get to, being only about 25km from Novaya Chara station or airport.

There are at least 40 glaciers in the region and new ones are being found each year. Their total area is just 15 square kilometres and they include stationary mountain glaciers and valley glaciers moving at between 3 and 6m a year.

The main climbing period is from 1 June to 15 September. Snow climbing is also possible from 1 February to 31 March and in November but it's not recommended outside these times.

The best place to obtain information about the routes is from Victor Stepanovich Ryzhi, who runs the BAM Turist Centre for Children in Kuanda. As well as writing a book on mountain climbing in the region, he also runs a service for serious mountain climbers. People write to him with their basic trip parameters and he provides advice on weather, preparation and routes. He charges a small price for this service.

If you are intending to climb to the top of a mountain, remember the Russian practice of swapping the letter left on the summit with one of yours. These letters each contain two parts. The first you send to the person who left it there and the second you send to the national association of Russian mountain climbers as proof that you made it.

Balbukhta (Балбухта) 1,615km

This railway siding is the spot where on 24 September 1984 the golden spike joining the eastern and western sections of the BAM was hammered in. There is a monument of sleepers and rails built in an A shape about 400m to the left and east of the station. The left side of the 'A' lists the names of stations from Ust-Kut to Balbukhta while the right side lists them from Tynda.

There are gold deposits nearby which will eventually be developed.

Kodar (Кодар) 1,664km

This stop consists of a small station which provides the guard for the 1.94km Kodar Tunnel (Кодарский тоннель). This tunnel goes through the Kodar mountains and separates the Lake Leprindo district from the Chara plains. The roof collapsed during the early stages of the tunnelling killing a worker. This revealed inadequate geological surveys and after several months of frenzied research, work resumed and the tunnel was completed on time

The remains of the Kodar gulag camp are about 10km from this station and the camp is described under *Novaya Chara*.

✕ Leprindo (Леприндо) 1,683km

Emerging from the tunnel you see to your left the beautiful 12km long Small Leprindo Lake (Озеро Малое Леприндо) and a few miles later you pass over a small bridge and to your right is the 22km long Big Leprindo Lake (Озеро Большое Леприндо).

The lakes are popular fishing spots and the train will usually stop somewhere along this stretch to let fishermen on and off. The lakes are well stocked with *sik, rolets, karus* and a unique red meat fish called the *kholetsk dovachan* (холец довачан). In addition, the lakes contain a unique variety of edible waternut called the *chilim* or *ro-gulnik* (чилим, ро-гульник). In winter, you will invariably see ice fishing on the lakes. This is a very beautiful area and waterfalls can often be seen tumbling down the steep sides of the Kodar mountains into the lakes.

Leprindo is typical of most stations on the BAM and consists of just one building. It is a lonely life.

Novaya Chara – Tynda
Новая Чара - Тында

Novaya Chara (Новая Чара)   1,734km
The town might be boring but the region is fascinating. Local attractions include the Kodar mountains, the Marble Canyon Gulag Camp, the mysterious Chara Sand Dunes and the BAM museum.

Novaya Chara is the administrative capital of the Kalaski *Raion* (Каларский район) and has a population of about 15,000. It was founded as a major BAM station and the vast majority of its citizens work for the railway. The original village of Chara, also known as Staraya Chara (Старая Чара), is 18km away to the north on the Chara River. The 851km long Chara River originates on the southern slopes of the Kodar Range, and flows along the Chara Depression before emptying into the Olekma River. It is navigable from the Olekma River 416km upstream. It is fed by rain, snow, glaciers and subterranean sources. High water is from May to September. The Chara freezes over in October and the ice breaks up in May.

The town of Novaya Chara is an excellent illustration of the process of temporary and permanent town development. See the *BAM Towns* section in *The BAM Zone* chapter for information on temporary and permanent settlements. In Novaya Chara construction of the permanent settlement was only half completed before funds ran out. Consequently, the town consists of two parts; a run down, shabby temporary settlement which has the shops, and a half built permanent part which has the apartment buildings and nothing else. Consequently, the permanent town dwellers have to walk at least a kilometre to the temporary settlement for shopping. The situation is symbolised by the partly built and fully vandalised building which was to be the permanent town's main shopping centre beside the hotel.

> **WHERE DID THE NAMES COME FROM?**
> Most of the region's towns, rivers and mountains get their names from the local indigenous people, the Evenk.
> Udokan (Удокан) means slowly rising region, Kodar (Кодар) means cliff and Muya (Муя) simply means water.
> Many Russians believe that the word chara (чара) refers to the old Russian metal cup common in 16th and 17th century households. Actually, the word is Evenk for a picturesque river crossing.

Getting there and away
There are daily trains arriving from the west including Kuanda (3:30 hours), Taksimo (5:40

204　BAM Mainline Route Description

hours), Severobaikalsk (15:00 hours), Taishet (36 hours) and Moscow (109 hours), and from the east Tynda (13:30 hours) and Neryungri (18:30 hours). There are daily flights to Chita. The airport is about 1km north of Old Chara.

Where to stay
The only place to stay in town is the Hotel Kodar (Гостиница Кодар)

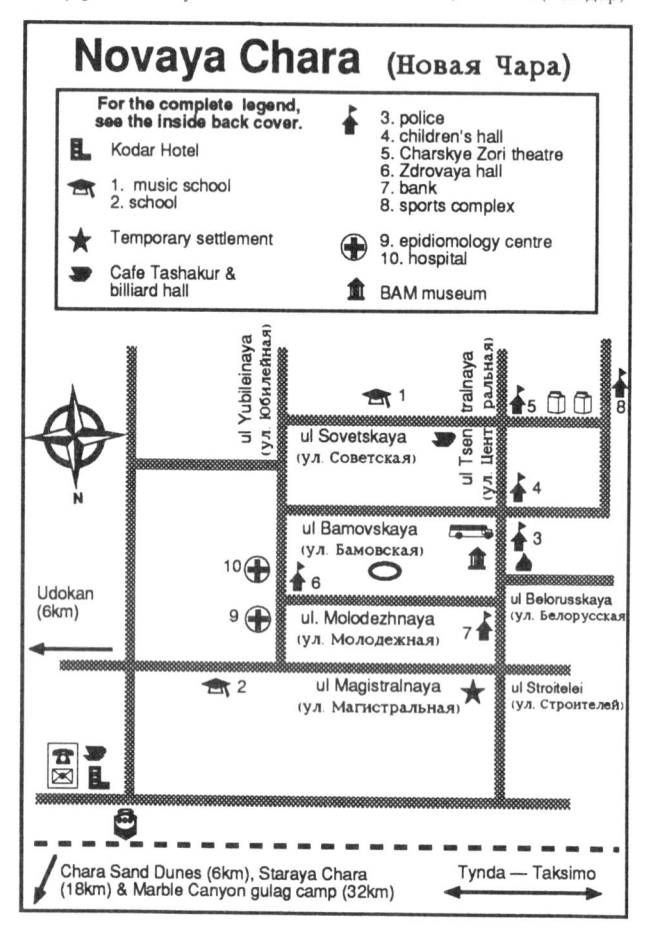

opposite the station. It is basic but has a hairdresser and cafe on the ground floor. Foreigners are charged 6 times the local price which makes the cost $30 a night. This pricing policy was probably introduced at a time when masses of foreign business people were expected when the competition was on to develop the nearby Udokan copper deposits. The influx never eventuated but the price remains. Check the register and it will probably show about 1 foreigner a month, ☎ 4-65.

Where to eat
The choices are limited unless you walk miles to the Cafe Tashakur. Strange as it might seem the best choice is the station's upstairs canteen. The hotel also has a cafe which never seems to be open.

What to see
Within town the only place of interest is the BAM museum. Its focus is, of course, on the heroic building of the BAM, but it also has a collection on the indigenous people and the early years of collectivisation, archaeological finds from the Chara Sand Dunes and memorabilia from the gulag camps. It is open every day except Monday from 10-17:00. Lunch break from 13-14:00. Director V Astrakhantseva-Nadelyaeva, 674159, Novaya Chara, BAM Museum, A-Ya51, ☎ 61-79, (Директор В Астраханцева-Наделяева, 674159 Новая Чара, Музей А-Я51).

Chara's BAM museum.

You may also come across someone selling a lilac coloured rock with black streaks in it called chariot. This semi-precious gemstone is found only in the Chara Valley and Muya Mountain Range.

For those botanically inclined, a five minute walk to the east along the BAM will bring you to a clump of Chozeniya trees. These trees are restricted to Lake Baikal with this one exception. How they got here and survive is still a mystery. From here and from the train, you can see two 200m high hillocks to the north which the locals laughingly call babagrud (бабагрудь) meaning *breasts* for obvious reasons.

Trips in the region

Staraya Chara (Старая Чара)
Despite its name meaning Old Chara, Staraya Chara is relatively young. It was founded in 1933 when the Soviet government's collectivisation policy forced the migrating Evenk to settle down to grow vegetables and raise livestock. As well as bringing the indigenous people under state control, this enabled teachers to instigate a successful literacy program which was a major state objective in the late 1920s and 1930s. Unfortunately the collectivisation was not a success as agriculture is unsuitable in most of the Chara basin which is affected by summer frosts and has large tracts of waterlogged land. Of the 6 original collective farms, the only remaining one is the Charski *Sovkhoz* which consists of 1,200 dairy cows and is 10km north of Staraya Chara.

The town now has a population of just 3,000 of which about 300 are Evenk. There is an Evenk museum.

While you can walk the 18km between Novaya Chara and Staraya Chara, a more comfortable trip is on one of the 4 buses a day that travel between the Airport, Staraya Chara and Novaya Chara, departing from Novaya Chara station at 8:00, 11:00, 15:30 and 17:00. The trip takes 20 minutes.

Chara Sand Dunes
An enjoyable half day trip is to the Sahara-like 6km long Chara Sand Dunes. How these dunes were created in the midst of 600m thick permafrost is still a mystery. The dunes were an important site for the indigenous people as a large number of stone arrows, axes and daily utensils from past millennium have been found there. These are on display in St Petersburg's Russian Museum of Ethnology and Novaya Chara's museum. The dunes are about 4km south-west of Staraya Chara and 6km north-west of Novaya Chara. You can see the dunes from the train as you depart Novaya Chara to the east.

Udokan copper mines

One of the main justifications for building the BAM was access to the nearby massive 1.2 billion ton Udokan copper ore deposit. This makes it one of the largest copper deposits in the world.

In the late 1980s, massive plans were made to construct the mine with the main processing centre at either the small base of Namingnakan (Намингнакан) (20km east of Novaya Chara) or at the geologists camp of Udokan (Удокан) (6km south of Novaya Chara). With the pursuit of foreign investment following the disintegration of the Soviet Union,

---

Russian Politics and Capitalism: A Recipe for Stagnation

The Udokan copper deposit is possibly the world's largest copper deposit and despite President Yeltsin giving the green light to proceed with a multi-million dollar feasibility study on 15 January 1993, not a ton of the ore has been dug up.

While the study was only for the mine's feasibility, the contract is enormously important as the winner will inevitably get the contract to build the copper mill, power station and housing for 2,000 workers.

Seven major western companies and one Russian consortium expressed interest in the project but eventually only one foreign company, Australia's BHP, and a Russian consortium, Udokan Mining Company, tendered for it. The latter won the contract and then the accusations started to fly over bias, impropriety and hidden agendas.

Firstly, it was claimed that the award process was a victim of political expediency by the Yeltsin government in the difficult months of late 1992. During this time, Yeltsin was faced with a hostile parliament, rising nationalism and falling popularity. The award of the contract to what appeared to be a Russian consortium was seen as a way to shore up his power base with powerful Russian civil and military industrialists as they would benefit from the work, and appeal to nationalists by portraying the contract's award as one that serves the best interests of Russia.

Secondly, it was claimed that the Udokan Mining Company consortium was in reality not Russian but substantially owned by foreign companies from Hong Kong and the US. One of the foreign businessmen behind the project was rumoured to be Hong Kong businessman, Mr Eddie Wong, and it has been reported that a key factor in the winning of the contract was Mr Wong's ability to secure a 25 year contract to supply 200,000 tonnes of copper concentrate a year out of the mine's total production of 360,000 to China.

Thirdly, it has been claimed that BHP's proposed three year program for developing the deposit was exceedingly slow and its true agenda was to prevent large amounts of copper entering the market which would destroy BHP's substantial profits for its existing, massive, world-wide copper interests.

Fourthly, it was claimed that there was a substantial conflict of interest in the panel that evaluated the two bids. Several of the panel's members were from the local region's government, the Chita Oblast, and the Chita Oblast was one of the shareholders of the Udokan Mining Company.

Whatever the truth, this story is indicative of the intrigues of government and business in the post-communist era.

Yeltsin opened the mine's development to joint ventures. See *Russian Politics and Capitalism* for a description of the resulting inaction. As neither a branch line to the area has been built nor has the geological research continued, it appears that nothing is expected to happen in the near future. If you visit Udokan by the dirt road just east of Novaya Chara, you will notice that the town is virtually deserted. Apparently everything worth anything was shipped away in 1994 when the future of the mine became apparent.

Lake Zapod day hike

A scenic lake with a great view of the mountains is located to the northwest of Staraya Chara. Lake Zapod (Озеро Запод) also known as Lake Otkaetkyel (Озеро Откаткёль) is about 30km from Novaya Chara. Its name, meaning *stack of hay*, describes the view of the nearby mountain of the same name. If you climb to the top of the mountain you will be rewarded by an awe inspiring view of the Kodar mountains which look as if they have risen sheer out of the ground. Before descending to the lake, have a look around for a freaky rock pillar which has a distinctive

---

MINING WITH ATOMIC BOMBS

The draft of the ninth 5-year plan authorised the Udokan program, but [publicly] did not go into detail. What the State secretly authorised was the use of a peaceful nuclear explosion on or near the surface of Drift Mine No 5. The explosives actually were delivered by the Trans-Siberian railway to Mogocha station and carried over the primitive winter road to Naminga during the winter of 1965-6. The Chara River, meanwhile, burst from its frozen surface and created a lateral river icing, which delayed the shipment. When the demolitions finally were delivered in late 1965, local geologists were evacuated beyond a 50-km radius of ground zero. An Evenk village was moved, but authorities in Moscow decided not to evacuate the larger settlement of Chara for fear that it would cause more harm from panic than would result from the potential exposure to radiation

Drift Mine No 5, it turns out, was the site of the poorest grade of ore, but if the experiment had succeeded there – and no one ever doubted it would – they would have proceeded to the sites of the richer ores.

The 'peaceful use of the atom' was planned for some time between January 2nd and 6th, 1966, a time when the winds were expected to be (and usually are) exceedingly low, but 'still they blow and do so unimpededly because there are no obstacles at Udokan's evaluation'. As in many parts of the Udokan basin, the rock is highly fragmented and latter-day experts are convinced that the potential radiation would have reached the water table and eventually the Lena River system. Although the Udokan explosion was called off at the last moment, the Brezhnev administration had planned to cordon off the region for ten years in order 'to let the radiation return to normal".

From "BAM after the fanfare: the unbearable ecumene" by Victor L Mote in *Soviet Environment: Problems, policies and politics*, Cambridge University Press, 1993.

male profile. The easist way to get to the lake is by road to the indigenous village called Kyust-Kemda (Кюсть-Кемда) to the north of Staraya Chara, and then walking the last 6km.

Marble Canyon Gulag Camp (Мраморное ущелье ГУЛаг)
This camp is probably the best preserved Stalin-era prisoner camp in Eastern Siberia. While it is not easily accessible and preparation is essential, it is well worth the effort.

The camp operated from 1949-1951 and was the biggest of the 10 camps in the Kodar mountains that mined uranium for the Soviet atomic bomb project. The guard's buildings and towers are extremely well preserved. You will notice that there are no prisoner barracks. This was because prisoners slept in canvas tents as wood was in short supply as it had to be carried up the mountains. There are also slag heaps and one accessible tunnel. In the tunnel there are respirators which were discarded when the camp was closed. The background radiation is now no higher than normal however as a precaution you should not enter the mine without a mask nor camp on top of the slag heaps. At the top of the canyon there are two graves. One is for an engineer N Azarovoi and another for a prison guard. The most difficult section of the canyon is at its entrance as it is very steep. Part way down the canyon you pass the

Marble Canyon Gulag Camp. Photo reproduced with permission from the BAM museum in Tynda.

remnants of the geologists camp and after another kilometre you reach the gulag.

There are many rumours about the size of the camps with estimates ranging up to 10,000. However the opening of Moscow's archives has revealed that the number was probably closer to 2,000. The one fact that no-one knows is the number of deaths. The records do not indicate this and as yet, no cemetery has been discovered.

Getting there
There are three main options to reach the gulag and these are briefly outlined below. It is advisable to get a copy of the map of the Kodar mountains around Chara including the Marble Canyon camp before embarking on these routes. The map and its purchase details are listed in the *Recommended Reading* section.

1: Walking from Staraya Chara
Day 1: Travel from Staraya Chara to a winter hut (зимовье) which is the start of the glacier gouged Sredni Sakukan River Valley (р. Средный Сакукан). Make sure you stay north of the river so you do not have to cross it later on.
Day 2: Walk to a collapsed hut (развалины) halfway up the valley.
Day 3: Walk to the creek opposite Marble Canyon. There is a collapsed hut here.
Day 4: Cross the river and walk to the gulag camp. After lunch walk out of the canyon up the valley until you reach the meteorological station. This comfortable building was built about 20 years ago by Irkutsk University climatology students.
Day 5: Based at the meteorological station, you can make an easy day return trip to Mount BAM. You walk through the mountain pass called Three Policemen (перевал Три Жандарма) which is between 2 glaciers. From here it is a 1km climb to the base of Mount BAM and back. You have to walk over a glacier but as it is gently sloping, you do not need special equipment. The view of Mount BAM is spectacular.
Day 6: The hardest day of the walk. You walk down the valley towards Marble Canyon but before you reach it, you turn left down the Baltiski River (р. Балтийский). Walk up the creek to the easy Baltiski pass (перевал Балтийский) and down the other side to the Byurokan River (р. Бюрокан).
Day 7: Walk down the Byurokan to its junction with the Verkhni Sakukan River (р. Верхный Сакукан). You can make a day trip from here to the nearby small Verkhni Sakukan Gulag camp.
Day 8: Cross the Verkhni Sakukan River, which is easily waded, to the BAM stop of Sakukan (Санукан). Catch the train back to Novaya Chara.

2: Helicopter from Staraya Chara
Day 1: Fly by helicopter from Staraya Chara to the meteorological station. This is a 30 minute trip. Walk to the entrance of Marble Canyon to inspect the graves. Return to the meteorological station and stay overnight.
Day 2: Fly by helicopter to the gulag camp. In the evening return to Staraya Chara.

3: Quick but economical visit from Staraya Chara
Day 1: Travel by tracked vehicle (like a tank but no gun and used for exploration work) halfway up the Sredni Sakukan River Valley. Walk from here to the meteorological station which is a 5 hour hike.
Day 2: Walk to the Marble Canyon and return to the meteorological station.
Day 3: Return by foot to the base of the Sredni Sakukan River Valley.
Day 4: Return by foot to Staraya Chara.

Notes
The bridge that crossed the Sredni Sakukan River infront of the Marble Canyon collapsed in 1992. To cross the river you may be able to walk across its remnants or walk up the valley to a narrower crossing point. It is worth finding out the water level before you depart from Novaya Chara for you may need inflatable rafts to cross the river after heavy rains.

It may be possible to travel the 20km to the base of the Sredni Sakukan River Valley in a four wheel drive vehicle depending upon the weather.

The Sredni Sakukan River Valley route is accessible from June to December but snow starts to fall in September. The route is totally impassable in April and May due to heavy snow falls.

A gun should always be carried because of bears, particularly just after they have risen from hibernation.

The 1994 cost of hiring a helicopter for a round trip over two days was $1,000, hiring a vehicle to the base of the Sredni Sakukan River Valley was $50 and the daily cost of a guide was $30.

Only attempt these trips with a guide who has actually been there before.

There are two other well preserved camps which are worth visiting. Don't be surprised if no-one knows of these as only a few Russian adventurers have ever visited them.

Verkhni Sakukan Gulag (Верхний Сакукан ГУЛаг)
Verkhni Sakukan Gulag operated for only one year until it was decided that the uranium ore at Marble Canyon was a better prospect. It is near

the junction of the Byurokan River and the Verkhni Sakukan River. Make your camp near the river junction and make a day return trip to the gulag which is about 2km away and 600m up the mountains. To get to the river junction, you go by train to the Sakukan BAM stop and walk on a rough track for about 20km alongside the Verkhni Sakukan River. A minimum of three days is required for this trip.

Kodar Station Gulag
This gulag does not appear to have a proper name so it has been called the Kodar Station Gulag as it is about 10km from the station. This gulag is smallest of the three camps and consists of 2 tunnels, 2 shafts and a few collapsed wooden buildings. It was only a small exploratory camp and does not even have a barbed wire fence around it. Getting there involves going on a dirt road to an Evenk reindeer herding camp. This is an interesting place to have lunch if it can be organised. About 3km away is the camp which is in the valley near the junction of the Khadatkand and Syalban Rivers (р. Хадаткaнд и Сюльбан). The background radiation is higher here than at the other camps so don't go into the tunnels without a respirator.

It is best to visit the camp in winter or late summer as rain turns the road to the Evenk camp into a quagmire. While the trip can be made in one day, it would be better to spend the night at the Evenk camp.

Kemen (Кемен)   1,755km
Near this station is the deepest permafrost on the BAM. Here the soil is frozen down to a depth of 600m.

About 5km to the west of this stop are the hot springs at Luktop (Луктор). The springs are near the railway line and can also be reached by the road from Novaya Chara which runs beside the railway. A small lodge is being built here by Novaya Chara's SMP 577 construction group. The water gurgles out of the ground at 60°C so you need to fill up the bath tubs and wait for them to cool before getting in.

Leaving Kemen, you start your assent of the Stanovoi Range. This section is double tracked and if you are lucky your train will pass another train providing an excellent photo of a snaking train with fabulous mountains in the background. The Stanovoi Range extends for 700km and large coal beds run its entire length. At the north east end of the range is Neryungri, site of one of the world's largest coal mines. This town is described in the *AYAM* section in the *BAM Branch Lines Route Descriptions* chapter.

Ikabya (Икабья)   1,772km
Ikabya was sponsored by the Georgian Komsomol Youth Organisation on the Bolshoi Ikabya River (р. Большой Икабья). About

10km to the east is the Evenk village of Chapo-ologo (Чапо-олого). The village has about 250 Evenks and they manage a polar fox farm. 20km from the village are famous hot springs on the shore of the Arbakhalir River (р. Арбахалир) but you can only reach them by the river or frozen winter river road. They are known as Charski Iztochnik (Чарский Източник). You can see Chapo-ologo on the banks of the snaking Bolshoi Ikabya River north of the train as you leave Ikabya. A short distance further on, you cross over the 8 span bridge across the Ikabya River which is one of the longest bridges on the BAM's central section.

Olongo (Олонго) 1,851km

Between Olongo and Khani is the triple border between the Republic of Sakha, Amur Oblast and Chita Oblast. The intersection is along the Khani Valley which the train travels through. The intersection is marked by a 2m long and 2m high white monument of a giant rail on the right. The monument also commemorates the highest point along the BAM railway which is 1,310m above sea level.

Khani (Хани) 1,879km

Khani is also called Luninskaya (Лунинская). It is the only BAM town in the Republic of Sakha (formerly Yakutia) and unlike the rest of Sakha, you do not need a visa to stop here. The town, located 1.5km into

Khani station with two workers heading off to the railyards.

Sakha, is situated in a very picturesque valley with snow capped peaks surrounding it. Trains normally stop here for between 5 and 40 minutes while the locomotives are changed. In this time, you can quickly run around town. The police station and post office are both at the station.

Outside of town, the only noteworthy place to visit is a geologist's tunnel 6km east of the station which was dug to get information on the region's geology before the BAM was built.

Goods are sometimes carted from Khani by a 199km road to the northern geological exploratory town of Torgo (Торго). Torgo is in the centre of a massive iron ore deposit. The road is virtually impassable except in winter. Like the Udokan copper deposits in Chara, the Torgo deposits were to be developed into a massive mining operation with a branchline to the BAM. This has also not eventuated and from reports, the town is virtually deserted.

The only accommodation in Khani is the Locomotive Brigade Hostel, ☎ 2-87 (Дом Отдыха Локомотивой Бригады).

Olekma (Олёкма)   1,934km
Olekma is named after the Olekma River, however the station is about 35km from the river. When the BAM was being constructed, barges were towed up the 1,435km long river from the Lena River to a landing on the Olekma and carted overland to the station. From Olekma to Larba, the BAM follows the course of the Olekma River and then the Nyukzha River. This route is very scenic and passes what in Russian is called *rock rivers*. These are the remains of rock slides with all the dirt washed away. The boulders can be up to 2m across and the rivers can be up to 500m wide.

Imangrakan (Имангракан)
Imangrakan is on the junction of the Imangra and Olekma Rivers.

Tas-Yuryakh (Тас-Юрях)   2,008km
Tas-Yuryakh is on the junction of the Tas-Yuryakh and Olekma Rivers.

Between Tas-Yuryakh and Yuktali stations you pass over the Olekma River. About 5km further on, you see a small town at the junction of the Yuktali and Olekma Rivers. This is the indigenous village of Ust-Nyukzha (Усть-Нюкжа) described under Yuktali.

Yuktali (Юктали)   2,028km
Yuktali is a small BAM town which has a Locomotive Brigade Hostel ☎ 3-38 (Дом Отдыха Локомотивой Бригады). This is a good place to stay overnight so that you can visit Ust-Nyukzha without rushing. Ust-Nyukzha is an ancient town and has an excellent

ethnographical museum and a *Sovkhoz* reindeer breeding farm. This well-known village is frequently visted by Russian groups. The BAM Kino Studios have made several films on the community and information on these is listed in the *Recommended reading* section.

🏠 Chilchi (Чильчи)   2,137km

The town is named after the Chilchi River which is an Evenk name. The town has a Locomotive Brigade Hostel, ☎ 2-74, (Дом Отдыха Локомотивой Бригады).

🏠 Lopcha (Лопча)   2,185km

Lopcha is a timber town with a Russian forestry camp and North Korean sawmill. Interestingly, the town once had a Russian club which studied the Juche philosophy developed by the now dead Great Leader and President Kim Il Sung of the Democratic Peoples Republic of Korea (DPRK), commonly known as North Korea. These clubs exist all over the world and are normally written off as left-wing loony groups.

So what is Juche? According to *A Sightseeing Guide to Korea*, published in the DPRK in 1991, "In a nutshell, the Juche idea means that the masters of the revolution and construction are the masses of the people and that they are also the motive force of the revolution and construction. In other words, one is responsible for one's own destiny and one also has the capacity to shape one's own destiny. The Juche idea is the guiding idea of the Korean revolution evolved by President Kim Il Sung. The Workers' Party of Korea and the Government of the Republic lead the revolution and construction, guided by the Juche idea." Impressive!

🏠 Larba (Ларба)   2,232km

Gold is mined here. About 30km upstream on the Nyukzha River is the tributary Urkima River. This is the location of a remote Evenk village called Ust-Urkima (Усть-Уркима).

🏠 Khorogochi (Хорогочи)   2,284km

The town has a Locomotive Brigade Hostel ☎ 2-31, (Дом Отдыха Локомотивой Бригады).

🏠 Kuvykta (Кувыкта)   2,334km

There is a reasonable quality road running from here to Tynda. The famous Moldovian poet Zhanna Ayarzhevkaya (Жанна Аяржевкая) lives here. She came here when the BAM was being built and remained. Another notable visitor was the cosmonaut Valentin Vitalevich Lebedev. However he left quickly after his whirlwind propaganda visit in the late 1970s. These visits by Soviet celebrities were common as they 'demonstrated' that the BAM was being built by everyone in the Soviet Union. The locals of Kuvykta were so pleased with his visit that there is a small space museum in town dedicated to his exploits. Valentin Vitalevich, was twice awarded the Hero of the USSR medal for his long duration space flights. His longest was in 1982 when he lived in space for 211 days, 9 hours, 4 minutes and 32 seconds. His first flight was in Soyuz 13.

Soyuz Space Craft

Soyuz 13 was launched on 18 December 1973 and was the forerunner of Soviet manned orbiting laboratories and space stations. It was the first Soyuz mission since the program started in 1967 that did not have a military component. The Soyuz is the first true manned spaceship as in the preceding 2 classes of spacecraft, the Vostok and Voskhod, the cosmonauts were merely passengers in virtually automatic craft. Not only could Soyuz cosmonauts perform critical orbital manoeuvres to complete a rendezvous and docking mission, but they could also carry out sophisticated earth and space science programs for periods of up to thirty days. The overall spacecraft weighed about 6,650kg and was nearly 7.5m long.

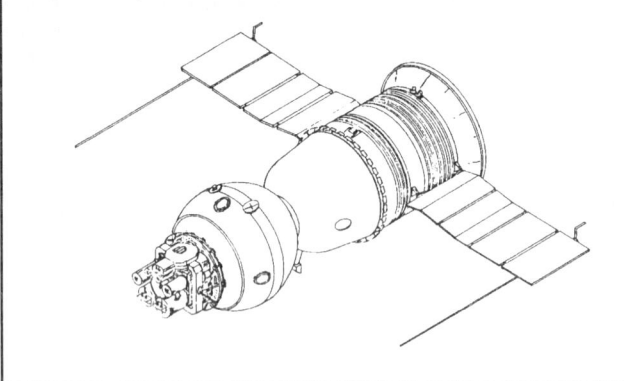

Tynda
Тында

Tynda (Тында)   2,364km
☎ area code: 416-56, ✉ Amurskaya Oblast, Tynda, 676080
Амурская Область, г. Тында 676080

Tynda is the capital of the BAM. It sits at the junction of the 4 sections of the BAM: eastern BAM, western BAM, AYAM and Little BAM. Tynda is the third largest town on the BAM with a population of 70,000. The main street, Krasnaya Presnya, is lined with 16 storey buildings which is very unusual for Siberia. Tynda's attractions include an excellent BAM museum, a local Evenk village and an excellent Russian *banya*.

The BAM headquarters is also based in Tynda which means that if you have a problem, you can take it to the top quickly. Whether they will do anything about it is another question. Not surprisingly, the Tynda station is the cleanest on the BAM.

Two full days are normally enough to see everything Tynda has to offer and there are several travel companies in town which can help you organise programs.

Tynda has a sister city relationship with Wenatchee of the USA. In the early 1990s, an exchange program for children of these two cities started.

Tynda was first joined, via the Little BAM, to the Trans-Siberian in 1937 when the village was known as Tyndinsky. In 1942 the line was pulled up and shipped to the Battle of Stalingrad. Workers started relaying the line in 1973

The gaint *Worker with the Sledge Hammer* sculpture is the best monument on the BAM. By a strange twist of fate, the power pole in front of the statue has tilted towards the worker so that now it looks like he is driving in the pole. The sculpture was built by workers of the BAM Bridge Building organisation, BAMmoststroi 10, and stands in front of their headquarters on ul Amurskaya.

Tynda (Тында)

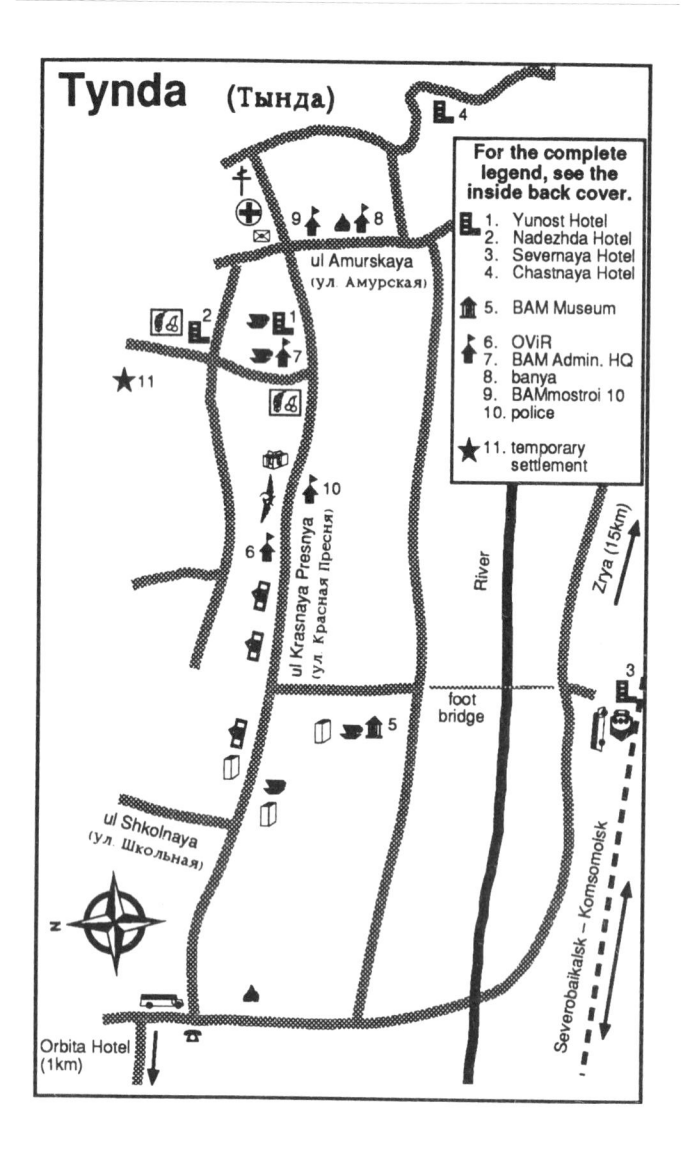

ul Amurskaya (ул Амурская)

ul Krasnaya Presnya (ул Красная Пресня)

ul Shkolnaya (ул Школьная)

River

foot bridge

Zeya (15km)

Severobaikalsk – Komsomolsk

Orbita Hotel (1km)

For the complete legend, see the inside back cover.

1. Yunost Hotel
2. Nadezhda Hotel
3. Severnaya Hotel
4. Chastnaya Hotel
5. BAM Museum
6. OViR
7. BAM Admin. HQ
8. banya
9. BAMmostroi 10
10. police
11. temporary settlement

and the new Little BAM reached Tynda in 1975. The early years of
Tynda were a litany of poor engineering with constant water and
heating shortages, inadequate housing, buildings subsiding into the
permafrost and power interruptions. The situation now is vastly
improved with the construction of a centralised heating system
consolidating the town's 38 separate heating boilers in 1977. Air
pollution was also a big problem due to the coal fired power station,
however this has closed with the supply of electricity arrived from Zeya
which is 225km kilometres away. Fogs are common in the morning but
disappear within a few hours of sunrise.

Getting there and away
There are daily trains arriving from every direction.

From the west they include Novaya Chara (14 hours), Taksimo (19
hours), Severobaikalsk (29 hours), Taishet (50 hours) and Moscow (123
hours).

From the south they include Bamovskaya (3:15 hours), Chita (24:40
hours), Irkutsk (42 hours) and Kislovodsk (Кисловодск) in south west
Russia near Stavropol. The Kislovodsk train No 687/261 departs 21:45
Monday and Thursday, and arrives from Kisolvodsk at 16:00 Tue and
Friday. There are also carriages, which are joined to other trains on the
Trans-Siberian, which go to Blagoveshchensk (15:40 hours), Khabarovsk
(23 hours) and Vladivostok (36 hours).

From the north they include Berkakit (4:50 hours), Neryungri (5:05
hours) and Aldan. From the east they include Fevralsk (18 hours), Novy
Urgal (27 hours) and Komsomolsk (40 hours).

There are two local trains a day which run down the Little BAM as
far as Murtygit and these offer a pleasant day trip.

There are flights from the Amur Oblast's capital of Blagoveshchensk.

Buses run along the Amur Yakutsk Highway northwards to
Neryungri (7 hours) and Mogot (2 hours), and southwards to Solovevsk
(Соловьевск), Urkan (Уркан) and Bolshoi Never (Большой Невер) on
the Trans-Siberian.

There is a railway ticketing office in the main street of Tynda which
saves you walking to the station. There is also an Aeroflot office on in
the main street, however it is hard to find as it is around the side of the
building.

Where to stay
Tynda has the dubious honour of having the most overpriced hotel in
Eastern Siberia. Hotel Yunost (гостиница Юность) is a crumbling multi-
storey 1970s hotel which has mostly small rooms with no facilities. They
have a pricing policy of charging foreigners 5 times the price for locals
which means that you can be set back a whopping $110 for a twin share

room! In the past, they could get away with this policy as there were no other accommodation options in the town. Nowadays there are a number of other choices, however most are not as centrally located as Yunost. Hotel Yunost, ul Krasnaya Presnya, ☎ 32-708 (гостиница Юность, ул. Красная Пресня).

The best accommodation in town is the Orbita Railway Hotel (гостиница Орбита) which is where senior railway officials stay when they visit Tynda. This building is a small mansion surrounded by gardens about 15 minutes walk from the city's bus station. The rooms are large, and there are several suites. The restaurant is excellent and there are several places for meetings. Well worth the $16 per person per night. To get to the hotel from the railway station, go along the road towards the centre of town and rather than turning up Krasnaya Presnya at the city's bus station, keep going straight ahead for another 500m. Turn left up ul Nadezhdy and take the left fork at its end. You then pass into the hotel's grounds which are surrounded by a large hedge. Orbita Railway Hotel, ☎ 33-64 (гостиница Орбита, ул. Надежды).

Another option in town is the Hotel Nadezhda (гостиница Надежда) which is just behind the Hotel Yunost. The hotel is an old *pioneer* building and the 3rd floor is a hostel with several beds in each room. The 4th floor is being renovated and will become a normal hotel. A cafe is being also built in the building. The building is owned by the extremely helpful Nadezhda Konstantinovna Nizova. The hostel rooms are $10 a night per person. Hotel Nadezhda, ul Festivalnaya 1, ☎ 29-278 home, ☎ 29-655 work (Надежда Константиновна Низова, ЧИН Торговый дом «Надежда», ул. Фестивальная 1).

At the railway station is the railway Hotel Severnaya (гостиница Северная), however they never seem to have any rooms.

The Chastnaya Hotel is in the old temporary settlement to the east. It is run by Lyudmila Viktorova and is easy to find as it is beside the town's bread factory. Chastnaya Hotel, ul Rushchskaya 4, ☎ 24-15 (Директор Людмила Викторова, гостиница Частная, ул. Рижская 4).

There are a number of hostels and hotels belonging to various BAM construction and operational organisations. Some may give you a room. They include:
Zheleznodorozhnikov Hostel for railwaymen, ul Amurskaya, ☎ 48-69 (Общежитие Железнодорожников, ул. Амурская).
Mosgiprotrans Hostel for constructors of the railway lines around Tynda, ☎ 34-11 (Общежитие Мосгипротранс).
Bamstroiput Hotel for constructors of the entire BAM railway, ☎ 36-53 (гостиница Бамстройпуть).
Bamstroimekhanizatsiya Hostel for organisers of mechanised units which supply the equipment for the BAM builders, ☎ 35-95 (Общежитие Бамстроймеханизация).

Where to eat
Restaurants are still fairly scarce around Tynda with the best two being the two storey bar and restaurant around the side of Hotel Yunost, and one beside Dom Kniga. There are also canteens in the BAM headquarters and near the railway library. Tynda is blessed with well

---

PIONEERS HOUSING

When the first wave of pioneers arrived in 1973 to restart the BAM, they had to live in tents to start with. They quickly assembled pre-fabricated houses or lived in metal vans which could be transported on sleds or wheels. However their greatest problem was heating in winter. A new style of round all-metal drum accommodation called tubs or *bochka* (бочка) houses offered a solution.

Entering the house, you find yourself in a small lobby with a shower on the right and drying cabinet for outdoor clothes on the left. Further on are the living quarters with a bedroom, kitchen and toilet. The living space of the *bochka* is 18 square metres and is intended for four occupants. Importantly, the house has an autonomous heating system and hot water system. This meant that *bochkas* were self-contained which is essential in towns being built. Unfortunately only a few of them were supplied to workers for a various reasons, including an inability to produce them in large numbers.

Pre-fabricated houses, *bochka* and vans were all expected to be removed when the BAM towns were constructed but as there is a lack of housing in most towns, many of the original inhabitants still live in them. A mixture of these houses can be seen up the hill behind the Nadezhda Hotel. There are signs for the BAM museum in this area but ignore them as the museum moved from here years ago.

stocked shops with the best being on ul Krasnaya Presnya. The state department store complex also has a range of railway hats and badges on sale. However as you need a railway purchasing permit to buy railway clothing, you may have to convince the salespeople with tales of being a collector in order to get them.

Visas
This is the only town on the BAM that still requires you to be registered by the police before you can get a room at a hotel. In the Soviet-era, it was a requirement that all visitors register with 24 hours of arriving in a hotel anywhere in the country. (Some Russian visas still have this requirement printed on them.) The registration requirement in Tynda is a legacy of these days and eventually it will disappear. Tynda's registration office is run by *OViR* and is located in the ground floor of one of the highrise buildings on ul Krasnaya Presnya. You should check upon arrival when it is open as it works only part days. It can take up to an hour to register and costs about $1.50. Sometimes you will be asked at the station for your registered visa in order to get a rail ticket.

Getting around
The station is about 2km out of town by a circuitous road route. However you can easily walk from the station to the centre of the town via a direct line over a foot bridge. Otherwise Bus № 5 runs regularly from the station down the main street of town. Be aware that the telephone and post parts of the post office are at different ends of the town. Past Hotel Yunosti on ul Krasnaya Presnya is a church being built next to the hospital.

What to see
For those interested in the BAM railway itself, this is the place to be. The headquarters of the BAM railway is here, as are the other numerous organisations including the Ministry of Transport Construction. The headquarters building (ul Krasnaya Presnya 47) has a railway ticket office there. To get in you need a railway employee's pass or you can try bluffing it.

The BAM museum is in the city's library building and is very good. The museum includes a model of what parts of the rail line were built when. It also contains displays of early settlers' equipment and gulag artefacts. It is open everyday except Friday from 10-18:00 with lunch 13-14:00. It is run by Tatyana Ivanovna Usova, ul Profsyuznaya 3, ☎ 32-483 (Татьяна Ивановна Усова, ул. Профсоюзная 3).

Next door to the *Worker with the Sledge Hammer* statue is the city's *banya*. This is a genuine *banya* with birch branches on sale, a pool, and wet and dry saunas.

There are two main markets in town which are more like bazaars. There are a surprising number of traders from the Central Asian republics at the markets and Turkish music is common. The main markets are behind Hotel Nadezhda and in front of the BAM headquarters.

Tynda is not much of a cultural centre, however the local Russian choir, Zernyshki (Зернышки), is worth hearing.

What's in the region

The most interesting place in the region is the indigenous Evenk village of Zarya (Заря) also known as Pervomaiskoe (Первомайское). The town is small with about 200 families. The main street, ul Centralnaya, is the only tarred road and it eventually peters out into a dairy farm. The most interesting aspect of the town is that it has a large school with about 1,000 students in it from several local Evenki villages. Combining their resources in this way has enabled the survival of the Evenki language and culture. Bus № 105 from Tynda's bus station travels to the village. The trip, which takes about 30 minutes, passes a stone bridge over the Getkan River. This functioning railway bridge is the only part of the original 1930s Little BAM railway left.

An excellent film on the Evenki was made by the BAM Film Studios

An Evenk and Russian sitting out the front of the Kolkhoz administration building and shop in the indigenous village of Zarya.

and they will supply a video copy of the film for a few dollars. They have also produced a number of films on the BAM. Victor Nikolaevich Pozharov, BAM Kino Studios, ul Krasnaya Presnya 34, ☎ 747-69, fax 22-004 (Виктор Николаевич Пожаров, Кино корреспондентский пункт МПС на БАМе, ул. Красная Пресня 34).

Getting assistance
The best source of information on what is happening in Tynda is the newspaper *Avangard* (Авангард) which is published 4 times a week. It is difficult to find it on the streets but it can be obtained from their office at ul Krasnaya Presnya 70 ☎ 213-97. Another source is the weekly *BAM* newspaper which lists events in Tynda and along the BAM.

There are a number of tourist companies in Tynda whose main business is organising trips for Russians into other countries. They are:
GeyaBAM: ul Profsyuznaya 4-42 ☎ 27-683, fax 32-335, telex 154128 KREDI SU. The director is Vladimir Kraenoperd (ГеяБАМ, ул. Профсоюзная 4-42, Директор Владимир Краеноперд). They also have a Moscow affiliate which is easier to fax to and they will pass the fax on. The Moscow company's fax is (095) 230-2919.
BAMtourist: BAMtourist, ul Krasnaya Presnya 27 ☎ 220-27, fax 209-47. The director is Natalya Philonenko (БАМТурист, ул. Красная Пресня 27, Директор Наталья Анатольевна Филоненко).
Inturist: This is the state travel company. ul Krasnaya Presnya 35, kv 3 (Интурист, ул. Красная Пресня 35, кв 3).
Tourism Department, BAM Railway Company: Each of the three sections of the BAM Railway has a tourism department. They have excellent access to railway hotels and specialist railway carriages. As each of the departments works independently and can organise your program along the entire BAM, you can contact any of the three, however the Severobaikalsk department (BAMtour) has the most experience with foreigners. This organisation should not be confused with the private company BAMtourist. Tourism Department, BAM, ul Krasnaya Presnya 47, ☎ 2-17-16, fax 23-329, telex 154215 DWC SU, The director is Lyudmila Yurevna Feninets (Отдел Туризма, ул. Красная Пресня 47, Директор Людмила Юрьевна Фенинец).

Tynda – Novy Urgal
Тында - Новый Ургал

Tynda (Тында)   2,364km
For information on Tynda, see the *Tynda* section in this chapter.

Bestuzheva (Бестужева)   2,391km

The station is named after a famous Decembrist family which saw all 3 sons participate in the anti-Tsar uprising on 14 December 1865. The St Petersburg uprising demanded a constitutional monarch rather than an omnipowerful Tsar. All 3 brothers were sentenced to death, which was later commuted to exile in Siberia. The first was Mikhail Aleksandrovich, a captain in the Moscow Imperial Guards Regiment, who led his regiment into Senate Square in St Petersburg and lined the soldiers up in front of the pro-government troops. He gave the command to open fire at the opposing forces and after his troops were routed by cannon fire, he tried unsuccessfully to rally them to storm Peter and Paul Fortress. His commuted sentence was 20 years in the Siberian city of Chita. The second brother was Nikolai Aleksandrovich, a lieutenant commander in the Naval Guards, who like his brother also led his troops into Senate Square in St Petersburg. He was sentenced to 20 years in the Siberian Nerchinsk mines. The last one was Aleksandr Aleksandrovich, a writer, who was exiled to Yakutia for his anti-Tsar writings and public meetings.

Accommodation can be organised at the Recreation Base, ☎ 38-83 (Бестужева База Отдыха). Just after you depart Bestuzheva, the line divides into the AYAM for Berkakit, Aldan and Yakutsk in the north and the BAM for Komsomolsk in the east.

Marevaya (Маревая)   2,452km

This moderate sized settlement was built by the Moscow Region BAM Construction company (ПодмосковскийБАМстрой). It has a North Korean logging camp nearby. Accommodation can be organised at the Railway Hostel, ☎ 2-71 (Общежитие).

Unakha (Унаха)   2,511km

There is another North Korean logging camp near this settlement.

Dipkun (Дипкун)   2,527km

This moderate sized settlement was built by the Moscow Region BAM Construction company (ПодмосковскийБАМстрой). Accommodation can be organised at the Railway Hostel (Общежитие).

Dess (Десс)   2,541km

This town derives its name from the Dess River, which eventually flows into the Zeya Reservoir.

Moskovski Komsomolets (Московский Комсомолец)

The station gets it name from Moscow's young communists who supposedly built it.

Tutaul (Тутаул)

This moderate sized settlement was built by the Moscow Region BAM Construction company (ПодмосковскийБАМстрой). It has a North Korean logging camp nearby. Accommodation can be organised at the Locomotive Brigade Hostel, ☎ 2-22 (Дом Отдыха Локомотивой Бригады).

Ulak (Улак)

This station is on the west bank of the Zeya Reservoir. 6km away is Gorni village, which has a population of 1,500, and the airport which services Verkhnezeisk.

Verkhnezeisk (Верхнезейск)   2,707km

Verkhnezeisk is a typical small BAM town and its averageness is what makes it worth spending 2 days here. It is large enough to have all of the aspects typical of BAM towns including a temporary settlement, shattered plans and isolation, yet small enough to be able to see everything and meet a range of people, which provides an insight into life in a rural town. Most importantly, its mayor, Vladimir Ivanovich Natresenyuk, is very happy to introduce you to all aspects of the town.

Verkhnezeisk is the name of the station while the town is called Zeisk. The name comes from the Zeya River which in Evenki means the blade of a knife, due to its narrow, fast flow as it cuts through the *taiga*. The town was hacked out of virgin *taiga* on the flat, marshy Verkhnezeskaya Plain (Верхнезейская Равнина). In the early 1970s when the BAM was being planned, it was stated that the town would be a major railway headquarters looking after a large section of the BAM. A town of 15,000 was planned with schools for 6,000 children, cinema, pool, maternity hospital and a large civic centre. However only the schools were built before the plans were changed and Zeisk became just a railway settlement. Consequently, like most other BAM towns, Zeisk has a large number of half built structures with large spaces between them in anticipation of future buildings.

When the wind blows in summer, dust swirls create a impression of a ghost town with the small number of people dwarfed by the scattered 5 storey accommodation blocks. This feeling is compounded by the lack of street names as the administration has held off naming them for over 15 years because they were waiting for decisions about the town's future. The inhabitants are also aware that they are under siege from the *taiga* and will tell you with great relish the story of a 17 year old who was eaten by a bear just 15km away in 1993.

The down sizing of the town was an enormous disappointment to the inhabitants who had given up everything to move here. In addition, the number of trains has been reduced to 2 passenger trains and 18 freight trains a day which has compounded the feeling of isolation. The town also lacks the typical Russian network of grandparents and relatives essential to compensate for the lack of child minding and other social services. The vast majority of inhabitants are young couples and there is only one *Great Patriotic War* veteran in town.

The town was sponsored by Ufa, which is in central Russia near the Kazakhstan border. The town's Central Asian inhabitants are not the original builders but people who have recently fled the ethnic problems in Central Asia and southern Russia. These people are welcomed by Zeisk's inhabitants as they increase the population and as everyone is an immigrant, there are no ethnic tensions as found in many established Russian towns.

One of the glimmers of hope for the town is the northern coal deposits at Elgynscoye in the Republic of Sakha. To mine the coal, a 320km railway line will have to be built from Zeisk, and the numerous foreign delegations have examined this possibility.

Verkhnizeisk was planned to be a small city but instead is a small town with shattered dreams.

Verknezeisk (Верхнезейск)

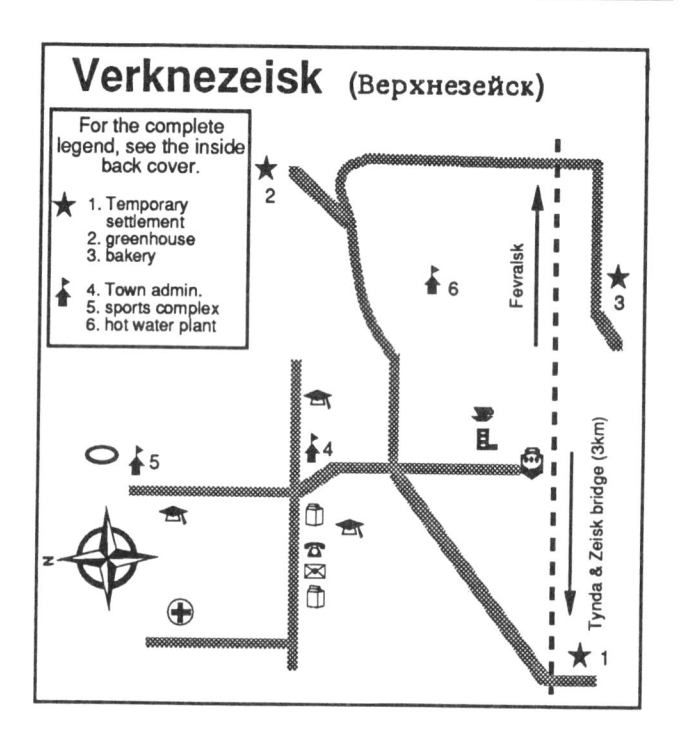

For the complete legend, see the inside back cover.

1. Temporary settlement
2. greenhouse
3. bakery
4. Town admin.
5. sports complex
6. hot water plant

Getting there and away

There is one daily train from the east, Tynda (8:50 hours) and one from the west, Fevralsk (9 hours), Novy Urgal (18 hours) and Komsomolsk (35 hours). There is also a daily local train running to the west as far as Dipkun (7 hours) departing at 07:30 and returning at 17:00 and one running to the east to Dugda (7 hours).

Flights arrive from Zeya and Blagoveshchensk at the Gorni airport on the other side of the Zeya Reservoir. To get there, walk across the Zeya Reservoir bridge or catch the local train to Ulak (Улак) and then walk 6km to Gorni village and airport.

From January to early April, it is possible to drive over the frozen Zeya Reservoir. It takes 3 hours to drive to Zeya. In summer, to drive to Zeya requires a long detour. You must drive 89km to Ogoron on the BAM then south to Zeya. The 8 hour trip is all on dirt roads.

Previously there was a regular hydrofoil which plied between Zeya and Zeisk. However under the government's user pays principle, the hydrofoil became more expensive than the plane and so was discontinued.

Where to stay
The only accommodation in town is the Locomotive Brigade Hostel just in front of the station. It has 25 rooms with 2, 3 and 4 beds per room and costs between $5 and $7 a bed, ☎ 2-14 (Дом Отдыха Локомотивой Бригады).

About 4km out of town is the old holiday camp, Nods. The camp is on the reservoir's shore and can accommodate 40 people. It has been closed but can be reopened for groups.

Where to eat
The only canteen in town is at the Locomotive Brigade Hostel.

What to see
The following description of the town's features is included not because they are unusual but because they are common to almost every BAM town. Their detailed description allows you to see and understand the reality of life in the BAM zone as you wander around the town.

Schools: There is one school and two kindergartens in town. These were built in anticipation of 6,000 students but today there are only 580. Typical of all of them is the multistorey Kindergarten №58. While the building is impressive, the equipment is limited due to a cut back in funds for schools. For a tour of the schools, contact Annya Forevnya Peshkovo, Middle School no 47, ☎ 2-81 (Ання Горьевня Пешковой, средная школа).

Temporary settlement: All BAM towns consist of a permanent and a temporary settlement. The temporary settlement is for the constructors of the permanent town and railway, and is normally a collection of ramshackle wooden buildings which are torn down when the work is completed. However in many BAM towns, the shortage of accommodation in the permanent settlement means that many people live in the temporary settlement. Zeisk is unusual in that demand for housing was less than expected and only 12 families out of the original 2,000 temporary settlement inhabitants remain in the temporary settlement. When most of the work was finished in 1988, constructors took everything that was portable including phones, the cinema and even the pool. Today, the temporary settlement is a sad collection of a few houses surrounded by collapsed and destroyed buildings, connected by dirt roads which look as if they haven't been graded since 1988.

THE MAYOR OF ZEISK

The Mayor of Zeisk, Vladimir Ivanovich Natresenyuk, is unusual. He is not an old party official only interested in power but just an ordinary man who really takes an interest in his town. The job is one with few privileges and perks and he even admits that he has a "position of power with no power". Power in a BAM town is divided between the railway and the civic authorities. However as the railway invariably owns all facilities including schools, hospitals, shops, houses and hotels, there is very little left for the civic authorities to manage. Therefore the mayor's main responsibilities are social services such as pensions, unemployment benefits and housing.

Housing is one of the biggest problems and even Vladimir Ivanovich does not have a flat in the town. The last mayor privatised the mayor's flat and bought it for himself. Consequently Vladimir Ivanovich lives on the outskirts of town in a wooden house.

Although 30 people are officially unemployed, he believes that there will be more jobless in the future. "I am trying to help but there are no jobs".

Vladimir Ivanovich's main job is simply talking to everyone, finding out what problems everyone has, helping with solutions and keeping everyone informed. In many ways a thankless task but one that he believes will develop a community spirit. As you drive around with Vladimir Ivanovich pointing to the vacant spaces where the pool, sporting complex and more apartment blocks should be, he speaks of everyone's resentment with Gorbachev's *perestroika* and Yeltsin's economic reform. "This has resulted in a lower standard of living for all. We are sick of talk and what we need is government help now!" Vladimir Ivanovich Natresenyuk, Mayor, 676239, Amurskaya Oblast, Zeisk *Raion*, Verkhnezeisk, ☎ 4-50, 4-36 (rail) (Владимир Иванович Натрасенюк, Администратор поселка, 676239, Амурская Область, ст. Верхнезейск).

Vladimir Ivanovich and his constituents holidaying on the nearby Zeya Reservoir's sandy beach.

SMP Construction Unit: Every reasonably sized BAM town has at least one construction unit called an SMP. These units construct railway buildings and lines. SMP 706 is based in Zeisk and while theoretically, it has 400 workers, lack of work and pay has meant that most of these workers have left or have another job.

Bakery: Bakeries are absolutely essential in every town as bread is the central element in a Russian meal. The Zeisk bakery is run by one woman who makes 300 loaves a day. The ovens are wood fired and while wood is delivered, she must chop it up. Occasionally there are bread shortages due to lack of ingredients but these are rare. The bakery's smell and bread making process make visiting here a must.

Greenhouse: The short 94 day growing season means that greenhouses are essential for all but the quickest growing plants. Zeisk has a typical commercial greenhouse which was built by the SMP to supply their workers' needs. The 40m long green house is heated to 28°C by a line from the city's central hot water circulation pipes and lit by electricity. However even with these, it is only practical to grown plants until mid October. The greenhouse is now run by one person who is having difficulty making it profitable with the recent substantial price rises for hot water and electricity.

Central heating plant: All hot water in the town is provided by the central heating plant powered by coal. The water is distributed by above ground pipes which should be covered with insulation and a protective metal skin. However insulation often falls off the pipes and is not replaced, resulting in a horrendous loss of energy in winter. The plant is worth visiting to appreciate the decrepit system.

Hospital: The town's medical complex consists of a polyclinic and a 100 bed hospital. These facilities lack a maternity ward which is surprising considering that most of the town's families are of child bearing age. Mothers normally deliver in the Tynda maternity hospital. A tour of the hospital provides a disturbing insight into the failing Russian medical services.

Commercial complex: The town's shopping complex is quite small with a bank, post office, food and clothing shops. They are all located in one area to minimise shopper's exposure to the winter temperatures.

What is in the region
The Zeya bridge over the Zeya Reservoir is the second longest bridge on the BAM. It is 1,100m long, stands 50m above the water and it took the

Private Enterprise Still Struggling in Siberia

In post-communist rural Russia, the introduction of self-employment, free markets and capitalism still have a long way to go. While goods trading and money market speculation may be accepted by the government, there is still a great deal of official resistance to private ventures in agriculture, manufacturing and professional services.

Victor P Sulitski is typical of the unconnected Russian who is struggling to run a business with his own hands. Victor was a naval dentist for years and would like to set up a private practice in Zeisk. However the government maintains a monopoly on dentistry and it is a criminal offence for dentists to work outside the government. So Victor established the first commercial fishing company on the Zeya Reservoir. He purchased licences for 50 nets along a 40km stretch and, with his 4 employees, catches a ton of fish a week. Despite the long hours and good catches, he is not making a good wage as the only purchaser is the state which pays him considerably below the market price. Life is very rough for Victor and his workers as during the fishing season they live under a canvas sheet on the fly invested shores of the lake. During winter, Victor lives by himself in an airless, underground shelter with a built in stove providing the only heat. From here he hunts bears and deer. Despite the long hours of arduous work and the short amount of time he spends with his wife in Zeisk, he is proud of his independence and would not return to a stifling state job. (Виктор П Сулицкий, Верхнезейск, ул. таежная 1).

Victor P Sulitski with his lunch of bread, *salo* and vodka. The western edge of the Zeya Reservoir used to be swamps but nowadays is a vast mat of trees, branches and twigs that are continually being washed up from the submerged forest.

Leningrad Bridge Building Company (Ленинградмостстрой) 9 years to build it. Because of its significance, it is guarded by a platoon of 30 soldiers. To walk across it or even to take photos of it is not possible without a pass from the guard's commanding officer.

On the north shore of the reservoir is the old Evenki village of Bomnak (Бомнак). About 120 families live here. When the reservoir was flooded, the village only lost one street. Buried here is G Fedoseev, the author of children's socialist heroic books including *By the Path of Experience* and *Pashka: From the Bear Ravine*. While there is a dirt road from Gorni to Bomnak, it is quicker to reach the village by boat across the 35km between Zeisk and Bomnak.

47km to the east of Bomnak on the Tok River is an old landing strip for American WWII Lend Lease aircraft. Planes landed here from the US and were refuelled before heading onwards to the war front.

Most of the railway line between Tynda and Komsomolsk was built by military railway troops. 4,000 of these soldiers were based around Zeisk providing timber and construction earthworks until they left in 1990. A number of their camps can still be found. One camp is on the outskirts of Zeisk, halfway between the temporary settlement and the bakery. Guard towers, barbed wire fences, demolished buildings and a statue to the construction achievements of soldiers can still be seen.

A much larger camp is the Forestry Battalion camp which cut timber from 1981 to 1988. The camp is spread over several square kilometres and a number of buildings still stand. There is also an enormous supply of wood just lying around. To get to the camp, you travel for about 1 hour towards Ogoron before turning off to the left on a track and go over the rails just before the graves of two railwaymen on the left embankment of the railway. This track leads for about 20 minutes until you reach the raised barrier of the camp's entrance.

Fishing is one of the highlights of the region. A large variety of fish can be caught including *shuka, som, taimen, shevak, kharius, lenok* and the rare *kasatka* (Касатка). Fishermen from as far away as Tynda come to the lake and spend a weekend fishing and camping before returning home with the month's fish. The most popular stop is the unmarked siding of Apetenolk (Апатенолк), 30 minutes from Zeisk.

Zeya Dam

The Zeya River was dammed with 115m high walls in 1972 to become the largest hydro-electric station in Eastern Siberia in 1975. The station provides power for both the Trans-Siberian which is 120km away and Tynda which is 300km away on the BAM. The other advantage of the dam is to regulate the downstream flow of the Zeya before it runs into the Amur. This stopped flooding, increased the area available for agriculture and enabled ships to travel up to Zeya more regularly. The

Zeya Reservoir is peculiar as it fills up during summer, not spring.

The filling of the dam did not have the human consequences of the Bratsk damming as the area was sparsely populated. The dam only drowned a children's camp and the gold mining village of Khvony (Хвойный). Khvony has since been rebuilt on a new site. The flooding was done without clearing the trees in the area which means that all the timber was wasted and boating is dangerous today as the trees are often just below the surface. The other towns on the reservoir are Snezhnogorski (Снежногорский) and Beregovo (Береговой), both of which are logging communities.

✕ Apetenolk (Апетенолк)   2,723km

From Verkhnezeisk you pass through the flat Verkhnezeskaya Plain (Верхнезейская Равнина) which contains numerous creeks and rivers flowing into the Zeya Reservoir. The unmarked siding of Apetenolk (Апатенолк) is the most popular stop for fishermen and is

The vertical tubes are designed to keep the ground frozen all year round which prevents it from subsiding. The tubes are filled with kerosene and penetrate several metres into the earth. As the kerosene absorbs heat from the ground, it vaporises and rises to the above ground part of the tube. The tube gives off heat which condenses the kerosene and the fluid then drips to the bottom of the tube where the process is repeated. While these tubes are effective, they are also very polluting as after a few years, they start leaking kerosene into the ground.

about 30 minutes from Zeisk. The stop is about 300m from the water's edge and fishermen then walk around the lake to their favourite spots. Along this stretch of the line you will see numerous kerosene tubes.

Ogoron (Огорон) 2,796km

The town was sponsored by Ulenovsk on the Volga River. There are considerable gas reserves between Ogoron and Verkhnezeisk but they are uneconomical to extract. After leaving the town, the train starts its long ascent over the Soktakhan and Dzhagdy Mountain Ranges (Хребети Соктахан и Джагды).

Moldavski (Молдавский) 2,820km

The station is named after Moldova from where its constructors came.

Miroshnechenko (Мирошниченко) 2,850km

Miroshnichenko was a hero of the civil war who single-handedly defended a bridge. There is a bust of Miroshnichenko at Fevralsk station. On 29 April 1984, the eastern section of the BAM was joined at this station.

The Tungala station is an excellent example of 1970s style architecture coupled with good permafrost design principles. The piers insulate the building from the ground which prevents the ground under the building from melting and subsiding.

Tungala (Тунгала)   2,863km
This is an usual looking station built on piers due to the permafrost. The town was sponsored by Novosibirsk.

Dugda (Дугда)   2,912km
This moderate sized settlement was built by the Moldovian BAM Construction company (МолдоваБАМстрой). This is the terminus of local trains which run to the east and west. Accommodation can be organised at the Railway Hostel (Общежитие).

Nora (Нора)
This station is named after the Nora River, a 305km tributary of the Selemdzha River.

Fevralsk (Февральск)   3,033km
Fevralsk is not the most attractive town but it offers several interesting side trips to unusual parts of the BAM Zone. The BAM town of 12,000 people had a difficult birth, as its site was badly chosen. It is located in a swamp on permafrost while solid ground is located just a few kilometres away. Consequently, in its early years the sewerage system collapsed, masonry became dangerously cracked and foundations sank. Today the town looks much older than its 20 odd years.

The town was mainly built by railway troops although the Moldovians sponsored it. In the early 1990s there were about 3,000 soldiers based around the town and the last left in July 1994. Despite their lasting legacy, including the 350 bed hospital, a hotel on the banks of the Selemdzha River and the partly built railway line to Ogodzha, there are no monuments in town to their work.

The monument on the station's platform is to the Russian Civil War hero, Miroshnechenko.

Trains normally stop at Fevralsk for 40 minutes which is long enough to dash the 500m from the station to the market on the outskirts of the town. For those less inclined to risk the trip, you can always go upstairs to the canteen in the station.

Getting there and away
There is one daily long distance train from the east, Tynda (18 hours) and one from the west, Novy Urgal (9 hours) and Komsomolsk (23 hours). There is also a daily local train running west to Dugda (Дугда) (5 hours) and one running east to Etyrken (Этыркен) (4 hours).

To the north, buses run on even days of the month to Ekimchan, departing at 15:45. To the south, buses run on odd days of the month to Svobodni (4 hours), Belgorsk (6 hours) and Blagovshchensk (8 hours). The 304km highway linking Fevralsk with Svobodni and Belgorsk on the Trans-Siberian Railway is one of only two paved roads in the BAM Zone. To the east, buses run on even days of the month to Novy Urgal departing at 7:30. These buses leave from the train station.

There are regular flights to Blagovshchensk, Svobodni and Ekimchan. Buses run 7 times a day to the airport which is 4km from Fevralsk.

Where to stay
A hotel is located in the station building. Its entrance is at the western end of the station. It has 10 standard rooms and one luxury room all of which are quite noisy, ☎ 22-90.

The best hotel is at the Rodina gold base. The hotel is part of the company's complex which includes the administration and equipment compounds. As well as having an excellent *banya*, it is an interesting place to stay as you gain an insight into the operations of a Russian gold mining company. Unfortunately it is a 20 minute drive out of town. Rodina Company, ☎ 31-126, 31-228.

Nearby the Rodina gold base is the old Railway Troops Officers' hotel. This has recently been renovated and is scenically located on the banks of the Selemdzha River. It is even more isolated than Rodina.

Another option for groups is the Byssa *Pioneer* Camp. This camp is located on the shore of the Byssa River (р. Бысса), about 4km from Fevralsk.

Where to eat
The canteen upstairs at the station always seems to be well stocked. The canteen is called Пenza (Пенза) and is named after the builders who came from this town about 400km from Moscow. There is also a Chinese/Russian restaurant in town.

What to see
The highlight of the town is the city baths which indicates Fevralsk's limited sightseeing possibilities! The *banya* consists of a municipal one on the ground floor and a private one upstairs. The contrast between the two in terms of facilities reveals that the town's power brokers live a good life. Asterid, the company that owns it, also has considerable commercial interests in the town and region. It is owned by the young entrepreneur Igor Yurevich Solomanov (Игорь Юрьевич Соломанов) ☎ 23-36.

6km away from Fevralsk is the 200 year old settlement of Fevralskoe. This community of only about 40 houses contains traditional Russian houses surrounded by the river and trees and is a refreshing contrast to Fevralsk's concrete apartment blocks surrounded by a wasteland.

If you are interested in the area's history, talk with the local historian, Galina Yakova, ul Ayanskaya 2a, kv25, ☎ 33-71 (rail) (Галина Якова, ул. Аянская 2а, кв 25).

Getting assistance
There are no tourist organisations in this town but the following 2 officials are useful contacts: Evgeni Nikolaevich Volga, Chief of Administration, ☎ 22-53, 32-62 (rail) (Евгений Николаевич Волга, Главный Администратор, п. Февральск). B N Bocharnkov, Deputy Chief of the Urgal Railway Department, Fevralsk Railway Station, ☎ 33-01 work (rail), 32-05 home (rail) (Б Н Бочарников, Зам. Начальника Ургальского отдела БАМж-д, ст. Февральск).

What is in the region
Rafting down the Selemdzha River (р. Селемджа) is a popular summer sport. The 647km long Selemdzha starts in the mountains to the north, flows past Ekimchan, Fevralsk, Svobodni and Blagoveshchensk before running into the Amur. The river is navigable from the Amur to the village of Norsk (Норск) which is 129km from Fevralsk, and occasionally as far as Ekimchan during highwater. Before the BAM was built, the Selemdzha was identified as a river of enormous recreational value. However the mining of railway ballast on its banks and upstream gold dredging of its tributaries has severely damaged the quality of the river. With a reduction in industrial activity and the settling of disturbed sediments, the river is slowly returning to normal. Rafting from Fevralsk to Svobodni takes a leisurely 3 days.

60km south of Fevralsk on the road to Svobodni is a famous sanatorium in the village of Byssa (Бысса). The sanatorium is based around a 42°C radon hot water spring and claims to be able to relieve arthritis and rheumatism. It can accommodate 50 people and was built by the Fevralsk gas production plant.

Future railway to Ogodzha
A railway line is currently being built to the coal rich region around the town of Ogodzha (Огод)а). The region contains a massive 131 million tons of coal. Ogodzha is 144km north of Fevralsk and when the line is finished, it will include 5 stations. By the beginning of 1995, only 23km of roadbed and 20km of rails had been laid by the railway troops who were building it. At the current rate it will take about 5 years to complete. The word Ogodzha means a 'sunny and warm valley' in Evenki.

Exploration of the Selemdzha Valley

The Selemdzha valley is a very beautiful and old area with several indigenous and ancient Russian villages. The most interesting route is a 600km loop starting in Fevralsk, through Stoiba, Ekimchan and Sofisk, and finishing in the BAM town of Novy Urgal. If you do travel the loop, you pass over the border into the Khabarovsk *Krai* before you reach the gold mining town of Sofisk (Софийск). There are regular buses from here through Ust-Umalta (Усть-Умальта) to Novy Urgal. However although Russian maps show that there is a road connecting Ekimchan and Sofisk, in reality this is little more than a dirt track. Scheduled buses run along the entire route except for this section and if you wish to travel it, you should hire a 4 wheel drive or try your luck at grabbing a rare lift.

The roads are better than most in rural Siberia as the gold mines pay for regular grading which reduces the repair costs for their large fleet of vehicles. If you are travelling between June and August, make sure you take mosquito repellent as the mosquitos are big enough to carry you off.

If you have limited time, the best and easiest trip is to Ekimchan. This 212km route takes 6 hours by car and you should stay overnight before returning the next day. The trip starts by taking you over the new railway line to Ogodzha, through the village of Fevralskoe to the Selemdzha River. A 24 hour car ferry takes your vehicle across the river

The 24 hour a day ferry which carries you across the Selemdzha River.

for $2.00.

The first village you pass through is Selemdzhinsk (Силемджинск) and the next is the ancient gold mining town of Stoiba (Стойба). This is about halfway to Ekimchan and it is a nice place for a picnic lunch on the banks of Selemdzha. The descendants of Volga Germans can be found here and in other nearby towns as they settled here during the 1800s colonisation of Siberia and in the 1930s when Stalin exiled them to Siberia.

A further 2 hours of driving will bring you to the area currently being dredged by giant 1940s-era dredges. The machines crawl along the rivers scooping up all the rock pebbles and water and mechanically shifting it. Any alluvial gold falls into a tray and the water and waste rock is flung out the back of the machine. The area laid waste by the machines remains scarred for decades as there is no rehabilitation process after dredging. The area has three dredges which work for 6 months of the year before the rivers freeze. Coming across them at night is quite surrealistic as the machines appear to be giant monoliths devouring all with spot lights like eyes looking for food. This region produces 26% of the gold in Amurskaya *Oblast*.

The next major town is Ekimchan (Экимчан) which is the regional headquarters of the Selemdzhski *Raion* (Селемджинский район). This is a small town which feels as if the twentieth century passed it by. Most of the buildings are wood, the streets are dirt broken up with patches of asphalt and the pavements are covered with wood. The town was founded in 1887 as a gold mining community and gets its name from the Evenki word for *older sibling*. It has a 16 person hotel. Contact the regional administrator, Sergei Nikolaevich Levanov, ☎ 21-311 (Сергей Николаевич Леванов, Главный Администратор, п. Экимчан). He has a fax but it is not connected as no-one can read the machine's Japanese instructions.

Tokur (Токур)

This town is more interesting to stay in than Ekimchan which is 12km away. Tokur is the commercial hub of the region even though it is a smaller town than Ekimchan and only founded in 1939. It is the headquarters of the company Olimp, and the Selemdzhinski gold mine. 3,000 people live in the town or work for these companies.

There are two hotels in town. One is the small, all-suite hotel in the administration block of Olimp and the other is the 21 room local hotel, 676561, Tokur, ul Sovetskaya 2, ☎ 22-524 (Амурская область, 676561, п. Токур, ул. Советская 2).

The best place to eat is at the excellent 5 table restaurant and bar owned by Olimp.

Feudal Capitalism

Tokur is a microcosm of the power shift occurring throughout Russian cities and towns.

In the past, Moscow-controlled massive industrial enterprises dominated the economic life of an area through their factories, farms, bakeries, hospitals, schools, telephone systems etc. The state, through the Communist Party, dominated local government and it often provided similar infrastructure for those not working for the enterprises.

Nowadays, with the disappearance of control from Moscow and the Communist Party, local private organisations have tried to fill the void. Unlike the old system, the new power blocks are locally controlled and much more reactive to the market. Rather than competing against each other, the power blocks respect each other's spheres of influence and often work cooperatively by dividing up the market.

Frequently, there are only one or two organisations in small towns along the BAM and each is like a feudal empire with staff personally loyal to their lord. Despite popular media coverage, these leaders are not always lazy ex-communist party hacks. Old boy political connections will only get you so far and building up a dynamic organisation requires business acumen and hard work. Nikolai Malik, the head of Tokur's dominant company, Olimp, is typical of the true entrepreneurs that Russia should be proud of.

Olimp's primary activity is distribution of goods. The company is blessed with many gold miners with high disposable income and very little to spend it on. Olimp buys in bulk imported confectionary, clothes and white goods, as well as supplying staples. Nikolai has expanded his work to such activities as importing fresh fish. In the past, the only fish available in the region's shops were frozen fish from the Pacific Ocean supplied by the state several months after it was caught. Seeing the demand for fresh fish, Nikolai hired planes to fly to the fishing villages and buy it as soon as it is brought on shore. With a fleet of trucks, he supplies fish and other goods to his shops and others in the region.

What makes Nikolai different from the vast majority of Russian businessmen who are simply traders is that he is investing in local production. In 1994 he purchased Tokur's bakery and has expanded it to produce a range of breads and cakes which the previously state owned bakery could never do.

Expanding into brewing beer was Nikolai's biggest investment. Establishing the brewery in 1995 cost $250,000 which included bringing Moscow technicians to Tokur to assemble the 40 tons of equipment. The plant now produces 63,000 litres per month for the region.

As well as distribution, Olimp has expanded into restaurants in Tokur, Ekimchan and Fevralsk.

Nikolai sees enormous opportunities in converting the region's timber wealth into furniture and semi-processed building materials. "Most companies simply try to export the timber which does not lead to many jobs nor help the Russian economy", he said. "If we can find a western company who could supply the technology, we would produce the wood products and benefit everyone." With so many successes already, Nikolai's ideas are destined to become reality sooner or later. Nikolai Malik, General Director, Olimp, Amurskaya *Oblast*, 676561, Tokur (Николай Малик, Генеральный Директор, Фирма Олимп, Амурская область, 676561, Токур).

Two interesting half day trips from here are to visit the Selemdzhinski Gold Mine and the Air Navigation Locator Station.

Selemdzhinski Gold Mine (Прииск селемджинский)
The Selemdzhinski gold mine was established in 1939 and since then, it has extracted 30 tons of gold from its 200km of tunnels. In its best year, it produced 1.5 tons, however today its 200 workers produce substantially less. The mine was a state company until it was privatised in December 1993. It is now 51% owned by shareholders.

Current production is being held back by a lack of investment and technology. The mine needs a refinery which extracts gold from the crushed rock. Otherwise, the ore has to be trucked to the BAM and then shipped to a refinery. This is how production has always been done but with the increase in the cost of freight and low extraction rates typical in Russian refineries, it is now not economical. Older refineries using mercury only extract about 60% of the gold, while the newer process using zinc and chlorine still only extracts 80%. So until a refinery incorporating foreign technology which can extract up to 99% of gold is built, the mined ore is piling up waiting to be processed.

A tour of the mine and its numerous tunnels is very interesting and make sure you visit the communist lecture theatre in the administration block. Contact Valentin Dovgaenko or Sergei Abramovich, Selemdzhinski Gold Mine, Amurskaya *Oblast*, 676561, Tokur (Валентин Довгаенко, Сергей Абрамович, Прииск селемджинский, Амурская Область, 676561, Токур).

Air Navigation Locator Station
On a nearby hill is an Air Navigation Locator Station. The station monitors and controls airspace within a 350km radius which covers the major Japan to Moscow flight path. Life here is extremely hard for the 20 technicians and air traffic controllers not only due to the isolated and harsh conditions on top of a mountain, but also because in 1994, their pay was up to 5 months late. With the arrival of the BAM, they were told that the station would move to Fevralsk in 1985. A decade later, they are still being told that there is no money for the move, despite the fact that their government organisation, AERO, receives about $150 million a year in fees for foreign airlines to fly over Russia.

The staff of the station are pleased to show anyone around and it takes about 30 minutes to reach from Tokur.

Zlatoustovsk (Златоустовск)
This town is 55km from Ekimchan and just before you reach it you come across the Evenk village of Ivanovskoe (Ивановское).

🏠 Zvonkov (Звонков)

This station is named after Vasili Vasilevich Zvonkov (1891-1965), a transport scientist. Vasili Vasilevich graduated from the Moscow Institute of Railroad Communication Engineers in 1917. During his career he taught at the Leningrad Institute of Waterway Transportation and the Military Transport Academy. From 1955 to 1965, he was deputy director of the Institute for Problems of Integrated Transport Systems of the Academy of Sciences. He was awarded the Order of Lenin, four other orders and numerous medals. He is unusual in that he only became a member of the Communist Party of the USSR late in his life in 1951.

🏠 Demchenko (Демченко)

This station was named after the Soviet hero, Maria Sofronovna Demchenko, who became famous for her exploits in the 1930s in harvesting a massive 24 tons of sugar beet per hectare. Such devotion to duty earned her an Order of Lenin.

🏠 Ulma (Ульма)

This station gets its named from the Ulma River which flows into the Selemdzha River.

After leaving Ulma, you pass the border of Amur *Oblast* and Khabarovsk *Krai*. Marking the border is a large monument to the military constructors who built most of the eastern section of the BAM. It looks like a giant "X" and is about 40km west of Ekyrken. The border also marks a time zone border. To the east in the Khabarovsk *Krai*, the time difference is 7 hours from Moscow while in western Amur *Oblast*, there is a 6 hour difference.

🏠 Etyrken (Этыркэн)   3,179

Accommodation can be organised at the Railway Hostel (Общежитие). After leaving Ekyrken, you ascend again as you pass through the Turana Range (Хребет Турана).

🏠 Alonka (Алонка)   3,264km

This medium sized town was built by the Moldovians. There are plans to dam the Bureya River (р. Бурея) in a narrow canyon near its junction with the Niman (р. Ниман). If this proceeds, Alonka will grow into a town of about 25,000.

🏠 Bureinski (Буреинский)   3,305km

This village is on the Bureya River (р. Бурея) near the ancient village of Ust-Urgal (Усть-Ургал).

> **LEARNING FROM NEAR DISASTER**
> Working in the *taiga* is dangerous, particularly in the spring thaw. In 1978, 6 railway builders were working in a quarry on a sand bar in the Bureya River, producing gravel for the rail bed. Suddenly the narrow riverbed turned into a violent torrent which prevented escape to the river bank. The water was rising rapidly so they took refuge on top of their truck. Uprooted trees and huge logs hurtled by, and it would have taken only one impact before the truck was overturned. After waiting a terrified night, they were rescued at dawn the next day. The experts learnt from their mistakes and decided to widen the network of automatic meteorological radio stations all along the eastern section of the BAM. These automatic meteorological stations, which are equipped with radio isotope generators that operate continuously for ten years, collect weather data and automatically transmit this information eight times a day to the Khabarovsk Metrological Centre. This information is processed and supplied daily to the surveyors and builders on the BAM.

Novy Urgal – Komsomolsk
Новый Ургал - Комсомольск

Novy Urgal (Новый Ургал) 3,315km
682071, Khabarovsk Krai, Verkhnebureinski Raion, Novy Urgal
(682071, Хабаровский Край, Верхнебуреинский район,
п. Новый Ургал)

Novy Urgal was founded in December 1974 when the first Ukrainian BAM builders arrived and is the headquarters of the eastern third of the BAM. Novy Urgal was sponsored by the Ukraine and many of its streets honour the builders with names such as Donbas, Kharkov, Carpathia, Dnieper and Kiev. An attempt has been made to incorporate traditional Ukrainian decoration into the multi-storey concrete buildings and the result is a chequered line along the top of the buildings.

Novy Urgal has a population of 14,000.

Getting there and away
There is one daily long distance train from the east, Tynda (27:00 hours), Fevralsk (9 hours), and one from the west, Postyshevo (7:50 hours), Komsomolsk (13 hours). There is also a daily local train running eastwards to Gerbi (Герби) (4 hours) and one running westward to Etyrken (Этыркен) (5:30 hours).

There is also a daily train south connecting with Izvestkovaya (Известковая) (12 hours) on the Trans-Siberian. A carriage of this train then joins a train to Khabarovsk (18 hours). There is a daily local train on this line which stops halfway to Izvestkovaya at Tyrma (Тырма) (5:45 hours). There are two daily local trains which run between Novy Urgal and its sister city, Chegdomyn, which is 17km away. Buses run 5 times a day between Novy Urgal and Chegdomyn.

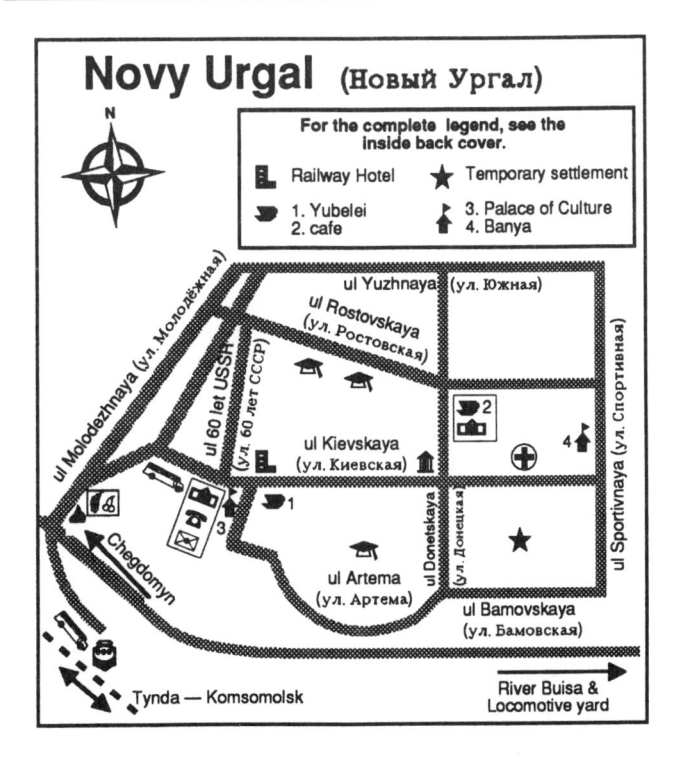

The regional airport is located at Chegdomyn and flights arrive from Tynda and Khabarovsk.

The road to Komsomolsk along the BAM is only drivable in winter, when it takes 16 hours.

Where to stay
The only hotel in town is the NGCh Railway hotel, ul Kievskaya 3. It has 8 hotel rooms with facilities and three floors of hostel accommodation, ☎ 64-06, manager Ekaterina Borisovna Prokopenko (Екатерина Борисовна Прокопенко, НГЧ Гостиница, ул. Киевская 3).

Where to eat
Novy Urgal is blessed with one of the best restaurants on the BAM, called Yubeleni (Юбелени). It is a canteen in the daytime and a restaurant at night. The manager takes a great deal of pleasure in his guests and will gladly prepare picnic lunches or food to your taste. Highly recommended.

What to see
The town has a BAM museum managed by the speed talker, Lyudmila Alexandrovna. BAM Museum, ul Kievskaya 7, 4th floor, ☎ 63-74 (Музей БАМа, ул. Киевская 7, Этаж 4, Людмила Александровна).

The market is on the eastern side of town in a pavilion which looks like a Chinese temple. It is actually North Korean and was given to the town as a sign of gratitude for allowing the North Koreans to work in the area.

To the north of the station are the railway yards. On the road to the yards are old steam train engine boilers which are used to supply hot water to the local villages. There is even one of these recycled locomotives providing steam in the railway yards.

The 2 bridges over the Bureya River are an impressive sight. In

A picnic at the popular dacha village on the banks of the Bureya River. The garages contain boats and farming tools.

BAM construction history, the bridges hold a special place due to the sacrifices and dedication of the railway troop builders. The wooden bridge for road traffic, was built in 1954, which was adequate for the small traffic from the only town in the area, Chegdomyn. However when it was decided to restart the BAM and build Novy Urgal, construction of a new metal bridge for rail traffic started. To get the bridge built in a hurry was a monumental task and it required working throughout the winter regardless of the temperature. Technically, soldiers and other workers are not obliged to work outdoors when the temperature falls below -45°C on windless days and -35°C when the wind is blowing. This regulation is due partly to human compassion and partly to preserving equipment as axes shatter and bulldozers rapidly fail in these sorts of temperatures.

The metal bridge was opened in record time on 22 April 1975 but on 20 July 1975, the largest flood in 300 years looked certain to wash the wooden bridge away. All along the Bureya River, villages were evacuated as the torrent washed trees and houses away. While the bridge could withstand the water, if trees got caught under it, the water pressure behind any obstacle would simply push the bridge over. As it was impossible to get within 2km of the bridge due to flooding, troops were lowered by helicopter to string a safety line across the top of it. Soldiers then stood on the bridge working to free any trees or other obstacles that got caught underneath it. The troops stood for hours in the freezing water, constantly afraid that the bridge would give way under them. It didn't and many won bravery medals that day.

The wooden bridge can be seen from the train and you will notice the enormous wooden shields around its piers which deflect trees and ice bergs. If you want to get a closer look at the bridges, you can hire a boat to take you up the Bureya River. There are dozens of boats located at the *dacha village* about 30 minutes by car from Novy Urgal.

Getting help

The company Standart is a private tin producer but also has excellent contacts and can organise specialist trips. The company's director is Nikolai Ivanovich Burov. ul Donetskaya 7, kv 9, ☎ 72-46 (home (rail)), ☎ 73-01 (work (rail)) (Стандарт, ул. Донецкая 7, кв 9, Николай Иванович Буров).

The head of the engineering section of the Novy Urgal railway department, Aleksandr Vasilevich Baranov is also well connected and can assist you in finding someone to help you. ul Donetskaya 13, kv 2,☎ 72-46 (home (rail)), ☎ 73-01 (work (rail)) (ул. Донецкая 13, кв 2, Александр Васильевич Баранов).

Chegdomyn (Чегдомын)
☎ area code: 421-70 ✉ 682080, Khabarovski Krai, Verkhnebureinski *Raion*, Chegdomyn (682080, Хабаровский Край, Верхнебуреинский район, п. Чегдомын)

Chegdomyn exists because of its coal deposits, which the indigenous Evenki knew about as the town's name means *black stone* in their language. The town is one of the oldest on the BAM as it was connected to the Trans-Siberian in the late 1940s. The line and town were built by Stalin's gulag prisoners and Japanese prisoners of war. A legacy of this is the name of the regions around the town. In a conventional Russian settlement, the satellite regions are called *microraions*. In Chegdomyn they are called Zones (Зона) which is the typical nomenclature for gulag settlements. Many other cities, such as Komsomolsk, were once also surrounded by Zones but it is a mystery why only Chegdomyn still retains this name. Chegdomyn is the administrative centre of the Upper Bureya *Raion* and is situated on the left bank of the Chegdomyn River.

Getting there and away
Trains running along the BAM do not pass through Chegdomyn as it is 17km north of the closest BAM town which is Novy Urgal. There is one daily long distance train running southwards from Chegdomyn, through Novy Urgal (32 minutes) and Izvestkovaya (Известковая) (12:30 hours) on the Trans-Siberian to Khabarovsk (18 hours). There are also two daily local trains which run between Novy Urgal and Chegdomyn.

Buses run 5 times a day between Novy Urgal and Chegdomyn. Buses also leave here for the north to Ust-Umalta (Усть-Уматьта) and Sofisk (Софийск).

The regional airport is located at Chegdomyn and flights arrive from Tynda and Khabarovsk.

Where to stay
The best hotel in town is the Bureya Hotel, with rooms starting at $16. ul Pionerskaya 1 ☎ 91-961 (гостиница Бурея, ул. пионерская 1). Another hotel is at ul Torgovaya 54 (гостиница, ул. Торговая 54).

What to see
Of all the BAM towns, this is the one where you will see the most North Koreans, wearing Chairman Mao style suits and Kim Il Sung badges on their lapels. This is because there is a North Korean consulate here. The consulate consists of barracks and administration buildings surrounded by a typical Russian 2m high concrete fence. Flanking the entrance is a large display window with colour photos revealing the 'great socialist

achievements', happy Korean life and the guiding hand of the now dead 'Great Leader" Kim Il Sung and the current leader, his son, the 'Dear Leader' Kim Jong Il. In many ways, the staged photos of waving Korean tractor drivers, smiling miners and sunbaking holiday makers are identical to those posters extolling the virtue of hardwork, communism and a spartan lifestyle during the Brezhnev's era.

The flag of the Democratic Peoples' Republic of Korea (DPRK), better known as North Korea.

Although the gate only consists of a boom bar, the guards at the front will quickly stop you from entering if you try unless you have an official reason. If you try to speak to one of the guards, invariably his partner will sprint off and return with a translator. While the translator understands Russian, he will invariably only say 'Nyet'.

Taking photos of a North Korean or of the consulate is highly risky. Your Russian guide will gleefully tell you the story of a German photographer who tried this and had his camera destroyed as a result. With each retelling, the story gets progressively more gruesome with the most outrageous version being that the photographer was set upon by a pack of chainsaw wielding Korean lumberjacks. Whatever the reality, there is some basis of truth. If you are determined to take a photo, do it from your car as you are leaving town.

What is in the region
One of the more popular places for locals is a sulphur water spring on the outskirts of town. The water continuously flows out of a pipe which is housed under a small pavilion. Everyone believes in the health benefits of the water, even the hospital which sends ambulances loaded with old milk churns to fill up with the water for patients. The spring is 30 minutes from town.

The most interesting place to visit is the coal mines. Coal was mined here for over 50 years and currently 2 million tons a year is extracted. There is one main open cut mine with three more planned. Unlike the mine at Neryungri, the Chegdomyn mine does not normally work around the clock. It produces only when it has to meet a government production target despite the fact that there is a shortage of coal in Russia.

NORTH KOREAN GULAGS

Strange as it might seem, Chegdomyn offers a rare and fascinating insight into one of the world's most secretive countries, North Korea. Officially known as the Democratic Peoples' Republic of Korea (DPRK), North Korea is the world's last communist cult-of-personality state. The country is run by the 'Dear Leader' Kim Jong Il who took over from his father, the 'Great Leader' and President, Kim Il Sung, when he died in 1994.

During the Soviet era, North Korea and the USSR were fraternal brothers bonded together against the capitalist threat from the 'puppet regime' of South Korea and the imperialist USA. As one reward for being communism's Asian bastion, North Korea was allowed to run logging camps in Eastern Siberia. Camps opened in 1967 in the Khabarovsk region and in 1975 along the BAM. The deal involved the Russians supplying logging equipment and fuel, in return for about 70% of the timber the Koreans felled. To reduce costs to a minimum, the Koreans ran their own market gardens which are believed by local Russians to be far more productive than those of the Russians.

The Soviet government didn't meddle in the operations of these camps and even allowed the Koreans to administer their own harsh laws. For example, if a Korean ran away from a camp, hoping to flee to China or South Korea, and was captured by the Soviet police, he was handed over to the North Korean camp authorities. These prisoners were chained and returned to North Korea to face probable execution. Today, the situation has changed slightly with the Russian police now less likely to try to capture defectors. For example, in 1992, 63 labourers fled the camps but only 19 were recaptured and handed back to the North Korean authorities.

It is claimed by some, such as Sergei Kovalyov, Russia's human rights ombudsman, that some of the camps are prison labour camps. He alleges that there is a secret protocol between the Russian and North Korean governments which gives North Korean intelligence

Propaganda pictures like the one above adorn the North Korean consulate in Chegdomyn. This statue symbolises the unity of a worker, peasant and intellectual towards building a society based on *Juche* (self-reliance). The imagery is Soviet socialist realist with the interesting twist of the intellectual being symbolised by the man in a Western suit holding a calligraphy pen.

services permission to have prisons on Russian territory. This has not been confirmed or denied by the Russian government but none of the numerous camps that can be seen along the BAM appear to be barbed wire encircled prisons patrolled by guard dogs. Most have a simple gate with the standard 2m high wooden or concrete Russian fence.

Few other Russians express concern about the North Korean presence as locals are conscious of the economic benefit of the Koreans' work. According to Russian forestry officials, timber cut by the North Koreans is 25% cheaper than timber cut by Russians and this differential is likely to increase as Russian labour costs rise. In 1992, the North Koreans produced 1.16 million cubic metres of cut timber and Russia earned US$4.75 million from exporting its share.

Despite this valuable hard currency income, the camps are winding down. Although figures are unreliable, it is estimated that there were about 20,000 North Koreans in Russia at their peak but by 1995, there were only about 10,000. In Tynda alone, the number has dropped from 6,000 to about 2,000. There are two main reasons for this. Firstly, the Russians are now demanding hard currency for fuel and equipment which the North Koreans don't have. Secondly, the cost of rail freight has risen astronomically so the profit margin on exporting timber is now small.

As a way of supplementing their income, the North Koreans are now building houses and hotels, and they are often preferred to Russians due to their high quality work and reliability. From anecdotal evidence it appears that the North Koreans have also become involved in drug smuggling in the Russian Far East. However the North Korean government denies any knowledge of this.

Despite, the problems, the economic benefits of having the North Koreans around are likely to ensure their presence for many more years along the BAM.

The Korean workers arrive normally for stints of three years and are allowed to return home twice in that time. Their salaries are paid to their families which is the regime's insurance that they will return home.

Urgal-1 (Ургал-1) 3,330km

The small village surrounding Urgal-1 was founded in the 1940s as the line to the Chegdomyn coal mines was being built. With the creation of Novy Urgal, which means New Urgal, most inhabitants abandoned Urgal-1 for the bigger settlement. Trains for Chegdomyn turn off the BAM near Urgal-1.

Soloni (Солони) 3,383km

This small town was built by the Tadzhikistan *Komsomol*.

Ducce Alin (Дуссе Алинь) 3,403km

Near this station is a 2km tunnel through the 1,302m Dusse-Alinski Mountain Range.

Suluk (Сулук) 3,421km

This small town, on the Suluk River, was sponsored by

Ducce-Alinski Tunnel (Дуссе-Алинский Тоннель)

Of all the tunnels on the BAM, this one has had the longest and most tragic history.

Work on the tunnel started in 1939 when prisoners from the BAM gulag complex, BAMLag, arrived on foot with only hand tools, one horse and a single motorised cart, and orders to dig a 2km tunnel as quickly as possible.

Conditions were extremely harsh, and starvation coupled with overwork was the most common cause of prisoners' death. The life of free workers was slightly better, however death was still common. For example, in 1940, the chief engineer, Vasily Konserov, was shot in the back by the military guard commander after a dispute. The death was officially called an accident and Konserov was buried with full honours, as he had previously received the Order of Lenin for constructing the famous Belomorski-Baltiski Canal.

A suitable replacement, the well known Moscow Metro engineer, Ratsboum, was forcibly volunteered to finish the tunnel. Upon arriving he was shocked at the condition of the prisoners and demanded immediate improvements, including giving the prisoners their meagre backpay. After some dispute, his superiors acquiesced to his demands, more afraid of not completing the tunnel on time.

Returning to work, Ratsboum was faced with a far greater problem. There was no survey equipment so the tunnel was being dug from both sides of the mountain using just line-of-sight. This meant that there was an excellent chance that the tunnels would never meet. The consequences of this happening would inevitably be a charge of deliberate sabotage followed by a firing squad. Luckily when the tunnels joined, they were out by only 20cm and Ratsboum's life was spared. Work continued on enlarging it until work halted in December 1942 due to the Second World War. In 1947, work recommenced and Ratsboum resumed his post. The tunnel was officially opened on Stalin's birthday in 1950. As part of the tunnel's decoration, a collage of four busts of Marx, Engles, Stalin and Lenin behind one another was chiselled into the rock face beside the entrance with the inscription 1947-1950 above it.

Despite its completion, the tunnel was never put into regular service as work on the line between the tunnel and Komsomolsk was stopped following Stalin's death. A small maintenance detachment remained until 1959 and then when it became obvious that the BAM's construction would not be resumed, the tunnel was abandoned. Subterranean water slowly trickled into the tunnel, the freezing of the water resulted in rock falls and eventually, the tunnel iced up.

Following the decision to restarting construction of the BAM, railway troops arrived at the tunnel in December 1974. Despite being abandoned for twenty years, the barracks were still in good condition and the soldiers moved into them. The camp's wire enclosures, guard towers and signs left no doubt as to the original builders and as excavation work commenced, more reminders, included frozen corpses, were unearthed. Letters about the gruesome finds started to be received by the soldiers' families and even a candlestick holder made from a skull was sent home as a souvenir.

The outcry from the soldiers' families quickly snowballed into a military commission sent from Moscow. In a great hurry, the camp underwent a *Potemkinski* renovation. Potemkin was a one-eyed general and lover of Katherine the Great, who would precede the Tsarina on her tours around Russia, ensuring that each village was freshly painted and festooned with banners, and

Khabarovsk *Komsomol*. After leaving Suluk, the train turns from the south east to the north east. You are now travelling up the Amgun Valley which is flanked to the north by the Bureinski Mountain Range and to the south by the Badzhalski Mountain Range.

Gerbi (Герби)   3,475km
This town, on the Gerbi River, is a railway settlement. It is the terminus for local BAM trains running to Novy Urgal in the west and Postyshevo in the east. Accommodation is available at the Locomotive Brigade Hostel (Дом Отдыха Локомотивой Бригады).

Urkaltu (Уркальту)   3,500km
This siding was where painted silver spikes were hammered into the track, signifying the completion of the 504km eastern section of the BAM in June 1978.

Amgun (Амгунь)   3,581km
This town is named after the 723km Amgun River that runs beside the train line. Permafrost is widespread in this region making the railway line construction very difficult. It was in 1989 between this station and Duki (Дуки), 50km away, that hikers found the wreckage of a American built DC-3 that had disappeared on 4 October 1938 while searching for the *Rodina* aircraft which had just crashed in the region. All 18 Russians on board the DC-3 were killed. The tail section of the DC-3 was recovered and now stands as a monument in Komsomolsk.

---

unsightly places and people hidden. As part of the camp's *Potemkinski* renovation, a cloth was tactfully draped over Stalin's bust.

The verdict of the commission was that the political education of the soldiers was poor and it was ideologically inappropriate for them to live in prisoners' barracks. So in just 10 days, the entire camp was levelled, including the cemetery, and all signs of the previous workers, including the busts and 1947-1950 inscription, were destroyed. The demolition work led to more grisly finds, among them numerous letters secreted away in the walls of the barracks. An example is: "To the beloved leader and Comrade Stalin, My wife went on a business trip and never came back. I myself was arrested at night and the term was 10 years. And when I asked why, I was told "you'll serve your term and then know". Pray find out the truth and restore justice."

To reopen the tunnel, the soldiers used the backblast from aircraft jet engines to melt the 32,000 cubic metres of ice that blocked the tunnel. Workers from both sides met on 11 April 1976 and the tunnel was officially opened in 1982 when the first train travelled from Novy Urgal through the tunnel to Komsomolsk. Sadly, the tunnel now just carries the letters "1982" on its portal with no mention of the previous tunnel builders.

Postyshevo (Постышево) 3,633km

Following the Second World War, worked resumed on the BAM until it was again stopped in 1949. During this time, the eastern segment of the line reached Postyshevo and this section of track remained in operation ever since.

Rodina - When Even A Disaster Breaks A Record

The 1930s were the golden age of Soviet aviation with records being broken virtually every second month. New planes were developed, aero clubs sprang up throughout the country and record breaking flights were common. Even though one such attempt resulted in the plane crashing, it only fuelled national pride.

In October 1938, an ANT-37 aircraft, nicknamed *Rodina* or homeland, left Moscow for the Russian Far East, crewed by three women in an attempt to break the non-stop distance record for women. The crew consisted of the navigator Marina Raskova, Captain Valentina Grizodubova and co-pilot Polina Osipenko. As soon as they passed the Urals, the weather turned ugly with a strong headwind and low visibility. Visual navigation became difficult and then the radio navigation signals stopped. They had no choice but to go on. When it became apparent that they were about to run out of fuel, Raskova was ordered to bail out as her position in the nose of the aircraft was deadly in a crash. She took her survival kit which consisted of a gun, matches and two bars of chocolate.

The plane struggled on for a few more kilometres before crashing. For the next 10 days Raskova struggled through the *taiga* until she reached the crashed *Rodina* and all the crew waited together until they were rescued. Despite the crash of the *Rodina* the flight captured the women's non-stop flying record with 26 hours, 29 minutes and more than 6,000km travelled.

This struggle captured the imagination of the Soviet people and when Raskova returned to Moscow, Stalin awarded her the Gold Star of the Soviet Union.

Raskova played a pivotal role in convincing Stalin to create women's air combat regiments following the Soviet Union's entry into the Second World War. Due to Raskova's personal fame, thousands of women applied to join her new regiment called the 587th Dive Bomber Regiment which later was designated the 125th Guards Bomber regiment. Eventually 1,000 were selected and training started in October 1941. Raskova trained herself and other pilots to fly the notoriously hard to handle Pe-2 divebomber. Unfortunately as the regiment was flying from their training base to the front, Raskova's plane crashed killing all aboard.

While her death was a tragic blow to all women pilots, she advanced the cause of women in her country. According to Anne Noggle in her excellent book, *A Dance with Death: Soviet Airwomen in World War 2*, "Without Marina Raskova it is doubtful that there would have been any women air regiments in the Soviet Union during World War 2". Her importance was also recognised by the US government when it launched a supply ship called Marina Raskova in California on 22 June 1943.

Urgal-1 is one of the oldest and possibly the most attractive of all BAM stations. It is unusually well maintained and has a delightful stained glass window in the booking hall.

The station was named after Pavel Petrovich Postyshevo (1887-1940) who was a prominent Ukrainian Bolshevik and ally of Stalin until his arrest in 1938. In 1930, Stalin named him secretary of the Ukrainian Central Committee and he ran the Party apparatus there until he disappeared.

The town, Berezovy (Березовый), has a different name from the station, and was sponsored by the Novosibirsk Komsomol. A 10 minute walk by foot brings you to the Amgun River (р. Амгунь) which is famous as one of the best fishing rivers in Eastern Siberia. In late summer and autumn, you can flyfish for dog salmon and hunchback salmon, while in winter you can icefish for *Brachymstax* salmon, taimen and grayling. You need a licence to fish but this is easily obtained once you arrive. The best fishermen in town are the father and son team of Victor Ivanovich and Genadi Viktorovich Shchus. They can organise a fishing trip if you write to them well in advance. 682638 Khabarovski *Krai*, Solnichny *Raion*, Berezovy, ul Parkovaya 18 (Виктор Иванович и Геннадий Викторович Щусь , 682638, Хабаровский Край, Солнечный район, п. Березовый, ул. Парковая 18).

About 8km down the Amgun River is the Old Believers village of Tavlinka (Тавлинка, Деревня староверов). Old Believers are devout followers of the Russian Orthodox Church as it was prior to the second half of the seventeenth century. It was at this time that the church underwent minor reforms which included a revision of the prayer book and new official statutes. Those that did not accept the reforms were labelled Old Believers and persecuted. Over the next 100 years they migrated eastward and at the height of persecution, hid their villages in remote *taiga*. Today descendants of these Old Believers exist just as they did then, shunning smoking and drinking. Tavlinka consists now of just 20 houses and has the feel of a dying community.

Another useful contact in Berezovy is the adventure club Azimut (Азимут) run by Adolf Vacelovich Bovogov, ☎ 292 and Sergi Chekashinm ☎ 423, 682638, Khabarovski *Krai*, Solnichny *Raion*, Berezovy, ul Novomotornaya 4a, kv 10 (Адольф Василевич Боговов и Сергей Чекашин, 682638, Хабаровский Край, Солнечный район, п. Березовый, ул. Новомоторная 4а, кв10)

Postyshevo is inconvenient to visit as there is only one long distance train a day in both directions and they both arrive in the early hours of the morning.

Evoron (Эворон)   3,697km

The station's name comes from nearby Lake Evoron (озеро Эворон) which means *ghosts of the lake* in Nanai language. The lake covers an area of 194 square kilometres, runs 30km north south and is about 12km wide. It is unusual in that eight rivers run into it and only one runs out. This outward flowing river is called Devyatka (Девятка) which means ninth. Lake Evoron area is a major resting place for migratory birds and the Wildlife Institute in Khabarovsk, which provides survey information for the government's nature resource management, has recommended that this area becomes a national park. Over 200 types of birds have been identified here.

In the late 1980s, it was planned to build a nuclear reactor at the lake. A combination of anti-nuclear protests in Komsomolsk and a cash shortage resulted in the 2.5 billion rouble project being dumped. However the lake suffered considerably in May 1993 when a massive oil spill in one of its feeder rivers flowed into the lake.

Kondon (Кондон)

5km from this station is the Nanai village of Kondon which is the location of one of Siberia's most important archaeological finds.

Archaeological digs first started in the 1930s with major finds near the old post office in the centre of the town and at another site 2km away known as Kukelev (Кукелев) on the banks of the Paltsem River (р. Пальцем). These sites were about 5,000 to 6,000 years old and revealed a highly organised society that had disappeared overnight. It appears that the village was attacked, everything was burnt down and the inhabitants fled never to return. Among the finds were wooden objects, combs made from animal bones and shards of pottery with a well known pattern of broad spirals. Then in 1965, workers discovered a statuette which for the first time, revealed the physical shape of the original inhabitants. Called the Nanai 'Venus', it confirmed the link between the past and present indigenous people. The statue was of a women with a soft oval face, broad cheekbones, a slender chin and small pouting lips. The woman's nose is long and thin like those of the North American Indians. The eyes exaggeratedly long and narrow, like arched slits, while the forehead low and upper part of the head is slanted back. Even in Kondon today, you can see women with these characteristics.

The Nanai 'Venus' provided the missing link between the ancient and current indigenous people of the Russian Far East.

There are no hotels in town, however very basic accommodation can be organised in the town's *Possovet*. There is a local museum in town, however most of the important archaeological finds are now at Novosibirsk 's museum of history and culture.

Gorin (Горин)   3,733km
This town is located on the Goryun River (р. Горюн) and is spelt in Russian either Goryun (Горюн), Goran (Горан) or Gorin. The BAM reached this town in 1942 but the rails were ripped up late that year to be used for the Stalingrad to Satarov line. The line was relaid in the 1950s and upgraded in the 1970s.

Khurmiuli (Хурмиули)   3,769km
This is a small indigenous village and is relatively famous for producing the first Nanai businessman of note, Inakenti Dyonovski.

Khalgaso (Хальгасо)   3,808km
This is the most easterly station managed by the BAM Railway Administration as the next station, Silinka, is run by the Far East Railway. For the really keen rail enthusiasts, this place is a must. When the line from Komsomolsk to Postyshevo was relaid in the late 1940s,

Lend-lease rails were used and today, you can still see the words *USA 1944* and *Colorado 1943* stamped on the rails. These rails are not used on the current BAM but on a siding running parallel to the BAM.

Beside the rails are the remains of a camp which started life as a hospital camp for forced labourers who laid the lines in the 1940s. The camp had two sections, Special Hospital Branch 3762 for Russian gulag prisoners and Camp No 5 for Japanese POWs. After the Soviet Union's gulag was closed in the 1950s, the camp was converted into a children's *Pioneer* camp. The camp was finally closed in 1984 when the BAM was completed and the number of trains rushing by presented a danger to young children. All that remains of the camp is the front gate and some rubble.

In the early 1990s, the Japanese built a memorial nearby honouring the Japanese POWs who died in the area. The Russian government has also indicated that it would like to built a similar memorial for the victims of Stalin's repression but does not have the funds to do so.

The site of the rails, camp and Japanese memorial is about 5km from the Khalgaso station and is relatively easy to find. Simply follow the road in front of the station to the village of Start (Старт). The town earned its name as a launching base for explorations to the north of Komsomolsk including Solnichny. 2km past Start, you pass a military settlement which houses a tank regiment. A further 1km on, the road does a left dog leg. Just before you cross over a railway line, take the left turn which runs parallel to the line through a rail lumber yard. About 400m further on, the road crosses the railway line and it is at this point that you will find the rails, camp remains and Japanese memorial.

Silinka (Силинка)   3,818km

Tin concentrate from the nearby Solnichny and Gorni mines is loaded here for smelting in China.

As you head towards Komsomolsk, you will pass an enormous antenna complex spread over several square kilometres. This is one of Russia's over-the-horizon (OTH) radars. This OTH radar is designed to watch the movement of aircraft, ships and strategic missiles between the Chinese coast and Guan Island. This is one of three such radar complexes in the Russian Far East with the other two at Nakhodka and Nikolaevsk-na-Amure. These radars are essential to early warning of incoming nuclear missiles and despite the conclusion of the Cold War, they are still highly secret. They have been codenamed Woodpecker as their radar signal produces a rapid click of 10.5 pulses per second.

Komsomolsk 2 (Комсомолск 2)   3,831km

A rail yard and suburban station 6km from the main Komsomolsk station.

Komsomolsk

Комсомольск

Komsomolsk 1 (Комсомольск 1)   3,837km
☎ code: 42141   ✉ 681021, Khabarovski Krai, Хабаровский Край

Komsomolsk embodies not only the ideals of the Communist Revolution but also the realities of Soviet socialism.

It was built in the unpopulated Russian Far East by fervent young communists as part of the 1930s nation-wide industrialisation campaign designed to propel the Soviet Union into the modern world. It was from these workers, who were members of the Young Communist League, or Komsomol, that the city got its name. The full name, Komsomolsk-na-Amure means Komsomolsk on the Amur River which distinguishes the city from the other Komsomolsks dotted throughout out Russia.

Despite its honourable background, Komsomolsk suffered under socialism and its trials have included mass arrests during Stalin's time, pollution and inadequate infrastructure. Today, Komsomolsk is suffering from high levels of unemployment and the population peaked at 312,400 in 1993 and is now declining as families leave for Khabarovsk and Vladivostok looking for work.

Despite this, Komsomolsk is the Russian Far East's fourth biggest city and has a lot to offer travellers. As well as being an attractive town on the beautiful Amur River, it is the gateway to the rarely visited northern areas of the Russian Far East, including Nikolaevsk via the Amur River, local towns including Solnechny and Amursk, and of course, the BAM.

History

Komsomolsk was built in a remote area of the Russian Far East with the closest settlements being a small Nanai indigenous village and the small Russian village of Permskoe founded in 1858. According to the 1890s *Geographical and Statistical*

THE EMBLEM OF KOMSOMOLSK WHICH IS ALSO CALLED THE CITY OF THE DAWN.

Dictionary of the Amur and Premorski Regions, in 1888, Permskoe consisted of just 26 farms, 78 adult males and 82 adult females. "The village provided supplies for the traders' and military's river boats and maintained a regional postal office."

The isolated site chosen for Komsomolsk may seem strange, however its remoteness was ideal for building a military industrial complex of aircraft, ship building and steel plants. The Chinese border was over 400km away, the Pacific Ocean was 450km down the Amur River while travellers on the Trans-Siberian would never get closer than 350km.

Komsomolsk was founded on 10 May 1932 when the advance party arrived from Khabarovsk on the river steamers Columbus and Comintern. Thousands of builders quickly followed and within 7 years, the town became the fourth largest in the Russian Far East. By the late 1930s growth had slowed due to workers' inexperience, harsh winters, and a lack of management and supplies. As Stalin's purges were sweeping the Soviet Union at this time, Komsomolsk's failure to meet targets became the justification for a local purge which started on the fifth anniversary of the city. The director of the steelworks, Amurstal, summed up the purging process in Komsomolskaya Pravda on 12 June 1937 with, "We are mercilessly rooting out this scum of wreckers". It was alleged that the 'wreckers' were very active and ingenious: they mixed sugar with concrete to lower its strength, they put glass into ball-bearings to cause accidents and destroyed vital blue-prints which delayed the growth of industry. The town's leadership was quickly eliminated amid claims of poor security which had led to "agents of foreign intelligence services, bandits and diversionists" penetrating the ranks of workers and technicians.

The victims of the Stalin's purges throughout the Soviet Union created a vast pool of labour and as Komsomolsk was in need of labour, Komsomolsk became the gulag capital of the Russian Far East. An estimated 900,000 prisoners tramped through Komsomolsk's camps. Thousands died and unmarked mass graves litter the city. For instance, the Sewing Machine Factory, railway park, Maternity Hospital No 1 and Dalstalkonstruktsiya Enterprise all sit on prisoner cemeteries.

As the *Great Patriotic War* progressed, Komsomolsk's gulag population of Soviet citizens decreased from 67,742 in 1942 to 28,073 in 1944. However this decline was more than offset by the flood of Japanese, and to a much smaller extent German, POWs. At its peak, the prison complex had 49,500 Japanese POWs which included 16,000 in 18 city camps and the rest working on the BAM and other projects in the region. In Komsomolsk, the Japanese worked in the steel plant, aircraft factory, brick plant, and repair plant. They also constructed most of the city's stone buildings including the Amur Hotel, Polyclinic No 7, High

School No 145 and 30th Anniversary of Oktyabr Cinema.

In 1990, Komsomolsk became the first Russian town to allow Japanese ex-POWs to return to honour their dead. Over the next few years, the Japanese built 16 memorials around Komsomolsk. Rumour has it that even then, the Russians were exploiting the Japanese as they charged them enormous amounts to build the memorials. Today, Komsomolsk has a sister city relationship with the Japanese city of Kamo.

Getting there and away
Komsomolsk is at the junction of an east, west and south rail network with daily long distance trains from all directions. From the east there are trains from Sovetskaya Gavin (13 hours), Vanino (12:30 hours) and Pivan (33 minutes). From the south there are trains from Irkutsk (82 hours), Khabarovsk (22 hours) and Vladivostok (35 hours). From the west, there are trains from Postyshevo (5:20 hours), Novy Urgal (13

Balancing Gender in Komsomolsk

The construction of Komsomolsk appealed to many communists who wanted adventure while building a brave new socialist world. They were invariably young and male, and the dearth of women made the population of Komsomolsk restless and transient.

This shortage created the Khetagurova Movement, which in conjunction with forced exile, became one of the major strategies for increasing the population of the Russian Far East in the 1930s. The movement was named after Valentina Khetagurova-Zarubina, the 22 year old wife of a major serving in the Special Far Eastern Army. She felt so much compassion for the single males in Komsomolsk who had little chance of finding a wife that she wrote an open letter to the women of the Soviet Union encouraging them to migrate to the Russian Far East. The letter was published on 5 February 1937 and appeared in numerous forms over the following years The needs of the Far East are great, she wrote. "We need fitters and turners, teachers and draftswomen, typists and accountants - all to the same degree. We want only bold, determined people, not afraid of difficulties". She described the Far East as an exotic dreamland, "where still a short time ago there were only deer, tigers and lions" and where "wonderful work, wonderful people and a wonderful future" would meet the girls. More importantly she implied that every girl would find a husband in the Far East and possibly even one who held a military rank or commanded a good salary. This appeal was picked up by others in the media such as Pavil Pavlenko who integrated it into one of his novels, "From the polar tundra down to Korea, everybody dreams of women. Nowhere else do people get married as quickly as there. Widows do not exist in the Far East. Only the oldest women overcome by senility remain single".

The Khetagurova movement was a brilliant success on paper, and by the end of 1937, over 70,000 Soviet girls had registered as volunteers for the Far East with 5,000 being selected in 1937 alone. How many actually married and stayed was never recorded.

262 BAM mainline route description

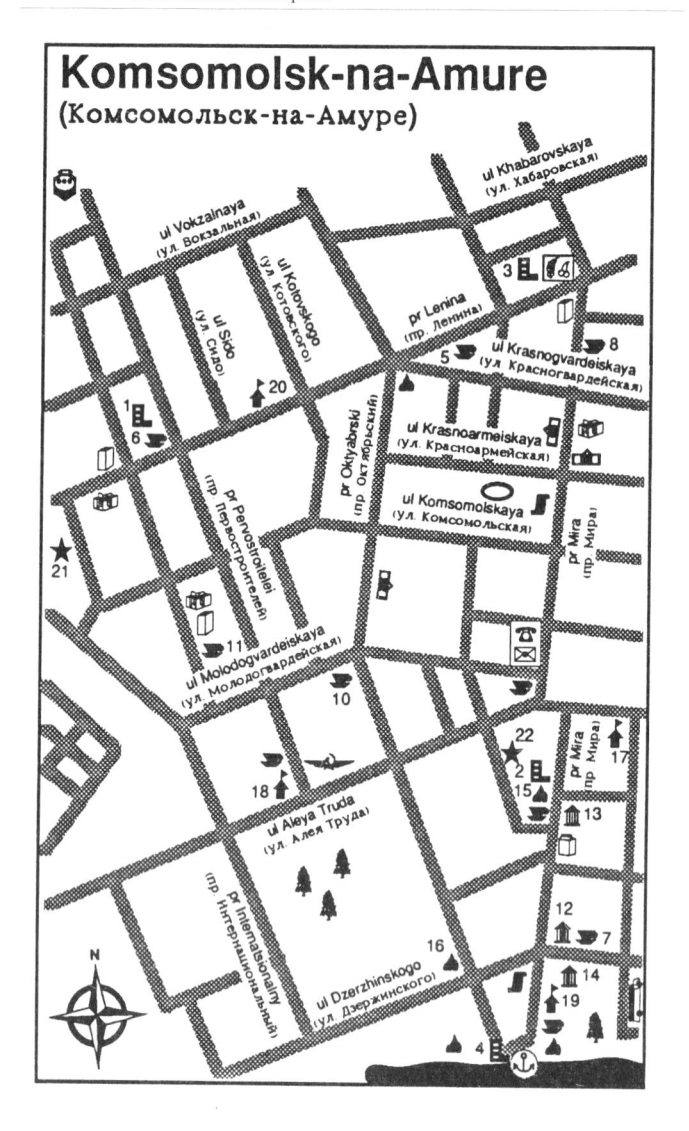

Komsomolsk-na-Amure
(Комсомольск-на-Амуре)

hours) and Tynda (41 hours). Several of the trains heading for Khabarovsk originate in Sovetskaya Gavin which means that it can be difficult booking tickets. Normally only when the train is approaching the station will the train conductor radio ahead the number of spare berths. Then there is a mad scramble at the ticket office to get one of these before the train arrives.

The Amur River offers an interesting way of arriving and departing. The river is navigable usually from 20 June to 31 August and there are regular hydrofoils to Khabarovsk and Nikolaevsk. There are also cruise ships that travel from China, through Blagoveshchensk, Khabarovsk, and Komsomolsk to Nikolaevsk.

There are regular flights from Khabarovsk, Nikolaevsk, Vanino, Bogorodskoe and several other rural towns. The airport is 27km out of town and there are 12 buses a day which make the 45 minute trip. The city's Aeroflot office is at pr Pervostroitelei 18, ☎ 303-93 (Агенство Аэрофлота, пр. Первостроителей 18).

Getting around
Komsomolsk is divided into two parts separated by the Silinka River. The northern part contain most of the industry while the southern part contains the city centre and residential areas. The main street is prospekt Mira which used to be prospekt Stalin until the late 1950s when this and 50 other street names were changed. Tram no 2 from the station goes past all 4 hotels before reaching the River Station on pr Mira.

Where to stay
There are four hotels to choose from.

Voskhod Hotel has the best facilities and is the closest to the station. It is expensive, charging foreigners four times the locals' price. This

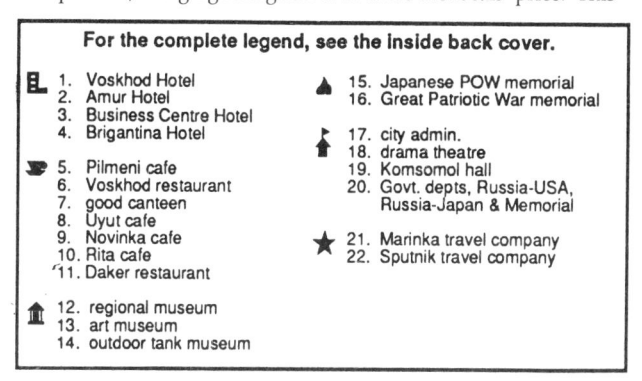

For the complete legend, see the inside back cover.

1. Voskhod Hotel
2. Amur Hotel
3. Business Centre Hotel
4. Brigantina Hotel

5. Pilmeni cafe
6. Voskhod restaurant
7. good canteen
8. Uyut cafe
9. Novinka cafe
10. Rita cafe
11. Daker restaurant

12. regional museum
13. art museum
14. outdoor tank museum

15. Japanese POW memorial
16. Great Patriotic War memorial

17. city admin.
18. drama theatre
19. Komsomol hall
20. Govt. depts, Russia-USA, Russia-Japan & Memorial

21. Marinka travel company
22. Sputnik travel company

means that it costs $50 for a room for two. There is a small cafe on the 8th floor, a ground floor restaurant and hairdresser. The hotel can send telexes on your behalf. The rooms are small but adequate with a toilet and shower. Hotel Voskhod, pr Pervostroitelei 31, ☎ 303-36 (Гостиница Восход, пр. Первостроителей 31). Buses 9, 20, 26 and 27 and Trams 1, 2, 4 and 5 all go past it.

Another good quality hotel is the Business Centre. It has a small number of rooms starting from $70 for a room for two. Hotel Business Centre, ul Khabarovskaya 47, ☎ 447-05 (Гостиница Бизнес-Центр, ул. Хабаровская 47). All trams go near it.

The most centrally located hotel is the down market Amur Hotel. The rooms start from $20 for a room for two. Most rooms have no facilities and the shower is on the ground floor. Often the haunt of shady businessmen and prostitutes. Hotel Amur, pr Mira 15, ☎ 430-74 (Гостиница Амур, пр. Мира 15). Trams 1, 2, 4 and 5 go past it.

The Brigantina Hotel at the River Station was renovated in 1994 and has very good rooms. The riverside rooms have an excellent view. The rooms start from $30 for a room for two. Hotel Brigantina, ul Naberzhnaya 1, ☎ 447-45 (Гостиница Бригантина, ул. Набережная 1). All trams except 5 go to it.

Where to eat

Komsomolsk has a good number of restaurants and canteens. Their locations are shown on the map. Of special mention is the Pilmeni Cafe which produces only *pilmeni*. These meat filled potato pastry dumplings are made on site with a small machine which is worth watching in action. Make sure you get the vinegar sauce and while these *pilmeni* are not as good as home made ones, they are quite tasty.

What to see

Regional museum

A good introduction to Komsomolsk is the Regional museum which is one of the best museums in the Russian Far East. It is unusually modern in its use of

A wintery day in Komsomolsk. The buildings are identical to those in European Russia.

dioramas, models and displays. There are displays of the local Nanai indigenous people, rural life in the late 1800s, the building of Komsomolsk, and the gulags in the region. Of interest are photos and documents of two Americans, Ann Stanley and Lloyd Patterson. These two ran the English language propaganda radio during the Second World War which broadcast into Japan, China and much of Asia.

If you are interested in indigenous culture, talk to the region's expert who works at the museum, Zoya Stepanovna Lapshana. The museum is open daily except Mondays from 10 to 17:00. Beside the museum is a canteen. Regional museum, pr Mira 8, ☎ 422-60 (Музей краеведческий, пр. Мира 8).

Art museum
The Art museum consists of two floors of art. The ground floor, where the toilets are located, has one room of western art with another room housing short term exhibitions. Upstairs is indigenous and peasant art. Art museum, pr Mira 16, ☎ 422-60 (Музей изобразительного исскуства, пр. Мира 16). There is also a commercial art shop at pr Pervostroitelei 20 (Художественная лавка, пр. Первостроителей).

Aircraft factory museum
The museum has good displays on the history of the nearby Yuri Gagarin Aircraft Factory with numerous displays of its aircraft including the Il-2, Mig-17 and SU-27. The museum is located about 20 minutes out of the centre of town on ul Kalinina near both the Kalinin monument and the 50th Anniversary Palace of Culture. Trams 4 and 5 go past it. It has irregular hours as most of its customers are Russian military personnel on organised tours. Aircraft Factory museum, ul Kalinina 7, ☎ 323-67 (Музей авиационного завода им Гагарина, ул. Калинина 7).

Tank museum
This open air museum consists of about 30 armoured fighting vehicles. It is located in the park next door to the regional museum. As it does not have a fence around it, it can be visited anytime.

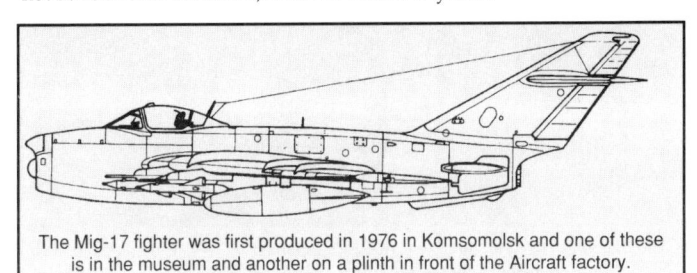

The Mig-17 fighter was first produced in 1976 in Komsomolsk and one of these is in the museum and another on a plinth in front of the Aircraft factory.

Japanese POW memorials
(Мемориал знак военнопленным, умершим в Комсомольске)
There are 16 memorial stones in and around Komsomolsk, marking cemeteries or camps of Japanese POWs. The central memorial is a large stone beside the Amur Hotel which was unveiled on 5 October 1991. This site was chosen because the POWs built the hotel.

Another important site is a graveyard where 1,513 Japanese were buried. This site is worth visiting although it is hard to find without a guide. To get to it, you travel down the Severno-Shasse highway (Северно Шассе) towards Solnechny for 20 minutes. When you come to an asphalt road to the left with a flag shaped sign on the corner stating Autobaz 8 (Автобаз 8), you take the small dirt road on the opposite side of the road. (If you reach 2 large power stations on your left, you have gone about 1km too far and need to go back and find the Autobaz 8 sign.) The dirt road peters out after about 100m and you need to walk a further 50m on a track which goes under a raised section of the insulated hot water tubes. The simple monument consists of a central pillar with Japanese writing on it.

Returning to Komsomolsk on the Severno-Shasse highway, you will pass a row of small red brick houses on the right. These are distinctively not Russian looking and were built by the Japanese.

The memorial marking the graves of 1,513 Japanese POWs. The sulphuric acid plant in the background is built on more graves.

Stalin's repression memorial stone
(Памятник знак Жертвам политических репрессий)
This stone is a memorial to those who suffered and died during Stalin's repression. The local government was pressured into creating this monument by an organisation called Memorial whose membership consists of relatives of repression victims.

One of the important functions of Memorial was to search for information on the death of their members' relatives and equally important, if they were posthumously rehabilitated. After Stalin's death many Russians who died in camps were secretly retried and many found not guilty. Although it was cold comfort for the victim, posthumous rehabilitation was important for relatives as without it, they were tainted with being a relative of an 'enemy of the state'. This allegation was sufficient to deny the relative from education, promotion, Communist Party membership and an internal passport which allowed them to leave their area. As the trials were secret, getting hold of documents relating to them was extremely difficult.

By the 1990s, these documents were no longer important due to the freeing up of society, however even now many relatives still do not know what happened to their loved ones.

Memorial ceased to exist in the early 1990s as the city administration took over its role of finding out information about former prisoners. However several ex-members claim that things have become worse as, while the government's policy is one of assistance, the reality is that the bureaucratic morass ensures that little happens.

The location of the stone, beside the City Court, is a poignant reminder of the failure of the Soviet justice systems. The stone was taken from the Mount Novaya quarry on the outskirts of Komsomolsk which was worked by prisoners.

Soldier-builders monument (Памятник войнам-строителям)
A half built monument near the central bus station best symbolises the collapse of communism due to processes such as *glasnost*. The monument was going to depict the 'heroic' arrival in 1934 of the construction troops who marched from Khabarovsk on the frozen Amur River.

However the reality was that while the soldiers did march over the ice, in front of them tramped prisoners who tested the ice and found the best route. Many prisoners died during this arduous trip. In addition, archives have revealed that these troops were the second military group to arrive but the exact date of the first is not known.

So today all that exists to commemorate communist propaganda is a 3m high concrete base with steel reinforcing sticking out of it. A monument is still planned for the soldier-builders as they did contribute

Travelling on the Amur River

The massive 4,440km Amur River forms in Mongolia and travels along the Chinese–Russian border before discharging into the Pacific Ocean just to the north of Nikolaevsk.

Foreigners travelling along the Amur River have not been a common sight in the past due to Soviet-era travel restrictions and a lack of information. However, the ease of organising a trip plus the number of interesting places en route which can only be reached by river, will ensure that foreigners are a common sight in the future.

Travelling on the Amur River
The hydrofoils and ferries officially run between 20 June to 31 August when the Amur is guaranteed to be completely clear of ice. Local ferries may start and end earlier depending of the river ice in their area of operation.

Tickets for the hydrofoils are bought at the river stations or if the town is small, on the vessel. As the price of tickets is expensive for locals, there are invariably spare berths. Remember to keep hold of your ticket as you may be asked to show it during the trip and when you get off the boat.

For people wanting an organised cruise along the Amur, one company doing this is Amurturist, based at Blagoveshchensk which is on the Amur River opposite the Chinese city of Hei Hei. Amurturist uses the 1994 refurbished luxury passenger liner, Mikluno Miklay, and offers a 13 day trip. The two deck liner has single and double cabins with shower, toilet, wash basin and airconditioning. The boat has walking decks, restaurants, bars and cinemas, and the crew provides regular entertainment on board. Almost half of the trip is along the Sino-Russian border and you will stop off at Khabarovsk, Komsomolsk, Nikolaevsk, Blagoveschensk as well as a number of "green stops" in picturesque places which are ideal for swimming, fishing and sports competitions. The price of the trip is $400 which includes accommodation, all meals and tours around the cities on route. Amurturist is run by president, Gennady Nikolaevich Trusnin. Amurturist, ul Kuznechnaya 1, Amurskoi Oblasti, Blagoveshchensk, ☎ (41622) 277 98, 903-77 or 231-22, fax 277-98, 231-22, telex 154113 TURNE SU (Амуртурист, г Благовещенск, Амурской области, ул. Кузнечная 1, президент Геннадий Николаевич Трушин).

In winter the Amur River freezes and becomes a road. The trip to Nikolaevsk takes 24 hours.

For more information on travelling on the Amur River, including places of interest, route description and suggested itineraries see *The Lena and Amur Rivers Guide* in the *Recommended reading* section.

Hydrofoil stops between Komsomolsk and Khabarovsk

Komsomolsk (Комсомольск)
Pivan (Пивань)
Amursk (Амурск)
Vosnesenskoe (Вознесенское)
Malmyzh (Малмыж)
Innokentevka (Иннокентьевка)
Slavyanka (Славянка)
Troitskoe (Троицкое)
Naikhini (Найхин)
Mayak (Маяк)
Chelny (Челны)
Elabuga (Елабуга)
Vyatskoe (Вятское)
Malyshevo (Малышево)
Vinogradovka (Виноградовка)
Khabarovsk (Хабаровск)

significantly to the city, however a more appropriate monument and site will be selected.

River Station (Речной вокзал)
The River Station was built to look like a steam ship when seen from the Amur River, and ferries and hydrofoils travel from here up and down the Amur. At one end is the ticket office with a small cafe. Look around for signs advertising sightseeing and disco boat cruises. At the other end of the building is the Brigantina Hotel. From the station, you can see Pivan on the opposite side of the river, the Amur bridge, and if you have binoculars, the never completed Pivan BAM tunnel.

On one side of the station is a memorial stone dedicated to the first builders who arrived on 10 May 1932.

On the other side is a memorial commemorating the 50th anniversary of the founding of Komsomolsk. Unveiled in 1982, the socialist realist monument of a young communist striding forward is symbolically located at the end of the Prospect of the First Builders, pr Pervostroitelei (пр. Первостроителей) which runs the 3kms from the railway station to the Amur River.

Brick and Towel memorial (Памятник Ю А Гагарину)
This is the locals' disrespectful name for the Yuri Gagarin Memorial which sits out the front of the Gagarin Aircraft Factory. The memorial depicts Gagarin holding a stylised book containing the Laws of the Cosmos (whatever they might be) with a cosmic train trailing behind him. From a distance, it looks like Gagarin holding a brick with a towel draped over his arm. The Aircraft Factory was renamed Gagarin Aircraft Factory to honour his three visits to the complex, although he

| Hydrofoil Timetable Between Komsomolsk and Nikolaevsk |||||
| From Komsomolsk ||| From Nikolaevsk ||
Arrive	Place		Arrive	Distance (km)
8:00 (departs)	Komsomolsk (Комсомольск)		18:45	
10:50	Kiselevo (Киселево)		15:05	212
11:15	Tsimmermanovka (Циммермановка)		14:40	235
11:40	Bystrinsk (Быстринск)		14:40	268
12:25	Sofiskoe (Софийское)		13:25	293
13:10	Mariinskoe (Мариинское)		12:15	329
14:20	Bulava (Булава)		11:15	357
15:05	Savinskoe (Савинское)		11:00	391
15:35	Bogorodskoe (Богородское)		10:25	417
16:40	Susanino (Сусанино)		9:10	473
17:15	Tyr (Тыр)		8:35	508
17:50	Takhta (Тахта)		8:00	525
18:50	Innokentevka (Иннокентьевка)		7:10	568
19:30	Bunkerovka (Бункеровка)			
20:00	Nikolaevsk (Николаевск)		6:30 (departs)	582

never worked there. To get to the memorial, take Tram No 4 or 5 to its terminus which is also a large market. It takes about 30 minutes to reach the memorial from the centre of town.

Great Patriotic War memorial
(Мемориал воинам, погибшим в годы 1941-1945)
This is the best sculpture on the BAM with the possible exception of the Worker with Sledgehammer in Tynda. This war memorial consists of 7 giant granite heads facing an eternal flame. It was sculpted by N S Ivleva who got the idea from reading a German officer's war diary. "We have marched through France and Belgium in just 3 days. We have conquered the Netherlands, but we are unable to take a single step in Russia. The Russians are firmly standing in our path like stone rocks and there is no way to pass around them or turn aside". Although the diary did not mention 7 'stone rock' Russians, the number was chosen because it is a lucky one in Russia, according to Ivleva.

Industry and its importance
There are three main industrial complexes in town: the Yuri Gagarin Aircraft Factory, the Amur Shipbuilding Factory and Amurstal steel works. It is possible to organise tours of these through any of the companies below.

The fabulous Great Patriotic War memorial.

Getting assistance

The best general travel company in Komsomolsk is Marika. The company is headed by Marina Aleksandrovna Kuzminovna who is one of the Russian Far East's experts on gulags, Japanese POWs and the history of the BAM. She has written three books on these subjects. She is currently the Secretary of the Japanese-Russian Friendship Society's Komsomolsk Branch and has organised a number of tours by ex-POWs from Japan. She was the Chairperson of Memorial and is also active in local politics. Marika, ul Shikhanova 10, ☎ 347-63, fax 402-69 (Экскурсионно-туристическая фирма Марика, ул. Шиханова 10).

Adventure travel is best organised through Exotur. This company's main activity is running outdoor programs for Russian and foreign youths groups and sportsmen. Exotur also runs a network of about 60 specialists who organise archaeological, ornithological, and ethnological trips for Russian and foreign scientists. It runs activities throughout the whole of Khabarovsk *Krai* and along the BAM. About 1,500 people use the facilities and experts of Exotur a year. It has connections with the city administration and even carries out ecological monitoring programs for a number of organisations. It has its own facilities including a newly renovated building (which was originally built by Japanese POWs) and large amounts of equipment including canoes, kayaks, rock climbing gear and tents. The company is run by the helpful Alexander F Shelopugin. Exotour Tourist Centre, pr Mira 43, ☎ 421-96, fax 421-96 (Александр Ф Шелопугин, Директор, Эхотур Туристнческий Центр, пр. Мира 43).

Another company specialising in running outdoor programs is Largi. The company is run by Aleksandr Melnichenko. Largi, pr Mira 52, office 26, ☎ 434-35, fax 402-69 (Александр Мелниченко, Директор, Фирма Ларги, пр. Мира 52, Офис 26).

Another option is Sputnik which mainly organises tours for Russians wanting to travel abroad. Sputnik, ul Sevastopolskaya 10, ☎ 472-25, fax 429-83 (Спутник, ул. Севастопольская 10).

A good source of information on what is happening is the local paper, the Dalnevostochny Komsomolsk, ul Kirova 31, ☎ 429-22 (Редакция газеты Дальневосточный Комсомольск, ул. Кирова 31)

Around Komsomolsk

Комсомольск Окрестности

This section contains information on places of interest around Komsomolsk which cannot be easily reached by train. If the places are near a railway station, such as the Japanese POW camp 26km out of Komsomolsk near Khalgaso station, then they are listed under the relevant station in the *Route Description* chapters.

Highlights around Komsomolsk include the Pivan BAM tunnel, birdwatching and skiing, and the towns of Solnechny, Gorny, Festivalny and Amursk. You can also take a local ferry to one of the nearby towns on the Amur River for an interesting day trip.

Getting around

Komsomolsk is the bus hub of the region and the following is the timetable for regional buses that leave from the central Bus Station near Komsomolsk's River Station. Bus Station, ul Haberezhnaya ☎ 38-62-91 (Автовокзал, ул. Набережная).

Pivan BAM tunnel

In 1939 work started on an 800m railway tunnel through a mountain that is virtually opposite Komsomolsk and to the north of Pivan. The tunnel was to link a planned 2.5km bridge across the Amur River and the railway line from Pivan to Sovetskaya Gavin. The start of the *Great Patriotic War* stopped the bridge although the tunnel was finished. Consequently, the tunnel, which was built at the cost of hundreds of gulag prisoners' lives, was never used. The tunnel's entrance, which

Bus timetable between Komsomolsk and regional towns

Bus number	Destination (Пункт Назн.)	Distance	Time (hours)	Frequency per day
102	Airport (Аэропорт)	27	0:45	12
104	Molodezhny (Молодежный)	34	1:00	6
106	Novi Mir (Новый Мир)	29	1:00	6
112	Pivan (Пивань)	23	1:00	7
111	Solnechny (Солнечный)	43	1:10	4
113	Ekon (Эконь)	25	1:00	3
220	Amursk (Амурск)	63	1:45	18
221	Elban (Эльбан)	85	2:00	2
222	Gorny (Горный)	61	1:45	2
283	Selikhino (Селихино)	76	2:00	5
286	Troitskoe (Троицкое)	230	5:00	Once on Sat & Sun
289	Innokentevka (Иннокентьевка)	182	4:00	Once on Sat, Sun, Tue & Fri

There are also buses to the following areas but you need to check the schedule at the Bus Station. A north east bus goes to Start (Старт), Khalgaso (Хальгасо), Lian (Лиан), Khurmuli (Хурмули), Dee (Деэ) and Gorin (Горин). A west bus goes to Bochin (Бочин). A south west bus goes to Molodezhny (Молодежный).

starts 100m above the river's water level, can be seen from Komsomolsk's River Station with binoculars. This side is very difficult and dangerous to get to as the mountain face is sheer.

The other side is much easier to get to and makes an interesting half day trip. To get to it, you go through Pivan past the disused brick works to the *dacha village*. In the village there are numerous confusing roads and you need to ask the way. Don't be surprised if many locals do not know where the tunnel is.

Once you reach the tunnel, you can walk in about 100m before you hit a fence which has been breached by vandals. It is possible to walk the length of the tunnel but it is dangerous and not recommended as the walls and roof are unstable. Walking through this monument to worthless labour is an eerie experience. Remember to take a torch.

There is a ferry between Pivan and Komsomolsk 12 times a day.

Skiing

There are several downhill ski runs near Komsomolsk and of course, cross country skiing can be done anywhere. The best runs with T-bars are three near Gorny in the Myao Chan mountains (Хребет Мяо Чан). Incidentally, the words Myao Chan mean *black head* in Evenk after the colour of the rocks, which you can't see in winter. There are several other runs in the region but their condition varies enormously. Rather than ski tows, some people hire a Buran Motor Sled to take them to the top of the run, then ski down. All of the local ski runs are controlled by Exotur of Komsomolsk. Skiing is possible from the start of November to mid May. The cost of an all inclusive day trip is about $50 from Komsomolsk with Exotur.

Bird watching and indigenous villages

There is an old forestry railway line which runs 20km to the north east of Komsomolsk, terminating at the logging town of Galichny (Галичный). Galichny is on the southern border of the Komsomolsk Nature Reserve (Комсомольский Заповедник) which is centred around the Gorin River and its eastern boundary is the Amur River. Where the Gorin flows into the Amur is the Nanai village of Bichi (Бичи) which can only be reached by boat. Nearby are other Nanai settlements of Dzemgi (Дземги) and Negigaltsy (Негигальцы). The Komsomolsk Nature Reserve is an excellent place for bird watching and over 240 species have been seen here. A regional bird expert is V A Kolbin (В А Колбин) who can be contacted through Exotur.

On the far side of the reserve is the Nanai village of Nizhnie Khalby (Нижние Халбы). This settlement is famous for its dance ensemble. There is a boarding school in the town for Nanai and Russian primary school children with classes taught in both languages. Nearby are spectacular cliffs which have spiritual significance for the Nanai. The village welcomes travellers and homestay can be organised there through Exotur.

The tin towns of Solnechny, Gorny and Festivalny

The three towns of Solnechny, Gorny and Festivalny could be known as the tin triangle, as they surround Russia's largest known deposit of tin. At one stage they were the industrial show pieces of the Far East but nowadays they are a shadow of their former selves. However they are worth a day visit and can be easily reached by local buses.

Solnechny is the regional capital, the largest of the three towns and at the junction of the roads to the other two. Solnechny is 43km north west of Komsomolsk while Gorny is 61km and Festivalny is 58km.

The Nanai called the region the Valley of Death and no people ever lived here. The reason for this is that the water is acidic and contains sulphur which has resulted in few animals living in the area.

Getting there and away
A day trip by local buses is an excellent way to see the region. There are 4 buses a day to Solnechny and 2 to Gorny.

The journey from Komsomolsk to Solnechny
In the late 1970s and early 1980s, the trip to Solnechny was on the communist tour circuit as the mountainous route is beautiful and you passed the 'major' socialist achievement of the bridge over the Tsurkul River (р. Цуркуль) where everyone was forced to marvel at the first rail bridge on the eastern sector of the BAM. While the road has deteriorated since then and no-one is very interested in the bridge, the trip is still pleasant. After leaving Komsomolsk, which is about 100m above sea level, you start to climb to 250m at Solnechny and 350m at Gorny. The change in height crosses a flora boundary and the dominant tree species changes from birches to pines.

Solnechny (Солнечный)
☎ area code: 421-48

Solnechny is a small modern city with about 20,000 inhabitants. The largest building is the headquarters of the mining enterprise which controls the mines of Solnechny, Gorny and Fevralsk. It dwarfs the city government building which symbolises where the real power lies. The Solnechny mines are on the other side of the Solnechny valley but can be seen from the town.

The downturn in demand for tin in Russia hit Solnechny hard and for over a year in the early 1990s, the workers were paid in white goods and canned food.

The best explanation of the Solnechny mine and its history can be found in the local museum, ☎ 91-2-11. Half of the museum is devoted to the history of the mine and of particular interest is the model of a smelter that was never built. Currently the tin concentrate is shipped to China for smelting there and the Russians would like to build a smelter locally. While the predicted 70 year life of the mines initially attracted considerable foreign interest in the early 1990s, nothing came of it as Russia's instability and the legal conditions of joint ventures scared off all investors. The other half of the museum is devoted to the region's geology. Of particular interest is the locally found semi-precious gemstone, Amethyst. This violet quartz is used in jewellery and is

---

Geologist Gets Glory but Little Else

There is a diorama in the Solnechny museum depicting the Solnechny tin ore discovery on 11 September 1955 by the Leningrad geologist, Oleg Nikolaevich Kabakov. Surrounding it are photos and documents proudly showing the torturous process of locating the deposit. This display demonstrates the prestige given to geologists during the Soviet era when they even had their own day of celebration. Geologists' Day was always on the first Sunday in April.

The Soviet media eulogised geologists as the great 'frontiersmen and women' who would locate the great wealth of frozen Siberia. There was no question that the mineral reserves existed, only when they would be discovered. Enormous effort was devoted to exploration and in 1971, there were 150 teams prospecting in the Far East. However, while the media gave praise, and the government allocated workers, more fundamental needs were often neglected. A letter in the newspaper *Pravda* on 16 November 1968 indicated the problems faced by geologists. The author complained about poor equipment, the entire lack of physical training for geology students, and most importantly, inadequate clothing. The geologist wanted an end to the old-fashioned 1800s-era wadded trousers and jackets which nobody wanted, and the introduction of the "type of comfortable clothes manufactured for tourists and only a dream for us".

A 1968 poster praising geologists. The message reads, *Mineral wealth is the main material for the development of heavy industry in the USSR.*

believed to be a cure for drunkenness if you carry it around with you.

A church is being built opposite the regional council building, which would have Lenin turning in his tomb.

The only accommodation in town is at the Zarya Hotel, pr Lenina 21a (гостиница Заря, пр. Ленина 21-а).

Gorny (Горный)

Gorny is a small, attractive township of 5,000 people. It is located in a pleasant, steep-walled valley with the Silinka River snaking through it. At the northern end of the town is the concentrator which extracts tin from ore. Although tin is the major product, copper, tungsten, lead and zinc are also concentrated here. The concentrator consists of a crusher which grinds the ore into small particles. The particles are washed over massive banks of vibrating tables and the each type of metal is separated on the basis of weight. At the end, the concentrated particles of metals are dried and loaded into giant bins and sent by truck to the BAM for smelting in China.

This process produces large amounts of tailings which are dumped on a massive heap 400m downstream of the concentrator. Behind the heap is the used water dam where any remaining metals hopefully sink to the bottom before the water flows back into the Silinka River.

As there are no chemicals used in the concentrating process, and no smoky chimneys in town, air pollution is zero. This helped Gorny win a Tidy Town Award in the mid 1980s. However, the Gorny and Solnechny concentrators are very polluting as a great deal of heavy metals leech from the tailings into the Silinka River. The river often has a bluish hue due to the copper wastes. The Silinka is one of the dirtiest rivers in the country and regularly features in the monthly ecological section of the regional newspapers, *Dalny Vostok* and *Tikhniokean Zvezda*.

A tour of the plant is quite scary with bank upon bank of tables vibrating away in dim light and no-one in sight. To organise a tour, go to the office and ask. They will either find someone to take you or simply say, "just wander around".

If you follow the single road through Gorny for another 11km you reach the famous lake of Amutinka (Оз. Амутинка) which translates as *black*. The lake is very cold as it is filled by the mountainous Amut River (р. Амут) and exits to become the Silinka River. The lake's water is pure and it is a very picturesque picnic spot. You need a 4 wheel drive to get there or good hiking boots.

Festivalny (Фестивальный)

This settlement is now virtually a ghost town with only about 100 people living there. Since the closure of the nearby underground Molodezhny mine, workers have moved to Solnechny. The remaining inhabitants either have retired or prefer to live in a house with a garden plot rather than in a multi-storey apartment building. There used to be an overhead bucket system which carried the ore to the Solnechny concentrator and its remains litter the sides of roads.

Amursk (Амурск)
☎ area code: 421-47

Virtually everything ever written about Amursk states that the city was founded in 1958 in order to build a giant industrial complex producing cellulose, which is the basic ingredient of paper. This was a lie. The real reason for building Amursk in a strangely remote, uninhabited area was the giant military industrial Amurmash complex (Амурмаш). Amurmash, which is short for Amur Machinery Enterprise, is officially described as producing non-standard equipment. In reality it produces tank shells and other ammunition. The enterprise consists of one building which is nearly 1km long. It can be seen on the left about 20 minutes out of town heading towards Komsomolsk. With the decrease in the defence budget, this factory is now producing buses and looking for overseas buyers for its munitions.

Amursk is an industrial town of 60,000 people. In 1958, construction of Amursk on virgin land was declared a new *Komsomol shock project* and volunteers were called from all over the Soviet Union. 900 workers arrived in the first week and the population grew rapidly despite the total lack of even rudimentary services. It may seem strange that people would volunteer to leave their comfortable homes for a rough life in the mosquito infested taiga, with winter temperatures as low as -40°C, however working on *shock projects* attracted greater wages, status and important access to limited goods such as books, carpets and cars.

Amursk was designed soon after the 1955 decree which renounced Stalinesque decorative, classically inspired buildings in favour of plainer, more easily constructed buildings. The architects of Amursk applied this decree to the letter and produced a fine example of post-Stalinest construction. Consequently Amursk has some of the country's ugliest concrete box apartment buildings totally devoid of decoration.

Getting there and away
Amursk is 63km south of Komsomolsk and 18km from the closest railway station of Mulki (Мылки). The easiest way to get there is on Bus № 220 from Komsomolsk which travels 18 times a day. Amursk originated buses include Bus № 103 which goes to Mulki station while Bus № 101 goes to Padali station (Падали), one station further south. Bus № 224 goes even further south to the large railway town of Elban (Ельбан).

Amursk (Амурск)

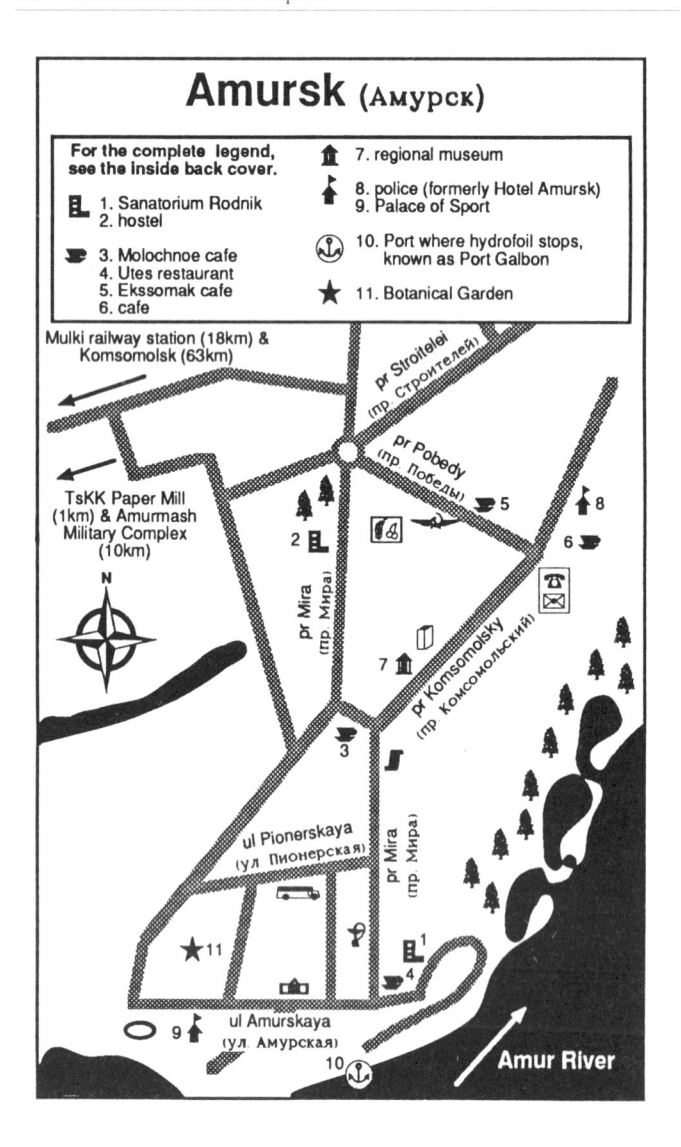

For the complete legend, see the inside back cover.

1. Sanatorium Rodnik
2. hostel
3. Molochnoe cafe
4. Utes restaurant
5. Ekssomak cafe
6. cafe
7. regional museum
8. police (formerly Hotel Amursk)
9. Palace of Sport
10. Port where hydrofoil stops, known as Port Galbon
11. Botanical Garden

Mulki railway station (18km) & Komsomolsk (63km)

TsKK Paper Mill (1km) & Amurmash Military Complex (10km)

pr Stroitelei (пр Строителей)

pr Pobedy (пр Победы)

pr Mira (пр Мира)

pr Komsomolsky (пр Комсомольский)

ul Pionerskaya (ул Пионерская)

pr Mira (пр Мира)

ul Amurskaya (ул Амурская)

Amur River

The most scenic route is via the Amur River on either a hydrofoil or local ferry from Komsomolsk or Khabarovsk. The Amursk River Station is just a floating barge with a few cabins and seats on it moored at the bottom of a cliff. Every winter the barge is moved to a place safe from the crushing effects of pack ice. The hydrofoil between Komsomolsk and Khabarovsk stops here as does the 7 times a day ferry between Amursk and Komsomolsk.

Where to stay
The best place to stay is the Sanatorium Rodnik, pr Mira 226, ☎ 236-21 or 264-53 (Родник, пр. Мира 226). Rooms cost $7. The only other option is a hostel at pr Mira 48 (Общежитие, пр. Мира 48). There was once a hotel in town called Amursk Hotel at pr Komsomolski 19 (Гостиница Амурск, пр. Комсомольский 19) but the building was taken over by the police and the town is now without a proper hotel. In the future it may be reopened.

What to see
The museum used to be devoted to the cellulose complex but since 1992, all reference to it has been removed. According to the museum's curator, Tatyana Ivanovna, "no one was interested". There is still one room dedicated to the early days of Amursk including a tent with wooden floors, stove and samovar. There is also one room devoted to the early settlers and more interestingly to the original indigenous people. On display are a number of archaeological finds that are over 5,000 years old, most of them recovered from the ancient settlement of Vosnesenskoe (Вознесенское) across the river from Amursk. The museum is located at pr Komsomolski, ☎ 245-533 (Краеведческий музей, пр. Комсомольский).

Amursk contains the third biggest greenhouse botanical garden in the Russian Far East, after Khabarovsk and Vladivostok. It has its roots in the Amursk Society of Young Fans of Cactuses formed in 1982. With support from members and the city council, the Botanical Gardens were created in 1988 and today have over 1,000 varieties of cactuses with the oldest being 25 years old and the heaviest being 1 ton. Its total collection contains 13,000 species of plants.

Before the collapse of the Soviet Union, 30,000 visitors used to marvel at the Gardens with their summer temperature of 30-35°C and winter temperature of 18°C.

However, with the collapse of the economy, few tourists visit the Gardens and the council now only pays wages and not capital repairs. In addition, the Gardens have been forced to save money by reducing the heating bill and in 1994, the winter temperature was just 8°C. Many plants unfortunately died.

To raise money, the Garden is now breeding plants and raising birds and tropical fish for sale as well as contracting for revegetation work.

TsKK paper mill
The industrial face of Amursk is TsKK or the Tsellyulosno-Kartony Kombinat (Цкк-Целлюлозно-картонный комбинат). This giant complex was the second cellulose and cardboard plant in the Russian Far East after the Japanese built a plant at Karufuto on south Sakhalin Island (which was occupied by the Soviets at the end of the war).

According to Soviet official history, for what it is worth, searching for a suitable location for such a plant started prior to the *Great Patriotic War* and was resumed in 1955. The plant started producing 75 tons a day of white cellulose from mainly silver fir trees supplied from 40 large logging camps. In 1992, TsKK consisted of 3 plants, 30 shops and 3,846 workers, producing amongst other things worked wood products, paper, cardboard, fodder yeast, ethylene spirit and fibre-board. The management will not disclose more recent figures but rumours floating around town all point to continual retrenchments and an eventual closure of the TsKK.

The biggest problem at the plant is air and water pollution. Despite claims that the 800,000 cubic metres of waste water a day discharged from the works remain in aerated ponds for several months before being pumped into the Amur River, untreated waste water often gets into the river. This often happens when the river floods bringing its water level above the height of the pond walls. The other problem is the stench. As you can imagine, millions of tons of rotting water lets off a horrendous odour. According to locals, the only relief comes when the wind blows away from the city or when it rains. The plant's management claims that the cost of cleaning up existing industrial pollution and installing new filtration equipment was 500 million roubles in 1992 and they do not have this money.

The main TsKK plant is about 1km from the city on the road to Komsomolsk. The end of the blue main building closest to the city is the area normally visited as it is the end of the production process.

Komsomolsk – Sovetskaya Gavan
Комсомольск - Советская Гавань

This section of the BAM was the only one completed during the *Great Patriotic War* and it played an important part in the Soviet seizure of Sakhalin and the Kuril Islands from the Japanese. Ironically, Japanese

POWs built a substantial part of the line. The 487km trip is quite slow due to the poor quality of the line. The trip is very scenic, passing through the Sikhote Alin mountain range before reaching the port cities of Vanino and Sovetskaya Gavan. From here, it is possible to catch a ferry across the Tatar Straits to Sakhalin Island.

The line is better serviced than the main part of the BAM and has three trains a day, two of which start in Khabarovsk and one near Vladivostok.

Until the early 1990s, the area was considered a border zone and both foreigners and Russians needed special permission to travel through it. The area was also restricted as it contained strategic reserves stockpiled in preparation for an invasion of Japan. As such, you will see a large number of military bases in the area which are either closed or being scaled down.

History of the line
The line was built in two stages; a 468km section from the right bank of the Amur at Pivan to Sovetskaya Gavan completed in 1945 and the 19km branch line from Komsomolsk to Pivan including the 1,437m Amur River bridge in 1975.

The 468km section was mostly built by gulag prisoners and POWs under the control of the Ministry of Internal Affairs' Construction Unit No 500. There were 6 major camps along the line with headquarters at Gursoe (Гурсое) and the main Japanese POW Camp No 1 at Vysokogornaya. In October 1945, Construction Unit No 500 consisted of a total of 124,000 workers which included 9,000 free workers, 2,600 escort guards, 1,600 railway troops, 34,000 Russian gulag prisoners, 12,800 exiled Russian ethnic minorities, 1,000 Germans POWs and 49,500 Japanese POWs.

The line was completed on 20 June 1945 and immediately started carrying soldiers to Vanino for the invasion of south Sakhalin Island which was held by the Japanese at that time. The first scheduled service started on 5 October 1946 but work continued for several more years building stations and improving the track.

Komsomolsk 1 (Комсомольск 1)   3,837km
For information on Komsomolsk, see the *Komsomolsk* section.

Amurski (Амурский)
This station, on the left bank of the Amur River, is the closest one to the Amur bridge.

Pivan (Пивань)   19km
This attractive settlement was built at the same time as

Komsomolsk to supply construction materials to the city. Nowadays, the brick factory, quarries and industrial railway lines lie abandoned around the mostly wooden town. Nearby is a *dacha village* where the exit to the Pivan tunnel lies. See the *Around Komsomolsk* section for more information on the Pivan tunnel.

Gaiter (Гайтер)   48km
To the south of the railway, you will see the large Khummi Lake (Оз. Хумми) which is really a bay on the Amur River.

Kartel (Картель)   60km
Near the station is the town of Bolshaya Kartel (Большая Картель) which was the site of a massive failed military project that very publicly revealed the huge waste and gross mismanagement of the

---

Amur Bridge

This 1,437m bridge spans the Amur River. Although it also carries road traffic, the bridge was primarily built to connect Komsomolsk on the left bank with the railway line to Sovetskaya Gavan on the right bank. The first train crossed over it on 26 September 1975 while it took another 7 years before it was opened to cars on 9 June 1982!

Before the bridge was built, transporting freight across the river was difficult. In summer, spring and autumn, train ferries would take 3 hours to transport rolling stock and many hours to load and unload. During winter, rails were laid over the frozen ice and the trains would go straight across it. There was normally a month's interruption to train services in between when ferries could not break through the ice or when the ice was too thin to support the rails. This twice yearly interruption would result in huge pile ups of up to 3,000 freight cars in yards on both sides of the river. Ice breaking ferries were tried in the early 1960s to overcome this problem but they were unsuccessful.

The Amur bridge is the longest of the BAM's 3,000 bridges and is considered one of the most innovative bridges in Russia. It was designed by Leningraders K S Shably and G L Katranov of the National Research Institute of Transport Engineering, and consists of eight 159m spans and five 33m spans. It used four techniques which were novel at the time. Firstly, it used 304 hollow ferroconcrete supports instead of the traditional solid footings to support the bridge. Secondly, it was fastened with thousands of high tension bolts which could each support 30 tons rather than the traditional tens of thousands of rivets. Thirdly, rails were directly bolted onto ferroconcrete slabs without the need for ballast, rather than onto sleepers supported by ballast. Finally, constructors used jet rock drilling for the first time in bridge construction.

Using these innovations plus overcoming the natural obstacles of great water depth, sharp fluctuations in the water level and fierce winter winds, it was hardly unexpected that the construction time doubled to over 10 years.

It is forbidden to stop on the bridge or even walk over it. The soldiers who guard the bridge at both end, enforce this law and will even stop you from taking photos.

Soviet military.

The Bolshaya Kartel saga started with an article entitled Mysteries of a Dead Object in the regional newspaper, *Priamurskie Vedomosti* (Приамурские Ведомости) on 27 November 1991. It was then given national exposure when the article was reprinted in the national newspaper *Izvestiya*. The article described a massive experimental radio locator station as part of an anti-missile defence system. It consisted of a 2km diameter circle with 300 steel antennas outside and 270 inside, and a monitoring complex. The complex was built by the Scientific Research Institute of Remote Radio Communication under the Ministry of Radio Industry with funds supplied by the Ministry of Defence. When it was finished in 1981, it was of limited success, because in its first year of operation it didn't work for 173 days and in just the first quarter of 1982, it stopped working on 106 occasions. It worked intermittently until 1983 when it was permanently shutdown, but it took until 1985 before it was decided to dismantle the complex. By then all the technical staff had left and there was no money or interest in actually carrying out the order. There was insufficient manpower to provide proper guarding and by the late 1980s, most of the valuable equipment and materials had been looted and the monitoring complex had been burned down.

The article decried the incredible waste and mismanagement and Gorbachev personally organised an investigation commission. Its conclusions were that between 6 and 20 million roubles (US$300,000 to 2,000,000) worth of precious metals and equipment had been stolen, however, strangely and probably for political reasons, the commission could not determine how much the project cost. In addition, the commission could not find anyone to blame so no charges were ever laid.

Until Gorbachev's policy of *glasnost* was introduced, this type of story was considered secret and never published. However *glasnost* opened a floodgate of exposes which contributed significantly to the rapid loss of confidence in the Communist Party, military and bureaucracy.

Today, the site remains unchanged and you can see part of the antenna complex from the railway and road.

Selikhin (Селихин)   71km

This is a large town where eastward bound trains normally stop for 20 minutes while westward trains stop for only 10 minutes. It is the southward turnoff for the road to Khabarovsk (300 km) and the northward turnoff to Cape Lazarev (500 km) near Nikolaevsk-na-Amure and Sakhalin Island. There are 5 buses a day to here from Komsomolsk. There are buses both north and south which may run as infrequently as once a week but none go as far as either Komsomolsk and Cape Lazarev.

Selikhin is also the junction of a railway branch line to the north. It goes through the villages of Machtovy (Мачтовый), Otkyabrski (Октябрьский), Chyni (Чучи), Nizhnetambovskoe (Ни)нетамбовское), Shelekhovo (Шелехово) and Yagodny (Ягодный) before terminating at Cherny Mys (Черный Мыс).

This railway was approved on 5 May 1950 by the Council of Ministers of the USSR and it was intended to reach Cape Lazarev where it would enter a 9km tunnel under the Tatar Straits before surfacing on Sakhalin Island. By 1953, 122km of rails had been laid as far as Cherny Mys and this length was opened for traffic. In March 1953 Stalin died and on 26 May 1953, the Council of Ministers stopped this and a number of Stalin's other pet projects. The line was transferred from the BAM Railway to the Far East Forestry Company (Гладальлеспром) and it became a forestry line. A few times, local and regional governments have proposed recommencing construction of the line to Nikolaevsk, however this is usually used as a vote winner for the isolated people to the north. The line does not carry passengers and consequently, is not shown on most railway maps of Russia.

Kun (Кун)   114km
The town near the station is not called Kun but Snezhny (Сне)ный). After leaving Kun, the train starts a long ascent through the chain of mountains which make up the Sikhote Alin Range (Хребет Сихотэ Алинь). The first chain you pass is the Khomi mountains.

Gurskoe (Гурское)   131km
This medium sized town derives its name from the Gur River which travels parallel with the railway for about 50km. Gurskoe was the location of the headquarters of the prisoner camps which built the railway and most of the buildings in town were constructed by prisoners.

Udomi (Удоми)   192km
This town partially owes it existence to being a passing loop stop. Due to the scheduling of trains along a single track line, eastward bound trains stop here for a few minutes in a siding, while westward bound trains don't stop at all.

Oune (Оунэ)   201km
At the 203km point is a memorial to the survey engineer, Arseni Petrovich Kuznetsov (1901-1943), who is buried on the eastern side of the nearby Peschanaya Mountain. The monument was built in the 1940s and is now crumbling. See under *Kuznetsovski* for more information on the surveyor.

Kuznetsovski (Кузнецовский)   222km

Contrary to what many Russians believe, the town is not named after the famous Russian Admiral Kuznetsov but rather the little known survey engineer, Arseni Petrovich Kuznetsov (Арсений петрович Кузнецов). Between 1935 and 1938 Arseni Petrovich surveyed much of the BAM and was then transferred to surveying the route for the Komsomolsk – Sovetskaya Gavan railway. When the war broke out, he was forced to resurvey the entire route as there was no metal for the planned bridges and little labour for the envisaged tunnels. The route finally chosen was significantly longer and more twisting than the original route but it could be constructed with less resources. He died in his office of a heart attack induced by overwork on 15 November 1943.

A monument was unveiled in Kuznetsovski on 1 July 1993 to commemorate the 50th anniversary of the joining of the east and west sections of the railway which occurred here.

Just beyond the town is the only tunnel on this section of the BAM. The 300m tunnel took prisoners 13 months to dig.

Vysokogornaya (Высокогорная)   239km

This town was the centre of the Japanese POW complex known as Camp Department No 1. Most of the town, including the station, was built by the Japanese. The train normally stops here for 30 minutes which is enough time to go to the popular bore beside the station to have a wash. The major occupations of the inhabitants are gold mining and logging.

The only accommodation is at the Locomotive Brigade Hostel (Дом Отдыха Локомотивой Бригады).

Datta (Датта)   259km

Why this station is called Datta is a mystery as the village of Datta is 160km away on the Pacific Ocean coast near Vanino.

Dzhigdasi (Джигдаси)   293km

The following story was told by N M Derevtsov, Veteran of Labour and former engineer on the Komsomolsk – Sovetskaya Gavan railway. He now lives in Kislovodsk near the Black Sea.

"Although the Japanese POWs left a legacy of buildings and railways, there were only a few instances when they left something more precious - descendants. One such instance occurred in the town of Dzhigdasi, and involved a Japanese engineer called Umoda and a Volga German telephonist named Marsha. Marsha was an internal exile as she and her parents had been deported to this region from their native Kazakstan during the *Great Patriotic War* due to Stalin's suspicion about their nationality's loyalty.

Initially, when the Japanese came to Dzhigdasi in 1943, they were always under close guard and officers were separated from enlisted men. Political education was an integral part of camp life and prisoners were divided into democrats and non-democrats with the latter, which included monarchists, considered anti-Soviet and requiring a more fundamental education. Political education included regular parades in support of communism, lessons on communist philosophy and the publication of a Japanese language communist paper called Symbol. While most of the Japanese paid little attention to education, Umoda, applied himself to learning Russian. Being a engineer, democrat and supervisor, he soon was trusted enough to walk around unescorted and because of his rare Russian ability, became a popular figure among the Russians. He developed a friendship with Marsha, and they spent as much time as they could together which was very limited as she worked all day and Umoda had to be back in camp before evening curfew.

The Japanese character Kotobuku meaning happiness.

Umoda told Marsha he loved her on her 18th birthday and gave her a beautiful red handkerchief which had on one side in exotic calligraphy the Japanese character Kotobuku meaning happiness. Unfortunately, the Japanese repatriation started in spring 1947 and he was one of the first to be shipped home. Unbeknownst to him, Marsha was pregnant with his child and returned to Kazakhstan to give birth to their child, Kolya. Despite all of her efforts, Marsha died without finding Umoda and telling him that he was a father. Kolya now lives in Germany and is still trying to trace his father."

Tuluchi (Тулучи) 322km

After leaving this town, the train passes over the Tumninski Range with the Primorski Range visible to the north.

Tumnin (Тумнин) 359km

There is a well known hot water spring about 10km out of this town along a dirt track. The town is named after the 364km Tumnin River which starts in the Sikhote Alin mountains and flows into the Tatar Straits. The railway runs through the Tumnin Valley until Vanino. This river is a major salmon spawning river and in August and September, fishermen will often sell jars of red caviar as the train stops along this section.

It is around this town and Vanino that most sightings have been made of the *Taiga Yeti*. About every six months the local newspapers report a new sighting of this monster, probably as a way of boosting circulation. The first real 'proof' was obtained in 1992 when footprints measuring 45cm were found. In the same year, the Yeti claimed its first victim who was a fit and healthy geologist who died of a heart attack when he saw the monster. If you do see the Yeti, don't be too worried as it appears he is a vegetarian having left the geologist's body untasted!

Ust-Orochi (Усть-Орочи)   399km
The Orochi is the Russian name for the local indigenous people who call themselves the Nanai. They mainly live in this area and around Komsomolsk. In 1979 there were just 1,200 left. They are commonly confused with the Oroki on Sakhalin Island, who are descended from Evenk, and the Orochony but the Orochi are a different ethnic group.

Mongokhto (Монгохто)   418km
Discretely hidden away from the station is the marine aviation base of Mongokhto. It was built as a staging post for lend lease goods flown from the US. There are claims that it is also the storage site of chemical weapons which pose a risk as their containers are physically deteriorating and the military has no money to destroy them.

There is also a road from here to the village of Datta on the Pacific Coast.

Vanino-Vokzal (Ванино-Вокзал)   453km
☎ area code: 421-76 ✉ Khabarovski Krai Хабаровский Край

Vanino is infamous throughout Russia as the port of departure for gulag prisoners to the death camps to the north. Nowadays, Vanino is one of the major Russian ports on the Pacific Ocean and the main gateway to Sakhalin Island.

Despite there being little to see in Vanino, travellers often prefer to stay here than the larger and more interesting Sovetskaya Gavan. The reason for this is that Vanino is easier to reach and is centrally placed for exploration of the region.

Getting there and away
There are three trains a day into Vanino, two of which start in Khabarovsk and one near Vladivostok.
There are no roads from Komsomolsk to Vanino.
There is an airport halfway between Vanino and the nearby city of Sovetskaya Gavan with flights to Komsomolsk, Khabarovsk and Yuzhno-Sakhalinsk on Sakhalin Island. Plane tickets can be bought at the railway station.

There are ferries which travel every second day to the port city of

Kholmsk on Sakhalin Island. The first ferry, called Sakhalin 1, was commissioned in June 1973 and carries passengers, railway wagons, cars and trucks. The 144km trip takes 9 hours. Tickets can be purchased at the railway station but you will have to show your visa with Sakhalin typed on it to get a ticket.

The easiest way to travel to Sovetskaya Gavan is to take Bus №101 from Vanino's central bus station which is near the light beacon in the middle of the main street. For information on the complicated train trip between Vanino and Sovetskaya Gavan, see under *Sovetskaya Gavan*.

VANINO LAMENT

The following is a song about the departure of gulag prisoners from Vanino to their probable death in the gulag camps of the north. As being sent from Vanino invariably meant that the prisoner would never return, most spouses never mentioned their disappeared partner and got remarried. This song describes this reality.

Following Stalin's death and the opening of prisons, many of the 'living dead' returned home to be ordered away by their former spouses afraid of the danger to their new family if another purge followed.

I remember that Vanino port, at the side of the steam ships so sullen, While we were going on board deep into those cold and dull holds.	Я помню тот ванинский порт, И вид пароходов угрюмый, Как шли мы по трапу на борт В холодные мрачные трюмы.
The sea fog was getting worse and worse, and the sea was beginning to roar ... Magadan appeared before us - "Capital of the Kolyma Territory".	Над морем сгущался туман, Ревела стихия морская. Стоял впереди Магадан - «Столица колымского края»
It was not a song but a moaning cry that came out of every heart: "Farewell the continent, farewell for good!" that was the roaring cry of the steamship.	Не песня, а]алобный крик Из каждой груди вырывался «Прощай навсегда, материк» Ревел пароход, надрывался ...
Everyone was seasick the prisoners embraced each other like brothers ... From time to time some curses came out of their mouths ...	От Качки тошнило, зэка Обнялись: как родные братья ... И Только порой с языка Срывались глухие проклятья ...
Be damned, Kolyma, that is like an alien planet, One can easily be driven mad There is no way back from here ...	Будь проклята ты, Колыма, Что назбана чудной планетой, Сойдешь поневоле с ума - Отсюда возврата уж нету ...
I know you are not waiting for me, and you don't read my letters. I know you are not going to meet me, and even if you do, you'll not recognise me.	Я знаю, меня ты не]дешь, И писем моих не читаешь, Я знаю - встречать не придешь, А если придешь - не узнаешь

Where to stay
The best hotel is opposite the station and is called Hotel Vanino, ul Chekhova 1, ☎ 51-228 (Гостиница Ванино, ул. Чехова 1). The director is Valintina Lvanovna Romanovna ☎ 519-07. Another option is the Hotel Komerchaya ☎ 506-81 (Гостиница Коммерческая). A more difficult place to organise is the 6 bed hostel at the Sports Complex near the hospital. Sergi Gorinov is its director, ☎ 512-24. There is also a hostel at the port but it is also difficult to organise accommodation there.

Where to eat
The best place to eat is the chic Cafe Odin (Кафе Один). The canteen at the station is large and open most of the time.

What to see
The only place of interest in town is the port and unless you have a ticket for the ferry, you won't see even this. During the communist-era the port was owned by its major user, the Sovetskaya Gavan Base of Ocean

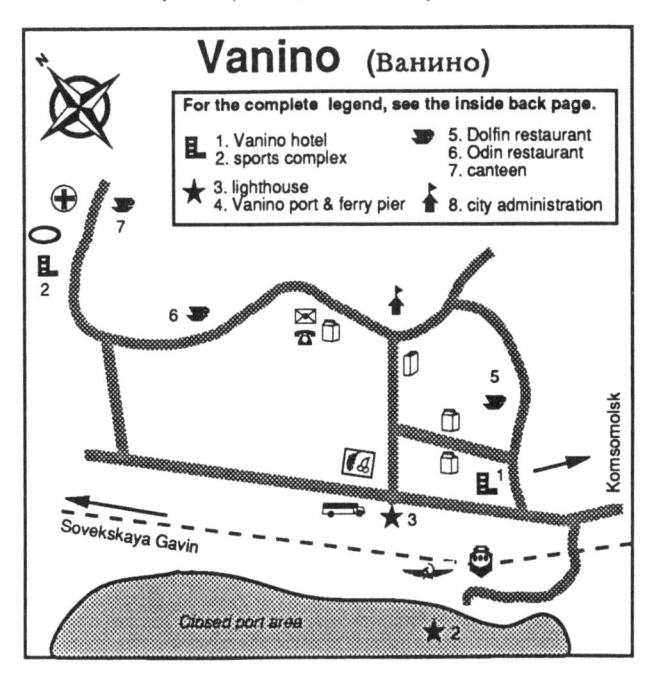

Vanino (Ванино)

For the complete legend, see the inside back page.

1. Vanino hotel
2. sports complex
3. lighthouse
4. Vanino port & ferry pier
5. Dolfin restaurant
6. Odin restaurant
7. canteen
8. city administration

Fishing Enterprise which is now called Morskie Resursy (Морские Ресурсы). However the port has now been privatised and is only interested in lucrative foreign ships which has been detrimental to the local fishing industry and railway. The problem is summed up in an article in the regional newspaper, *Tikhookeanskaia Zvezda* on 4 August 1993. "Formerly one could make arrangements with the port director for unloading the vessel, refuelling it, for servicing it ... now at the port there are several commercial entities for loading and unloading ... Fuel is no longer an obligation of the port but must be arranged with a company which has more interest in supplying foreign vessels for hard currency than supplying a domestic fishing company ... In fact, fuel was

---

VANINO TRANSIT CAMP

Before World War Two, the main transit camp for gulag prisoners to the northern goldfields of Kolyma, Magadan, Sakhalin, Kamchatka and to the uranium mines of Primorski Territory was Nakhodka, near Vladivostok. However with the opening of the BAM, part of the transit camp moved to Vanino. These camps were like giant slave markets with representatives from various camps coming to select the fittest workers. For instance, one large mine in the region had a contract with the NKVD (the KGB forerunner) to supply 12,000 prisoners a year.

Most prisoners only stayed in Vanino for a few days, which was just as well as they mostly slept in tents or out in the open. However some were unlucky enough to be caught there at the end of the navigational season or when something unusual happened, such as when the harbour was blocked when a load of explosives for the Kolyma mines blew up on board the ship, Dalstroi, in 1946.

The following description of the Vanino transit camp was written by Solomon M, in *Magadan*, 1971. "When we came out on to the immense field outside the camp, I witnessed a spectacle that would have done justice to a Cecil B DeMille production. As far as the eye could see, there were columns of prisoners marching in one direction or another like armies on a battlefield. A huge detachment of security officers, soldiers and signal corpsmen with field telephones and motor-cycles kept in touch with headquarters, arranging the smooth flow of these human rivers. I asked what this giant operation was meant to be. The reply was that each time transport was sent off, the administration reshuffled the occupants of every cage in camp so that everyone had to be removed with his bundle or rags on his shoulder to the big field and from there directed to his new destination. Only 5,000 were supposed to leave, but 100,000 were part of the scene before us. One could see endless columns of women, of cripples, of old men and even teenagers, all in military formation, five in a row, going through the huge field, and directed by whistles or flags. It was more than three hours before the operation was completed and the batch I belonged to was allowed to leave for the embarkation point."

The numbers described by M Solomon may be somewhat exaggerated as archives have revealed that there were only ever a maximum of 10 permanent and transit camps in Vanino with a total population of 15,000. Another description of the horrors of Vanino's transit camps can be found in *Kolyma: The Arctic Death Camps* by Robert Conquest, 1978.

sold to foreigners at the same time that the ferry between Vanino and Sakhalin didn't run 'because of lack of fuel'".

Foreign ships are a common sight in Vanino, particularly from Japan and the Chinese port of Taijin, and the town is awash with second hand Japanese cars, Chinese plastic toys and imported food.

Getting assistance
Staff at the Vanino Sea Port's International Department can assist in organising hotels and other arrangements. However, they may be expensive. Anya Ilkhovskaya (Аня Ильховская) speaks excellent English but her boss and head of the department, Valeri Sabinov (Валерий Сабинов) does not, ☎ 57-637, fax 514-82, telex 141156 PIRS SU.

Sovetskaya Gavan-Sortirovka (Oktyabrski)
(Советская Гавань-Сортировка (Октябрьский)) 461km

This station is the Sovetskaya Gavan marshalling yards and is still 26km from the Sovetskaya Gavan passenger station. You change trains here for Sovetskaya Gavan if you are on a long distance train, however you do not need to change trains if you are on a local train. The town is quite large as it is the region's main railway depot. There is a railway hostel here.

There is a road from here to the closed naval base called Zavety Ilicha (Заветы Ильича) which translates as The Legacy of Vladimir Ilich Lenin.

Desna (Десна)   476km
This station serves the village of Maiski (Майский).

Sovetskaya Gavan-Gorod
(Советская Гавань-Город)   487km
☎ area code: 421-71 ✉ 682880, Khabarovski Krai
Хабаровский Край

From the day the gulf of Sovetskaya Gavan was discovered in 1853 by Admiral Boshnyak, the area has been militarily significant both as a naval base and as forward defence against Japan.

The gulf's headwater is about 2km wide and flanked by Cape Menshevik and Cape Putyatina. The gulf consists of three bays; the Severnaya (south), Zapadnaya (west) which is also known as Konstantin and Yugo-Zapadnaya (southwest) which is also known as Khadzhy Gulf.

The gulf provides one of the few good deep harbours in the Far East and although the bay ices over from November to April, ships can move in and out with the assistance of ice breaking tugs. Fogs are common during May, June and July. The gulf was an ideal invasion place for the Japanese who occupied parts of the Far East until 1922. At that time, the lower half of Sakhalin Island, which is about 120km away, was occupied by the Japanese. For this reason, there are numerous old trenches, bunkers and observation points built before the *Great Patriotic War* dotted around Sovetskaya Gavan's coastline.

Sovetskaya Gavan was one of the 3 most important naval bases of the Pacific Fleet and at its height in the 1950s and 1960s, it normally had 7-10 major surface combatants such as cruisers, destroyers, frigates, coastal patrol ships and submarines and 80 small support vessels harboured there. The base also housed a submarine school.

The navy started using the base for fitting out half built ships and submarines from the Komsomolsk shipyards when the first floating dock of 5,000 tons arrived in 1939.

After the Soviet occupation of Sakhalin Island, which removed the direct Japanese threat, the region's priority shifted from forward defence to the support of Soviet forces on Sakhalin. The post war Soviet strategy was to prepare for an invasion of Japan by dispatching forces through Sakhalin across the narrow straits to secure Japan's Hakkaido Island. The Japanese's response was a strategy called Look North which involved placing their most powerful defence units on Hakkaido. The Fleet Air Arm airbase at Sovetskaya Gavan provided, and still does, long distance reconnaissance bombers including Tu-16 Badgers and Tu-142 Bears.

To support the Soviet strategy, about 20% of the Russian Far East's 11 million tons of war matériel was stored in the region's coastal area.

With the collapse of the Soviet Union, the military forces in the area have been disbanded or significantly reduced. Vessels are now rare in the Zavety IIicha naval base, which can be seen from the road that connects Vanino and Sovetskaya Gavan, and no construction work is carried out anymore. Few planes fly out from the military airport and troops aren't seen that often around Sovetskaya Gavan.

Commercial activity has now replaced the military focus in the region. The Sovetskaya Gavan port is now owned by the Terminal company which is made up of numerous Far East, Altai and Yakutian enterprises. From the number of imported Japanese cars, babies and status-symbol big dogs in town, it appears that many locals have prospered because of this arrangement.

The city has actively sought international connections and already has sister city agreements with Everet in USA, Rymo in Japan, and the Port of Sligo in Ireland. Of particular interest to foreign companies are forestry concessions. Australians are particularly active in the area which is ironic considering that an Australian company held the last concession of the Czarist period at the turn of the century.

Sovetskaya Gavan has a population of about 40,000. This is lower than the peak of 50,000 in 1959 which coincided with the height of the Cold War but significantly higher than the low of 26,000 in 1967.

The city was originally known as Imperatorskaya Gavan or Emperor's Harbour, and in 1926, became Sovetskaya Gavan. The city administration has so far resisted pressure to return to its original name.

Getting there and away

Getting here by train is not straight forward. Although there is a Sovetskaya Gavan station and the long distance trains have Sovetskaya Gavan written on their destination plates, these trains do not actually reach Sovetskaya Gavan. Instead the trains terminate in the Sovetskaya Gavan marshalling yards called Sovetskaya Gavan-Sortirovka (Советская Гавань-Сортировка), which is also known as Oktyabrski (Октябрьский). Sovetskaya Gavan-Sortirovka is 8km from Vanino and 26km from Sovetskaya Gavan. At Sovetskaya Gavan-Sortirovka, passengers change for a two carriage local train for the final leg of the journey. This transfer usually means that you arrive in Sovetskaya Gavan 2 hours after you depart Vanino. The journey is reversed when you depart Sovetskaya Gavan.

Beware the timetable at Sovetskaya Gavan station which states the time of departure for the train at Sovetskaya Gavan-Sortirovka even though it just says Sovetskaya Gavan. The connecting train from Sovetskaya Gavan to Sovetskaya Gavan-Sortirovka leaves Sovetskaya Gavan about 90 minutes before the long distance train to Khabarovsk departs Sovetskaya Gavan-Sortirovka.

Be warned that if you catch Train № 251, you will arrive at midnight in Vanino and two in the morning at Sovetskaya Gavan. This is a dreadful time to arrive in any town but particularly bad in Sovetskaya Gavan as the station is stuck in the middle of nowhere about 8km from the town. To get to the city, you walk through the forest for 200m up a hill until you reach a bus shelter on the road. Bus № 1 goes to the city. To get to the station from the city, get off at the second stop. Unfortunately, it appears that very few taxis wait at the station. The 8km railway extension to the city has been planned for decades but work has yet to start. The station's ticket office hours are 11:30 to 14:30 and 17:00 to 20:00.

There are also local trains which run daily between Sovetskaya Gavan and Vanino, but Bus № 101 from Sovetskaya Gavan to Vanino is more convenient. The bus departs from the Victory Square beside the hotel in Sovetskaya Gavan.

There is an airport between Vanino and Sovetskaya Gavan with flights to Komsomolsk, Khabarovsk and Yuzhno-Sakhalinsk on Sakhalin Island.

Plane tickets are sold at the Aeroflot office on ul Goncharova (ул. Гончарова).

Where to stay
Sovetskaya Gavan has a large hotel, however due to the difficulties of getting to the city, most travellers stay in Vanino. Sovetskaya Gavan Hotel, ul Pionerskaya 14, ☎ 31-783 or 31-614 (Гостиница Советская Гавань, ул. Пионерская 14).

There is a business centre in town which can possibly organise travel arrangements. Business Centre, ul Lenina 12, ☎ and fax 34-851 (ул. Ленина).

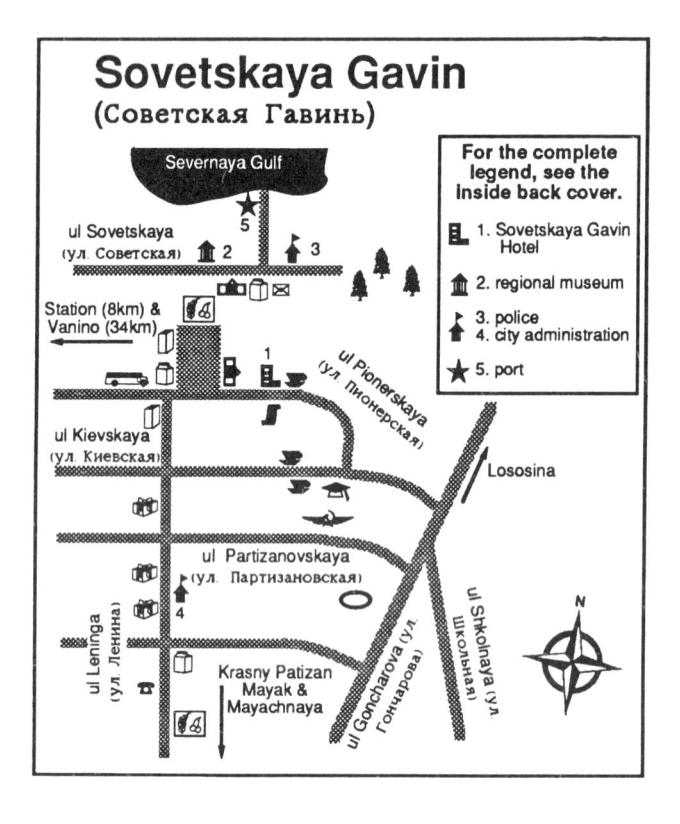

Where to eat
There are limited choices in this city with the only restaurant being at the Sovetskaya Gavan Hotel. As Sovetskaya Gavan is the base for much of the northern Pacific Ocean fishing fleet, the shops are stocked with excellent fish. Kamchatka crabs are quite common as the crab beds to the north produce about 80% of the world's canned crab. In addition, the city's cannery produces tins of red caviar which fill the local shops.

What to see
The regional museum contains a small collection on the revolutionary and gulag-era history of the region plus excellent material on the indigenous people. It also has a room of stuffed animals and birds including a rare Amur tiger. It is open all days except Saturday and Monday from 10:00 to 18:00 with a lunch break from 13:00 to 14:00. It is located at ul Sovetskaya 29 (музей, ул. Советская 29).

The only part of the port that is easily accessible is near the museum. Until 1992, a ferry used to leave this pier for Vanino. If demand increases, it may be resumed.

An interesting day trip is to the Pacific Ocean to see the remains of anti-Japanese paranoia. To get there, you catch a bus for 30 minutes to the village of Lososina (Лососина). As you walk through the town you pass a monument to Admiral Boshnyak who discovered Sovetskaya Gavan's harbour in 1853. 300m from the bus is a junction with the good quality road veering to the right. Take the dirt track to the left and after 3-4km (40 minutes) you come to the sea with a road leading to a lighthouse which is called mayak (маяк) in Russian. From here you can see Vanino and Sakhalin with binoculars. 300m to the right of lighthouse is a 2 storey building with a radar dish on its roof. 500m to the left are concrete artillery bunkers which are 2m high, 2.5 wide, 3m long and are made of 50cm thick walls. All the guns have been removed. These fortifications and the trenches were built prior to the *Great Patriotic War* as a defence against the Japanese.

In front is a small island and although it is possible to climb down to the sea, it is dangerous. In October and November locals collect edible sea weed which is called sea cabbage (морская капуста) from the base of these cliffs. As can be seen by the surrounding 50cm high stunted pines and mountain ashes, the wind is extremely strong, so harvesting the seaweed is both dangerous and freezing work. The return walking trip from Lososina takes 4 hours.

Another day trip to the coast is to visit the Krasny Partizan Lighthouse (Красный партизан Маяк) and memorials on Cape Nikolaya (Мыс Николая). Beside the lighthouse is a memorial with a beautifully decorated bell which was the original lighthouse bell and dates from 1895. Also beside the lighthouse is a monument dedicated to the lighthouse keepers who were tortured to death by the White Army in 1919.

The lighthouse is in a naval area which was once closed, but now no-one seems to mind you wandering in. To get there, take the bus from Sovetskaya Gavan to Mayachnaya (Маячная) and then it is a short walk to the lighthouse.

BAM Branch Lines Route Descriptions

Route Description Legend

✗ station only

🏠 village

▦ town

Chegdomyn – Novy Urgal – Izvestkovaya	298
Komsomolsk – Khabarovsk	300
Bamovskaya – Tynda (The Little BAM)	304
Khrebtovaya – Ust-Ilimsk	307
Tynda – Neryungri – Aldan – Yakutsk (AYAM)	308

Chegdomyn – Novy Urgal – Izvestkovaya
Чегдомын - Новый Ургал - Известоковая

This 360km railway was the first part of the BAM to be built. It connects the Trans-Siberian station of Izvestkovaya with the BAM town of Novy Urgal, before terminating 32km later at Chegdomyn. The line was built to ship coal out from the massive Chegdomyn coal deposits. Much of it was built by Japanese POWs and Japanese graves litter the area.

Getting there and away
The line is basically used for freight and there is only one passenger train a day that travels its full length. This train runs between Chegdomyn and Khabarovsk, although one carriage may join another train bound for Vladivostok.

There are daily local trains from both ends of the line, Chegdomyn and Izvestkovaya, which travel as far as Tyrma which is halfway along the line.

There is no road between Chegdomyn and Izvestkovaya.

Chegdomyn (Чегдомын)   0km
For information, see under *Chegdomyn* in the *BAM mainline route description* chapter.

Urgal 1 (Ургал 1)   17km
Urgal 1 is located at 3,330km on the BAM. For information, see under *Urgal 1* in the *BAM mainline route description* chapter.

Novy Urgal (Новый Ургал)   32km
Novy Urgal is located at 3,315km on the BAM. For more information, see under *Novy Urgal* in the *BAM mainline route description* chapter.

Elga (Эльга)   75km
Elga is near the small port village of Chekunda (Чекунда) on the Bureya River. There are no regular passenger vessels from here down the Bureya.

Tyrma (Тырма)   191km
This is a railway town and there is accommodation at the Locomotive Brigade Hostel (Дом Отдыха Локомотивой Бригады). A local train runs from here to Chegdomyn in the north and another train

runs to Izvestkovaya in the south. The town is on the banks of the 334km Tyrma River, which flows into the Bureya River. This is the burial site of many Japanese POWs and is a popular pilgrimage site for Japanese.

🏠 Yaurin (Яурин)   303km
The Yaurin River snakes along beside the railway from near Tyrma until it crosses under the railway near Yaurin.

🏠 Perevalny (Перевальный)   309km
Just to the south of this railway station is the border of the Jewish Autonomous Region.

🏠 Kuldur (Кульдур)   330km
This is the location of the Kuldur Health Resort which is famous throughout Russia. The balneological resort is located in the scenic Kuldur River valley where the summer is moderately warm with a mean July temperature of 18°C but the winter is very cold with a mean January temperature of -27°C. The attraction of the resort is the therapeutic 72°C hot mineral water which has a chemical formula of:

$$F_{0.012} H^2 SiO^3{}_{0.108} M_{0.4} \frac{(HCO_3 + CO_3) 37 C 127}{(Na + K) 95 Ca 3} \qquad T\ 72°C \quad pH\ 9.3$$

Bathing in the cooled water is allegedly good for patients with skeletal-muscular, gynaecological, dermatological, nervous or digestive disorders. The health resort actually consists of two sanatoriums; Kuldur and Zhemchuchina Khingana. Kuldur (Кульдур) is located 2km from the station and is the main health resort. Zhemchuchina Khingana (Жемчужина Хингана) is located in town and designed for parents with children from 7 to 14. Its accommodation is mostly twin share rooms. It is necessary to book to stay in either of these sanatoriums. 682032 Khabarovsk *Krai*, Evreiskaya Autonomous *Oblast*, kurort Kuldur, sanatoriums Kuldur and Zhemchuchina Khingana (682032 Хабаровский край, Еврейская Автономная Область, курорт Кулдур, санаторий Кульдур или Жемчужина Хингана).

🏠 Izvestkovaya (Известковая)   360km
This town is on the Trans-Siberian and despite it being the junction of the Chegdomyn – Trans-Siberian line, most of the Trans-Siberian express trains do not stop here. It is a typical small town of about 2,000 people with a canteen, post office, dairy farm and market but little else. The old part of town, with its rustic wooden buildings and household garden plots, is hidden in the trees to the west of the town. It is not recommended to stop here unless you have to change trains.

Komsomolsk - Khabarovsk
Комсомольск - Хабаровск

This is probably the least interesting railway section in the Far East. There are only 5 reasonable sized towns en route with the rest of the stops being either forestry camps or railway sidings. The route is mostly flat as it runs across the Amur River flood plain. There is no road along the length of the railway as the Komsomolsk to Khabarovsk highway is 100km to the east on the other side of the Amur River.

As well as the 4 long distance trains a day from Komsomolsk to Khabarovsk, there are a number of local trains along parts of the line. The best advice for travelling on this route is to catch one of the overnight trains and sleep through the journey.

Komsomolsk (Комсомольск)   0km
Beside the railway is a good road which goes 78km to the village of Teisin on Lake Bolon. A few kilometres out of Komsomolsk is the turn off to the east to the small town of Molodezhny (Молодежный). For information on this city, see the *Komsomolsk* section in the *BAM mainline route description* chapter.

Khurba (Хурба)   7km
This small town is wedged between the Big Khurba and Little Khurba Rivers (р. Хурба).

Mylki (Мылки)   22km
This is the closest station to the industrial city of Amursk. Although there is a railway line to the city, it only carries freight trains. There are regular buses between Mulki and Amursk. For information on Amursk, see under *Amursk* in the *Around Komsomolsk* section in the *BAM mainline route description* chapter.

Raz. 303km (Раз. 303км)   36km
Surrounding the station is the small town of Izvestkovy (Известковый).

Elban (Эльбан)   63km
This is one of the biggest towns on this railway. It has a machine building plant, dairy farms and a large number of vegetable farms.

Teisin (Тейсин)   73km
Besides the station, there is nothing at this stop. However 5km east of here is the old village of Teisin which is on the edge of Lake Bolon. The road from Komsomolsk terminates here.

Kharkovsk (Харьковск)
This station is named after the west Russian city of Kharkov.

Bolon (Болонь)   ·99km
This 5,000 inhabitant railway and logging town takes its name from the nearby Lake Bolon. The town is wedged between the Alyur and Syumnyur Rivers (р. Алюр и Сюмнюр) which flow into the lake. The lake is also know as Bolen, Nuri-Odzhal or Boulen-Odzhal and is the largest lake in the flood plain of the lower Amur, being 338 square km, 70km long, 20km wide and having an average depth of 3m. In the centre of the lake is the volcanic island of Yadasen (о. Ядасен). The lake flows into the Amur River along a 9km channel and on its shores is the village of Achan (Ачан). This indigenous village is believed to the first settlement on the Amur River.

The Lake Bolon area is a major stopping place for migratory birds so the Wildlife Institute in Khabarovsk, which provides survey information for the government's nature resource management, has recommended that this area becomes a national park. Over 200 types of birds have been identified here.

A 1936 poster announcing the imminent arrival in Komsomolsk of the railway line from Khabarovsk.

From Bolon town, you can reach the lake by a 10km road. On the lake's shore is the village of Dzhuen (Джуен).

Sanboli (Санболи)   202km
There is a dirt road from Sanboli to the Trans-Siberian Railway. The road skirts to the north and west of the Vandan Mountain Range

(Хребет Вандан). Nearby are about 17 caves with the longest being 300m. The region is very hilly as the station on the Amur River flood plain is at 150m above sea level while the 848m Mount Elovaya (г. Еловая), the highest peak of the Vandan Mountain Range, is just 6km away from Sanboli.

Litovko (Литовко)   220km
This is the major railway town between Komsomolsk and the Trans-Siberian. There is a railway hostel here. 3km from the station is the village of Ukrainka (Украинка).

Dalnevostochny (Дальневосточный)   231km
The small forestry settlement around the station is known as Lesnoi (Лесной).

Darga (Дарга)   291km
Less than 1km east from here is the ancient Russian village of Golbuchnoe (Голубичное) on the Darga River.

Utiny (Утиный)   319km
This railway siding is named after the poet, Iosif Pavlovich Utkin (1903-1944) who was born in a village in the Khabarovsk region. His works were first published in 1922 and he won fame with the narrative poem, the *Tale of Motele the Redhead* (1925) which deals with the changes introduced by the October Revolution in a small Jewish town. He was the author of the narrative poem, *My Beloved Childhood* (1933) and of the collections, *A First Book of Poems* (1927) and *Lyrics* (1939). The combination of revolutionary fervour and tender lyricism made Iosif Pavlovich's poetry popular, especially among the youth of the 1920s and 1930s. His published poetry includes, *Verses from the Front* (1942) and *On the Motherland, Friendship and Love* (1944). He died in an aeroplane crash while returning from the German-Soviet war front in 1944.

After leaving Utiny, the train soon crosses over the Turguska River (р. Тунгуска) which is the northern boundary of the Jewish Autonomous Republic. This region was established in 1935 to create a homeland for Russian Jews. The area was virtually uninhabited as it is unsuitable for agriculture. Settlement has progressed slowly and today about 100,000 people live in the region which has its capital at Birobidzhan. Just 5% of the population is of Jewish descent. Some of the station signs are written in Hebrew.

Volochaevka 2 (Волочаевка 2)   330km
This is a large railway complex 9km before the junction of the line to Komsomolsk and the Trans-Siberian. Trains from Komsomolsk

for the west (Irkutsk) go through Volochaevka 2 and join the Trans-Siberian at Volochaevka 1. Trains from Komsomolsk for the east (Khabarovsk) go through Volochaevka 2 and join the Trans-Siberian at Dezhnevka.

Volochaevka is famous as the scene of a major battle during the Russian Civil War. The Battle of Volochaevka ran from 5 to 14 February 1922 in the vicinity of the railway station and was one of the last operations battles of the Russian Civil War in the Russian Far East. In late 1921, General Molchanov's White Guard forces launched an offensive from the Maritime Region to the north and on 22 December 1921, they seized Khabarovsk and advanced westward to Volochaevka. After a defeat near the railroad station, the White Guard forces (4,500 men, 63 machine guns, 12 artillery pieces and 3 armoured trains) were forced onto the defensive. The Red Forces were under the command of V Blyukher (7,600 men, 300 machine guns, 30 artillery pieces, 3 armoured trains and two tanks) and attacked on 5 February. Although the temperature was as low as -35°C, the poorly equipped Red troops attacked the enemy without pause. The Whites' defences were finally broken on 12 February and by 14 February, the communists had retaken Khabarovsk.

There is a hotel in Volochaevka.

Dezhnevka (Дежневка)   336km
This is the actual junction of the Trans-Siberian and the line to Komsomolsk.

Priamurskaya (Приамурская)   357km
This town is just on the border of the Jewish Autonomous Region. The only thing of interest in the town is the silica brick factory which produces insulation bricks for furnaces. After leaving the town, you cross 3km of swamp and small streams before reaching the 2.6km bridge across the actual Amur River.

Amur (Амур)   365km
The settlement of Amur sits on the right bank of the Amur.

Khabarovsk 1 (Хабаровск 1)   374km
Khabarovsk was founded as a military outpost in 1858 and today it is the second largest city in the Russian Far East with over 600,000 inhabitants.

Khabarovsk is a fascinating city and you can spend several days exploring it. The city is well covered in other guidebooks, such as *Russia by Rail* by Athol Yates or the *Trans-Siberian Handbook* by Bryn Thomas, so refer to these for information.

Bamovskaya – Tynda (The Little BAM)
Бамовская - Тында (Маленький БАМ)

This 180km stretch connecting the Trans-Siberian Railway to the main BAM line was the first section of the BAM to be built. It offers a striking contrast to the busy Trans-Siberian. The unelectrified Little BAM has only one track which winds through the *taiga*, compared to the two or three track electrified Trans-Siberian with its broad curves cut through farming land. Six long distance trains crawl along the Little BAM daily at 46km/h compared to the 50 trains screaming along the Trans-Siberian at 100km/h.

The railway roughly parallels the Amur Yakutsk highway which runs from the nearby Trans-Siberian station of Bolshoi Never (Большой Невер), through Tynda to Yakutsk. Although buses run between this highway from the Trans-Siberian to Tynda, trains are cheaper and more regular.

The Little BAM was first proposed in the early 1930s as part of the initial BAM concept. Originally it was envisaged that the line would run north from the Trans-Siberian station of Urusha (Уруша), however in 1933 the planners opted for a new location 64km to the east. A new station was built here called BAM, which was renamed Bamovskaya to prevent confusion with the railway line. Work started in early 1933 with many of the original workers being prisoners in Stalin's gulags. The Little BAM officially reached Tynda on 7 November 1937. Until the invasion of Russia by Germany in June 1941, when all work on the BAM stopped, Tynda was simply a supply base for the railway lines being pushed north, east and west.

In 1942 the line was pulled up and shipped to the war front and it was only on 5 April 1972, that work started on rebuilding the Little BAM. Virtually nothing of the old line remained as the *taiga*, permafrost and swamps had reclaimed the old embankments and even buildings. It is interesting that it was two years later that the first trainload of the Komsomol arrived on 3 May 1974 and it is this date that most Soviet-era books name as the start of the Little BAM.

As this was the first section of the BAM to be laid, it attracted enormous media attention within the Soviet Union. Daily building achievements and statistics were splashed over the front pages of newspapers such as "On 10 May 1972, work started on the first bridge" and "On 14 September, No 1272 Diesel Locomotive pulled the first passenger train to the first completed station of Shtrum".

On 9 May 1975, to coincide with the anniversary of the defeat of

Germany in World War II, the Little BAM was officially opened. Over its 180km length, 104 large and medium bridges and 140 other structures were built and 10.7 million cubic metres of earth and road metal were used.

Getting to the Little BAM

There are 6 long-distance trains a day which travel on the Little BAM. They travel between Moscow–Tynda, Chita–Tynda, Kislovodsk–Tynda, Kharkov–Tynda, Blagoveshchensk–Tynda and Khabarovsk–Neryungri.

Although Russian maps show that the Little BAM is connected to the Trans-Siberian at Bamovskaya, the truth is that the Little BAM branches at Shtrum station with the one branch connecting the Trans-Siberian at Bamovskaya and another branch connecting the Trans-Siberian at Goreli (Горелый). Trains from the west (Moscow, Irkutsk) to Tynda use the Bamovskaya branch with those from the east (Khabarovsk) use the Goreli branch.

If you are on a through train to Tynda from either the west or east, there is not a problem. However if you have to change trains, then it can be difficult. As few Trans-Siberian trains stop at Bamovskaya or Goreli (unless they are going on the Little BAM), the closest major stations where all Trans-Siberian trains stop are at Skovorodino (Сковородино) on the eastern side of the Little BAM or Erofei Pavlovish (Ерофей Павлович) on the western side. You should get off at one of these stations and change trains for one of the Little BAM trains.

There are also two local trains a day which run on the Little BAM from Tynda to Murtygit, which is two stations north of Bamovskaya. Why doesn't it go through to the Trans-Siberian you may ask? Firstly, Murtygit is a medium sized working town while few people work in either Shturm or Bamovskaya. In addition, Bamovskaya is managed not by the BAM Railway but by the Zabaikalsk Railway (Забайкалск)

Many of the stops on this line are little more than logging settlements.

and if the train stops there, it has to pay a service fee to the Zabaikalsk Railway Administration.

Bamovskaya (Бамовская) 0km
There is not much to Bamovskaya. It is a small town, with a sprinkling of stores, no hotel and only a few trains a day stop there. The best thing in Bamovskaya is the big word "BAM" in white blocks lying on the sloping ground infront of the station. It is not advisable to get off an express train here without knowing when your connecting train up the Little BAM will arrive.

Shtrum (Штрум) 18km
This unremarkable 2 house (and one track repairing machine) station is the first station owned by the BAM railway on the Little BAM.

Murtygit (Муртыгит) 49km
This medium sized town was built by the Voronesh Komsomol from western Russia. You will see the word Voronesh (Воронеж) with the year 1977 written in white brick on the red water tower next to the station. This is the terminus for local trains which run on the Little BAM from Tynda. A crashed American Lend Lease WW2 bomber was found about 12km from Murtygit in 1993 but it has yet to be recovered as there is no money to restore it.

The town has two Railway Hostels (Общежитие): a larger mixed sex one ☎ 2-84 and a male only one ☎ 4-20.

Anosovskaya (Аносовская) 82km
You will notice that the station looks as if it's about to fall down. This is because its foundations have sunk into the earth due to engineers ignoring the lessons of permafrost construction. By the time the evidence of inadequate construction had become indisputable, other Little BAM towns had been built and were similarly suffering, including Murtygit where both the school and sewage treatment plant collapsed.

The town has a Railway Hostel (Общежитие) ☎ 2-75, -13, 2-89 or 2-07

After leaving, Anosovskaya, you pass through the Yakan mountains on the most windy part of the route.

Zabolotny (Заболотчое) 113km
This station deserves its name which is derived from the word meaning *swamp*.

Belenkaya (Беленькая) 133km
This town was sponsored by the city of Orenburg (Оренбург) in

the South Urals.
The township is about 500m north of the station. There were Stalin-era gulag camps around the town.

Accommodation can be organised at the Locomotive Brigade Hostel ☎ 2-23 (Общежитие).

Seti (Сети)   160km
This is the headquarters and largest of North Korea's logging camps in the Tynda area. There used to be about 5,000 North Korean workers in the region but this has been dramatically reduced over the last few years. You can see their camp from the railway on your right as you approach the station from the south. You can wander to the camp but don't attempt to take photos. An explanation of the North Korean camps is included in under *Chegdomyn* in the *BAM mainline route description* chapter.

The other notable aspect of Seti is that it has a UFO society of 5 people which has 'sighted' a 3m high Yeti in the area.

Tynda (Тында)   180km
See under *Tynda* in the *BAM mainline route description* chapter.

Khrebtovaya – Ust-Ilimsk
Хребтовая - Усть-Илимск

The 214km railway between Khrebtovaya and Ust-Ilimsk was primarily built for the construction and maintenance of the Ust-Ilimsk hydro-electric station. The railway line, opened in 1970, passes through very scenic countryside and is a pleasant 4 hour trip.

Getting there and away
There is only one passenger train a day along the line. This train starts in Ust-Ilimsk, goes through Bratsk, joins the Trans-Siberian at Taishet before terminating in Irkutsk. There is no road parallel with the railway as the road connecting Bratsk with Ust-Ilimsk is on the other side of the Ust-Ilimsk Water Catchment Basin (Усть-Ильимское Водохранилище).

Khrebtovaya (Хребтовая)   0km
Khrebtovaya is located at 575km on the BAM. For more information, see under *Khrebtovaya* in the *BAM mainline route description* chapter.

🏠 **Igirma** (Игирма)   70km
This station serves the town of Novaya Igirma (Новая Игирма) which means *New Igirma*. The town is on the south bank of a flooded valley with the original Igirma village 30km to the south east. A reasonable road from Khrebtovaya ends at Novaya Igirma.

🏠 **Tubinskaya** (Тубинская)   160km
Tubinskaya is located on the north side of the flooded valley which used to be known as the Tuba River and is now known as Tuba Straits (Залив Туба).

Ust-Ilimsk (Усть-Илимск)   214km
☎ area code: 39-535

The town is located on the junction of the Angara and Ilimsk rivers and owes its existence to the Ust-Ilimsk hydro-electric dam. The power station is one of 3 giant hydro-electric stations on the Angara River with the others being in Bratsk and Irkutsk. Work started on the dam in 1963 with the building materials being floated down the Angara or trucked from Bratsk. Much of the 4,320MW capacity of the Ust-Ilimsk hydro-electric station is used to power the BAM. The dam and town are built on permafrost and consequently all the buildings, most notably the station, are built on insulated piles.

The main part of Ust-Ilimsk and its station are located on the eastern shore of the Ust-Ilimsk Water Catchment Basin with the port on the western shore. The station is 12km from the town and there are regular buses between the two. One of the most unusual aspects of Ust-Ilimsk is that the first cellar phone system in Russia was built here. It has only a few users and it is a mystery why this town of 100,000 was chosen.

Ust-Ilimsk can be reached by daily train from Khrebtovaya (4 hours), Bratsk (8:30 hours), Taishet (15 hours) and Irkutsk (26:30 hours).

Ust-Ilimsk can also be reached by daily buses from Bratsk and flights from Bratsk, Irkutsk and Krasnoyarsk.

Tynda – Neryungri – Aldan – Yakutsk (AYAM)
Тында - Нерюнгри - Алдан - Якутск (АЯМ)

While the AYAM (АЯМ) technically describes the 1,230km railway from the Amur River to Yakutsk (Амуро-Якутская Магистраль), most people and this book use the word AYAM to mean the 1,046km Bestuzhevo to

Yakutsk section of the AYAM. Bestuzhevo is 27km north of the BAM capital at Tynda. The section from the Amur River to Tynda is commonly known as the Little BAM.

The 1,046km AYAM is divided into 3 sections with the last one still to be completed.

- The first 210km section from Bestuzhevo to Berkakit, with a short branch line to Neryungri coal mine, was completed in 1978.
- The second 380km section from Berkakit to Aldan and Tommot was opened to freight traffic in January 1994 but in, January 1995, it was still not open to passenger trains.
- Work has only recently started on the third 456km section from Tommot to Yakutsk and it is unlikely that it will be finished before the turn of the century.

The building of the AYAM is a monumental construction project in terms of overcoming the natural barriers of permafrost, rivers and mountains. When it is completed, the railway will require some 200 bridges, 21 of which will be more than 1km long, 85 million cubic metres of moved earth and land fill, 540 structures other than bridges, 7 major railroad stations, six new settlements and 2,100 workers to staff the new line.

The Republic of Sakha (Caxa)

The Republic of Sakha, previously known as the Yakut Autonomous Soviet Socialist Republic, is a vast, virtually uninhabited land. It has just 984,000 inhabitants in its 3.1 million square kilometres which is just one person per 3 square kilometres.

The largest ethnic group is indigenous Yakuts, followed by Russian, Ukrainian, Evenki, Tatar, Even and Yakaghin. The vast majority of the government, police and senior business leaders are indigenous Yakuts.

Sakha is far more autonomous than other regions in the Russian Far East as it has an elected president and parliament, greater economic self-determination and its own visa requirements.

> **THE AMUR YAKUTSK HIGHWAY**
> Before the AYAM was built, a road from the Trans-Siberian to Yakutsk was hacked out of the *taiga*. Known as the Amur Yakutsk Automobile Highway (Амуро-Якутская автомобильная магистраль), the 1,777km road is mostly dirt broken up with patches of asphalt. The road in winter is notorious with its treacherous ice patches and steep descents, and you will see memorials along the road to the drivers who have died on the highway. The route is even more demanding in winter because trucks can't stop moving in the -50°C temperature as their tyres and engine blocks freeze and shatter.

Republic holidays
19 June: Independence Day of Sakha.
Last Sunday in March: Day of Reindeer Herders (День Оленевода).

Visas
To enter Sakha, you need the names of the towns you wish to visit on your Russian visa. This rule is enforced by the railways and airlines as you must show your visa before they will sell you a ticket. However, the only place that your visa will be checked in Sakha is at the airports. There is no checking of visas on the AYAM trains from Russia.

The visa requirement was introduced in 1994 as a way of reducing the visitors to the region, which in turn reduces the consumption of limited food and goods. In addition, the visa system allows the government to control the visits of foreign businessmen which ensures that they are informed of all commercial activity.

The fine for not having a visa is $2.50 but there may be additional arbitrary punishments applied.

If you want to go to Sakha it is best to get one or more Sakhian towns listed on your visa before your leave home. This is done by asking the organisation who send you a visa invitation to list towns on their invitation. If you arrive in Russia without them on your visa, it is virtually impossible to find any place outside of Sakha to add them. Even in Tynda, there appears to be no-one with the authority to issue a visa for this area. The only way to get permission once you are in Russia is to get a telegram or letter from someone in the region. This is normally sufficient to be able to buy a rail or airline ticket. Once you arrive, you can then go to the police station to get the visa.

If you do not have a contact to get an invitation from, try the friendly chief of the Berkakit administration and write that you will pay $20 for a telegram inviting you to Sakha. Stepan Andreevich Podolon, Head of City Administration, 678923 Berkakit, ul Bamovskaya, ☎ (0204) 27-463 home (Степан Андреевич Подолон, Главный Администратор, Поселковый Совет, 678923, Беркакит, ул. Бамовская).

Tynda (Тында) 0km
See *Tynda* in the *BAM mainline route description* chapter.

Bestuzheva (Бестужева) 27km and 0km
See *Bestuzheva* in the *BAM mainline route description* chapter.
Just after you depart Bestuzheva, the line divides into the AYAM to the north and the BAM mainline to the east.

Gilyu (Гилю) 19km
Gilyu is located on the northern side of the Gilyu River and is the

start of a scenic ascent through the Stanovo mountains.

Mogot (Могот)   44km

Mogot is a small industrial town with 2 storey buildings. There is a North Korean timber complex on the outskirts of the town and there was a Stalin-era gulag camp nearby.

This town is one of the best examples of poor construction on the BAM. The town rests on permafrost and as such, it is essential that all buildings rest on piles which insulate the buildings from the ground and prevent subsidence. Although the piles should have been driven many metres through the permafrost, many didn't even go down 2 metres. During the town's first summer when the top layer of the permafrost melted, the piles sank and dragged down the buildings. By spring 1981, the town's heating pipes, water mains, and its sewerage system were out of order, the pavements had collapsed and the administration and shopping block were boarded up due to the danger of further collapses. The town's administration appealed for help but the construction authority, the Ministry of Transport Construction, denied responsibility. Today, the patched-up town again has most of its facilities although it looks years older than it actually is.

Accommodation can be organised at the Railway Hostel ☎ 4-29 (Комната Отдыха).

Rikhard Zorge (Рихард Зорге)

2:20 hours after leaving Tynda as you approach Rickhard Zorge, you will see the Amur Yakutsk highway crossing over the railway. This road passes over the AYAM another three times before your train reaches Berkakit.

Yakutski (Якутский)   80km

Between the stations of Yakutski and Nagornaya Yakutsk, you pass over the unmarked border of the Amur *Oblast* and the Republic of Sakha.

Nagornaya Yakutsk (Нагорная Якутск)   93km

This station services the medium sized town of Nagorny (Нагорный) which means uplands. After leaving Nagornaya Yakutsk, you pass through a 1.2km tunnel.

Zolotinka (Золотинка)   135km

There's not much to this settlement except for the Olensky *Sovkhoz* reindeer breeding farm. Near the station is the start of a popular rafting route down the Iengra River (р. Иенгра) to the Timpton River (р. Тимптон) which takes you to the town of Chulman. There were Stalin-era gulag camps around Zolotinka.

Accommodation is available at the Railway Hostel No 1 ☎ 2-67 (Общежитие №1).

Several kilometres north of Zolotinka the train passes over the Iengra River. Guarding the bridge is a large military post. From the height of the bridge you can see the plan of the camp and most notably, the zig-zag trenches along both sides of the banks designed to repel a water-borne attack.

2km past the bridge on the left is the old town of Iengra (Иенгра).

Berkakit (Беркакит)   192km

The word Berkakit means *place of death* in Yakut, although why it is called this is not known. The AYAM arrived at Berkakit in 1977. The nearby city of Neryungri is a better place to stay however if you want to organise a trip on a freight train to Aldan, you have to come here as explained below. As all trains that go to Neryungri also stop at Berkakit, which is 15 minutes by rail to the south of Neryungri, refer to *Neryungri* for information on getting there and away.

The only accommodation in town is the Locomotive Brigade Hostel, ☎ 20-43 (Дом Отдыха Локомотивой Бригады).

Travelling by freight train to Aldan
Currently the railway to Aldan from Berkakit carries only freight trains as it is under the control of the Ministry of Transport Construction (MTC) which is not allowed to run passenger trains.

Railways in Russia are constructed by the MTC on behalf of the Ministry of Railways and the MTC will operate the line for anywhere from a few months to several years. Only after MTC are confident that the line has stabilised and there is no chance of derailments will ownership be transferred to the Ministry of Railways.

The MTC freight trains on the Neryungri – Aldan section are managed by OVE or the Department of Temporary Exploitation (ОВЭ-Отдель Временной Эксплуатации). Currently, the headquarters of OVE for the Berkakit-Aldan section of the AYAM is at Lesnoi settlement (п. Лесной) which is 20 minutes on foot from Berkakit station towards Neryungri. If you want to travel on a freight train to Aldan, then you have to talk with the Chief of Freight Traffic at Lesnoi. Oleg Murkhin, ☎ 06-214 (Олег Мурхин, ОВЭ, 678923, п. Лесной). However be warned, travelling in a freight train can be very slow. On one trip, it took the author 14 hours to travel the 280km to Aldan.

The trains for Aldan depart from the OVE freight yard which is on the other side of Neryungri. Buses to the OVE freight yard depart from Lesnoi at 7.15 and 16:00.

If you travel in a freight train to Aldan, you will invariably travel in the guards' van. The van is a converted passenger wagon with a stove, beds, wash basin and batteries to run the van's electric lights. The guards are called *Vagonshchiki* (Вагонщики) and their main role is to load and unload the wagons. They sometime check the wagons on route but this is normally the job of rail wagon checkers who are based at stations. Vagonshchiki normally work 15 days on and 15 off but this varies depending on how long each trip lasts.

Neryungri-Passenger (Нерюнгри-пасс.) 202km
☎ area code: 841147
✉ 678922, Yaktskaya-Sakha Republic, Neryungri
678922, Якутская-Саха Республика, г. Нерюнгри

Neryungri-Passenger station is the main passenger station for Neryungri and should not be confused with Neryungri-Gruz. (Нерюнгри Груз.) also known as Ugolnaya (Угольная) which is 8km further on and is the Neryungri freight station.

Neryungri is the second largest city in the Republic of Sakha, with a population of about 70,000. The town was a Komsomol project which is reflected in the large number of communist statues in the town. In addition to these reminders, you will notice an extraordinary number of large signs proclaiming that you are in Neryungri.

Neryungri was a rural village with a population of 1,000 before 1970. Following the discovery of one of the world's largest coal deposits, a geological and working settlement was quickly built in 1972. The settlement quickly grew until in 1974, it was granted the title of a *city*.

Today, Neryungri consists of five and nine storey apartment buildings with wide streets. The architectural style is late 1970s functional concrete boxes. The buildings are all built on piles due to permafrost and are designed to withstand powerful earthquakes.

The town has only limited recreational facilities and this, combined with the harsh -50°C winter temperature, results in annual labour turnover of more than 20%.

The town has a reputation for being an environmental disaster with air pollution many times higher than the permissible Soviet limit. There is no doubt that in the past the town has been permanently encased in smog but with the closing down of the coal-powered electricity generating plants and the opening of Serebyani Bor hydro-electric power station, this problem has disappeared. However, waves of dust still blow through the town from the mine on hot, windy summer days.

Getting there and away
From the south, trains arrive from destinations including Berkakit (15 minutes), Tynda (5 hours), Novaya Chara (19 hours), Taksimo (24

hours), Severobaikalsk (34 hours), Taishet (55 hours) and Moscow (128 hours), Bamovskaya (8:15 hours), Chita (29 hours), Irkutsk (47 hours) and Kislovodsk in the south west of Russia near Stavropol. There are also carriages which are joined to other trains from Blagoveshchensk (21 hours), Khabarovsk (28 hours), Vladivostok (41 hours) and Komsomolsk (45 hours).

The nearest airport is 45km away at Chulman and flights arrive from Moscow, Barnual, Chita, Novosibirsk, Irkutsk, Rostov-na-don, Kemerovo, Khabarovsk, Aldan and Yakutsk.

A bus to Tynda departs from the station every Monday, Wednesday, Friday and Sunday at 14:00. There is also a bus that travels the 648km from Neryungri to Bolshoi Never on the Trans-Siberian.

A bus runs every day to Aldan and departs at 7:15 from Neryungri railway station, 7:30 at Neryungri, 8:05 at Chulman airport and 14:00 at Aldan. The trip to Aldan is quite expensive at $35.

Bus №102 runs about every hour between Berkakit and Neryungri.

Where to stay
The closest hotel to the centre of town is Hotel Timpton which has 30 rooms, with triple rooms costing $15 per person and twin rooms $20 per person. There is a Chinese restaurant and cafe in the hotel. Hotel Timpton, ul Yuxhno-Yakutskaya, ☎ 42-410 (Гостиница Тимптон, ул. Южно-Якутская). Another option is Hotel Sosnovaya which has single rooms at $30. Hotel Sosnovaya, ul Bolnichni Kompleks, ☎ 42-141 (Гостиница Сосновая, ул. Болничны Комплекс). The only other hotel is Hotel Severnaya which has deluxe single rooms at $30 and normal single rooms $15, ☎ 417-55. You can also stay at the NGRES hydro-electric station hotel at Serebyani Bor which is about 30 minutes out of Neryungri. NGRES Hotel, Serebyani Bor (Гостиница НГРЭС, Серебяный бор).

Getting assistance
In the Soviet-era, the youth wing of the national tourist company, Intourist, controlled Sputnik. Sputnik is now independent and its 2 branches in Neryungri are run by Klavdiya Kokhonkova. The company can organise city and coal mine tours, hiking, museum trips, homestay, interpreters and transport. Sputnik, ul Karla Marksa 20, kv 71, ☎ 498-56, fax 445-91, (Клавдия Кохопкова, Спутник, ул. Карла Маркса 20, кв 71) and pr Druzhby Narodov 21, ☎ 408-65 (Спутник, пр. Дружбы Народов 21). For hikers, rafters and other adventurers, your best contact is the Serebyany Bor Adventure Club run by Volodya Shesbakov, ul Teologov 61-1, kv 3 (Володя Шесбаков, Турист клуб «Серебяный бор», ул. Теологов 61-1, кв 3) and Sergei Oriov, ul Mira 7, kv 40 (Сергей Ориов, Турист клуб «Серебяный бор», ул. Мира 7, кв 40).

What to see
There is not much to see in Neryungri except the museum and the church built in 1994, however there is plenty to see in the region.

What to see in the region
There are several interesting attractions in the region.

There is a reindeer breeding farm near the BAM station of Zolotinka, which is also the start of a popular summer rafting route down the River Timpton (р. Тимптон) to Chulman. The river is ideal for inexperienced rafters. See under *Zolotinka* for more information.

A popular swimming spot with a rare sandy beach is close to Neryungri on the Chulman River. To get to it, you go just past the junction of the Neryungri spur line and the AYAM. You can see the beach from the road.

A pleasant half day trip is out to the hydro-electric power station at Serebyany Bor (Серебяный бор). You can visit the station, and Sputnik occasionally organises hang gliding in the area around the reservoir. You can eat at the Olongro restaurant (Олонгро ресторан) ☎ 520-59 and stay at the NGRES Hotel (НГРЭС).

Around Neryungri are a number of mineral springs which are popular picnic spots. The most popular ones are the hot springs called Nakhot (Нахот) about 30km north of Chulman and the cold water

Building the onion domes for Neryungri's Russian Orthodox Church.

316 BAM branch lines route descriptions

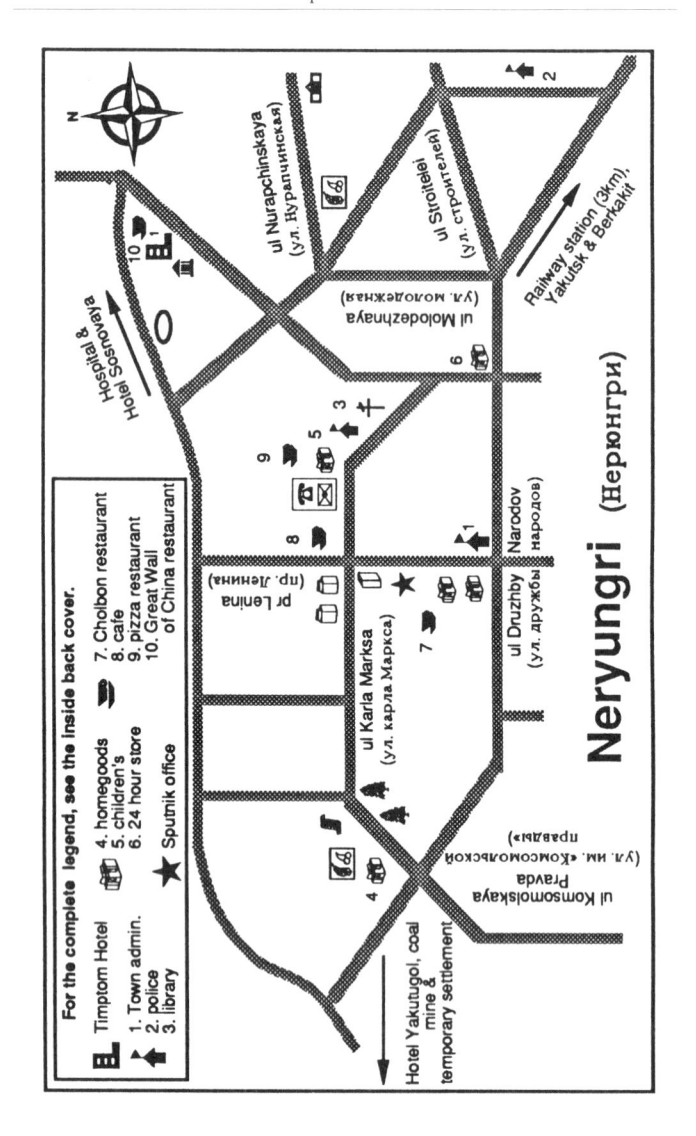

springs 5km south of Berkakit.

Neryungri Sputnik also organises visits to the granite plant 10km north east of Berkakit, although why you would want to visit it is a mystery.

However the best attraction in the area is the Neryungri Coal Mine.

Neryungri Coal Mine

Visiting the Neryungri coal mine is a must. It is one of the world's largest open cut coal mines with 12 million tons of coal a year being dug up. At this rate, the mine will be exhausted by 2007 but this is of no great concern as the Neryungri coal mine is just one field in the 40 billion ton South Yakutia coal basin.

Everything about this mine is big. The trucks are massive, the crushing plant is huge and the coal trains are never ending. Even the roads are built for giants with 60cm thick reinforced slabs of concrete rather than asphalt. The best way to appreciate the sheer size of the mine is to fly over it. Another way is to drive around the mine from one open cut pit to the next. There are no restrictions on doing this but be aware that you are sharing the road with 200 ton trucks which have an unchallengeable right of way.

The first stop on a tour of the 3,000-employee mine is the mine's

Everything is dwarfed by the massive 200 ton trucks used to haul coal from the pits.

headquarters. This 9 storey building is about 10km out of Neryungri on the road to the mine. This is the end of most bus routes to the mine. You can catch Buses № 3 and 6 from the town to this stop. There is no museum in the building, but it has a good canteen and several well stocked shops on the ground floor. One kilometre further on, to your right, is the headquarters of the mine's truck company, ATA Yakutugol (АТА Якутуголь), and its giant repair workshop is a further 500m onwards. You can wander around this workshop without a pass and crawl over the mammoth 2,300 horsepower trucks with their 5 metre diameter tyres.

This workshop only maintains 170 big dump trucks out of the mine's fleet of 2,500 vehicles. The majority of these giant tip trucks are 180 ton Russian Belaz, 120 ton Japanese Komatsu and 200 ton US Dresser trucks, however there are also a few US Caterpillar trucks. The average cost of each truck is about $2 million.

Maintaining the fleet is demanding as the trucks have to work 24 hours a day, 365 days a year in temperatures as low as -50°C. In summer, the problems are just as bad with coal dust storms choking and even destroying the truck's engines. The drivers work 12 hour shifts with 2 months of holidays a year. They are only allowed to drive for 5 months each year as longer exposure to the continuous vibration and constant physical effort in controlling a 200 ton truck can do them permanent damage. The workers spend the remaining 5 months a year working in the vehicle repair shops and on other less demanding jobs in the mine. In addition to the Russian maintenance staff, 9 foreign specialists work at the mine, maintaining their respective company's vehicles.

Another interesting place to visit is the coal washery at Ugolnaya, 8km northwest of Neryungri. This complex is the largest and most modern washery in Russia and annually reduces 9 million tons of dug up coal to 5 million tons of coal concentrate ready for exporting. Trucks dump their loads of coal into the washery's crushers which reduce lumps of coal to 0.3mm fragments. The coal is then concentrated by flotation and solid-magnetic suspension. The wet concentrate is then conveyed to one of four giant driers which remove all moisture. The dry concentrate is then carried by conveyers the length of a football field to waiting coal trains. 870 workers run this computer controlled plant.

Denisovski (Денисовский)   221km
Most of the inhabitants of this town work in the underground coal mine.

Chulman (Чульман)   232km
Chulman is the region's airport and is 30km north of Neryungri.

The town sits on the right bank of the Chulman River opposite a spectacular white limestone cliff that rises on the left bank. It was from this that the town derived its name which means *white rock* in the Evenk language. Nowadays the cliff is grey with soot from an old 72MW coal power station. Chulman has two industries; underground coal mining and limestone mining.

Chulbass (Чульбасс)   246km
When the rail builders named this small town, they were optimistically expecting that the region would boom. The name of this station derives from the words Chulman Basin (Чульманский Бассейн) which signifies a giant industrial area similar to the heavily industrialised Donbass or Donets Basin in European Russia.

Taezhnaya (Таежная)   351km
After this stop, the train passes over the highest ridge between Tynda and Aldan and the mountains here are permanently covered in snow. About 40km to the east was a Stalin-era mica gulag complex around Kankunsky (Канкунский). There is a turnoff for the small Kankunsky settlement on the Amur-Yakutsk Highway near the station.

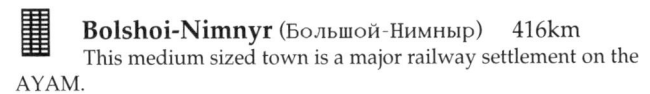

Bolshoi-Nimnyr (Большой-Нимныр)   416km
This medium sized town is a major railway settlement on the AYAM.

Kosarevski (Косаревский)   470km
This station is also known as Orochen 1 (Орочен 1). About 2km from the station, is the gold mining village of Lebedinaya (Лебединая) which means swans. Freight trains often terminate at Kosarevski and to get the last 16km to Aldan, you can catch one of the regular buses from Lebedinaya to Aldan, which take 40 minutes. You can also catch a bus to the larger village of Yakokit (Якокит) to the east, from where regular buses also travel to Aldan.

Aldan (Алдан)   486km
☎ area code: 411-45
✉ 678900, Yaktskaya-Sakha Respublika, Aldan
678922, Якутская-Саха Республика, г. Алдан

Aldan exists for its gold and mica. When gold was found in the 1920s, the indigenous village in the area was called Nezhametny which became the Aldan settlement in 1924. It became the city of Aldan in 1939 and the city council always has a celebration on its anniversary on 15 July. The town now boasts a population of 30,000 with 60,000 in the region.

10km to the south of Aldan is the satellite town of Leninski which was known as Nizhnestalinsk (Нижнесталинск) or Lower Stalin until 1962.

The power behind the town is Aldanzoloto (Aldan Gold Co) which has its headquarters 27km away in the smaller but wealthier town of Nizhne-Kuranakh.

Aldan was closed to foreigners from the 1930s to the early 1990s and then opened for a few years until the Sakhian government redeclared it a closed town in 1992. The government did this because it was concerned about the possibility of gold theft in the guise of business. This means you should have Aldan on your visa to buy a ticket to the city. However, if you arrive by train or bus, no-one checks.

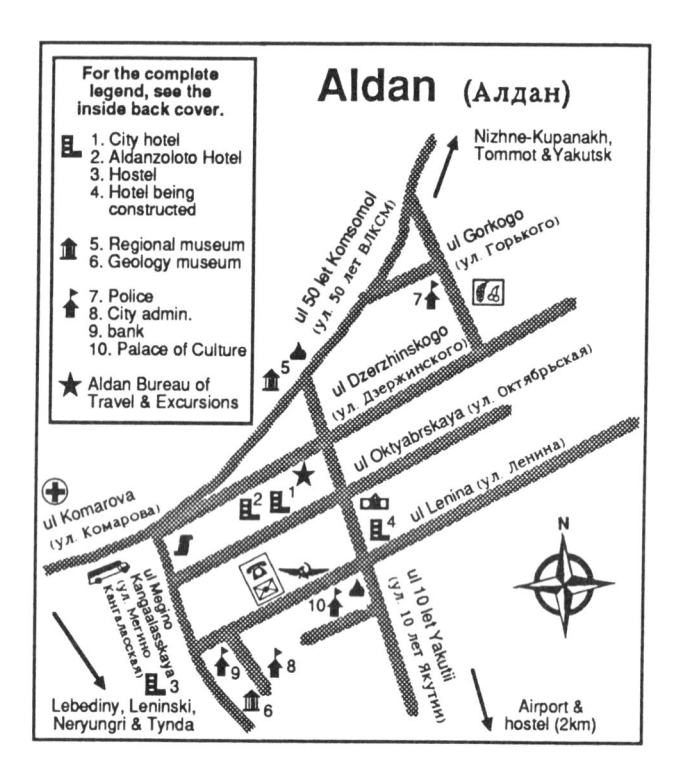

Aldan (Алдан)

For the complete legend, see the inside back cover.

1. City hotel
2. Aldanzoloto Hotel
3. Hostel
4. Hotel being constructed
5. Regional museum
6. Geology museum
7. Police
8. City admin.
9. bank
10. Palace of Culture

★ Aldan Bureau of Travel & Excursions

Streets: ul 50 let Komsomol (ул. 50 лет ВЛКСМ), ul Gorkogo (ул. Горького), ul Dzerzhinskogo (ул. Дзержинского), ul Oktyabrskaya (ул. Октябрьская), ul Lenina (ул. Ленина), ul Komarova (ул. Комарова), ul Maginо-Kangalasskaya (ул. Мегино-Кангаласская), ul 10 let Yakutii (ул. 10 лет Якутии)

To: Nizhne-Kupanakh, Tommot & Yakutsk; Lebediny, Leninski, Neryungri & Tynda; Airport & hostel (2km)

Getting there and away
Although freight trains reach Aldan, it will be a few years yet before passenger trains make it. For information on how to catch a freight train, see under *Berkakit*.

A more reliable way of travelling between Neryungri and Aldan is on a bus. There are daily buses departing Aldan at 7:00 and arriving at 1:25 at Chulman airport, 2:00 at Neryungri and 2:15 at Neryungri railway station. The trip is $35.

Local buses run daily between towns such as Kanku (Канку), Nizhni-Kuranakh, Khatystyr and Tommot. Buses run to Yakutsk on Wednesday and Saturday for $35.

There are flights from Yakutsk, Chulman and Khabarovsk.

Where to stay
The only public hotel is a two storey, wooden hostel with a number of shared rooms. The price is $5 a bed. There is also a hotel owned by Aldanzoloto and a workers' hostel which may give you a room. A multi-storey hotel is being built in the centre of town but when it will be completed is unknown as it is currently in its seventh year of construction. A better place to stay is in Nizhne-Kuranakh as there is a very good hotel owned by Aldanzoloto.

Getting assistance
This is one place where it is great to have someone who can organise accommodation and access to the museums. The best contact is Olga Yakovlevna Korneva, Director of the Aldan Bureau of Travel and Excursions, ul Dzerzhinskovo 30,☎ 229-63, fax 235-76 (Дириктор Ольга Яковлевна Корнева, Алданского Бюро Путешествий И Экскурский, ул. Дзержинского 30). Another contact would be the Director of Aldanzoloto in Nizhne-Kuranakh, (Алданзолото, п. Нижне-Куранах). There is also an office of Yakutsk Intourist (Якутинтур) however it does not seem to be very active.

What to see
There is a regional museum and a geological museum in Aldan. The first contains halls dedicated to the history of gold mining in the region, the creation of the town and work from local artists. The second displays the history of the geologists who worked for the company Aldan Geology Co and the region's rocks.

There is the usual collection of monuments to revolutionary leaders, WWII heroes and explorers dotted around the town.

However the most interesting sights are not in the town but around it. A nice day trip is to the Yakutian indigenous village of Khatystyr (Хатыстыр) which is 60km away on the Aldan River. The main occupations of the inhabitants are reindeer breeding and fishing. To get there you need to catch a bus which goes through Nizhne-Kuranakh.

On all the roads out of Aldan, you will notice that the river valleys have been stripped of all vegetation. These valleys have been dredged for alluvial gold and as there are no regeneration programs, they will stay barren for decades.

Aldan is also the location of one of the strangest headstones in Russia. About 8km south of Aldan on the Amur Yakutsk highway is a gravestone with a pair of bicycle handlebars sticking out of it. It is common for drivers who get killed on the road to have steering wheels attached to their headstones but a bicycle is unique.

Gluboki-Kuranakh (Глубокий-Куранах)   519km

This station serves the medium sized settlement of Nizhne-Kuranakh (Нижне-Куранах). This town houses the headquarters of the region's largest gold mining company, Aldanzoloto. The town has excellent facilities including a hotel, brewery and salami factory. There is a road from here to the Yakutian indigenous village of Khatystyr (Хатыстыр) which is 30km away on the Aldan River.

Yakokit (Якокит)   533km

This stop should not be confused with Yakokyt (Якокут) village which is 42km south of here. Near the railway station is a *pioneer* camp.

Tommot (Томмот)   568km

This small city is on the Aldan River and in the past, boats sailed from Yakutsk, up the Aldan River via Khandyga and Ust-Maya to Tommot. Tommot is the furthest upstream point that can be reached on the Aldan River. The town is an iron and steel centre and coal is shipped in from Neryungri and iron ore from the nearby Aldan deposits. Although by early 1995, the railway had yet to reach Tommot it was expected within a year.

Pravaya Lena (Правая Лена)

This station is on the right bank on the Lena River. A 10km bridge being built across the river will be the biggest construction on the AYAM and is expected to take at least 8 years to build.

Yakutsk (Якутск)   1,046km

Yakutsk is the capital of the Republic of Sakha. This fascinating city can be reached by bus from Aldan or Tommot, river cruiser from Ust-Kut on the BAM or plane. For more information on the river trip, see *Ust-Kut* in the *BAM mainline route description* chapter. For detailed coverage of Yakutsk, see the *Trans-Siberian Handbook* by Bryn Thomas.

APPENDIX

Russian language guide	A2
Railway dictionary	A4
Buying a ticket	A6
Booking accommodation	A10
Glossary	A11
Recommended reading	A14
Timetables	A19

Russian language guide

Путеводитель по Руссому Языке

The following table shows the English letter equivalant for Russian letters, with the following simplification rules: ый = y, ий = i.

You may notice that some of the stations have a different spelling than the nearby town, eg Kholodnaya station but Kholodnoe village. This is because Russian has different spellings for adjectival endings. In addition, in this book there are a few Russian words, notably well known place names, which have not been transliterated using the following table. Instead these words adopt the spelling which has been common in the past.

Russian	English	Pronunciation	Russian	English	Pronunciation
а	a	**f**ar	т	t	**t**rain
б	b	**b**et	у	u	m**oo**ve
в	v	**v**odka	ф	f	**f**rost
г	g	**g**et	х	kh	lo**ch**
д	d	**d**og	ц	ts	lo**ts**
е	e	**y**et	ч	ch	**ch**illi
ё	e	**yo**ghurt	ш	sh	**sh**ow
ж	zh	trea**s**ure	щ	shch	fi**sh**
з	z	**z**ebra	ъ		hardens the following letter
и	i	**s**eek			
й	i	**b**oy			
к	k	**K**iev	ы	y	**di**d
л	l	**L**enin	ь		softens the preceeding letter
м	m	**M**oscow			
н	n	**n**ever			
о	o	**o**ver	э	e	m**a**p
п	p	**p**eter	ю	yu	**u**nion
р	r	**R**ussia	я	ya	**y**ak
с	s	**S**amarkand			

Basic English Russian phrases

The following is the bare minimum needed for non-Russian speakers to get around. The first part is a small basic dictionary and pronunciation guide. The second part consists of specialised dictionaries of words and phrases not covered in phrase books.

Rather than trying to pronounce these phrases, it is better to simply point to them.

The basics

English	Pronunciation	Russian
yes	da	да
no	nyet	нет
please	poz**halu**ista	пожалуйста
good day	zd**rast**vuite	здравствуйте
hi	zd**rav**stvui	здравствуй
thankyou	spas**iba**	спасибо
goodbye	dasved**ani**ya	до свидания
bye	pa**ka**	пока
please give me	**dai**te poz**halu**sta	дайте пожалуйста
call me a doctor	**pozo**vite **vrach**a	позовите врача
do you have ... ?	u vas yest ...	у вас есть ...
Cheers!	**za vash**e z**dor**ove	за ваше здоровье
good	khoro**sho**	хорошо

Useful Railway Expressions

Here is my ticket.	Вот мой билет.
Please show me my place.	Покажите; пожалуйста; мое место.
Please wake me in an hour before we arrive at ...	Разбудите меня, пожалуйста; за час до прибытия в ...
Please wake me at ...	Разбудите меня в ... часов
Where is the restaurant car?	Где находится вагон-ресторан или буфет?
Where is the toilet?	Где находится туалет?
May I smoke here?	Здесь можно курить?
Please bring me a (another) blanket.	Принесите, пожалуйста; 9еще одно0 одеяло.
What is the next station?	Какая следующая станция?
How many minutes will the train stop here for?	Сколько минут стоянка поезда?
I am late for the train.	Я опоздал на поезд.

Railway dictionary
Словарь железнодорожных терминов

касса		ticket window
	предварительная касса	for tickets after 24 hours
	в день отправления касса	for tickets within 24 hours
	текущая продажа билетов	for tickets within 24 hours
	воинская касса	for military personnel
	Интуриста касса	for foreigners
	часы работы с 8 до 20	working from 08:00hrs to 20:00hrs
	круглосуточная касса	open 24 hours
	обед 13 до 14	lunch break from 13:00hrs to 14:00hrs
	перерыв	break
	технический перерыв 10.15 до 10.45	technical break from 10:15hrs to 10:45hrs
расписание		timetable
	Чет. (четным числам)	even days of the month (ie 2, 14, 28 of May)
	Неч. (по нечетным числам)	odd days of the month (ie 1, 13, 27 of May)
	вых (по выходным)	weekends and public holidays
	раб (по рабочим дням)	weekdays
	От. (отправление)	departure
	Пр. (прибытие)	arrival
	Пл. (платформа)	platform
	станция назначения	station of destination
поезд		train
	скорый поезд	fast train
	транзитный поезд	transit train
	пассажирский поезд	passenger train
	пригородный поезд	suburban train
	фирменный поезд	deluxe express train (it always has a name such as *Rossiya* (Moscow to Vladivostok train)
	поезд опаздывает	train is late
	поезд не останавливается	train does not stop
	поезд не заходит на станцию	train does not stop at the station

Railway dictionary

вокзал, станция — station
- начальник вокзала — station master
- дежурный по станции — station attendant
- справка — information

вагон — carriage
- СВ (спальный вагон) — 2 berth compartment carriage
- мягкий вагон — 2 berth compartment carriage
- купейный вагон — 4 berth compartment carriage
- плацкартный вагон — open sleeping carriage
- общий вагон — open sitting carriage
- беспересадочный вагон or отцепной вагон — wagon which separates and joins another train partway through the journey

билет — ticket
- туда — one way
- обратно — return
- полный — adult
- детский — child
- место — berth number
- верхнее место — upper berth
- нижнее место — lower berth
- проездной билет — pass such as a monthly pass
- льготный билет — discount ticket for pensioners, students etc
- зона — price zones

время — time
- московское время — Moscow time
- местное время — local time

на поезде — on the train
- бригадир поезда, начальник бригады проводников — head conductor
- проводник — conductor
- стоп-кран — emergency stop handle
- багажная полка — baggage rack
- одеяло — blankets
- бельё — sheets
- постельные принадлежности — rolled up mattress and pillow

Buying a ticket
(покупка билета)

Step 1: Try to decipher the timetable at the station. Write your destination and date of departure in Russian letters. Go to the information *kassa*.

Please help me. I don't speak Russian. Please read the question I point to with my finger and write the answer.

1. I want to go to .... on ....../....../......
2. I want to go to .... as soon as possible.
3. When is the next train with spare places? .... (Moscow time)
4. What times do the trains depart from here? .... (Moscow time)
5. What is the number of the train that leaves at ....? Train number ....
6. What is the cost of a:
   SV .... roubles/dollars
   coupe .... roubles/dollars
   platskart .... roubles/dollars
   obshchei .... roubles/dollars
7. Are there .... tickets available for this train. Yes or No?
8. Why can't I buy a ticket?
   - no train.
   - train is fully booked.
   - you have to buy a ticket at window ....
   - you can only buy a ticket .... hours before the train arrives.
9. Which ticket window should I go to .... ?
10. What platform does the train leave from .... ?
11. When does the train arrive at ....? It arrives at (Moscow time) ....
12. How many hours does it take to get to ....?

Thank you for your help.

Buyingaticket A7

Будте любезны, помогите мне. Я не говорю по-русски. Пожалуйста; прочтите вопросы на которые я укажу пальцем; и на пишите ответ.

1. Я хочу поехать до .... на ...../...../.....
2. Я хочу поехать до .... на ближайшем поезде.
3. Когда следущий поезд с указанными местами .... часов (Московское время)?
4. Когда отправляется поезд отсюда .... часов (Московское время)?
5. Какой номер у поезда который отправляется до ....? поезд №.............. ?
6. Сколько стоит билет в
   СВ .... рублей/долларов
   купе .... рублей/долларов
   плацкарт .... рублей/долларов
   общий .... рублей/долларов
7. Есть ли .... место на этом поезде. Да или Нет?
8. Почему я не могу купить билет?
   - нет поезда.
   - нет мест.
   - вы должны купить билет в кассе № ....
   - вы можете купить билет за .... часов до прибытия поезда.
9. К какому окну мне подойти .... ?
10. С какой платформы отправляется поезд .... ?
11. Когда поезд прибывает в ....? оезд прибывает в часов .... ? (Московское время
12. Сколько часов поезд идет до ....?

Большое спасибо за помощь.

Step 2: Complete all the information on the card and give it to the ticket seller.

Good day. I don't speak Russian. I have written what I want.

1. I want to buy .... SV / coupe / platskart / obshchei tickets to .... departing on train number .... on ..... /...../.....
2. I want to go to .... as soon as possible.
3. What is the cost of all these tickets ? .... roubles/dollars
4. Why can't I buy a ticket?
    - no train.
    - train is fully booked.
    - you have to buy a ticket at window ....
    - you can only buy a ticket .... hours before the train arrives.
9. If there are no tickets on my first choice, please give me tickets for ..... /...../....

Thank you for your help.

Notes

Здравствуйте. Я не говорю по-русски. Я написал что я хочу.

1. Я хотел бы купить .... СВ, купе, плацкарт, общий билет до .... на поезд № .... который отправляется до ..../..../....

2. Я хочу поехать до .... как можно скорее (на ближайшем поезде).

3. Сколько стоят эти билеты .... рублей/долларов?

4. Почему я не могу купить билет?
   - нет поезда.
   - нет мест.
   - вы должны купить билет в кассе № ....
   - вы можете купить билет за .... часов до прибытия поезда.

9. Если нет мест на этот поезд, я хочу купить билеты на ..../..../..../

Большое спасибо за помощь.

Booking accommodation
(Бронирование Проживания)

It is best to book accommodation in advance and the easist way to do that is to send a telegram to the hotel. Copy the Russian on the sample booking telegram below onto a blank telegram form found at post offices and fill in the relevant details. The top section is left blank as it is completed by the post office staff. The cost of a local telegram is about $1.00.

МИНИСТЕРСТВО СВЯЗИ РОССИИ	ПЕРЕДАЧА
ТЕЛЕГРАММА	___ го ___ ч. ___ м.
	Номер рабочего места
	Автоответ пункта приема
№_____	Передал _____
___ сл. ___ го. ___ ч. ___ м.	Служебные отметки

Категория и отметки особого вида If the telegram is urgent, write "срочная" here)

Куда, кому The address goes here. It is best to include the telephone number of the receiver also so the post office can ring them.

Забронируйте 1-местный / 2-местный номер на 1 / 2 человека
(Book me 1-bed / 2-bed room for 1 / 2 people)

в ваших гостинице / доме отдыха локомотивой бригады / общежитие / коттеджах
(in your hotel / locomotive brigade hostel / hostel / cottages)

на 1 / 2 / 3 дня. Приезд поездом ☐   ☐/☐/19☐.
(for 1 / 2 / 3 days. We arrive on train № ☐ on ☐/☐/199☐.)

☐
(Signed)

Glossary
(Толковый Словарь)

These words are the main foreign words and abbreviations used in the text.

AYAM (АЯМ): The initials of the Amur-Yakutsk Mainline railway which technically starts at the Amur River and finishes at Yakutsk. However in this book, the popular definition of the AYAM is used which means the railway from Tynda to Yakutsk (Амуро-Якутская Магистраль).

BAM (БАМ): The initials of the Baikal-Amur Mainline railway which technically starts near Lake Baikal and finishes at the Amur River. However in this book, the popular definition of the BAM is used which encompasses the BAM mainline from Taishet on the Trans-Siberian to Sovetskaya Gavan on the Pacific Ocean coast plus all of the BAM branch lines (Байкало-Амурская Магистраль).

BAM mainline: The backbone of the BAM which stretches from Taishet to Sovetskaya Gavan.

BAM Zone (Зона БАМа): The development area around the BAM which is up to several hundred kilometres wide.

banya (баня): Russian sauna.

bolota (болота): A swamp.

СССР (СССР): Abbreviation for Union of Soviet Socialist Republics (Союз Советских Социалистических Республик).

coupe (купе): An carriage with four berths per cabin. The most common carriages for foreigners.

dacha (дача): Usually a very small cottage on a small farm plot owned by city dwellers.

dacha village (дачный посёлок): A suburb on the outskirts of most towns where most dachas are located.

Decembrist (Декабрист): A revolutionary who took part in the 14 December 1865 uprising in St Petersburg, demanding a constitutional monarch rather than an omnipowerful Tsar.

derevnya (деревня): A village or hamlet. There are numerous other words for village, such as *khutor* and *stantsiay*, but with the exception of *derevnya* and *selo*, these words are only of historical significance.

elektrovoz (электровоз): An electric locomotive.

GES (ГЭС): A hydro-electric station.

glasnost (гласность): A Gorbachev-era buzz word meaning

political and media openness.

GOELRO (ГОЭЛРО): From the initials of the 1920's Government Plan for the Electrification of Russia (Государственный план электрификации России) which shaped and still shapes the electrification policy in Russia today.

gorod (город): A city with a minimum population of 12,000 and at least 85% of its employed population engaged in non-agricultural work.

Great Patriotic War (Великая Отечеcкая Войнa): The Soviet Union only fought in the Second World War from 1941 to 1945 and this is their term for this war.

gulag (ГУЛаг): From the initials of the organisation which ran prison camps, the Main Department of Corrective Labour Camps (Главное Управление Исправительных Лагерей). The word is now used to mean a prison camp of the Stalin-era.

homestay (домашнее условие): Accommodation in a Russian family home.

Intourist (Интурист): Russia's largest travel company.

izba (изба): A wooden rural house.

kassa (касса): A ticket window.

KGB (КГБ): The initials of the Soviet secret police (Комитет Государственной Безопасности) which operated from 1956 to 1991. It is now called the FSK or Federal Counter-Intelligence Service (Федеральная Служба Контрразведки).

kladbishche paravozov (кладбище паравозов): A steam engine graveyard.

kolkhoz (колхоз): A collective farm.

kombinat (комбинат): A large industrial complex.

kompot (компот): A fruit drink made of berries.

Komsomol (Комсомол): Abbreviation for the Communist Youth League (Коммунистисческий Союз Молодёжи) which represented 14 to 27 year olds.

Komsomol Shock Project (Всесоюзная ударная Комсомольская стройка): A nationally significant project managed by the Komsomol.

Krai (Край): A territory.

KSO (КСО): Abbreviation for the search and rescue teams for people lost in the wild (Контрольно-Спасательный отряд).

kurort (курорт): A health resort or a town of sanatoriums.

lyuks (люкс): A deluxe hotel room.

Little BAM: The railway connecting the Trans-Siberian at Bamovskaya to the BAM at Tynda.

manevrovy (маневровый): A shunting locomotive.

militsia (милиция): police.

microraion (микрорайон): A satellite town or suburb.

myaky (мягкий): A first class sleeping carriage with two beds only in the compartment. Synonym for *SV*.

novy (новый): New.

Oblast (Область): A region.

obshchi (общий): An open carriage with no reserved seating or sleeping benches.

Oktyabrenok (Октябрёнок): The communist-era national youth organisation for young children from 7 to 9 years of age.

OViR (ОВиР): The Ministry of Internal Affairs' department that registers and extends visas for foreigners. It also issues passports for Russians. (Одел Виз и Регистраций).

parokhod (пароход): A steamship.

parovoz (паровоз): A railway steam engine.

pereval (перевал): A mountain pass.

perestroika (перестройка): A Gorbachev-era buzz word meaning restructuring.

permafrost (вечная мерзлота): Ground that is permanently frozen.

Pioneers (Пионер): The communist-era national youth organisation for young children from 9 to 14 years of age.

ploshchad (площадь): A city square.

poezd (поезд): A train.

posolok (посёлок): An urban settlement with a minimum population of 3,000 and at least 85% employed in non-agricultural work.

pr. or pr-t (пр. или пр-т): Abbreviation for prospekt (проспект) meaning avenue.

provodnik (проводник): A train conductor.

Raion (Район): A district.

raz (раз.): Abbreviation for razezd (разьезд) which is a railway siding.

salo (сало): Smoked, cured or salted pig fat still attached to the rind which is eaten in thin slices.

samovar (самовар): A hot water urn.

sanatorium (санаторий): A health resort often built near mineral springs or mud pools.

selo (село): A rural village.

sortirovka (сортировка): A marshalling yard where passenger trains join, separate or wait.

Soviet (Совет): A council.

sovkhoz (совхоз): A state owned collective farm.

stary (старый): Old.

SV (СВ): Abbreviation for a first class sleeping carriage with two

beds only in the compartment (спальный вагон). Synonym for *myaky*.
teplokhod (теплоход): A motorised ship.
teplovoz (тепловоз): A diesel locomotive.
tonnel (тоннель): A tunnel. The word can also be spelt tunnel (туннель).
TOTs (ТОЦ): The Russian equilivant to a mall where a number of shops are all located in one place (Торговый Обшественый Центр).
Trans-Siberian Railway (Транс-Сиб): The 7,200km railway stretching from Moscow to Vladivostok.
turist (турист): This word used to carry a significantly different meaning to the English word *tourist*. *Turist* traditionally meant adventure travel such as mountaineering and camping, while *tourist* usually referred to a traveller on a packaged holiday or one who stayed for a short time in a city. However the Russian word *turist* is is now commonly used to mean the same as the English *tourist*.
ul. (ул.): Abbreviation for ulitsa (улица) meaning street.
vetka (ветка): A railway branch line.
vokzal (вокзал): A railway station.
zakaznik (заказник): A nature sanctuary.
zapovednik (заповедник): A large nature reserve.
zheleznaya doroga (железная дорога): A railway.

Recommended reading
(Что ещё можно прочитать)

To be able to fully appreciate what you are seeing, it is recommended that you read as much as you can about the countries and regions you are visiting.

BAM railway
The Second Trans-Siberian Railroad: The new stage in the development of the USSR's eastern region by Leonid Shinkarev, 1977. Interesting Soviet propaganda.
Trailblazing Through the Taiga and *Working for Present and Future Generations* by Yuri Kazmin. These enjoyable socialist realist novels were written in the 1930s during the first stage of the BAM.
The Mainline of My Youth by Nikola Nikolarov, 1932. The story recounts the author's experiences working on the first stage of the

BAM. Nikolarov was the son of the famous Bulgarian revolutionary and general secretary of Comintern, Vasily Kalarov.
The Great Baikal-Amur Railway by V I Malashenko, 1977. Another piece of Soviet propaganda.
The BAM Zone Fishing Guide by Athol Yates. This booklet includes information on fishing locations, types of fish, bait and fishing techniques plus details of the BAM Zone's nautre reserves.
Siberian Lena and Amur Rivers Guide by Athol Yates. This booklet includes information on travelling along the Lena and Amur Rivers which connect with the BAM. Included are maps of Nikolaevsk-na-Amure and Yakutsk. The booklet is an excellent supplement to the *Siberian BAM Railway Guidebook*.

General Russian guidebooks

The following are good general guidebooks to Russia and include at least a mention of the BAM or the BAM Zone.
Russia by Rail by Athol Yates.
Trans-Siberian Handbook by Bryn Thomas.
Lonely Planet Siberian Guide.
The Trans-Siberian Rail Guide by Robert Strauss.
Trekking in Russia and Central Asia: A Travellers Guide by Maier Frith.

Russian travellers tales and interesting books

The Trans-Siberian Railway: A Traveller's Anthology by Deborah Manley.
The Big Red Train Ride by Eric Newby.
The Great Railway Bazaar by Paul Theroux.
Off the Map: Bicycling across Siberia by Mark Jenkins. A novel about the author's bike ride along the Trans-Siberian route from Moscow to the Pacific Coast in 1993.
Russian National Parks, an article in *Surviving Together*, Spring 1993, which covers the problems facing managers of Russian national parks.
Red Planes Fly East by Piotr Pavlenko (1899-1951). A communist novel about the settlement of Siberia in the 1930s which captures the enthusiasm of opening up a brave new world. The book served to encourage people to live in eastern Siberia, and advocated the Khetagurova movement. Pavlenko's other books include *In the East*, which became a film in 1937 called *In the Far East*.
The Soviet Far East in Antiquity by A P Okladnikov, 1963. An excellent overview of Siberia's ancient people by Russia's greatest

ethnographer.
Farewell to Matyora by Valentin Rasputin. The novel is the tragic story of the flooding of the Bratsk region which necessitated 249 settlements being moved and resulted in serious social problems. Rasputin also wrote a number of other stories about his local area, Lake Baikal and Irkutsk, including *You Live and Love, Going Downstream, Unexpected Trouble, Borrowed Time* and *Money for Maria*.
Behind the Urals: An American Worker in Russia's City of Steel by John Scott. This 1942 book is the autobiography of an American who volunteered to work in the newly developed city of Magnitogorsk. Although this city is thousands of miles from Komsomolsk, the two cities were founded about the same time and experiences parallel each other.
How the Steel Was Tempered by Nikolai Ostrovsky. This 1952 book portrays the enthusiasm of the early years of Communist power. The anti-hero of this novel was so popular that a future BAM town will be named after him. This book is great, and don't let any literacy critic tell you it's a worthless piece of socialist realism.
A Journey From St Petersburg to Moscow by Alexander Nikolaevich Radishchev. Written in the late 1700s, this book should be called A Journey from St Petersburg to Moscow via the BAM Zone. It details the author's life including his 10 year exile in the Ilimsk prison, near Bratsk, at the western end of the BAM. It portrays the brutality and ugliness of rural Russian life admirably.
A Dance With Death: Soviet Airwomen in World War II by Anne Noggle. This excellent 1994 book covers in detail the life of air navigator Marina Raskova, her place in aviation history and her crash in the BAM Zone.
Living Ethics by Elena Ivanovna Rerikh. This book is the foundation for the Sun City to be built at Severobaikalsk. See under *Severobaikalsk* in the *BAM Mainline Route Description* chapter for more information on Rerikh.
Bear Hunting with the Politburo by Craig Copetas. The real story of doing business in the new Russia is a gem that gives the real feel of Siberia's "wild-west" capitalism.
Forever Flowing by Vasily Grossman, 1972, *Kolyma Tales* by Varlam Shalamov, 1980, *Kolyma: The Arctic Death Camps* by Robert Conquest, *Magadan* by Michael Solomon M, *One Day in the Life of Ivan Denisovich* by Aleksander Solzhenitsyn, *Forced Labours in Soviet Russia* by David Dallin and *A World Apart* by Gustav Herling all describe the horrors of Stalin's gulag camps. Several make specific mention of the BAM.

Arctic Mirrors: Russia and the Small Peoples of the North by Yuri Slezkine, 1994. An excellent review of the past and present policies of the Russians towards the indigenous people of Eastern and North Siberia. Other important books on indigenous people include:
A History of the Peoples of Siberia: Russia's North Asian Colony 1581-1990 by J Forsyth, 1992.
Popular Beliefs and Folklore Traditions in Siberia, edited by V Dioszegi, 1968.
The People of Siberia, edited by M G Levin and L P Polapov, 1964.
Crossroads of Continents-Cultures of Siberia and Alaska, by William W Fitzhugh and Aron Crowell.
Shamanism-Soviet Studies of Traditional Religion in Siberia and Central Asia, edited by M Mandelstam Balzer.
Shamanism: Archaic Techniques of Ecstasy by M Eliade, 1974.
Karl Marx Collective: Economy, Society and Religion in a Siberian Collective Farm by C Humphrey, 1983.
A Field Guide to Birds of the USSR by V E Flint, R L Boehme, Y V Kostin and A A Kuznetzov, 1984. This is the best book on birds of Siberia.
Russian Birds of Prey and Owls Newsletter, Eugen Potapov, Edward Grey Institute of Field ornithology, Department of Zoology, South Parks Rd, Oxford OX1 3PS, UK, email: potapov@vax.oxford.ac.uk.

Maps

A range of interesting Russian maps of cities and regions are available from Four One Company, 523 Hamilton Rd, London Canada N5Z 1S3, tel: (519) 433-1351, fax: (519) 433-5903.
The best hiking and adventure map of north Lake Baikal is the *Across the North West Baikal Area* map, produced by BAMTour. It has topographical details of the area including suggested routes and a list of the passes and their difficulties. Copies can be obtained for $15.00 from Red Bear Tours, 320B Glenferrie Rd, Malvern, Melbourne, Victoria, 3144 Australia, tel: (613) 824 7183, fax: (613) 822 3956, email bmccunn@werple03.mira.net.au
A map of the Kodar Mountains including Marble Canyon (Gulag camp location), Novaya Chara and Staraya Chara is also available for $15:00 from Red Bear Tours.

Videos

Road to the Ocean. A 1945 black and white film on the construction of the Komsomolsk to Sovetskaya Gavin line.
Iron Road. A 1992 film revealing the truth of the 1945 construction

of the Komsomolsk to Sovetskaya Gavin line.
BAM 20th Anniversary. A 1994 film commemorating the construction of the BAM.
The above films are only available from Marina Kuzmina, Russia, 681013, Komsomolsk-na-Amure, ul Vokzalnaya 37-4, kv 10, tel: (4272) 347-63 (Марина А. Кузьмина, Россия 681013, Комсомольск-на-Амуре, ул. Вокзальная, 37-4, кв 10).
Aerograd. This 1935 Mosfilm is one of the most unforgettable Soviet films of the 1930s about the construction of a fictitious eastern Siberian city, Aerograd. To build it, the communists fought against the Japanese saboteurs and Russian Old Believers. May be available from your obscure video shop.
Blue Eye. A video by Scadia Productions on Lake Baikal and seal hunting.

Getting information by email
Email is a very good source of information as you get up to date information and communication instantaneously across the world. Because the addresses of the electronic providers change regularly, the best way of tracking down everything that is currently running is to find a file called Post-Soviet Study Resources on the Internet, which is compiled by Ian Kallen. The best way to find this is simply to do a gopher search for Post-Soviet Study and see where it turns up.

There are a number of listservers which are worth joining and their addresses include:
- friends@solar.rtd.utk.edu (Russian general events)
- fsu@sovset.org (CIS issues)
- h-russia@uicvm.uic.edu (Russian history)
- seelangs@cunyvm.cuny.edu (Russian linguistics)
- rushist@earn.cvut.cz (Russian history)
- omri-l@ubvm.cc.buffalo.edu (Russian news digest)
- travel-l@vm3090.ege.edu.tr (general worldwide travel listserver)

Bulletin boards include:
- soc.culture.soviet
- alt.current-events.russia
- talk.politics.soviet

Timetables
(Расписание)

The timetables are listed in the following order:

BAM Mainline
　　Taishet – Bratsk – Lena (Ust-Kut)
　　Lena (Ust-Kut) – Severobaikalsk
　　Severobaikalsk – Tynda
　　Tynda – Novy Urgal – Komsomolsk
　　Komsomolsk – Sovetskaya Gavan

BAM Branch Lines
　　Chegdomyn – Novy Urgal – Izvestkovskaya
　　Komsomolsk – Khabarovsk
　　Bamovskaya – Tynda (The Little BAM)
　　Khrebtovaya – Ust-Ilmisk
　　Tynda – Neryungri – Aldan – Yakutsk (AYAM)

At the head of each timetable are the trains travelling within and through this section of railway. The timetable is for the fastest train on the section and the departure times are Moscow time. The figures in brackets are the length of time the train stops at the station. Remember that the stopping times depend on which way the train is travelling.

The BAM Mainline distance is measured from Taishet which is the junction of the BAM and Trans-Siberian. Branch line distances are measured from the BAM.

Remember that the timetables are indicitive and may vary over time.

　　Raz. is short for razezd (разезд) which translates as siding.

BAM Mainline Timetable

Map 1: Taishet – Bratsk – Lena (Ust-Kut) section

75	Tynda – Moscow	76	Moscow – Tynda
77	Neryungri – Moscow	78	Moscow – Neryungri
15	Bratsk – Irkutsk	16	Irkutsk – Bratsk
87	Ust-Ilimsk – Irkutsk	88	Irkutsk – Ust-Ilimsk
91	Lena – Moscow	92	Moscow – Lena
197	Severobaikask – Krasnoyarsk	198	Krasnoyarsk – Severobaikalsk
265	Tynda – Taishet	266	Taishet – Tynda

This timetable is for Train №75.

0	Taishet (Тайшет)	1:07		339	Gidrostroitel (Гидростроитель)	7:52
10	Akulshet (Акульшет)			366	Zyuba (Зюба)	
30	Kostomarovo (Костомарово)			379	Pashenni (Пашенный)	
48	Toporok (Топорок)			405	Kezhemskaya (Кежемская)	
57	Nevelskaya (Невельская)	2:10		418	Mamyr (Мамырь)	
97	Parchum (Шарчум)			437	Rechushka (Речушка)	
117	Novochnka (Новочунка)	3:13		463	Vidim (Видим)	
120	Sosnovye Rodniki (Сосновые Родники)			482	Sokhaty (Сохатый)	
		3:32		503	Chernaya (Черная)	
142	Chuna (Чуна)	3:47 (10)		518	Svedneilimskaya (Среднеилимская)	
154	Isykan (Изыкан)			546	Zhelezny (Железный)	
167	Targiz (Таргиз)			554	Korshunukha-Angarskaya (Коршуниха-Ангарская)	11:18 (15)
177	Chuksha (Чукша)			564	Sibirishnaya (Сибиришная)	
191	Keshevo (Кешево)			575	Khrebtovaya (Хребтовая)	
210	Toreya (Торея)			592	Krastovaya (Крастовая)	
226	Ornevka (Огневка)			612	Semigorsk (Семигорск)	
246	Turma (Турма)			623	Merzlotnaya (Мерзлотная)	
259	Balaga (Балага)			649	Kamanova (Кайманова)	
269	Vikorevka (Вихоревка)	6:24		663	Ruche (Ручей)	
283	Morgudon (Моргудон)			674	Yantal (Янталь)	
292	Anzebi (Анзеби)	6:56		683	Kuta (Кута)	
303	Galachinski (Галачинский)			715	Ust-Kut (Усть-Кут)	
314	Bratskoe More (Братское Море)			722	Lena (Лена)	14:34 (20)
325	Padunskie Porogi (Падунские Пороги)	7:36				

Map 1: Lena (Ust-Kut) – Severobaikalsk section

75	Tynda – Moscow	76	Moscow – Tynda
77	Neryungri – Moscow	78	Moscow – Neryungri
91	Lena – Moscow	92	Moscow – Lena
197	Severobaikask – Krasnoyarsk	198	Krasnoyarsk – Severobaikalsk

This timetable is for Train №75.

722	Lena (Лена)	14.54		931	Ulkan (Улькан)	20:30
736	Lena-Vostochnaya (Лена-Восточная)			954	Umbella (Умбелла)	20:57
				983	Kunerma (Кунерма)	21:36
761	Chudnichy (Чудничый)	16:27		998	Delbichinda (Дельбичинда)	
786	Zvezdhaya (Звездная)	17.07		1015	Daban (Дабан)	
823	Niya (Ния)	17:50		1029	Goudzhekit (Гоуджекит)	
854	Nebel (Небель)	18:31		1043	Tuya (Тыя)	
890	Kirenga (Киренга)	19:40		1064	Severobaikalsk (Северобайкальск)	23:10
904	Okunaka (Окунайка)					

Map 2: Severobaikalsk – Novaya Chara – Tynda section

75	Tynda – Moscow	76	Moscow – Tynda
77	Neryungri – Moscow	78	Moscow – Neryungri
87	Ust-Ilimsk – Irkutsk	88	Irkutsk – Ust-Ilimsk
197	Severobaikask – Krasnoyarsk	198	Krasnoyarsk – Severobaikalsk
201	Tynda – Severobaikalsk	202	Severobaikalsk – Tynda
603	Novy Uoyan – Severobaikalsk	604	Severobaikalsk – Novy Uoyan
607	Novaya Chara – Kuanda	608	Kuanda – Novaya Chara
609	Novaya Chara – Kuanda	610	Kuanda – Novaya Chara
611	Taksimo – Novy Uoyan	612	Novy Uoyan – Taksimo
613	Taksimo – Novy Uoyan	614	Novy Uoyan – Taksimo
673	Tynda – Yuktali/Lopcha	674	Yuktali/Lopcha – Tynda
675	Tynda – Yuktali	676	Yuktali – Tynda

This timetable is for Train №75.

1,064	Severobaikalsk (Северобайкальск)	23:45	1,599	Taku (Таку)	
1,104	Nizhneangarsk (Нижнеангарск)	0:13	1,615	Balbukhta (Балбухта)	
1,120	Kholodnaya (Холодная)		1,632	Syulban (Сюльбан)	
1,141	Kichera (Кичера)	0:51	1,652	Naledny (Наледный)	
1,177	Kiron (Кирон)		1,664	Kodar (Кодар)	
1,196	Angoya (Ангоя)	1:46	1,683	Leprindo (Леприндо)	13:20
1,207	Ogdynda (Огдында)		1,694	Sallikit (Салликит)	13:37
1,224	Ogne (Огней)		1,714	Sakukan (Сакукан)	14:01
1,242	Anamakit (Анамакит)	2:34	1,734	Novaya Chara (Новая Чара)	14:24 (33)
1,257	Novy Uoyan (Новый Уоян)	2:56 (10)	1,755	Kemen (Кемен)	15:17
1,275	Bakany (Баканы)		1,772	Ikabya (Икабья)	14:40
1,292	Raz. 555km (Раз. 555км)		1,803	Ikabyakan (Икабьякан)	
1,312	Churo (Чуро)		1,826	Mururin (Мурурин)	
1,330	Kyukhelbekerskaya (Кюхельбекерская)	4:25 (11)	1,851	Olongo (Олонго)	
1,346	Kovokta (Ковокта)		1,879	Luninskaya (Лунинская)	
1,359	Angarakan (Ангаракан)			Velbemkan (Вельбемкан)	
1,385	Raz. 635km (Раз. 635км)	5:33	1,934	Olyokma (Олёкма)	19:17
	Raz. 651km (Раз. 651км)			Imangrakan (Имангракан)	
	Raz. 673km (Раз. 673)		2,008	Tas-Yuryakh (Тас-Юрях)	
	Raz. 686km (Раз. 686)		2,028	Uyktali (Юктали)	21:35
	Severomuisk (Северомуйск)	7:15		Taluma (Талума)	
	Arkum (Аркум)		2,074	Dyugabul (Дюгабуль)	22:22
	Ulgi (Ульги)			Unkur (Ункур)	
1,400	Muyakan (Муякан)		2,137	Chilchi (Чильчи)	22:28
1,462	Ulanmakit (Уланмакит)		2,185	Lopcha (Лопча)	0:40
1,484	Taksimo (Таксимо)	9:11	2,204	Elgakan (Эльгакан)	
1,507	Raz. Lodya (Раз. Лодья)		2,232	Larba (Ларба)	1:40
1,522	Raz. Aku (Раз. Аку)		2,257	Lumbir (Лумбир)	
1,548	Shivery (Шиверы)		2,284	Khorogochi (Хорогочи)	2:50
1,558	Kora (Койра)			Kutykan (Кутыкан)	3:23
1,576	Gorbachevskaya (Горбачевская)		2,334	Kuvykta (Кувыкта)	3:57
1,577	Kuanda (Куанда)	10:55	2,343	Kuryan (Курьян)	
1,586	Raz. 884km (Раз. 884км)		2,364	Tynda (Тында)	5:00

	Map 3 & 4: Tynda – Novy Urgal – Komsomolsk section		
203	Komsomolsk – Tynda	204	Tynda – Komsomolsk
671	Dipkun – Tynda	672	Tynda – Dipkun
	Dugda – Verkhnezeisk		Verkhnezeisk – Dugda

This timetable is for Train №204.

2,364	Tynda (Тында)	8:55	3,179	Etyrken (Этыркэн)	6:36
2,376	Shakhtaum (Шахтаум)			Amgan (Амган)	7:09
2,391	Bestuzheva (Бестужева)			Shugara (Шугара)	7:36
	Dzhalingra (Джалингра)			Tuyun (Туюн)	8:03
	Amut-Ozerny (Амут-Озерный)			Stlannik (Стланник)	8:37
2,452	Marevaya (Маревая)	10:54	3,264	Alonka (Алонка)	9:10
	Emeka (Эмейка)			Kychyranky (Кычыранкы)	9:46
	Kuduli (Кудули)			Chebangda (Чебангда)	10:13
	Khaimkan (Хаимкан)		3,305	Bureinski (Буреинский)	10:43
2,511	Unakha (Унаха)		3,315	Novy Urgal (Новый Ургал)	11:10 (40)
2,527	Dipkun (Дипкун)	12:10 (15)	3,330	Urgal 1 (Ургал1)	12:13
2,541	Dess (Десс)		3,342	Chemchoko (Чемчуко)	
	Moskovski Komsomolets		3,357	Mugule (Мугуле)	
	(Московский Комсомолец)		3,366	Turuk (Турук)	
	Utuga (Утугай)		3,374	Mukunga (Мукунга)	
	Tutaul (Тутаул)	13:42	3,383	Soloni (Солони)	13:25
	Klepikovo (Клепиково)	14:07	3,393	Naldi (Нальды)	
	Pervoprokhodsty		3,403	Ducce Alin (Дуссе Алинь)	
	(Первопроходцы)	14:29	3,412	Avakha (Аваха)	
	Baralis (Баралус)	15:01	3,421	Suluk (Сулук)	14:29 (6)
	Mulmuga (Мульмуга)	15:35		Raz. 106km (Раз. 106км)	
	Mulmugakan (Мульмугакан)		3,441	Mogdi (Могды)	
	Ulak (Улак)		3,458	Orokot (Орокот)	
2,707	Verkhnezeisk (Верхнезейск)	17:16	3,475	Gerbi (Герби)	15:52
2,723	Apetenolk (Апетенолк)	17:47	3,487	Talidazhak (Талидажак)	
2,751	Izhak (Ижак)		3,500	Urkaltu (Уркальту)	
2,774	Ulyanovski Stroitel		3,513	Badzhal (Баджал)	
	(Ульяновский Строитель)	19:35	3,532	Dzhamko (Джамку)	17:11
2,796	Ogoron (Огорон)		3,533	Sektali (Сектали)	
2,820	Moldavski (Молдавский)		3,561	Zanga (Энга)	17:45
2,833	Ulagir (Улагир)		3,581	Amgun (Амгунь)	18:13
2,850	Miroshnichenko (Мирошниченко)		3,598	Sonakh (Сонах)	
2,863	Tungala (Тунгала)	21:33	3,614	Ebrun (Эбрунь)	
	Kamnega (Камнега)		3,633	Postyshevo (Постышево)	19:09 (25)
	Tangomen (Тангомен)			Raz. 311km (Раз. 311км)	
2,912	Dugda (Дугда)	22:43		Raz. 324km (Раз. 324км)	
	Nora (Нора)	23:24	3,657	Bolen (Болен)	20:11
	Meun (Меун)	0:06	3,678	Moni (Мони)	20:43
2,975	Drogoshevsk (Дрогошевск)	0:40	3,697	Evoron (Эворон)	21:16
	Skalisty (Скалистый)	1:21	3,720	Kharpichan (Харпичан)	21:41
	Chervinka (Червинка)	1:53		Kondon (Кондон)	
3,033	Fevralsk (Февральск)	2:18 (40)	3,733	Gorin (Горин)	22:06
	Zvonkov (Звонков)		3,758	Mavrinski (Мавринский)	
	Demchenko (Демченко)		3,769	Khurmiuli (Хурмиули)	23:02
	Isakan (Исакан)		3,793	Lian (Лиан)	23:35
3,118	Isa (Иса)	4:53	3,808	Khalgaso (Хальгасо)	0:03
3,134	Gvozdevski (Гвоздевский)		3,818	Silinka (Силинка)	0:23
	Mustakh (Мустах)		3,831	Komsomolsk 2 (Комсомолск 2)	0:40
	Ulma (Ульма)			Komsomolsk 1 (Комсомолск 1)	1:00

Map 4: Komsomolsk – Vanino – Sovetskaya Gavan section

187	Sovetskaya Gavan – Khabarovsk	188	Khabarovsk – Sovetskaya Gavan
251	Sovetskaya Gavan – Khabarovsk	152	Khabarovsk – Sovetskaya Gavan
921	Sovetskaya Gavan – Khabarovsk	922	Khabarovsk – Sovetskaya Gavan

This timetable is for Train №188.

0	Komsomolsk11 (Комсомольс 1)	11:45		(Высокогорная)	19:15 (25)
	Novy Mir (Новый Мир)		259	Datta (Датта)	20:09
	Amurski (Амурский)		279	Kenaga (Кенага)	20:42
19	Pivan (Пивань)	12:40	293	Dzhigdasi (Джигдаси)	21:00
27	Kumte (Кумтэ)	12:55	307	Koto (Кото)	21:19
48	Gaiter (Гайтер)	13:22	322	Tuluchi (Тулучи)	21:44
60	Kartel (Картель)	13:39	337	Akur (Акур)	22:06
71	Selikhin (Селихин)	13:55(20)	359	Tumnin (Тумнин)	22:43
82	Eldigan (Эльдиган)	14:31	385	Khutu (Хуту)	23:13
101	Poni (Пони)	15:00	395	Imbo (Имбо)	23:30
114	Kun (Кун)	15:27	399	Ust-Orochi (Усть-Орочи)	23:43
131	Gurskoe (Гурское)	16:00		Chepsary (Чепсары)	0:08
143	Pochepta (Почепта)	16:20	418	Mongokhto (Монгохто)	0:29
158	Uktur (Уктур)	16:42	422	Landyshi (Ландыши)	0:45
166	Aksaka (Аксака)	16:54	432	Dyuanka (Дюанка)	1:07
180	Kenai (Кенай)	17:20	443	Toki (Токи)	
192	Udomi (Удоми)	17:38		Chudinovo (Чудиново)	
201	Oune (Оунэ)	17:54	453	Vanino-Vokzal (Ванино-Вокзал)	1:55
208	Kosgrambo (Косграмбо)	18:07	461	Sovetskaya Gavan-Sort.	
214	Otkosnaya (Откосная)	18:22		(Советская Гавань-Сорт.)	
222	Kuznetsovski (Кузнецовский)	18:44	476	Desna (Десна)	
228	Sollu (Соллу)		487	Sovetskaya Gavan-Gorod	
239	Vysokogornaya			(Советская Гавань-Город)	2:15

BAM Branch Lines Timetables

Map 4: Chegdomyn – Novy Urgal – Izvestkovaya section

659	Novy Urgal – Tyrma	76	Tyrma – Novy Urgal
661	Tyrma – Izvestkovaya	662	Izvestkovaya– Tyrma
663	Chegdomyn – Izvestkovaya	16	Izvestkovaya – Chegdomyn

This timetable is for Train №663.

0	Chegdomyn (Чегдомын)	4:50	191	Tyrma (Тырма)	12:12
17	Urgal 1 (Ургал 1)	5:17 (3)	204	Alanap (Аланап)	12:33
32	Novy Urgal (Новый Ургал)	6:20		Tarakelok (Таракелок)	13:13
55	Adnikan (Адникан)	6:56	238	Ekhilkan (Эхилкан)	13:36
75	Elga (Эльга)	7:37	262	Zimove (Зимовье)	14:14
	Dolina (Долина)	7:56	281	Talandzha (Таланджа)	14:54
106	Yagdynya (Ягдынья)	8:36	303	Yaurin (Яурин)	15:28
	Korchagin (Корчагин)	9:14	309	Perevalny (Перевальный)	15:42
136	Ushman (Ушман)	9:56		Kuldur (Кульдур)	16:24
151	Sogda (Согда)	10:26	343	Brusit (Брусит)	16:42
158	Moshka (Мошка)	10:43	360	Izvestkovaya (Известковая)	17:05
	Malinnik (Малинник)	11:16			

Map 4: Komsomolsk – Khabarovsk section

67	Komsomolsk – Khabarovsk	68	Khabarovsk – Komsomolsk
187	Sovetskaya Gavan – Khabarovsk	188	Khabarovsk – Sovetskaya Gavan
251	Sovetskaya Gavan – Khabarovsk	152	Khabarovsk – Sovetskaya Gavan
921	Sovetskaya Gavan – Khabarovsk	922	Khabarovsk – Sovetskaya Gavan

Note: The final destination of trains 187/188 is Tikhookeanskaya.

This timetable is for Train №67.

0	Komsomolsk 1 (Комсомольск 1)	15:55	211	Raz. No 12 (Раз. №12)		
7	Khurba (Хурба)		220	Litovko (Литовко)		21:03
22	Mylki (Мылки)	16:43	231	Dalnevostochny (Дальневосточный)		
30	Malmyzh (Малмыж)		244	Forel (Форель)		
36	Raz. 303km (Раз. 303км)		259	Vandan (Вандан)		
42	Podali (Подали)		266	Yubilein (Юбилейн)		
53	Ulbinka (Ульбинка)		274	Dzhelyumken (Джелюмкен)		
63	Elban (Эльбан)	17:39	291	Darga (Дарга)		
72	Teisin (Тейсин)	17:52	291	Partizanskie Sopki (Партизанские Сопки)		
81	Mengon (Менгон)	18:03	309	Dzharmen (Джармен)		
89	Kharkovsk (Харьковск)		319	Utiny (Утиный)		
99	Bolon (Болонь)	18:25	330	Volochaevka 2 (Волочаевка 2)		23:09 (20)
107	Yuzhny (Южный)		336	Dezhnevka (Дежневка)		
116	Raz. No 21 (Раз. №21)		347	Nikolaevka (Николаевка)		
136	Khevchen (Хевчен)		357	Priamurskaya (Приамурская)		
147	Raz. No 18 (Раз. №18)		365	Amur (Амур)		
168	Selgon (Сельгон)	19:39	374	Khabarovsk 1 (Хабаровск 1)		0:33
183	Nuskhi (Нусхи)					
202	Sanboli (Санболи)					

Map 3: Bamovskaya – Tynda section (The Little BAM)

77	Neryungri – Moscow	78	Moscow – Neryungri
203	Tynda – Vladivostok	204	Vladivostok – Tynda
279	Tynda – Blagoveshchensk	280	Blagoveshchensk – Tynda
191	Tynda – Chita	192	Chita – Tynda
225	Tynda – Khabarovsk	226	Khabarovsk – Tynda
533	Tynda – Kharkov	534	Kharkov – Tynda
6063	Tynda – Murtigit	6064	Murtigit – Tynda
	Tynda – Kislovodsk		Kislovodsk – Tynda

This timetable is for Train №78.

0	Bamovskaya (Бамовская)	2:30	94	Silip (Силип)		
18	Shtrum (Штрум)	2:55	113	Zabolotny (Заболотное)		
49	Murtygit (Муртыгит)	3:52	133	Belenkaya (Беленькая)		5:37
65	Purikan (Шурикан)		160	Seti (Сети)		
82	Anosovskaya (Аносовская)	4:41	180	Tynda (Тында)		6:35

Map 1: Khrebtovaya– Ust-Ilimsk section

| 87 | Ust-Ilimsk – Irkutsk | 88 | Irkutsk – Ust-Ilimsk |

This timetable is for Train №88.

0	Khrebtovaya (Хребтовая)	11:45	139	Tushama (Тушама)	14:19
19	Hachalny (Начальный)	12:02	160	Tubinskaya (Тубинская)	14:48
42	Balarikha (Балариха)	12:25	183	Diabazovy (Диабазовый)	15:24
70	Igirma (Игирма)	12:54	214	Ust-Ilimsk (Усть-Илимск)	16:00
94	Rudnogorsk (Рудногорск)	13:27			

Map 5: Tynda – Neryungri – Aldan – Yakutsk section (AYAM)

77	Neryungri – Moscow	78	Moscow – Neryungri
279	Tynda – Blagoveshchensk	280	Blagoveshchensk – Tynda
191	Tynda – Chita	192	Chita – Tynda
225	Tynda – Khabarovsk	226	Khabarovsk – Tynda
533	Tynda – Kharkov	534	Kharkov – Tynda
	Tynda – Aldan		Aldan – Tynda

This timetable is for Train №78.

0	Tynda (Тында)	6:55	306	Ogonor (Огоньор)	
12	Shakhtaum (Шахтаум)		321	Tit (Тит)	
27	Bestuzheva (Бестужева)		331	Yangi (Янги)	
19	Gilyui (Гилюй)		351	Taezhnaya (Таежная)	
44	Mogot (Могот)	8:35	365	Mikhailovka (Михайловка)	
	Rikhard Zorge (Рихард Зорге)		379	Vasilekka (Васильекка)	
80	Yakutski (Якутский)		396	Nikolkin-Klyuch (Николкин-Ключ)	
93	Nagornaya Yakutsk (Нагорная Якутск)	9:45	416	Bolshoi-Nimnyr (Большой-Нимныр)	
113	Ayam (Аям)		437	Yuuma (Юума)	
	Kholodnikan (Холодникан)		454	Seligdr (Селигдр)	
135	Zolotinka (Золотинка)	10:33	470	Kosarevski (Косаревский)	
	Okurdan (Окурдан)		486	Aldan (Алдан)	
177	Oborcho (Оборчо)		503	Tomyorak (Томёрак)	
192	Berkakit (Беркакит)	11:45 (10)	519	Gluboki-Kuranakh (Глубокий-Куранах)	
202	Neryungri-Passenger (Нерюнгри-пасс.)	12:10	533	Yakokit (Якокит)	
210	Neryungri-Freight (Нерюнгри Груз.)		548	Ene (Энье)	
221	Denisovski (Денисовский)		559	Dyamovski (Дямовский)	
232	Chulman (Чульман)		568	Tommot (Томмот)	
246	Chulbass (Чульбасс)			Amga (Амга)	
256	Tenismy (Тенисмый)			Dobrolet (Добролет)	
271	Chulmekon (Чульмекон)			Olen (Олен)	
288	Khatymi (Хатыми)			Pravaya Lena (Правая Лена)	
				Yakutsk (Якутск)	

Master Route Map

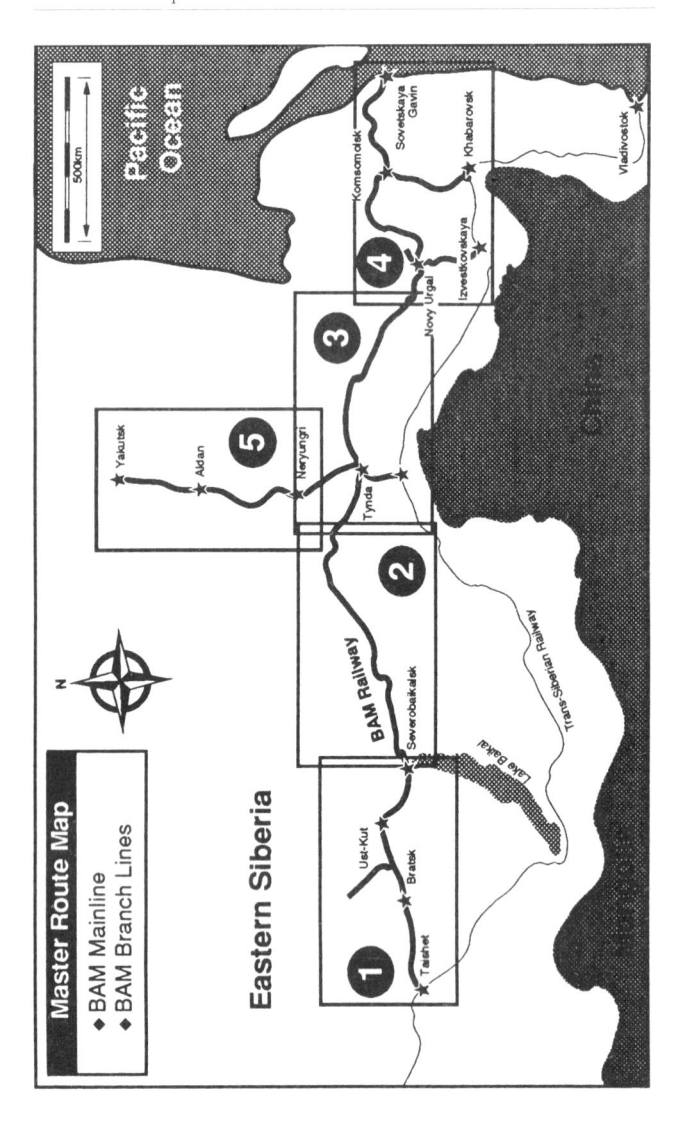

Map 1

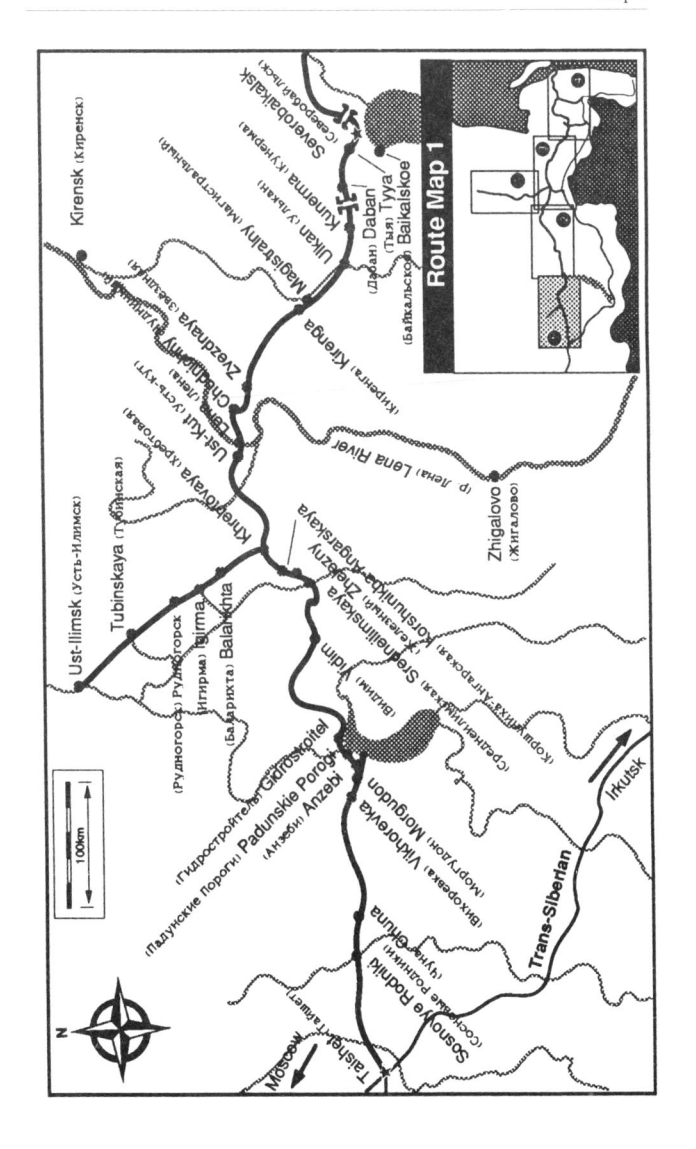

Map 2

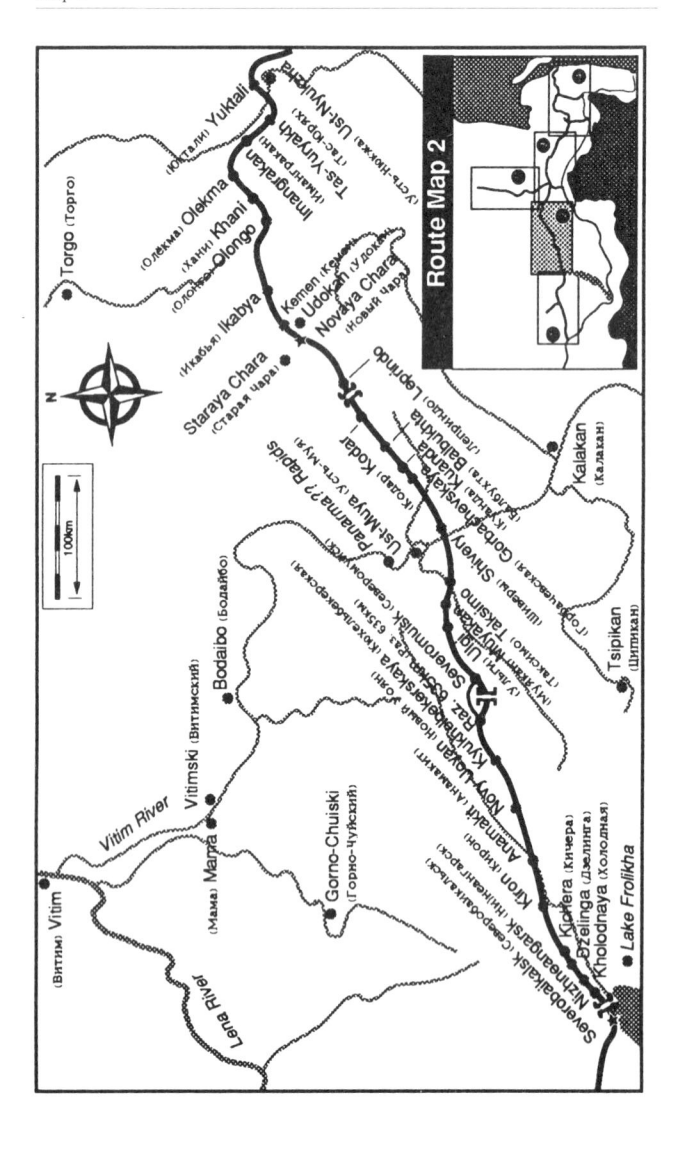

Map 3

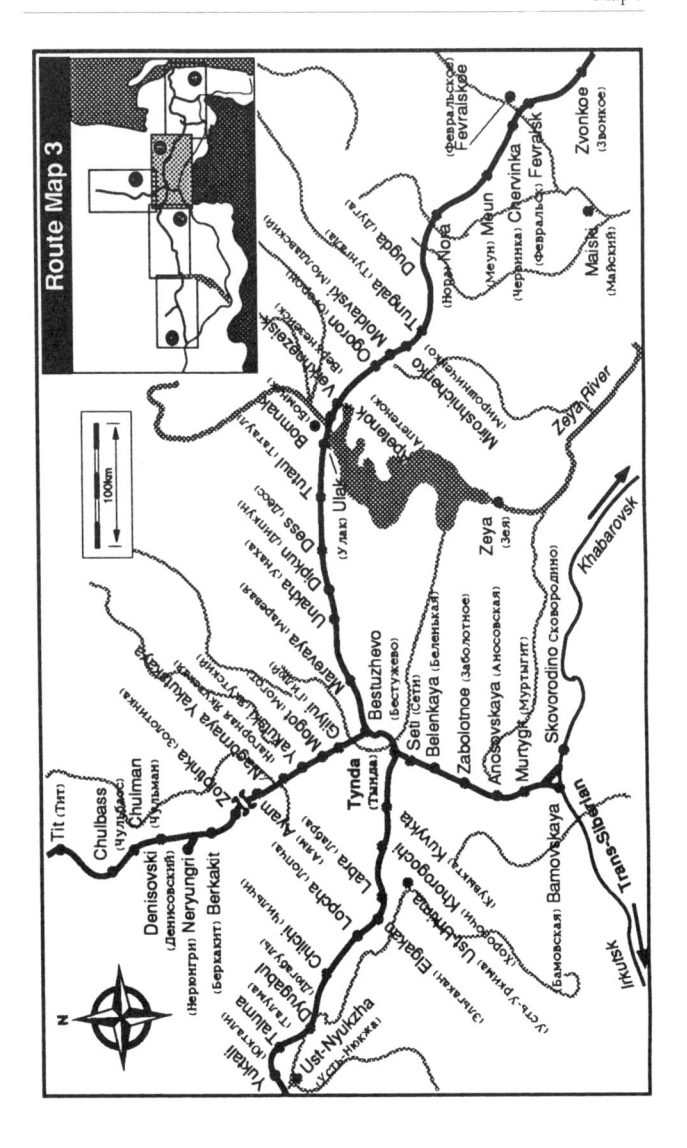

Map 4

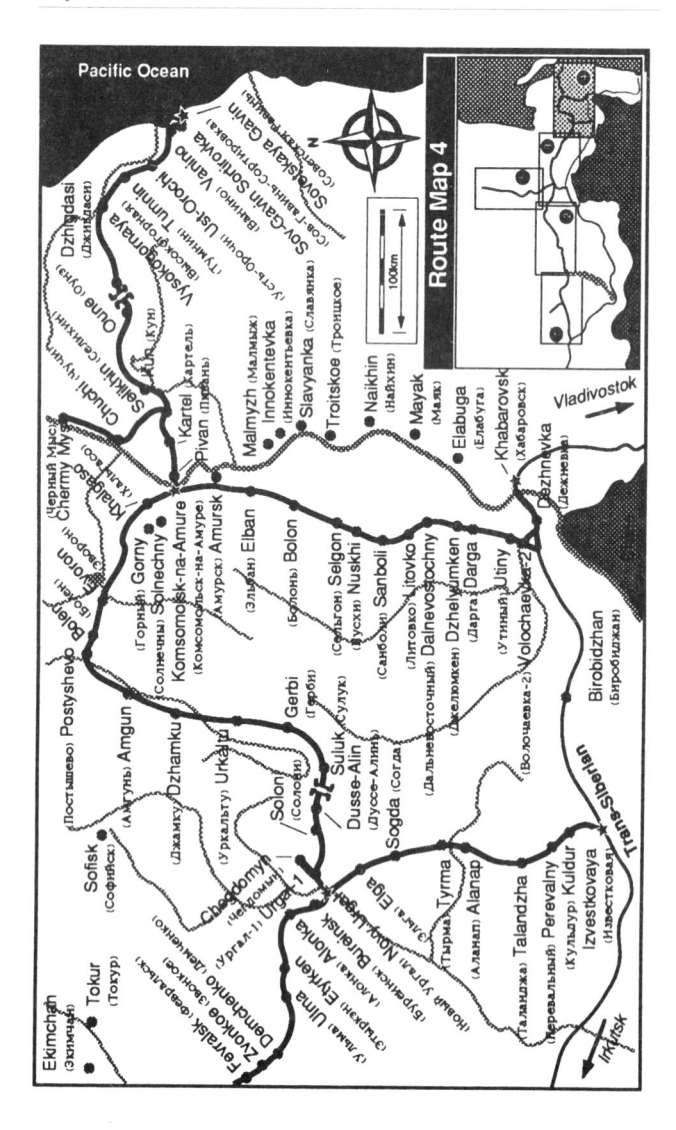

Map 5

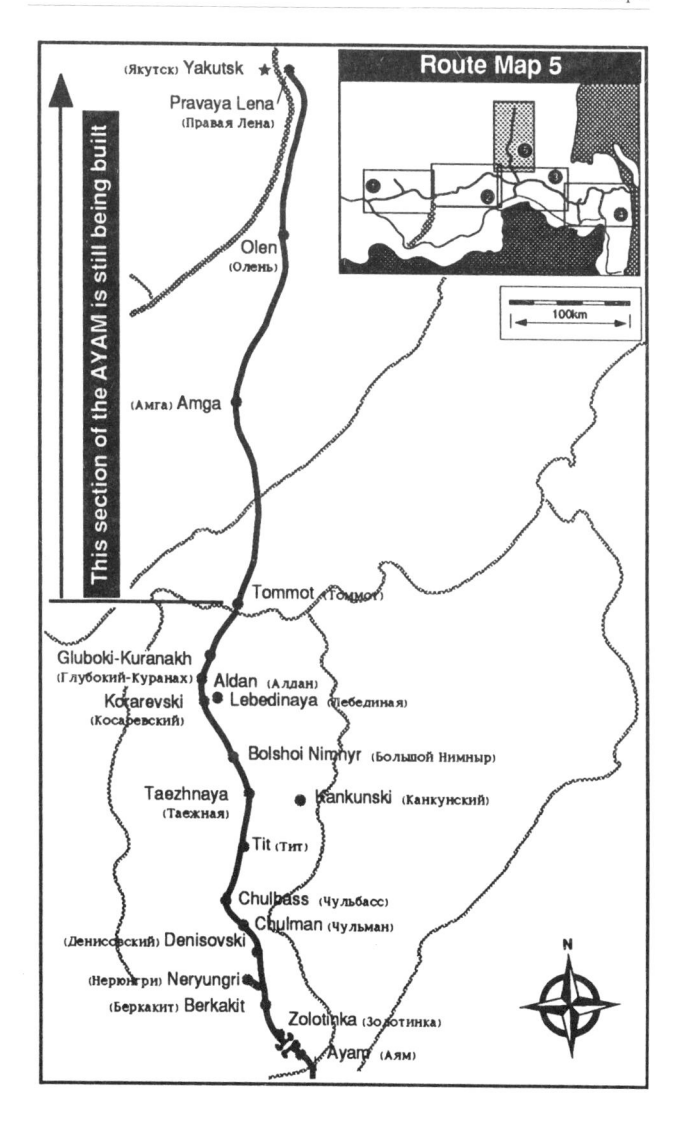

Index

Указатель

Map references are in **bold** type.

abbreviations A4-A5, A11-A14
accommodation 43, 93, 109-11, 121-22, 123, 238, 299
Achan (Ачан) 301
adventure travel 37, 91, 93, 146, 199-201, 257, 271
agriculture 40, 58-61, 206, 215, 243, 311
air travel 106
aircraft, historical 32, 186, 233, 253, 254, 257-58, 265, 269-70, 287, 306
Akikan gulag camp 22, 166-67
alcohol & legal drinking age 65, 132-34
Aldan (Алдан) 44, 312-13, 319-22, **320**
Alonka (Алонка) 243
Amgun (Амгунь) 253
Amur (Амур) 303
Amur-Yakutsk Highway 304, 309, 311, 319
Amursk (Амурск) 41, 47, 277-80, **278**
Amurski (Амурский) 281
Anamakit (Анамакит) 179
Angoya (Ангоя) 47
animals 69-73, 94, 164, 172-3, 227
Anosovskaya (Аносовская) 27, 306
Anzebi (Анзеби) 138-39
Apetenolk (Апетенолк) 234-35
architecture 40, 41, 42, 47, 255, 277
art galleries 161, 265
atomic bomb mining 208
AYAM 14, 15, 52, 308-322
Baikolskoe (Байкальское) 39, 170-71
bakeries 46, 231
Balbukhta (Балбухта) 14, 201
BAM construction history 1-34, 158, 175,193-94, 201, 217, 221, 253, 257-58, 280-81, 282, 284, 285, 304-05, 338-39
BAM museums 161, 222, 246
BAM underwater tunnel 22, 284
BAMlag gulag 10, 20-22, 252
Bamovskaya (Бамовская) 10-13, 304, 306
banks 48
banya 48, 222, 237
Bargalino (Баргалино) 191-92
Barulnaya (Барульная) 138
bears 70, 227
Belenkaya (Беленькая) 27, 306-07
Berezovy (Березовый) 255
Berkakit (Беркакит) 312-13
Bestuzheva (Бестужева) 225, 310
Bichi (Бичи) 273
bicycle riding 164
bird watching 94, 256, 273, 301

black market 101
boats, see hydrofoils, river cruisers
Bodaibo (Бодайбо) 10, 31
Bolon (Болонь) 301
Bolshaya Kartel (Большая Картель) 282-83
Bolshoi-Nimnyr (Большой-Нимныр) 319
Bomnak (Бомнак) 223
booking & buying rail tickets 90-92, 114, 116-120, 167, A6-A8
booking accommodation 122, A10
booking tours 89-92
botanical gardens 279
Bratsk (Братск) 10-11, 41, 44, 46, 140-44, **141**
Bratsk Porozhski (Братск Порожский) 138
Bratskoe More (Братское Море) 139
Brezhnev, Leonid 2, 4-5, 12, 13, 58, 171
bribes 127
budgeting & costs 92-93
Bureinski (Буреинский) 243
Buryat indigenous people 70-74, 75, 184
buses 121
cafes 123
canteens 123
cars & car rental 106
caviar 67
caving 146-47, 302
Chapo-Ologo (Чапо-Олого) 213
Chara sand dunes 206
Chara, see Stara Chara or Novaya Chara
Chegdomyn (Чегдомын) 10, 40, 248-49
Chekanovski (Чекановский) 139
Chekunda (Чекунда) 298
chemical weapons 287
Cherny Mys (Черный Мыс) 284
Chilchi (Чильчи) 215
Chulbass (Чульбасс) 319
Chulman (Чульман) 11, 318-19
Chuna (Чуна) 138
churches 161, 276, 315
cinema 37
clothes to take 102, 104, 115
coal mines 11, 227, 248, 249, 313, 317-8
Cold War & spying 2-3, 30-34
communist propaganda 16, 254, 274, 304
construction problems 23-30, 142, 156-58, 177, 180-84, 219, 236, 304, 306, 311
Cossacks 131-32
costs & budgeting 92-93
country life 39-40, 59
coupe railway carriages 109-11
credit cards 101-02, 104
crime & safety 79-80, 111, 128-29, 132
currency 101-02

customs 132-34
Daban (Дабан) 155
dacha 59, 138, 144, 247, 273
Dalnevostochny (Дальневосточный) 302
Darga (Дарга) 302
Datta (Датта) 285
Decemberists 161, 180, 193, 225
Delbichinda (Дельбичинда) 155
Demchenko (Демченко) 243
Denisovski (Денисовский) 318
Desna (Десна) 291
Dess (Десс) 225
Dezhnevka (Дежневка) 303
Dipkun (Дипкун) 47, 225
drinking water 98, 102, 113-14
drunken forests 54
Dugda (Дугда) 47, 236
Duki (Дуки) 253
Dusse Alin (Дуссе Алинь) 11, 29, 251, 252-53
Dzelinga (Дзелинга) 45, 179
Dzemgi (Дземги) 273
Dzhigdasi (Джигдаси) 285
Dzhuen (Джуен) 301
earthquakes 50-51, 158
education 162, 178, 199-200, 226, 229, 273
Ekimchan (Экимчан) 40, 239-40
Elban (Эльбан) 277, 3000
electricity 101
Elga (Эльга) 298
Energetik (Энергетик) 140
English language 89
entertainment 37, 128
environmental problems 55-57, 142, 143, 155, 159, 164, 208, 240, 256, 276, 280, 313, 319, 322
Etyrken (Этыркэн) 243
Evenk indigenous people 75, 206, 223-34, 242, 308, 319
Evens indigenous people 75, 309
Evoron (Эворон) 256
exchange rate 101
expenses 92-93
farming 40, 58-61, 206, 215, 243, 311
Festivalny (Фестивальный) 276-77
Fevralsk (Февральск) 40, 47, 236-38
fire trains 85-86
fish & fishing 67-69, 94, 155, 164, 196-199, 202, 232, 234-35, 255, 286, 290-91, 295
flora & fauna 51-54, 62-64, 66-73
food 58-67, 93, 94, 115, 124-25
food preserving 59, 65-66
food, where to eat 93, 123-24
forest fires 49
freight train travelling 312-13
fur farms 171, 213
Gagarin, Yuri 269-70
Gaiter (Гайтер) 282
Galachinski (Галачинский) 139
Galichny (Галичный) 273
gender issues 254, 261

geology 3, 10, 274, 275, 321
Gerbi (Герби) 253
German POWs 15, 22, 260, 281
getting sick 98-100, 104
getting there & away 95
Gidrostoitel (Гидростоитель) 140
gifts 104, 132
Gilyui (Гилюй) 310-11
glaciers 49-50, 200-01
Gluboki-Kuranakh (Глубокий-Куранах) 322
Golbuchnoe (Голубичное) 302
gold mines & dredges 187-88, 214, 238, 240, 241, 242, 319-20, 322
Gorbachev, Mikhail 5, 6, 7, 14, 15, 283
Gorbachevskaya (Горбачевская) 193
Gorely (Горелый) 305
Gorin (Горин) 257
Gorny (Горный) 226, 276
Goudzhekit (Гоуджекит) 155-56
Great Patriotic War 3, 4, 22, 154, 217, 227, 257, 260, 265, 270, 280-81, 285-86, 292, 295, 304-05
greenhouses 61, 231
guidebooks 89, A15
gulag camp remains 22, 166-67, 202, 209-212, 319
gulag life 20, 21, 139, 168, 288
gulags 10, 11, 15, 23, 136, 138, 189, 248, 252-53, 257, 260-61, 267, 272, 281, 282, 284, 285, 287-88, 290, 304, 307, 311-12
Gurskoe (Гурское) 284
hard currency 101-02
health precautions 98-100, 104
helicopter hiring 106
hiking 94, 164, 169-70, 196, 208-09
holidays 94-95, 310
homestay 122
hospitals 98-100, 104, 231
hostels, railways 93, 121-22
hot water 45, 113-14, 231
hotels 43, 93, 121-22, 123
hydrofoil 107-8, 143, 144, 152, 156, 160
Igirma (Игирма) 308
Ikabya (Икабья) 212-13
Imangrakan (Имангракан) 214
indigenous people 69-76, 141-42, 161, 170-71, 184, 215, 223, 265, 301, 309
individual travel 89
industries 3-8, 60-61, 142-44, 185-86, 207-08, 214, 227, 235, 274-77, 280, 317-18, 319, 320, 322
insects 98-100
internet A18
Irakinda (Иракинда) 188
Irkutsk (Иркутск) 160-61
Ivanovskoe (Ивановское) 241
Izvestkovaya (Известковая) 11, 13, 299-300
Japanese POWs 22, 248, 258, 260-61, 266, 280-81, 285-86, 298, 299
Jewish Oblast 299, 302, 303

Kalakan (Калакан) 188
Kankunsky (Канкунский) 319
Kartel (Картель) 282-83
Kazachinskoe (Казачинское) 154
Kemen (Кемен) 212
KGB 131
Khabarovsk (Хабаровск) 149, 303
Khalgaso (Хальгасо) 257-58
Khani (Хани) 27, 213-14
Kharemika (Харемика) 171
Kharkovsk (Харьковск) 301
Khatystyr (Хатыстыр) 321-22
Kholodnaya (Холодная) 39, 166
Khorogochi (Хорогочи) 215
Khrebtovaya (Хребтовая) 147
Khrushchev, Nikita 4, 6, 47, 58
Khurba (Хурба) 300
Khurmiuli (Хурмиули) 257
Kichera (Кичера) 47, 178
Kirenga (Киренга) 154
Kirensk (Киренск) 10, 149
Kodar (Кодар) 45, 201-02
Kodar mountains 50, 200-01, 208-09
Kodar station gulag 202, 212
Komsomol 12, 14, 15-18, 32, 33, 37, 199, 259-260, 261, 269
Komsomol shock project 8, 12, 15-18, 277, 313
Komsomolsk-na-Amure (Комсомолск-на-Амуре) 4, 10, 11, 41, 42, 44, 45, 59, 60, 68, 69, 96, 258, 259-71, **262**
Kondon (Кондон) 256-57
Korshunikha-Angarskaya (Коршуниха-Ангарская) 145-47, **145**
Kosarevski (Косаревский) 319
Kuanda (Куанда) 37, 40, 47, 68-69, 193-201, **194**
Kuldur (Кульдур) 299
Kun (Кун) 284
Kunerma (Кунерма) 12, 43, 155
Kuvykta (Кувыкта) 215-16
Kuznetsovski (Кузнецовский) 285
Kyukhelbekerskaya (Кюхельбекерская) 180
Lake Baikal 7, 50-51, 156, 159, 160, 169-70, 179
Lamaism 170-71
Larba (Ларба) 215
laundry 122-23
Lebedinaya (Лебединая) 319
Lena (Лена) 148-150
Lena-Vostochnaya (Лена-Восточная) 150-51
lend lease 233, 257-58, 287, 306
Lenin, Vladimir Ilich 58, 291
Leninski (Ленинский) 320
Leprindo (Леприндо) 202
Lesnoi (Лесной) 302, 312
libraries 45, 89
Litovko (Литовко) 302
living conditions 25, 36-48, 58-66, 193-94, 226-231, 313
locomotives 81-84, 85
Lopcha (Лопча) 215
Luninskaya (Лунинская) 213-14
Magistralny (Магистральный) 12, 154
mail 43-44, 125-27
Maiski (Майский) 291
maps A7, M1-M5
Marble Canyon gulag camp 209-211
Marevaya (Маревая) 47, 225
markets 45-46
medical precautions & services 98-100, 104, 231
military 2-3, 19-20, 45, 131, 258, 260, 265, 267, 277, 281, 283, 287, 291-92, 295-96, 303, 312
militsia 128-132
Miroshnichenko (Мирошниченко) 14, 235
Mogot (Могот) 311
Moldavski (Молдавский) 235
money 101-02
Mongokhto (Монгохто) 287
Morgudon (Моргудон) 138
Moskovski Komsomolets (Московский Комсомолец) 226
mountaineering 169-70, 200-01
Munok (Мунок) 154
Murtygit (Муртыгит) 306
museums 46, 66, 144, 145-46,150, 161, 205, 206, 215, 222, 246, 264-65, 275, 279, 295, 315, 321
mushrooms 67
Muya (Муя) 191-92
Muyakan (Муякан) 184
Mylki (Мылки) 277, 300
Nagornaya Yakutsk (Нагорная Якутск) 311
Nakhot (Нахот) 315-17
Nanai indigenous people 72, 75, 256-57, 273-4, 287
Negigaltsy (Негигальцы) 273
Nelyaty (Неляты) 191-92
Neryungri (Нерюнгри) 44, 50, 133, 313-18, **316**
Neryungri coal fields 11, 313, 317-18
newspapers 12, 13, 30, 31, 32, 34, 37, 89, 224, 260, 271
Nezhametny (Нежаметны) 319
nightlife 37, 128,
Nivkhi indigenous people 72, 75
Niya (Ния) 47
Nizhne-Kuranakh (Нижне-Куранах) 322
Nizhneangarsk (Нижнеангарск) 11, 12, 40, 51, 175-78, **175**
Nizhnestalinsk (Нижнесталинск) 320
Nizhnie Khalby (Нижние Халбы) 273-74
Nora (Нора) 236
North Korea 215, 225, 226, 246, 248-49, 250-51, 307, 311
Novaya Chara (Новая Чара) 11, 22, 39, 45, 203-06, **205**

Novaya Igirma (Новая Игирма) 308
Novy Uoyan (Новый Уоян) 179
Novy Urgal (Новый Ургал) 39, 42, 244-247, **245**
October revolution (1917) & Civil War (1918-21) 235, 236, 295-96, 303
Ogadzha (Огоджа) 238
Ogoron (Огорон) 235
Oktyabrski (Октябрьский) 291
Okusikan (Окусикан) 180
Old Believers religion 255-56
Olekma (Олекма) 214
Olkhon Island (Ольхон Остров) 160
Olongo (Олонго) 47, 213
Onakorchanskaya bay (Онакорчанская Бухта) 170-71
Orochen (Орочен) 319
Orochi indigenous people 75, 287
Osinovka (Осиновка) 140
Oune (Оунэ) 284
Padali (Падали) 277
Padunskie Porogi (Падунские Пороги) 140
Palace of Culture 45, 94, 161-62
Parama Rapids 188-91
passports & visas 93, 102, 118, 222, 309, 310
Pereval (Перевал) 79
Perevalny (Перевальный) 299
permafrost 27-29, 49, 234, 253
Pervomaiskoe (Первомайское) 223-34
photography 33, 249, 282, 307
Pivan (Пивань) 11, 272-73, 281-82
planning a trip 88-104
plants 51-54, 62-64, 66-67, 94
police 128-132
pollution 55-57, 142, 143, 155, 159, 164, 208, 240, 256, 276, 280, 313, 319, 322
Polovinka (Половинка) 12
Port Novobratsk (Порт Новобратск) 138
Postyshevo (Постышево) 11, 47, 68-69, 254-56
POWs 15, 22, 248, 258, 260-61, 266, 280-81, 285-86, 298, 299
Pravaya Lena (Правая Лена) 322
pre-history 206, 256-57, 279
Priamurskaya (Приамурская) 303
prisoners, see gulag, German POWs, Japanese POWs
queues 128
rafting 94, 164, 188-92, 238, 311, 315
rail tickets, booking & buying 90-92, 114, 116-120, 167, A6-A8
rail travel 108-20
railway construction workers 15-23
railway electrification 9, 11
railway infrastructure 10-13, 78-81, 291, 305, 309
railway operation 78-82
railway stations 42-43, 79
railway troops 19-20, 15, 130-31, 233, 236, 247, 252-53, 281
railway workers 81-82, 312-13

railway, also see trains
Raz. 303km (Раз 303км) 300
Raz. 635km (Раз 635км) 180
recommended reading A14-A18
religion 74-75, 76, 161, 174, 255-56, 276, 315
Reorich, Elena Ivanovna 174, 178
repair trains 84-85
restaurants 124
Rikhard Zorge (Рихард Зорге) 311
river cruisers 107-08, 147, 152-53, 268-69, 279
roads 304, 305, 309, 311, 319
rock rivers 51, 214
rolling stock 82-86, 312-13
rural life 39-40, 59
Russian language 101, 154, A2-A9, A11-A14
Russian Orthodox Church 161, 315, 276
Russian Spring Fever 98-100
safety & crime 79-80, 111, 128-29, 132
Sakha, Republic of 308-10
Sakhalin Island 281, 287-88
sanatorium 122, 238, 299
Sanboli (Санболи) 301
schools 162, 178, 199-200, 226, 229, 273
seals 94, 164, 172-3
Selemdzhinsk (Силемджинск) 239-40
Selikhin (Селихин) 283-84
Serebyany Bor (Серебяный Бор) 313, 315
Seti (Сети) 307
Severobaikalsk (Северобайкальск) 7, 8, 11, 41, 42, 45, 47, 156-63, **157**, 164, 174
Severomuisk (Северомуйск) 180, 181, 182-84
shamans 74-75, 76
Shivery (Шиверы) 192
shopping 43, 104, 126
Silinka (Силинка) 258
skiing 156, 164, 169, 273
Skovorodino (Сковородино) 305
smoking 114
Sofisk (Софийск) 239
Solnechny (Солнечный) 61, 274-76
Soloni (Солони) 47, 251
Solzhenitsyn 136
Sosnovye Rodniki (Сосновые Родники) 138
Sovetskaya Gavan (Советская Гавань) 6, 10, 11, 41, 44, 291-96, **294**
space travel 146, 147, 154, 215-16, 269-70
springs, water 154, 156, 171, 179, 212, 213, 238, 249, 315-17
Stalin, Joseph 4, 11, 47, 252-3, 254, 255, 260
Staraya Chara (Старая Чара) 39, 206
Start (Старт) 258
steam locomotives 150
Storm (Штурм) 306
Suluk (Сулук) 47, 251-53
Sun City 175
Taezhnaya (Таежная) 319
taiga 51-53, 69, 99

Taishet (Тайшет) 6, 10, 11, 136-37, **137**
Taksimo (Таксимо) 11, 47, 184-87, **185**
Tarasova (Тарасова) 154
Tas-Yuryakh (Тас-Юрях) 214
Tatar Straits 22, 281, 283-84
Tavlinka (Тавлинка) 255-56
taxis 121
Tayura (Таыура) 154
Teisin (Тейсин) 301
telegrams 125-27
telephones 43-44, 78-79, 125-127, 308
tic, Ixodes 98-100
tickets, booking & buying rail 90-92, 114, 116-120, 167, A6-A8
tiger, Siberian 72-73
time zones 166, 192, 243
timetables, boats 152-53, 160, 268-69
timetables, trains A19-A25
tipping 127
toilets 114, 115, 120-21
Tokur (Токур) 240-42
Tommot (Томмот) 322
Tonnelni (Тоннельный) 180
town, types of 38-42, 44-45, 181, 226-27, 229
train carriages 83-84, 108-15
train safety & crime 79-80, 111, 128-29, 132
trains, accommodation 109-11
trains, life on board 111-14
Trans-Siberian railway 2, 3, 5, 6, 8, 9, 95-96, 142, 177, 219, 237, 248, 244-45, 260, 298, 299, 300, 301, 302, 303, 304, 305
travel tips 88-104, 125
travel agents 89-92
travel information, finding additional A14-A18
travel insurance 101
travel itineraries 96-98
travellers' cheques 101-02, 104
trekking 164, 169-70, 196, 208-09
Tsars 2, 9
Tubinskaya (Тубинская) 308
Tuluchi (Тулучи) 286
Tumnin (Тумнин) 286-87
tundra 52, 69
Tungala (Тунгала) 47, 235, 236
Tungara (Тунгара) 42
tunnels 10, 11, 12, 14, 22, 24, 29-30, 155, 165-65, 201-02, 251, 252-53, 272-73, 282, 285, 311
Tutaul (Тутаул) 226
Tynda (Тында) 6, 10, 11, 12, 13, 27, 28, 41, 42, 44, 47, 217-224, **218**
Tyndinsky 217
Tyrma (Тырма) 298
Udokan (Удокан) 11, 27, 203, 207-08
Udomi (Удоми) 284
Ugolnaya (Угольная) 313, 318
Ulak (Улак) 226
Ulgi (Ульги) 184
Ulkan (Улькан) 154
Ulma (Ульма) 243

Unakha (Унаха) 225
uranium mining 209, 211-12
Urgal (Ургал) 10, 11, 13, 39, 42, 47, 251, 255
Urkaltu (Уркальту) 253
Urusha (Уруша) 304
Ust-Ilimsk (Усть-Илимск) 308
Ust-Kut (Усть-Кут) 10, 11, 13, 41, 43, 60, 147-51, **151**
Ust-Muya (Усть-Муя) 39, 191-92
Ust-Nyukzha (Усть-Нюкжа) 11, 39
Ust-Orochi (Усть-Орочи) 287
Ust-Paramsk (Усть-Парамск) 189-92
Ust-Urgal (Усть-Ургал) 243
Utiny (Утиный) 302
Utkin, Iosif Pavlovich 302
vaccinations 98-100
Vanino (Ванино) 41, 42, 287-91, **289**
vegetarians 124-25
Verkhnezeisk (Верхнезейск) 41, 43, 45, 47, 68-69, 226-31, **288**
Verkhny Sakukan gulag camp 211-12
Verkhnyaya Zaimka (Верхняя Заимка) 167
Vidim (Видим) 145
Vikorevka (Вихоревка) 138
visas & passports 93, 102, 118, 222, 309, 310
vodka 65, 132-34
volcanoes 196, 301
Volochaevka 2 (Волочаевка 2) 10, 302
Vosnesenskoe (Вознесенское) 279
Vysokogornaya (Высокогорная) 42, 285
washing 122-23
water, drinking & hot 45, 98, 102, 113-14, 231
weather 49, 94, 104, 309, 313
what to take 102-04
Wildlife Institute of Khabarovsk 72-73, 301
Yakokit (Якокит) 319, 322
Yakuts indigenous people 75, 309, 312, 321-22
Yakutsk (Якутск) 27, 149, 322
Yakutsk, Republic of 308-310
Yakutski (Якутский) 311
Yanchukan (Янчукан) 180
yachting 162-63
Yaurin (Яурин) 299
Yeltsin, Boris 6, 207-08
yeti 286-87, 307
Yukhta (Юхта) 154
Yuktali (Юктали) 214-15
Zabolotny (Заболотное) 306
Zarya (Заря) 223-24
Zavety Ilicha (Заветы Ильича) 291
Zeya (Зея) 46
Zheleznogorsk-Ilimsky (Железногорск-Илимский) 145-47, **146**
Zhelezny (Железный) 145
Zlatoustovsk (Златоустовск) 242
Zolotinka (Золотинка) 311-12, 315
Zvezdhaya (Звездная) 12, 151-54
Zvonkov (Звонков) 243